The Politics of
Oil-Producer Cooperation

The Political Economy of Global Interdependence

Thomas D. Willett, Series Editor

The Politics of Oil-Producer Cooperation, Dag Harald Claes

States, Banks, and Markets: Mexico's Path to Financial Liberalization in Comparative Perspective, Nancy Auerbach

The Political Economy of European Monetary Unification, second edition, edited by Jeffrey A. Frieden and Barry Eichengreen

Peace, Prosperity, and Politics, edited by John Mueller

Financial Market Reform in China: Progress, Problems, and Prospects, edited by Baizhu Chen, J. Kimball Dietrich, and Yi Feng

Institutions, Transition Economies, and Economic Development, by Tim Yeager

Capital Controls in Emerging Economies, edited by Christine P. Ries and Richard J. Sweeney

Exchange-Rate Policies for Emerging Market Economies, edited by Richard J. Sweeney, Clas Wihlborg, and Thomas D. Willett

Political Capacity and Economic Behavior, edited by Marina Arbetman and Jacek Kugler

Judging Economic Policy: Selected Writing of Gottfried Haberler, edited by Richard J. Sweeney, Edward Tower, and Thomas D. Willett

Interest Groups and Monetary Integration: The Political Economy of Exchange Regime Choice, Carsten Hefeker

Growth, Debt, and Politics: Economic Adjustment and the Political Performance of Developing Countries, by Lewis W. Snider

Establishing Monetary Stability in Emerging Market Economies, edited by Thomas D. Willett, et al.

The Politics of
Oil-Producer Cooperation

Dag Harald Claes

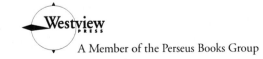

Westview
PRESS
A Member of the Perseus Books Group

The Political Economy of Global Interdependence

Copyright © 2001 by Westview Press, A Member of the Perseus Books Group

Published in 2001 in the United States of America by Westview Press, 5500 Central Avenue, Boulder, Colorado 80301-2877, and in the United Kingdom by Westview Press, 12 Hid's Copse Road, Cumnor Hill, Oxford OX2 9JJ

Find us on the World Wide Web at www.westviewpress.com

Library of Congress Cataloging-in-Publication Data
Claes, Dag Harald
  The politics of oil-producer cooperation/Dag Harald Claes.
    p. cm.—(The political economy of global interdependence)
  Includes bibliographical references and index.
  ISBN 0-8133-6843-X (pbk.)
    1. Petroleum industry and trade—International cooperation–Political aspects.   I.
Title.
  II. Series

HD9560.6.C53   2000
338.2'7282—dc21

                                                                00-044774

The paper used in this publication meets the requirements of the American National Standard for Permanence of Paper for Printed Library Materials Z39.48-1984.

PERSEUS
POD
ON DEMAND   10   9   8   7   6   5   4   3   2   1

In Memoriam
Sonja Claes
(1927–1997)

Contents

List of Tables and Figures		xi
Acronyms		xv
Acknowledgments		xvii

1	**Introduction**	**1**
	1.1 Oil as International Politics, 2	
	1.2 International Cooperation, 3	
	1.3 International Political Economy, 6	
	1.4 The Multilevel Approach, 8	
	1.5 Relations to Economic Theory, 20	
	1.6 A Note on Sources, 27	
	Notes, 31	

2	**Market Context**	**35**
	2.1 Market Structure, 36	
	2.2 Market Power, 44	
	2.3 The Era of the International Oil Companies, 51	
	2.4 The OPEC Era, 60	
	2.5 Structural Effects of the Price Increases, 70	
	2.6 New Market-Power Relations, 77	
	2.7 Conclusion, 88	
	Notes, 91	

3	**Political Context**	**95**
	3.1 Politicization, 96	
	3.2 Oil and Security, 99	
	3.3 The Iran-Iraq War, 101	
	3.4 The Iraq-Kuwait War, 107	
	3.5 Internal Threats, 114	
	3.6 Political Cooperation Between the Gulf States, 121	
	3.7 Conclusion, 126	
	Notes, 127	

4.0   OPEC as an International Organization   131
4.1   Institutional Approaches, 131
4.2   The Organizational Structure of OPEC, 142
4.3   Institutional Functions of OPEC, 144
4.4   Conclusion, 164
      Notes, 166

5   Price and Production Policy of OPEC Countries   171

5.1   The Redundant Cartel:
      OPEC Price Policy, 1971–1981, 172
5.2   The Effective Cartel:
      OPEC Quota Policy, 1982–1985, 182
5.3   The Defected Cartel:
      OPEC Market-Share Policy, 1986–1998, 188
      Notes, 198

6   Country Case I: Saudi Arabia—A Hegemonic Power   201

6.1   A Dynamic Approach to Hegemony, 204
6.2   The Making of a Hegemon, 207
6.3   The Incapable Hegemon, 1973–1981, 218
6.4   The Benevolent Hegemon: Swing Producer,
      1982–1985, 225
6.5   The Coercive Hegemon, 1986–1996, 231
6.6   The Mixed Strategy, 1999–2000, 233
6.7   The Relative Power of the Hegemon, 234
      Notes, 237

7   OPEC: A Successful Cartel?   239

7.1   Conditions for Cartels, 240
7.2   Cartel Behavior, 243
7.3   OPEC as a Price-Maker, 247
7.4   Quota Compliance, 253
7.5   The Profits of Cooperation, 269
7.6   A Cartel or a Success?, 273
      Notes, 278

8   Extending the Cooperation:
    OPEC and the Non-OPEC Producers   281

8.1   The Non-OPEC Producers in General, 282
8.2   The OPEC–Non-OPEC Bargaining, 289
8.3   Explaining Non-OPEC Cooperative Behavior, 292
      Notes, 295

9   Country Case II: Norway—From Free-Riding to Cooperation   297

    9.1   Domestic Factors in International Relations, 299
    9.2   The Bargaining Process, 301
    9.3   The Bargaining Game Between OPEC and Norway, 316
    9.4   Explaining the Norwegian Policy Change, 326
    9.5   Conclusion, 346
    Notes, 348

10 Oil-Producer Cooperation and the Study of
    International Political Economy   353

    10.1   Empirical Findings, 353
    10.2   The Explanatory Model Revisited, 361
    10.3   The Value of Combining
          Political Science and Economics, 366
    10.4   Theoretical Implications, 371
    Notes, 378

References   379
Index   395

Tables and Figures

Tables

1.1	World proven reserves, production, growth, and decline in reserves, and R/P ratios, 1970–1993	22
1.2	Investment per additional daily barrel of capacity	24
2.1	Proved reserves at end of 1975, 1985, and 1995	37
2.2	Refinery capacity and throughputs, 1995	38
2.3	The division of the Turkish Petroleum Company in 1928	54
2.4	Ownership shares in Middle East production distributed to companies	56
2.5	Producing countries' dependency on the majors, 1970	62
2.6	Taxonomy of trading	79
2.7	Principal foreign downstream acquisitions of petroleum-exporting countries, 1983–1990	84
3.1	Saudi Arabian and Iraqi share of OPEC production, July 1990 and 1991–1994	113
3.2	Democracy indexes for the OPEC countries, 1970–1996	115
3.3	Classification of the regimes of OPEC countries	117
4.1	Secretaries-general of OPEC	145
4.2	Key ministerial committees of the OPEC conference	146
4.3	Organizations and state power	151
5.1	Regional crude supply gains and losses, August 8–October 20, 1990	191
5.2	Iraqi and Saudi Arabian production, July 1990, and average, 1991–1994	192
6.1	Share of total exports, selected countries, 1950–1965	209
7.1	Conditions affecting the incidence of cartelization	240

7.2   Cartelization of international oil   242
7.3   OPEC cartel strategies, 1973–1999   247
7.4   Correlation between price and production
      by time periods   248
7.5   Correlation between price and production
      by price movements   250
7.6   OPEC quotas, 1982–1998   256
7.7   Correlation between production and quotas   259
7.8   OPEC and Saudi Arabian production, quotas,
      and overproduction, April 1982 to December 1995   259
7.9   OPEC members' overproduction correlated with
      other members' overproduction, March 1982–July 1990   267
7.10 Relationship between others' overproduction
      and own overproduction   268

8.1   Categories of non-OPEC producers   282
8.2   Characteristics of selected non-OPEC producers,
      1985–1986   290
8.3   Selected non-OPEC producers' production growth,
      from previous year   291

9.1   Pressure exerted on Norway by OPEC, 1983–1987   320
9.2   Norway's accommodation of OPEC, 1983–1987   320
9.3   Norwegian conditions for cooperation, 1983–1987   322
9.4   Correlation between positions by major parties in
      committee recommendations to parliamentary
      propositions on petroleum-related issues, 1970–1994   335
9.5   Common positions between Labor and the
      Conservative Party on petroleum-related issues in
      parliamentary committees   336

Figures

1.1   Explanatory model of the book   19
1.2   Model of the industrial organization of the
      international oil market   27

2.1   Market concentrations: 5, 10, and 15 largest
      producing countries, 1965–1995   40
2.2   Market shares, 1965   41
2.3   Market shares, 1995   42
2.4   Trilateral oligopoly   47

2.5   Conflictual aspects of intergroup relations   48
2.6   Cooperative aspects of intergroup relations   49
2.7   The Red Line   55
2.8   Energy demand, 1950–1999   58
2.9   Primary energy consumption, 1950 and 1995,
       different fuels   59
2.10   Selected OPEC countries' production, September
       1972 to April 1974   65
2.11   Monthly oil prices, 1973–2000   66
2.12   Spot and official prices, July 1978–July 1983   71
2.13   Oil consumption in barrels per thousand GDP,
       1960–1993 (1980 $)   72
2.14   Oil consumption, 1965–1999   73
2.15   Trends in taxation of petroleum products   75
2.16   Market shares, 1965–1999   76
2.17   OPEC member countries' estimated current
       account balance, 1972–1998   86
2.18   Changes in control over the vertical production chain   88
2.19   International oil companies' and producing
       countries' share of product chain   89

3.1   Categories of politicization   98
3.2   Iranian and Iraqi production, 1976–1989   105
3.3   Democracy index of OPEC members by region,
       1970–1993   116
3.4   Iranian, Iraqi, Kuwaiti, and Saudi Arabian oil
       production, 1976–1995   125

4.1   Production, quotas, and monitoring   156

5.1   Iranian, Iraqi, and Saudi Arabian monthly
       production, 1976–1981   176
5.2   OPEC production and spot prices, 1976–1998   180
5.3   Average production, January 1981–March 1982,
       and production over March 1982 quota   184
5.4   Saudi Arabian and other OPEC production, 1985–1986   190
5.5   Brent oil price, January 1999–June 2000   196

6.1   The hegemonic cost-minimization model   206
6.2   OPEC and Saudi Arabia GDP, 1960–1998   228
6.3   Saudi Arabian government budgets, selected
       years, 1971–1996   229
6.4   Saudi production and spot oil price, 1982–1985   230

6.5 Share of OPEC production for Saudi Arabia, Iran, and Iraq, 1965–1998   236

7.1 Kuwaiti, Nigerian, and Libyan oil production, 1974–1975   252
7.2 IEA estimates of OPEC production, 1977 and 1982, and actual production   254
7.3 OPEC production and quotas, April 1982–April 2000   258
7.4 N-person prisoner's dilemma   261
7.5 OPEC countries' overproduction and R/P ratio   263
7.6 OPEC countries' overproduction and share of total production   265
7.7 N-person chicken   266
7.8 OPEC revenue, price, and production, 1972–1995   271
7.9 Value of OPEC members' oil exports, 1960–1998   272
7.10 Crude oil prices, actual and successive International Energy Workshop polls   274

8.1 Market share of OPEC, former Soviet Union, and other non-OPEC, 1988 and 1998 (%)   284
8.2 Russian oil exports outside former Soviet Union, 1990–1997   285
8.3 US oil production, consumption, and imports, 1965–1999   286
8.4 Chinese oil production and consumption, 1988–1998   288

9.1 The threat game-tree   318
9.2 Actual, planned, and reduced Norwegian oil production, 1986–1991   325
9.3 Norwegian oil production, 1971–1999   328
9.4 Brent Blend oil price, 1976–1995 ($ and NOK)   330
9.5 The petroleum sector share of GDP and total exports, 1972–1999   333
9.6 Paid taxes from the petroleum sector, 1971–1999   334
9.7 Agreement in parliamentary committee remarks between Labor and the Conservative Party regarding petroleum issues and all issues, 1970–1994   337

Acronyms

API	American Petroleum Institute
Aramco	Arabian American Oil Company
BNOC	British National Oil Corporation
BP	British Petroleum
CENTO	Central Treaty Organization
EIA	Energy Information Administration
ENI	Ente Nazionale Idrocarburi
FTC	Federal Trade Commission
GATT	General Agreement on Trade and Tariff
GCC	Gulf Cooperation Council
IEA	International Energy Agency
IOC	International oil companies
IPC	Iraq Petroleum Company
IPE	International Political Economy
IPEX	International Petroleum Exchange
mbd	Million barrels per day
NIOC	National Iranian Oil Company
NOK	Norwegian krone
NYMEX	New York Mercantile Exchange
OECD	Organization for Economic Cooperation and Development
OPEC	Organization of the Petroleum Exporting Countries
PDVSA	Petróleos de Venezuela SA
PEMEX	Petroleos Mexicanos
PLO	Palestinian Liberation Organization
SoCal	Standard Oil of California
Statoil	The Norwegian State Oil Company
UAE	United Arab Emirates

Acknowledgments

This project was initiated and completed while I was at the Fridtjof Nansen Institute. Most of the work was done in the intermediate period while I was research fellow and assistant professor in the Department of Political Science at the University of Oslo. I thank both institutions for providing necessary funding for this project.

Several people commented on different sections of the manuscript. I thank you all, not mentioned nor forgotten. Glenn Martin and Paula Reedy copyedited the manuscript and improved it considerably. In the process from thesis to book I benefited from the stimulating research environment at the ARENA program at the University of Oslo, and from trying to tackle the penetrating comments of Professors Thomas D. Willett and Arthur Denzau. At Westview Press, David McBride and Christine Marra provided excellent editorial assistance.

None of the above-mentioned persons bear any responsibility for any misjudgments or errors that may be present in the final text. My wife, Lene, had to put up with an uninspired, inattentive, and tired husband for several years. I can only hope that I will be able, to some extent, to make up for it. My daughter, Sofie, was born in the middle of the work on the thesis. At that moment the importance of my doctoral thesis suffered a dramatic relative deprivation. Also at this very moment of writing I hear her calling, "Pappa, Pappa," reminding me of the completeness of life, rather than the problems of conflicting interests.

Dag Harald Claes
Langhus, July 2000

1

Introduction

The Politics of Oil

What determines the cooperative behavior among the oil-producing countries?
That is the question this book seeks to answer. The cooperation between
the oil producers has been the topic of many studies in the field of energy
economics. This study approaches this well-known topic from the theoretical field of political science, in particular from the subdiscipline
known as International Political Economy (IPE). The study is based on the
view that understanding the cooperation between oil producers is a
question of understanding interactions of politics and economics.

Three analytical beliefs guide the study. First, the economic models of
the oil market are not sufficient in understanding the cooperative behavior of the governments of oil-producing states. "Oil, unlike other commodities, has a universality of significance which in the real world places
limits on the application of economic rationale to the evolution of the industry" (Odell 1996:38). The economic models are valuable but need to
be supplemented by models and approaches that are capable of integrat-
ing an understanding of the policies of oil-producing states and the economic factors of the international oil market. This study provides such an
approach.

Second, our understanding of the oil producers' behavior, and for that
matter most aspects of international politics, will increase if we are able
to understand the dynamic relationship between factors at different analytical levels. To grasp how different factors interrelate, more complex
models are required. This study thus applies a multilevel approach in explaining the cooperative behavior of oil-producing states (Rosenau 1990).

Third, this is a study of the policy of oil-producing states, not a testing of
their behavior against models of optimal economic behavior. Nor is it a historical study revealing new empirical facts. It is an example of what Bates
et al. (1998) calls "analytical narrative." This study is "motivated by a de-

sire to account for particular events and outcomes" (Bates et al. 1998:3), while at the same time acknowledging "the benefits to be gained from the systematic use of theory" (Bates et al. 1998). The reader will thus find that most chapters in this book are a combination of narrative and analysis.

1.1   Oil as International Politics

Susan Strange found energy to be a topic between the study of economics and the study of political science, thus demanding a political-economy approach: "what is needed . . . is some analytical framework for relating the impact of states' actions on the markets for various sources of energy, with the impact of these markets on the policies and actions, and indeed the economic development and national security of the states" (Strange 1988:191).

Economic models of the market behavior of oil-producing states have been developed on the basis of the assumptions underlying the behavior of economic entities (i.e., firms). The fact that the cooperation between oil producers since 1971 has been a cooperation between states, not firms, makes these models incapable of fully explaining their behavior. "Recognizing that the members of OPEC (Organization of Petroleum Exporting Countries) are national governments, not private businesses, conventional economic analysis of cartels must be blended with political analysis" (Willett 1979a:52). The rationale of states is different from the rationale of firms. States have a more complex set of interests, and tend to place primacy on security interests. Furthermore, states are more complex organizations that contain more potential for internal conflicts over aims and means. Finally, states have to pay attention to aspects at the societal level in a way that firms seldom have to do[1]—if for no other reason than that the leadership of the democratic states usually seeks re-election, and leaderships of nondemocratic states seek to avoid revolution. This makes it necessary to supplement the economic understanding of the cooperation between the oil producers with an understanding of the behavior of oil-producing *states*. Only through a combination of political and economic analysis can one gain a better understanding of the intrinsic world of international oil, as "the economics of oil influence the politics of oil, and vice versa" (Amen 1996:360). This study seeks such a combination.

The international oil market is, of course, not isolated from the rest of the international economy. The changes in the oil market can be a result of not only an individual actor's non-oil interests and behavior but also the actor's position in a more general international political structure. To capture this aspect of the international oil market, Simon Bromley, in his study of US oil policy, develops what he calls a conjunctural approach, combining realism with orthodox economics: "By . . . placing the developments of US oil policy in the context of its wider management of the world economy and nation-state system, [the approach] demonstrates the central role which oil played in the organization of US hegemony" (Bromley 1991:242). His conclusion is that the explanation of oil-market development is connected with the overall development of the international postwar economic system:

> The economic crisis can be more readily understood as the results of general contradictions within the maturation of postwar capitalism, evidenced also in an overall shift of US hegemony to an increasingly unilateral and predatory form; and second, the response of the United States to these wider challenges played a significant role in the origins of the oil price increases. (Bromley 1991:242–243)

A similar proposition is put forward by Karlsson (1993:12, my translation):

> The fundamental . . . hypothesis in the study is that the control and power in the international oil economy has been the key *grundbulten* in the US-controlled world order. . . . When this key is disturbed so is the position of the hegemonic power (the US), and its ability to control the world order. The understanding of the international oil market is substantially limited if the question is not related to the control over the world order and the development and change of the world economy.

As will become clear in the rest of this book, I do not subscribe to this understanding. First, the role of the United States is overemphasized. The United States has been a policy-taker in the international oil market since the beginning of the seventies. It has primarily struggled to compensate for its lack of influence in this market, using whatever power it found available: diplomatic skills, economic rewards, and military force. The use of these instruments has been a sign of weakness, not strength. Second, there are several political aspects of the international oil market worth studying that are not related to general international politics or superpower relations. Third, the interaction between the oil market and international politics can fruitfully be approached through perspectives that focus on the political interests of market actors like the oil-producing states. This is a basic idea in Chapter 3.

1.2 International Cooperation

This study is about the cooperation of states, more specifically about a certain group of states—the oil producers.[2] This calls for some remarks about what is meant by cooperation. Axelrod and Keohane (1986:226) argue that "cooperation occurs when actors adjust their behavior to the actual or anticipated preferences of others." Milner (1997:7) finds an agreement on this definition a "notable feature of the recent literature on international cooperation." It follows from the definition that actors' preferences are essential—both the preferences of others and the actors' preference for adjusting its own policy to the others actors' preferences. This implies that the actors all assume that cooperation will be beneficial: "What counts as cooperation thus depends on the presence of two elements: *goal-directed* behavior that seeks to create *mutual gains* through policy adjustments" (Milner 1997:8).

The definition also implies that cooperation is impossible between actors whose preferences are perfectly contradictious. In such cases of pure conflict, there is no room for adjustments. Nor is there any need for adjustment of behavior or cooperation if the actors' preferences over outcomes are identical, unambiguous, and perceived by all actors. Most prominent are the cases where actors have both common and conflicting interests at the same time. In such cases cooperation might realize outcomes that represent Pareto-improvement, as opposed to the outcomes generated by the actors' individual rational behavior. "To arrive at the Pareto-optimal outcome requires that all actors eschew their dominant strategy. In addition, they must not greedily attempt to obtain their most preferred outcome once they have settled at the unstable outcome they prefer to the stable equilibrium" (Stein 1990:32). Arild Underdal (1987:175) points out that sellers in a market can "simultaneously compete for market shares, face product prices as collective goods (externality), and stand a chance of increasing cost-efficiency by coordinating R&D or production or distribution activities (synergy)." The relationship between oil producers is a prominent example of such a combination of common and contradicting interests.

One particular issue in the theoretical debate in the study of international relations is the role of international institutions in the promotion of cooperation between states. Keohane (1989:3) argues that "there is . . . ample evidence to conclude both that states have mutual interests and that institutionalization is a variable rather than a constant in world politics. Given these conditions, cooperation is possible but depends in part on institutional arrangements. A successful theory of cooperation must therefore take into account the effects of institutions." Even in cases where actors have identical preferences, the need for some institutions can emerge if, for instance, there are several equilibrium points with equal payoff to the actors.[3] This creates a need for coordination, and some form of institutionalization of the interaction is likely.

There are several ways in which international institutions can increase cooperation between states. First, institutions can provide the actors with necessary information about the other actors' preferences. Second, institutions can provide negotiation frameworks that reduce transaction costs and thus increase the effectiveness of inter-state transactions (Keohane 1989:111). Such frameworks can also help coordinate actors' expectations by establishing conventions. Third, institutions can change the cost-benefit calculations of states, or the incompatibilities of their positions, by providing an arena for issue-linkages, mediating between states, and providing instruments for verification that actors are abiding with agreements, or sanctions for those who are not. Fourth, institutions can "frame" how decisionmakers view their collective options, as well as contribute to the creation of collective identities. This list does not exhaust the possible ways that institutions can influence cooperation between states, but it highlights some of the aspects to be discussed in Chapter 4.

Empirical studies of cooperation might address different aspects of cooperation. Throughout this study, four aspects will be prominent: First, the *substantive scope* of the cooperation—that is, the parts of the producers' oil policies that are subject to collective decisionmaking. In this study the main focus will be the price and production policies of the oil-producing countries. Second, the *depth* of cooperation. This pertains to the strength and autonomy of the collective institutions compared to the sovereignty of the individual state in the formation and implementation of policy. This aspect can vary from loose targets for the producers' price and production policies to having a supranational institution deciding the price and production levels for all member states. Third, the *effectiveness* of the cooperation. This aspect focuses on the outcome of the cooperation, and can be defined as the extent to which the oil producers reach their substantive objectives. In this study the effectiveness is measured against the noncooperative outcome, that is, from a situation of competitive behavior among the oil producers. If the producers' income rises above the assumed income in a competitive market situation, it becomes meaningful to discuss the extent to which this increased income level is a result of cooperative behavior. Without such an increased income level, the question of effectiveness becomes empirically less relevant. Fourth, the *costs* connected with the cooperation. This includes two types of costs: first, and most important, the opportunity costs, which are the "sacrifices" by the individual oil producer when behaving cooperatively compared with a situation where it behaves competitively; and second, the transaction costs connected with conducting the cooperation, such as the costs of running the secretariat, holding meetings, and so on. The beneficial effects will have to be evaluated against the existence of such costs.

1.3   International Political Economy

This is a study in the tradition called International Political Economy (IPE), as it focuses on the political aspect of the relationship between states in an economic issue area. This is in line with the way Robert Gilpin (1987:9) employs the concept of political economy

> simply to indicate a set of questions to be examined by means of an eclectic mixture of analytic methods and theoretical perspectives. These questions are generated by the interaction of the state and the market as the embodiment of politics and economics in the modern world. They ask how the state and its associated political processes affect the production and distribution of wealth and, in particular, how political decisions and interests influence the location of economic activities and the distribution of the costs and benefits of these activities.

Although I do not subscribe to the notion of the market as the embodiment of economics but rather seek to identify the market actors in a more concrete way, the key question of this study is, as for Gilpin, "how political decisions and interests influence economic activities."

The developments in the oil market, especially OPEC's gradual control of it, created problems for the economic understanding of the market mechanisms; "there is currently no economic model that describes the process of price determination under OPEC" (Tourk 1977:322). "With regard to theoretical issues, it remains an open question how best to design a model of the behaviour of OPEC" (Gately 1984:1113). On the other hand, the theoretical problem had long been apparent, and internally in the United States, oligopoly and effective cartel formation had been familiar phenomena: "Perhaps the most remarkable failure of modern value theory is its inability to explain the pricing, output and other related decisions of the large, not quite monopolistic firms which account for so large a proportion of our output" (Baumol 1959:13).[4]

The development of the oil market in the seventies led to disagreement among economists how to interpret the development. "There are basically two explanations of what happened in 1973–74. The one most widely accepted by economists is that OPEC effectively cartelized the world oil market, exploiting its power to raise prices above competition levels by restricting production. . . . The other explanation argues that OPEC was largely irrelevant as an organization and that its members acted competitively" (Gately 1984:1101).[5] Even individual economists' comprehension of OPEC as a market actor changed over a few years of market turmoil. Two quotations from works by Robert Pindyck illustrate this point: "OPEC's behaviour is surprisingly predictable, since the cartel is most likely to take only those actions that are in its best economic interest" (Pindyck 1978:37); "economic rationality probably applies even less to OPEC than to many other economic agents" (Pindyck 1982:179).

When economic models fail, economists resort to the explanation that political factors disrupted the "natural" market development. This kind of disruption has occurred several times during the last thirty years, and made international oil a highly fluctuating business. The major oil market "shocks" of this period were (i) the 1973 Arab-Israeli War; (ii) the 1979 Iranian revolution; (iii) the 1980 outbreak of the Iran-Iraq War; and (iv) the 1990–1991 Iraq-Kuwait War. During, or in the aftermath of, all these political events, the price of oil changed dramatically, and the structure of the oil market was affected in a fashion unexplainable by economic models of the oil market. The fact that economic rationality is unable to explain the actors' behavior leads to the question what kind of logic would actually explain it. One possibility is that market behavior, unexplained by economic rationality, is in fact impossible to explain, and subsequently doomed to be left to chance or idiosyncratic events. The tendency to highlight the so-called oil shocks promotes a picture of the oil market during the last thirty years as one left to chance. Such a view is just as wrong as the belief that economic models fully explain the behavior of oil-producing states. What is called for is the development of models able to *combine* economic and political factors.[6] The above-mentioned political events have to be viewed together with the changes in the oil market caused by equally dramatic economic events such as (i) the Tehran-Tripoli agreement of 1971; (ii) the establishment of the OPEC quota system in 1982; (iii) OPEC's changed market strategy of 1985; and (iv) Saudi Arabia's strategy connected with the Iraq-Kuwait War in 1990.

The cooperation between oil producers is influenced by the actors' interests and behavior outside the oil market. States tend to have many interests outside a particular market; firms, few. One of the most prominent scholars of oil-market economics admits that states have a complex set of interests, but disregards the possibility that non-oil interests can affect the state's oil-market behavior:

> Some models have governments making oil production decisions for noneconomic reasons. This confuses means with ends, and getting with spending. A state seeks first to survive; then, to cultivate its garden, or spread the true faith, or bash its neighbors, or anything else. But whatever the objectives, the more wealth the better. A state that deliberately avoids wealth-maximizing is a special story, which had better be a good one. (Adelman 1993b:17)

Obviously Adelman's proposition "the more wealth the better" is correct, but for states' wealth might be a way of achieving security and vice versa. It is an empirical question, when and how (Keohane 1984:23). The statement "the more wealth the better" seems trivially true, but if the security of the state is threatened, no amount of wealth can compensate for the possible cessation of its existence.

In an earlier study I applied the concept of politicization to the relationship between OPEC and Norway in the international oil market (Claes 1990). The actors' motives were expanded to encompass motives unrelated to the oil market (read: political) and likewise the actors' available means. In that study, politicization denoted the linkage of economic matters to a political decisionmaking level, in line with the perspective outlined by Hirsch and Doyle (1977:11–13). Politicization was perceived to occur when an actor in a given market allowed its political aims outside the market concerned to affect its economic objectives and behavior in the market; or when an actor in a given market employed political means for purposes of achieving economic objectives *in* the market. This perspective will be further developed in Chapter 3.

This study tries to combine economic theories and theories of political science. The underlying assumptions regarding actors' motives and interests in political science are different from those of economics. Hveem (1996:37) has pointed out an important aspect of this difference: "economic theory tends to treat states and international organizations . . . exactly as they treat individuals and firms. . . . Neoclassical economics does, in other words, not bother to analyze the actors' motives and interests." An overriding aim of this book is to grasp the complexity of factors influencing states' motives, interests, and behavior. This calls for a multilevel approach, which means that theories at different levels of analysis are included in order to explain the oil-producer cooperation. As pointed out by Milner (1997:6): "variations across countries, as well as over time and among issue areas within the same country, suggest that neither national nor the international level of analysis is sufficient to explain the patterns of cooperation that we observe in world politics." An argument for an approach that combines structural and behavioral aspects is presented in the next section.

1.4   The Multilevel Approach

James Rosenau has argued in favor of more complex models in the study of international relations. "Scientific convention stresses that theory should be parsimonious, that the complexity inherent in the interaction of a large number of variables precludes meaningful theoretical insights" (Rosenau 1990:23). I subscribe to this principle. However, parsimonious models run into some difficulties: "Virtually by definition, parsimonious theories are compelled to ignore the multiple macro and micro levels at which the sources of turbulence stir and gather momentum" (Rosenau 1990). This book will forsake parsimony in order to "acknowledge multiple layers of causation" (Rosenau 1990).

This variety of theoretical approaches can lead to an incoherent approach. However, the aspects of oil-producer cooperation examined here are not empirically arbitrary. As will become evident during the empirical analysis in this study, the aspects discussed complement each other and are interrelated. They are also theoretically complementary, as they highlight different aspects of what is called the situational analysis. "Situational analysis has as its primary objective the explanation of the actions undertaken by political actors in given situations" (Farr 1987:49). There are two components of the situational analysis: the situation model and the principle of rationality. The principle of rationality is discussed in section 1.4. The situational model contains the natural environment, the social environment, and the problem-situation in which the actor finds itself (Farr 1987:50). "The physical surroundings contain aspects that are naturally given or given by prior human activities. . . . The social surroundings contain the relevant behavior of other actors, the social relations between actors and institutions. . . . The problem situation is the choice the actor faces" (Hovi and Rasch 1996:74, my translation). A similar model of actors' behavior is given by Elster (1989c:13–14):

> A simple scheme for explaining an action is to see it as the end result of two successive filtering operations. We begin with a large set of all abstractly possible actions that an individual might undertake. The first filter is made up of all the physical, economic, legal and psychological *constraints* that the individual faces. The actions consistent with these constraints form his *opportunity set*. The second filter is a mechanism that determines which action within the opportunity set will actually be carried out. . . . In this perspective, actions are explained by opportunities and desires—by what people can do and what they want to do.

The model presented by Elster is more general than the one outlined by Farr and by Hovi and Rasch, as it does not specify the mechanism by which the actor chooses among different possible actions. The situational model assumes that the actor makes a rational choice between possible actions. Some aspects of the discussion in this book suggest that the oil producers in some instances have not adhered to the principle of rationality.[7]

Based on the situational approach, the understanding of structure in this book is not one of structure as a direct causal factor in itself, but as a *constraint* on the behavior of the actors, individually and in common, and thus on the outcome of their cooperative efforts.[8] These constraining aspects will be split in two parts: the structural level and the institutional level. The structure is definitely something the actors regard as given. The institutions are more susceptible to change due to changes in the behavior of the actors. However, in this book the main focus will be the constraining effects of the institutions, not how or why the oil producers created the cooperative institutions in the first place (see Chapter 4).

The Structural Level

Empirically, the structural features of the international oil market to be discussed in this study are factors such as the degree of horizontal and vertical integration, the demand elasticity, and the barriers to entry (see Chapter 2). Furthermore, as the cooperation among oil producers is a matter of intergovernmental cooperation, the importance of the international political structure, in particular for the security interests of these states, is discussed in Chapter 3.

These structural aspects influence the utility of the policy choices of all market actors, and subsequently they limit the possibility of establishing successful oil-producer cooperation. At any given point in time, when actors make decisions, they will tend to regard the structural aspects as given. This does not imply that the actors' behavior does not influence the market structure. Several aspects of the actors' behavior discussed in this book can be regarded as basic moves (Snyder 1972:222). Basic moves are to be understood as an actor's behavior altering the set of possible outcomes of a negotiation, or, in this case, of the bargaining relationship between the oil producers. This points to the understanding in the book of a dynamic relationship between structure and behavior.

A prominent advocate—if not *the* prominent advocate—of structural explanations is Kenneth Waltz. He argues that "systemic effects cannot be reconstructed from the system's interacting parts since the parts behave differently because they are parts of a system. The constraints and incentives of a system, its dynamics, change if its structure changes or is transformed. To explain outcomes, we have to look at a system's dynamics and not just at the characteristics and the strategies of the units" (Waltz 1986:342). However, structural explanations have little value unless it is shown how these factors have influenced an actor and its intentions.[9] Hollis and Smith (1991:118) end their discussion of the structural approach like this:

> since the structure shows itself only in the behavior of the units, and since
> functional explanations must involve purposive behavior by the units, there

is no way of inferring that the units are merely dependent. . . . changes within and between the units are the only plausible explanations of change in the system. . . . the case rests with Waltz's remark . . . that "the shaping and shoving of structures may be successfully resisted."

As Hollis and Smith indicate, Waltz does not exclude the role of actors' behavior and interaction in explaining the outcome. In fact, he seems to be in agreement with the multilevel approach outlined here: "Structures condition behaviors and outcomes, yet explanations of behaviors and outcomes are indeterminate because both unit-level and structural causes are in play" (Waltz 1986:343). We are probably at a point where different scholars emphasize different aspects of a complex reality and thus reach different conclusions without being in disagreement on the fundamental ontology. Axelrod and Keohane (1986:253), for instance, regard the role of the units as more active, doing more than just resisting the "shaping and shoving" of structures: "We have also found that states are often dissatisfied with the structure of their own environment. We have seen that governments have often tried to transform the structures within which they operate."

It makes a difference whether the actors are merely resisting the structure or trying to transform it due to dissatisfaction with it. The latter indicates more autonomous actors than the former. The statement by Waltz that "states can more readily change their system than transform it" (1986:342) implies that he believes that states can transform the system. Differences in emphasis do, however, have methodological implications, as pointed out by George, Farley, and Dallin (1988:9):

> Of particular interest here is the emphasis Axelrod and Keohane [1986] place on the need for moving beyond the structural form of the hypotheses to empirical analysis of the decision-making processes of the actors and the strategic interaction between them [they continue in a footnote]. That is, not simply to make assumptions about what goes on in the Black Box of decision making and the Black Box of strategic interaction but, insofar as possible, to study directly the processes of decision making and interaction.

This is essential to the aim of this study. Far too many studies of the international oil market make crude assumptions regarding actors' interests, behavior, and interaction. The result is an overemphasis on structural aspects of the market.[10] An approach that combines structural and behavioral aspects can yield new and better understanding of the international oil market, and such a thematically focused study can contribute to the understanding of international economics and politics, of which the international oil market constitutes an interesting and important aspect.

Walter Carlsnæs contributes to the agent-structure debate by introducing time as a part of the theoretical model (Carlsnæs 1992). This opens the possibility to include both the impact of structure on agents and the impact of agents on structure, by modeling the relationship as a dynamic process. This pragmatic approach seems far better than trying to resolve ultimately the causal relationship between actors and structure. The position taken in this study is that the agent-structure debate is and will be unsolvable. It is trivially true that "both agents and social structures interact reciprocally in determining the foreign policy behavior of sovereign states" (Carlsnæs 1992:250). This probably goes for all human decisions. We can discuss how and to what extent structures influence a particular behavior and vice versa, but this is obviously an empirical question.

In Chapter 2 I try to explain the possibility of oil-producer cooperation on the basis of changes in the market structure and the accompanying distribution of power among three groups of market actors: the producer countries, the consumer countries, and the international oil companies. First, the discussion concerns the extent to which the fundamental aspects of the market structure of the international oil market limit the oil producers' freedom of action in such a way that they influence the possible cooperation between them. Second, there is the question to what extent the market power of other actors, such as the consuming countries and the international companies, limits the success of cooperation between the oil producers. Changes in market structure and market-power distribution are assumed to constrain the opportunity set for possible successful oil-producer cooperation. The argument is based on theories of industrial organization. In Figure 1.2 the model of industrial organization of the international oil market is introduced. The figure explicitly outlines the causal relationship between market structure, market behavior, market power, and the so-called performance, which in this book is narrowed down to the possibility of producer cooperation. The empirical contents of these concepts are further developed in Chapter 2. It should be noted that the structural aspects of the oil market discussed in Chapter 2 form a basis for the discussion in all the following chapters, as the arguments in the other chapters are all dependent on the structural changes identified in it.

In Chapter 3, on the political structure, theoretical problems connected with the understanding of states as rational actors emerge. In that chapter the actors are regarded as having a complex set of interests. It follows that the actors might have difficulties identifying the optimal choice of action, or that their behavior in different situations might be contradictory. This leads us to the study of the behavior of states as complex actors, which is a substantial field in the theoretical literature on foreign policy, in particular following the seminal work of Graham Allison (1971). In Chapter 3 this problem is confined to the possible contradiction between the welfare interests and the security interests of the oil-producing states, and the implication of this contradiction for the cooperation between such states. The organizational unity of the state is subsequently preserved in Chapter 3, while the interests are regarded as more complex than in Chapter 2.

The Institutional Level

In Chapter 4 the discussion focuses on an intermediate level between the structure, which the actors take as given, and their individual behavior or interaction. This level is occupied by institutions. The institutions are created by the oil producers but still constrain the same actors' behavior. "Institutions are the rules of the game in a society or, more formally, are the humanly devised constraints that shape human interaction. In consequence they structure incentives in human exchange, whether political, social or economic. Institutional change shapes the way societies evolve through time and hence is the key to understanding historical change" (North 1990:3). Interstate cooperation of certain degrees of time and space demands some forms of institutionalization. To some extent the institutions play the same role as the structure, in as much as institutions "constrain activity, and shape [actors'] expectations" (Keohane 1989:3). However, institutions often are more easily influenced by the actors' behavior. Institutions are created by the actors, and thus their autonomy has been a much-debated issue in the study of international politics. In the case of the oil-producer cooperation, the formal organization OPEC is the dominant manifestation of this institutionalization. This organization has a low score on the scale of autonomy (see Chapter 4).

The question is to what extent membership in the organization OPEC influences the members' behavior, their objectives, and their collective identity. Generally, institutions are regarded as at the same time constraining and enabling actors' behavior. In Chapter 4, institutions are primarily seen as constraining the actors' behavior by their role in providing information, creating decisionmaking rules, monitoring agreements, framing decisions, and forming common identities. This is to some extent contrary to the conventional view of OPEC. The traditional approach to the study of OPEC has been the role of the organization in controlling the oil market and thus enabling the members to reap huge profits on their oil exports. These aspects are discussed in Chapter 2 as part of the relationship between the structure of the international oil market and the behavior of oil producers, oil consumers, and the international oil companies. In the rest of the study the focus is on the cooperation *between* oil producers. Given this aim, the organization is directed to the aim of achieving a collective good for the oil producers: a higher oil price. Accordingly, the role of the organization is primarily to curb individual members' incentive to cheat or behave as free riders. The argument in Chapter 4 assumes that institutions might obtain sufficient autonomy to influence the actors' behavior. Once an institution has been created, there are some additional costs connected with the dissolution of the organization, regardless of its substantive value or importance. In the case of OPEC, this phenomenon is certainly present. Even in times when the members of the organization have disregarded the common policy formulated during its deliberations, a dissolution of OPEC would most certainly have created a more severe and lasting market disruption, a development most of the members would regard as catastrophic. The organization has obtained a certain degree of autonomy, and thus it has a certain independence from the will of the members.

The Level of State Interaction

Due to the above-mentioned insufficiency of a purely structural explanation of oil-producer cooperation, the attention is now turned to the interaction between the actors. The importance of this level is argued by Arthur A. Stein (1990:53):

> State behavior does not derive exclusively from structural factors like the distribution of power; neither can such behavior be explained solely by reference to domestic sectors and interests. Structure and sectors play a role in determining the constellation of actors' preferences, but structural and sectoral approaches are both incomplete and must be supplemented by an emphasis on strategic interaction between states.

The meaning of the word "cooperation" includes an assumption of such strategic interaction between two or more entities. As pointed out above, the bargaining between the oil producers includes both cooperative and conflictual incentives. Compared to the basic moves at the structural level, this level focuses on the negotiatory moves or communication moves (Snyder 1972:222). These are moves, among a set of actors, within a structurally constrained bargaining relationship. The market behavior of the actors is influenced by changes at the structural level, but not completely determined by it.

In Chapters 5 to 8 the actors' objectives are regarded as limited to their interests as oil producers—to maximize revenues from their oil production. In this chapter, cartel theory is combined with insight from the theory of collective action. The theory of collective action, developed by

Mancur Olson (1965), is used to discuss the issue of quota compliance, which is one aspect of cartel theory.[11]

Chapters 5 to 8 are based on the second part of the situational analysis, the principle of rationality. This concept needs some clarification. The principle implies that an action is regarded as explained when it can be shown that the action was adequate given the actor's perception of the situation (Hovi and Rasch 1996:75). In itself this does not include assumptions regarding the actor's desires. However, Donald Davidson (1980:11) has argued that "at least in a vast number of typical cases, some pro attitude must be assumed to be present if a statement of an agent's reasons in acting is to be intelligible." This connects the action with the desires. Davidson's general argument goes as follows: "Whenever someone does something for a reason . . . he can be characterized as (*a*) having some sort of pro attitude toward actions of a certain kind, and (*b*) believing . . . that his action is of that kind" (Davidson 1980:3–4). These two aspects are named the primary reason. Davidson claims that "the primary reason for an action is its cause" (Davidson 1980:4).[12] Elster (1985:2–3) spells out this point as follows: "we must require, first, that the reasons are reasons for the action; secondly, that the reasons do in fact cause the action for which they are reasons; and thirdly, that the reasons cause the action 'in the right way.' Implicit in these requirements is also a consistency requirement for the desires and beliefs themselves." This links the action with the reason, but the theory also tells us how this reason emerges: "An action, to be rational, must be the final result of three optimal decisions. First, it must be the best means of realizing a person's desire, given his beliefs. Next, these beliefs must themselves be optimal, given the evidence available to him. Finally, the person must collect an optimal amount of evidence" (Elster 1989c:30). This outlines the understanding of the individual actor as a rational actor. The approach to the interactional level is thus understood as the meeting of two rational actors.[13]

The next step of this book is to ask whether we discover additional aspects of the oil-producer cooperation if we modify and supplement the principle of rationality. It might be that the principle of rationality is insufficient to explain the actors' behavior in particular instances, although it holds true that actors act rationally most of the time.

The behavior of an actor in a policy area can change as its interests become relatively less important due to changes of the opportunity set in another policy area. The world is complex, and it is impossible for the decisionmaker to have information about all issues in order to calculate the utility connected with each policy option. Rational choice theorists' assumptions regarding the actor's knowledge seem too strong. Simon (1976:81) calls for loosening the assumptions: "Rationality implies a complete, and unattainable, knowledge of the exact consequences of each choice. In actuality, the human being never has more than a fragmentary knowledge of the conditions surrounding his action." This bounded rationality challenges the presumption of consistency: "Beliefs and desires can hardly be reasons for action unless they are consistent" (Elster 1985:4). Regarding the actor's desires, Elster (1985:6) states that "the consistency criteria for preferences involve, minimally, *transitivity*: if I prefer *a* to *b* and *b* to *c*, I should prefer *a* to *c*. More complex consistency criteria are required when preferences are defined for options with a more complex internal structure." In the study of interaction between actors, the rational choice is a framework for game theory. Also in game-theoretical studies, simplifications are necessary: "a usual procedure when applying game-theoretical models is to perceive the players preferences as exogenous. . . . This means for practical purposes that preferences are assumed to remain unaffected by which moves have been conducted during the game. For instance, the preferences are assumed to be unaffected if the actors in the game enter into an agreement" (Hovi 1992:16, my translation). As Hovi points out, the above assumption "undoubtedly represents a substantial simplification in relation to the real world" (Hovi 1992:16). This does not imply any rejection of the principle of rationality. It does, however, call for an inclusion of the process of weighing the different interests. It also opens up the possibility that desires are more volatile and unpredictable. In this study the parsimony of game theory has been sacrificed in order to make a more fine-grained discussion possible and thus increase the validity of the study of actors' interaction.

The Level of Individual State Behavior

The fourth level is the domestic aspects of the formation of states' policies in the international oil market. The need for including even studies of individual actors is proposed by Hollis and Smith (1991:143). Having concluded that the structural approach is insufficient, they proceed by studying the units and their relations by discussing game theory. This still leaves at least two problems unsolved:

> One is the psychology of the individual human decision-makers and how it functions in small decision-making groups. The other is the bureaucratic organization of the domestic process of making policy and translating it into decision and implementation. (Hollis and Smith 1991:143)

The cooperation between oil producers is influenced by factors within the individual states. Several aspects of the domestic policy-making process of many oil producers could be relevant to this study. It has been necessary to limit this part of the book to two case studies: first, a case study of Saudi Arabia, focusing on the kingdom's role as a hegemonic power among the oil producers (see Chapter 6); and second, a case study of Norway, focusing on the consequences of its increased market share for the country's policy toward oil-producer cooperation (see Chapter 9).

The assumption of a unitary actor, which has prevailed throughout the previous levels, is now abandoned. The actors are assumed not only to have a complex set of interests, as is the case in Chapter 3, but also to be organizationally heterogeneous, modestly in Chapter 6, and more fundamentally in Chapter 9.

Keohane and Nye (1977:27) argue that "when there are multiple issues on the agenda, many of which threaten the interests of domestic groups but do not clearly threaten the nation as a whole, the problems of formulating a coherent and consistent foreign policy increase." In Chapter 6, Gilpin's (1981) theory of hegemonic stability is modified to explain better the fall of hegemony. In the discussion of Saudi Arabia's role in the oil-producer cooperation, the policy dilemma of the House of Saud becomes evident—the royal family wishes to provide external security through a military alliance with the United States, but runs the risk of provoking internal disruption by becoming too Westernized. The oil policy is balancing between the large exporter dominating the market and the large OPEC ally being exploited by the smaller members. The chapter does not include domestic factors as such, but shows the policy dilemma of an individual actor, and thus increases the complexity of the approach compared with that of the previous chapters.

The theory adapted in Chapter 9 is a combination of bargaining models of the relationship between OPEC and Norway, and models of the formation of public policy in Norway. The aim is to understand how the free-rider strategy, pursued by Norway in the seventies, became increasingly difficult to sustain as the Norwegian oil production and the share of the total market increased. Compared with Chapter 6, this chapter increases the complexity of the approach further by arguing that the organizational structure of the individual state also is complex, leading not only to inconsistent interests but also to inconsistency in behavior among different parts of the state. "Domestic politics and international relations are often somehow entangled, but our theories have not yet sorted out the puzzling tangle. It is fruitless to debate whether domestic politics really determine international relations, or the reverse. The answer to that question is clearly 'both, sometimes'" (Putnam 1988:427). The model is further complicated because Norway was, and is, in a bargaining relationship with the OPEC members, and the fact that Norwegian domestic actors, like the executive and the legislature themselves, are not unitary actors. The formalized model of the two-level game provided by Milner

(1997) is thus used as a framework for the empirical discussion on the Norwegian policy toward OPEC, although it is not applied explicitly.

Propositions and Model

A multilevel approach such as the one outlined above unavoidably generates a complex set of explanatory propositions. This increases the possibility of incoherence and internal contradictions in the approach chosen. This section will explicate the propositions of the different chapters and establish the relationship between them. It is argued that the multilevel approach applied in this study is based on complementarity of the different parts.

The first proposition is that the success of oil-producer cooperation has been constrained both by fundamental economic factors, such as demand elasticity and lack of barriers to entry, and by other actors' behavior in the international oil market, such as that of the oil-consuming countries and the international oil companies. The difference between the short-term inelasticity and the long-term elasticity of crude oil demand inflicted the short-term beneficial oil-producer cooperation with considerable costs in the long run. The strategy that was profitable in the short term became costly in the long run. In addition, other actors amplified this effect, making the oil producers' attempt to govern the international oil market even harder than the structural effects would have implied. These aspects of oil-producer cooperation are discussed in Chapter 2.

The second proposition discussed in this book is that the institutionalization of cooperation between oil producers has made the cooperation more successful than would otherwise have been the case. The establishment of OPEC and the subsequent working of this organization are assumed to have benefited the oil producers. Chapter 4 discusses how the members, through institutional mechanisms, have tried to overcome the individual members' incentives to act as free riders.

The third proposition is that the collective action of the oil producers has created an additional profit to the producers. The empirical discussion in Chapter 5 first establishes the extent of collective action by the oil producers. Second, it focuses on the bargaining process leading to such collective action. In Chapter 7 the distribution of the costs and benefits resulting from the collective strategy is also highlighted. Chapter 6 focuses on the role of Saudi Arabia, on the basis of the hypothesis that large producers are more likely to contribute to the provision of a collective good than are smaller actors.

The fourth proposition of this study is that the oil-related decisions made by oil-producing states are influenced by interests outside the international oil market. States have more on their minds than profit. In

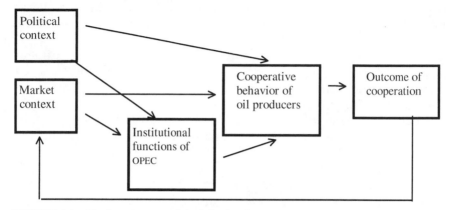

FIGURE 1.1   Explanatory model of the book

Chapter 3 the consequences for oil-market behavior of states' security interests are examined. The question discussed is to what extent the security interests of the oil-producing states have had a negative effect on their incentives to cooperate in the oil market, and their ability to work jointly to achieve cooperative decisions and thus beneficial outcomes.

The fifth proposition follows from the third one, as Saudi Arabia is identified as the actor having in certain periods carried a heavier burden than the rest of the members of OPEC. The proposition is that the OPEC cooperation has been dependent on Saudi Arabia's performing a role as a hegemonic power. This proposition is discussed in Chapter 6.

The sixth proposition suggests that the larger a country's share of the total market becomes, the less likely it is that this country will pursue a free-rider strategy. The case of Norway illustrates this point and other bargaining aspects of the oil-producer cooperation. Since Norway has gone from being an insignificant producer to becoming the world's second-largest oil exporter, a case study of this country provides a diachronic approach to the question of why an individual oil producer chooses to cooperate. These aspects are discussed in Chapter 9, which also includes a discussion of the proposition that changes in domestic factors influence the willingness of a state's authorities to indulge in producer cooperation.

The relationship between the key variables included in this study can be illustrated in a model (see Figure 1.1). The model suggests how the different aspects of the study are related. It does not imply that the study includes estimations of the direction and strength of causality. The model thus has an illustrative function. As pointed out in section 1.2, the

dependent variable in this book is the outcome of oil-producer cooperation. This outcome is determined by the intentions and behavior of the
oil producers. These, in turn, are determined by three independent variables: the market context; the political context; and the institutional
functions of the oil-producer organization, OPEC. Besides indicating the
relationship between the explanatory factors in the study, the model in
Figure 1.1 also indicates the dynamic approach of this book. Structure
and behavior are intertwined, and the outcome of the oil-producer cooperation at time t_1 will influence the structure at time t_2. It is left to the discussion in the individual chapters to substantiate the contents of the different explanatory factors. The aspects of the overriding research
question and the model outlined in this section will be dealt with in the
conclusion (Chapter 10), where the findings of the different chapters are
drawn together.

The different chapters in this book all deal with the same empirical
phenomenon, the cooperation between oil producers during a thirty-year
period, from 1971 to 2000. Each chapter approaches different aspects of
this phenomenon, from underlying structural constraints, through the
bargaining between OPEC members, and to the strategy of an individual
actor like Norway. The chapters are thus on different levels of analysis,
and they apply different theories. The following section places this study
in relation to existing economic literature on oil-producer cooperation
specifically and the international oil market in general.

1.5   Relations to Economic Theories

In the study of the international oil market, several economic models
have been applied. Fundamental assumptions, methodology, and episte-
mology vary in the different models. Robert Mabro (1992) has categorized the economics of the oil market into four different lines of research:

1.   those based on the understanding of oil as an exhaustible resource
2.   those focused on aspects related to industrial economics
3.   those making game-theoretical simulation exercises
4.   those conducting econometric testing of oil-market price behavior

Although none of these lines of research provides a satisfactory answer
about what determines the price of oil, Mabro obviously recognizes the
merits of all of the four research streams. The present study relates to the
economic lines of research as follows: the fourth line, dealing with econo-
metrics and predictions, is of little relevance, as this study deals with past
experiences and is aimed at explaining, not predicting. The third line,
game-theoretical aspects, forms the theoretical basis for the discussion in

Chapter 7 and parts of Chapter 9. The game theory presented in this study is, however, far from the one presented by Mabro. The game theory in this study highlights some key aspects of the strategic interaction of specific actors, in particular situations, in the history of oil-producer cooperation. The line of research mentioned by Mabro is a microeconomic variant of game theory that builds theoretical comprehensive models of behavior of all market actors. In Chapter 2, concepts taken from the second line, industrial economics, will be applied. The theoretical foundation of this line of research is outlined in the next subsection. First it is necessary to present the argument of those who refute the first line of research, the one based on the understanding of oil as an exhaustible resource.

Hotelling and Exhaustible Natural Resources

The first line of research mentioned above "has its true source in a seminal article published by Professor Hotelling in 1931" (Mabro 1992:2). In short, the Hotelling (1931) rule states that an exhaustible resource can be regarded as a fixed asset that the owner can either extract or leave in the ground. The problem for the owner is to maximize the profit over the total extraction time. If oil is extracted immediately, the value of it equals the interest rate (provided that the social discount rate equals the market interest rate). The only reason to leave the oil in the ground is a perception of future price increase. It follows that the price must rise at the interest rate or the discount rate for the profit of leaving the oil in the ground to be equal to the profit of extraction.[14]

Hotelling's work has inspired a tremendous number of energy economists. One of, if not *the*, most prominent energy economists, Morris A. Adelman, has on several occasions argued against the applicability of the Hotelling rule to the international oil market. In a more recent contribution, he states that "the Hotelling Rule and Hotelling Valuation Principle are thoroughly discredited. A valid theory was joined to a wrong premise, the fixed stock. It gave results contrary to fact" (Adelman 1993b:8). The argument is partly based on an empirical observation that the physical limit of oil is not a restriction on the consumption of oil. But it is also based on an understanding that the physical or geological amount of oil is irrelevant to the working of the oil market currently and for the foreseeable future. "The total mineral in the earth is an irrelevant non-binding constraint. If expected finding-development costs exceed the expected net revenues, investment dries up, and the industry disappears. Whatever is left in the ground is unknown, probably unknowable, but surely unimportant: a geological fact of no economic interest" (Adelman 1993a:220).

TABLE 1.1   World Proven Reserves, Production, Growth, and Decline in
Reserves (all in 10 x 9 barrels), and R/P Ratios (years), 1970–1993

Year	Proven Reserves	Production	Net Growth or Decline in Reserves	R/P Ratio
1970	533	17.4	45	
1971	578	18.3	22	33.2
1972	600	19.3	-23	32.8
1973	577	21.2	14	29.9
1974	591	21.2	11	27.9
1975	602	20.2	11	28.4
1976	613	21.9	-18	30.3
1977	595	22.6	-7	27.2
1978	588	22.9	22	26.0
1979	610	23.7	-2	26.6
1980	608	22.8	11	25.7
1981	619	21.3	46	27.1
1982	665	20.1	10	31.2
1983	675	20.0	1	33.6
1984	676	21.1	23	33.8
1985	699	20.5	9	33.1
1986	708	21.4	45	34.5
1987	753	21.9	91	35.2
1988	844	22.8	76	38.5
1989	920	23.5	48	40.4
1990	968	23.8	7	41.2
1991	975	23.7	22	43.1
1992	997	23.9	10	41.8
1993	1,007	23.7	2	42.5

SOURCE: Odell 1991:4, 1994:93.

From a straightforward empirical perspective, the overall situation regarding oil reserves has been calculated by Peter Odell (1991), who argues, in accordance with Table 1.1, that the world is running into oil, not
out of oil. The basic assumption for the Hotelling argument, the fixed
stock, has in fact been a substantially increasing stock during the last
thirty years, measured as proven reserves.[15] The real world would be
perverse according to the Hotelling theorem, as it is a correlation between increased production and increased reserves. Since 1945 the relationship has been as follows: The more oil that has been found, developed, and produced, the higher the estimation of remaining reserves has
become. Geological knowledge and extraction technology have something to do with this development. Without going into detail on this

point, the conclusion is that the world has so far been moving away from the development prescribed by Hotelling (1931).

Geologically, there is a fixed amount of physical oil reserves in the world. The argument is that this fact is of no relevance to the actors in the oil market. In particular instances in the history of the oil industry, oil has been perceived as scarce. This understanding has not been based on any measurement of a substantial fall in remaining oil reserves but rather on the experience of dramatic price increases. This fallacy is all too obvious: The price increase is understood as signaling a scarcity. The perception of scarcity leads to projections of continuous prices increases, which again are taken as evidence of scarcity. When the oil price increased in 1973–1974 and 1979–1980, it was expected to continue to increase. As can easily be argued with the benefit of hindsight, this was totally wrong. (This will be discussed in further detail in Chapter 2.) In this setting the Hotelling theorem might have some value, however, as it can explain the decisionmaking problem of an owner of an oil field or oil reserves. If the owner believes that prices will increase more than the return on investments, he or she might tend to postpone extraction. "Nobody would sell his or her shares in Shell at £5 per share today if there was a belief that the price is going to rise to £6 in a month or so" (Mabro 1992:3). This gives the Hotelling theorem some credibility. However, the owners of the resources are often states, which tend to spend the money they earn. To forgo income today often means hard political choices and bargaining with either other parts of a ruling elite or the population in its capacity as voters. Thus the difference between the logic of companies and the logic of states have implications for the relevance of the Hotelling theorem.

Adelman argues that the cost of replacing the produced reserves is a better measure of scarcity: "The early-warning signal of scarcity is a persistent rise in development costs and in the in-ground value of oil reserves" (Adelman 1993a:276). The trend since 1945 is not clear-cut. The overall costs of developing oil have varied, and producing countries differ regarding the level of replacement costs and to what extent the replacement costs are rising or falling. Adelman's sample of key OPEC countries indicates that a large portion of the world's oil reserves is located in countries with falling replacement costs (see Table 1.2).

It is also important to note that for a large part of the reserves being extracted today—as in most parts of the Middle East—the selling price is well above what is needed to cover costs and earn a fair profit. Thus, the incentives for cost-cutting in these areas are few. In other areas, such as the North Sea, where profit margins have come under pressure, substantial cost-cutting efforts have been successfully implemented. The conclu-

TABLE 1.2   Investment Per Additional Daily Barrel of Capacity ($)*

Country	1985	1989–90
Abu Dhabi	2,912	2,033
Algeria	4,570	3,533
Indonesia	5,908	5,637
Iran	NA	1,433
Iraq	NA	145
Kuwait	1,455	895
Libya	24,199	NA
Nigeria	3,179	2,611
Qatar	1,331	1,408
Saudi	692	373

*All dollar amounts in this book are in U.S. dollars.
SOURCE: Adelman 1993b:6.

sion is thus that there are no signs today that overall replacement costs are increasing.

The other important questionable assumption in the Hotelling paradigm is the linear-cost assumption. It is understandable that Hotelling understood the world in this way, as he wrote his paper in the thirties, when most oil was extracted in low- and stable-cost areas with an abundance of oil reserves. Today, however, even in low-cost areas, fast increase in extraction is impossible or at least very costly. Accordingly, no matter what the incentives for increased extraction are, the physical conditions and economics of increased extraction prohibit such increases in depletion rates, at least in the short run. Furthermore, increasing production to a maximum depletion rate takes time.

> Therefore we should expect to see production in the lower-cost areas grow faster than the high-cost. This is precisely what we saw before 1973. Then there was an abrupt turnaround. High-cost areas expanded drilling mightily while low-cost cut back. It was water flowing uphill. The only theory which explains it is monopoly, whether of one or a small group trying to act as one, to restrain output to maintain prices. (Adelman 1987:47)

This powerful argument is important for the focus of this study. In these terms it is the degree of monopoly behavior by the oil-producing countries that is the focus of this study.[16]

The conclusion that oil prices would continue to increase was also reached through analysis of the oil-producer cooperation. Dermot Gately (1995), with the benefit of the hindsight, cites Fesharaki (1981:304): "as to the extent of the price increases [in the 1980s], one can only say with certainty that real prices will not be allowed to decline again." The following conclusion was reached by Øystein Noreng (1978:101):

A low level of oil imports into the OECD (Organization for Economic Cooperation and Development) area will not silence the demands within OPEC for price increases, as long as the oil price remains below the cost of alternative energy sources. . . . many OPEC countries with large populations and small oil reserves are likely to have trade balance deficits by the early 1980s. They will then have the choice of reducing their domestic programs of social and economic development, increase their oil exports, or pressing for a hike in the oil price. The last option is the most acceptable to them because their ability to increase exports is limited and a loss of income is obviously undesirable.

Here it is the likely policy of the oil producers that leads to the conclusion that prices will increase. This is in accordance with the mechanisms that, later in the eighties, caused Adelman to reach the above-mentioned conclusion of "water flowing uphill." These aspects of the oil-producer cooperation are fully developed in Chapter 5.

The Industrial Organization of the International Oil Market

Having argued that the Hotelling tradition has limited relevance given the present state of the oil market, I now turn to the second of Mabro's streams of research: industrial economics:

The second stream consists of work in the more traditional field of industrial economics. Its origins are much older [than those of the first stream]; and the most notable contributions preceded the oil shock of 1973. Recall Paul Frankel (1946), Edith Penrose (1968), Helmut Frank (1966), Jack Hartshorn (1962) and Morris Adelman (1972), among others, who despite their fundamental differences in approaches and fundamental differences in views were all concerned with the economic variables that matter (costs; prices, behavior of firms; scale, vertical integration and industrial structure; transfer prices and tax optimization), and with the central issue of political economy, the relationship between government and industry. (Mabro 1992:4)

Mabro finds that this tradition "dwindled to a trickle" (1992:4) after 1973.[17] However, Chapter 2 will discuss the structural conditions for oil-producer cooperation from this perspective. But first some basic concepts in the literature of industrial organizations will have to be presented.

Most textbooks on industrial organization start with a variant of a model describing the relationship between the basic characteristics of the

industry, the market structure, the actors' behavior, and the ultimate outcome in the forms of prices, patterns of profit, technological progress,
and distributional effects (Scherer and Ross 1990:5; Greer 1984:10; Shepherd 1990). Except for Chapter 2, this study is about the behavior of a
specific group of market actors—the oil producers. In Chapter 2, the focus is on the context of the oil-producers' cooperation. The context consists of two elements, which I have called market structure and market
power. The market structure consists of a vertical and a horizontal structure. The market power is related to the distribution of ability to influence market developments among three groups: the consuming countries, the international oil companies, and the producing countries. The
problem then arises as to how basic characteristics, market structure, actors' behavior, and, for instance, price developments are related to each
other. Figure 1.2 presents a standard textbook version of the industrial organization, including some key concepts used in this study.

The factors included in the market structure box were traditionally
considered exogenous given and not subject to possible influence by the
market actors. Analysts soon discovered that this was not so. The "old"
industrial economists hold on to the notion that the main flow in Figure
4.2 was going from structure through behavior to performance:

> The causation flows mainly downward, . . . At each point in time, the mar-
> ket's structure usually influences the behavior of the firms as they decide
> how strongly to compete or collude with each other. . . . Careful mainstream
> researchers have always recognized that cause and effect are mixed to some
> degree, but logic and business experience have strongly suggested that the
> causation usually flows mostly downward. (Shepherd 1990:7)

The "new" industrial economists thus emphasize

> a number of serious deficiencies. In particular, while it may be possible to
> identify a relationship between, for example, industry profitability and mar-
> ket concentration, there is no reason to believe that such a positive correlation
> tells us anything about causation. . . . What this points to is a difficulty in the
> traditional approach in identifying which of the relevant economic phenom-
> ena are exogenous and which are endogenous. Developments in the new in-
> dustrial economics suggest that most of the factors that enter into market
> structure, conduct, and performance are endogenous. They are derived from
> the basic economic conditions that characterize the market under investiga-
> tion and the strategic interactions of the players in those markets. . . . Firms do
> not merely react to given external conditions, but try to make their economic
> environment as beneficial to themselves as possible, taking into account that
> their competitors will do likewise. (Norman and La Manna 1992:1–2)

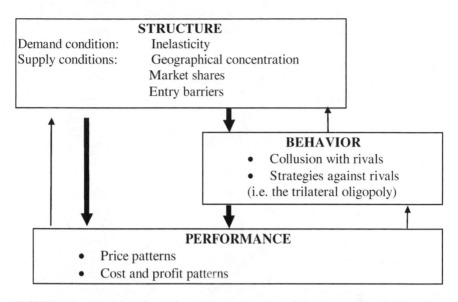

FIGURE 1.2   Model of the industrial organization of the international oil market

This leads to the fundamental proposition of Chapter 2, namely, that the aspects of the market structure cannot be separated from the aspects of the actors' behavior. The dynamic relationship created between structural change and the actors competing for market power is an important foundation for the rest of the book. A study of the success of the oil-producer cooperation has to discuss how this cooperation is affected by and affects the behavior of other actors and the market structure. Chapter 2 outlines the market structure, but the arguments in all the following chapters are based on the understanding of (i) a dynamic relationship between the oil-producer cooperation and changes in the market structure, and (ii) the producers as a group in a strategic interaction with other market actors—the international oil companies and the oil-consuming countries.

1.6   A Note on Sources

As a consequence of the multilevel approach advocated in section 1.4, the empirical analyses in the different parts of this study are partly based on secondary sources. "Secondary research differs from *primary research* in that the collection of the information is not the responsibility of the analyst. In secondary research, the analyst enters the picture after the data collection effort is over" (Stewart and Kamins 1993:3). There are obvious disadvantages connected with the use of secondary sources:

> Data often are collected with a specific purpose in mind. . . . the data collected might be so extensive that the individual whose job it is to interpret the findings can potentially arrive at many different, even conflicting conclusions, all of which might be supported by some subset of the data. . . . the secondary data are aggregated in some form, and the unit of aggregation may be inappropriate for a particular purpose. . . . finally, secondary data are, by definition old data. (Stewart and Kamins 1993:6)

These aspects have to be given particular consideration when using secondary sources. Some advantages of using secondary sources can also be noted: "it is less expensive to use secondary data than it is to conduct a primary research investigation" (Stewart and Kamins 1993:5). In this study the use of secondary sources has facilitated a more complex analysis than would have been possible if all aspects discussed had been based on primary research. This weighing toward more variables and fewer primary sources has been a conscious choice. However, there are several topics in this book that are based on primary research, meaning that the data have been collected by me. In the following paragraphs the data used in the different chapters are outlined, and some methodological aspects discussed. First, however, some comments are necessary about the use of sourcebooks and compiled statistical material.

This study covers a thirty-year time span, from 1971 to 2000. Several economic factors are presented in charts. The data on prices and production are taken from reliable sources, widely used as references in the oil industry. Most price data in the book are based on the prices reported in OPEC *Bulletin*. These monthly average price data are based on *Platt's Oilgram Price Report*, which is regarded as reliable in reporting the spot crude oil prices. The monthly production data are taken from the publication *Petroleum Economist*, a well-known source of information on the international oil market. Annual production data have been taken from *BP Statistical Review of World Energy*. This publication is perhaps the most-cited reference for oil-market data, and is regarded as highly reliable. Production figures vary somewhat between different sources, but not in a way that should make the discussion in this book uncertain. In addition to these statistical reports, three sourcebooks have been used. *Energy in the World Economy—a statistical review of trends in output, trade, and consumption since 1925* (Darmstadter et al. 1971) is a compilation of statistical information on world energy until 1970. There is no analysis conducted in this source. The same goes for *Oil Economists' Handbook* (Jenkins 1986), which is a compilation of statistical information and a dictionary of oil-related terms. OPEC *and the World Energy Market—a comprehensive reference guide* (Evans 1990) describes the events in the oil market and the decisions of OPEC and the members' behavior in the market on a year-by-year basis from 1960 to 1990. The text presented in this book is mostly descriptive, providing "wide-ranging factual coverage . . . designed to provide a rounded historical perspective" (Evans 1990:xxi). This publication is largely a textual presentation, and the possibility of interpretations and errors is greater than in the above-mentioned statistical compilations. This has partly been compensated for by a substantial reliance on *Official Resolutions and Press Releases—1960–1990* (OPEC 1990). This compilation, published by The Secretariat of the Organization of the Petroleum Exporting Countries in Vienna, provides the full texts of the decisions of OPEC, and can in my opinion be regarded as just as good as having the original texts.

The data in Chapter 2, which form the basis for the inference of a causal relationship between market structure, market power, and the possibility of producer cooperation, are of two different kinds: statistical data on the historical developments in important economic variables constituting the market structure, and a historical description of the relationship between the three groups constituting the trilateral oligopoly. The first kind of data is utilized through a descriptive economic method presenting the changes in the economic variables. On this basis, it is argued that the conditions for producer cooperation are better given a favorable development in such factors. The historical narrative regarding the changes in market power is utilized in the same manner, describing the changes in control among the international companies, the consuming countries, and the producing countries, and suggesting that certain constellations of power between these groups favor the establishment of cooperation between the oil producers. In Chapter 2, these two kinds of data and the connected reasoning are linked as the presentation is structured according to the historical changes in these variables and the dependent one—the oil-producer cooperation. None of the data presented in this chapter are especially uncertain. They are all very well established and largely noncontroversial in the literature on the oil market.

Chapter 3 includes, in section 3.5, data from the Polity III project, which are used to describe the level of democracy among the OPEC countries. The validity and reliability of these data are discussed in Jaggers and Gurr (1995). The coding of the Democracy Indexes referred to in Table 3.2 obviously involves an element of subjectivity: "Given the paucity of democracy as an analytical concept, the empirical variability of current measures of regime type can be attributed, at least in part, to differences among researchers" (Jaggers and Gurr 1995:469). Intersubjective agreement seems a reasonable criterion for relying on the data, at least for the use made of them in this study: "The stronger the correlations between our measures and others' indicators of regime traits . . . the higher our confidence in the empirical validity of our indicators and data" (Jaggers and Gurr 1995:473). The measures applied are highly correlated with measures used by other scholars of democracy (Jaggers and Gurr 1995:475).

The data in Chapter 4 are mostly primary data on the decisions made at the OPEC conferences or by different ministerial committees. Most of these are compiled and published by the organization itself (OPEC 1990). There is no reason to doubt the reliability of these data. However, they should not be interpreted as telling the whole truth about the decisions. In every organization that involves bargaining between states or other actors, there might be hidden agendas and double meanings related to both the bargaining process and the subsequent outcome. To some extent this has been taken into account, as I have included both direct statements from the actors and the evaluation of different events by commentators or in secondary literature.

As in Chapter 2, the data used in the empirical discussion in Chapters 5 and 7 are a combination of statistical data on economic factors and historical narratives. Here the theme is the internal bargaining between oil producers, and not, as in Chapter 2, the market structure and the relationship between oil producers and other groups in the international oil market. The data on quotas are non-disputable, as they are taken directly from OPEC resolutions and are reported verbatim in Table 7.6. The significance of the calculated OPEC revenue in Figure 7.8 is, however, more questionable, as no cost estimates are included. It is simply a multiplication of price and production on a monthly basis. The reason for this is that the intention regarding this figure is only to give a general picture of the development, and that estimates of production costs are one of the most uncertain issues in the statistics of the international oil industry. For example, Morris A. Adelman, a prominent scholar, made estimates on the basis of the following assumption: "It is assumed that drilling costs are the same across all nations and are equivalent to the U.S. drilling costs since no country-specific drilling costs are available" (Adelman and Shahi 1989:3).

The account of the development of the Saudi Arabian hegemony in Chapter 6 is based on secondary literature, both on Saudi Arabia's role in the oil market and on the more general development of the state and the policy of the Saudi Arabian regime.

Chapter 9 includes an account of the bargaining relationship between OPEC and Norway in section 9.3. Here, newspapers are a prominent source of information. In many cases these news reports refer only to statements made by the actors in the bargaining process. In such cases the methodological uncertainty is related to the accuracy of these references. In cases where the journalists have interpreted aspects of the bargaining situation on the basis of interviews with actors involved in the process or their own judgments, the reliability is further weakened by the journalists' possible inaccuracy and misunderstanding of aspects of the situation. In my use of such secondary sources, the primary aim has been to cite the facts drawn from primary sources, and as far as possible avoid the interpretation of the secondary author (see Moravcsik 1998:83). The insight into this bargaining process gained from more official sources is slim, as the official statements made about the bargaining with OPEC are all part of the bargaining itself. The possibility of revealing information to the opponent made most official statements vague and inane. In section 9.3 the weaknesses of section 9.2 are somewhat countered as the general aspects of the bargaining relationship between OPEC and Norway are discussed in terms of game theory. Both of these sections could have been presented individually. My argument is that the reliability and validity of the arguments in the chapter as a whole are strengthened by discussing the same aspects both in a fine-grained empirical fashion and in a more general, game-theoretical way. Section 9.4 deals with the domestic factors influencing the Norwegian policy toward oil-producer cooperation. Here, the data are of different kinds. First, I use some economic data regarding the importance of the oil sector in the Norwegian economy. Second, data on the political disagreements in the Norwegian parliament regarding oil issues are presented. Third, some secondary sources and reported statements by ministers are given. These sources are reliable in the quoting of statements. The secondary sources range from graduate theses to renowned scholars on Norwegian oil policy.

Notes

1. Environmental activists attacking oil installations and public criticism of relations with regimes abusing human rights are two examples of situations where oil companies are confronted by society in a manner similar to that characterizing the relations between state and society.

2. Even a further specification might be necessary. The study primarily deals with the net exporters of crude oil, in other words, those oil producers who operate on the international oil market. Much attention will be devoted to the members of the Organization of the Petroleum Exporting Countries (OPEC), although Chapter 9 is a case study of a non-OPEC producer, namely, Norway.

3. "A point such that neither side can profitably move away from it is regarded as an *equilibrium point* and the strategies which give it as *equilibrium strategies*" (Nicholson 1992:93).

4. Monopolization had to a great extent been rendered a legal question—how legislation could prevent the formation of such groups. In the international oil

market this legal aspect of the problem did not arise. What did emerge was what we can call the ideological attacks on OPEC for destroying the liberal world economic system of free trade.

5. This division of the economics models is also present in the oil-market models in Crémer and Isfahani (1991) and in Mabro (1992).

6. The argument is not limited to the introduction of political factors. Approaches which combine the study of the oil market with factors other than politics can increase our understanding of the oil market. Øystein Noreng (1997) has conducted a study of the relationship between oil and religion.

7. In Chapter 4 the logic of appropriateness is presented as another way actors choose between different possible actions. In Chapter 3 the complexity of states' interests modifies the actor's ability to make rational calculations of utilities connected with the different possible actions, and thus the actor's rationality is weakened. Finally, in Chapter 9 the inclusion of the domestic political structure in the analysis of a particular actor reveals a decisionmaking process so complex that the state cannot be regarded as a unitary actor, and thus a weaker principle of rationality is called for.

8. In this book the structure of the international oil market is applied simply, according to the meaning suggested by Edith Penrose (1987:80): "a framework within which activity is carried out and which is itself not easily changed" (i.e., factors the oil producers take as given).

9. Walter Carlsnæs, lecture, September 13, 1991, Department of Political Science, University of Oslo.

10. I am indebted to Bent Sofus Tranøy for pointing out this implication.

11. Adelman's argument, cited in section 1.2, that oil producers try to maximize wealth is the basis for the discussion in Chapter 5. The way the oil producers achieve it is through collective action in which the other producers influence the individual actor's calculation of the rational choice. The rational choice thus becomes a more complex calculation than in a situation where the actor makes its choice in isolation. The actor interacts strategically with its environment, and the environment thus cannot be treated parametrically in the rational decision process.

12. With this understanding, Davidson includes what Elster calls intentional models in the category of causal models: "I want to defend the . . . position that rationalization is a species of causal explanation" (Davidson 1980:3). This goes along the argument presented by Searle (1983:115): "some philosophers have been so impressed by the peculiarities of human action that they have postulated a special kind of causation that goes with agents. According to them there are really two different kinds of causation, one for the agents and one for the rest of the universe." Searle, however, argues that "since Føllesdal's article [Føllesdal 1971] on the subject, it has been widely accepted that certain forms of causal statements are inten[t]ional" (ibid.:117). Elster, however, argues that "it is clear that for practical purposes we may treat intentional and causal explanations as wholly distinct" (1985:23).

13. John Harsanyi (1986:89) defines game theory as "the theory of rational behavior by *two or more* interacting rational individuals, each of them determined to

maximize his own interests, whether selfish or unselfish, as specified by his own utility function."

14. This argument assumes that the income from oil sales is used in such a way as to generate social benefits equal to the general interest rate level.

15. Proven reserves are "generally taken to be those quantities which geological and engineering information indicates with reasonable certainty can be recovered in the future from known reservoirs under existing economic and operating conditions" (*BP Amoco Statistical Review of World Energy 1999*).

16. A much-debated theme in short-term analysis of the supply side of the oil market is the study of production capacity and capacity utilization. This topic will not be a prominent part of this study. Some readers might find this lack of emphasis on capacity strange. Two arguments explain this: First, the public information on countries' oil-production capacity is inherently uncertain. Second, the installed production capacity is important in understanding short-term constraints on producer behavior. In the longer run, as in this book, capacity for many producers becomes a question of investment capital for exploring and developing new production capacity. Such decisions are a matter of political considerations of the economic interests of the state. This is a topic studied in this book. But for these producers, capacity is not a constraining issue in the longer term.

17. This was partially due to the importance attributed to OPEC after this year, in particular the political aspects of the OPEC era, such as ideological attacks on OPEC as a cartel and its role in the north–south divides and the Arab-Israeli conflict. "There is no point pretending in these circumstances that the study of OPEC can be fully objective" (Mabro 1992:5).

2

Market Context

The aim of this chapter is to discuss the structural conditions for oil-producer cooperation. The argument put forward is that the success of the cooperation between the oil producers has been constrained both by fundamental economic factors (such as changes in demand and lack of barriers to entry) and by the behavior of other actors (international oil companies and consuming countries). These two sets of factors (denoted as market structure and market power) interact during the time period in question, changing the conditions for the success of the oil-producer cooperation. The market power of other actors and the structure of the international oil market are factors outside the direct control of the oil-producing countries' governments. These governments accordingly tend to regard such factors as given when forming their own oil policies. The oil producers' own behavior, in turn, influences the other actors' behavior and the structure of the market, and thus creates changes in the conditions for the oil-producer cooperation itself at a later stage. As pointed out by Carlsnæs (1992), the relationship between actors' behavior and structure should be regarded dynamically (see section 1.4). The studies of the international oil market during the last decades have to include a dynamic understanding of the relationship between structural factors and the behavior of market actors. This is the aim of sections 2.3 to 2.6.

The concepts of market structure and market power will be developed in sections 2.1 and 2.2. For the purpose of this study, the most important aspects of the market structure are the demand elasticity and the number of oil producers. The most prominent aspect of the market power is the control over the oil resources, trading mechanisms, and the taxation strategies of consuming countries. The importance of these aspects is outlined at the end of sections 2.1 and 2.2.

2.1   Market Structure

The aim of this section is to describe the structure of the international oil market. The concept of market structure generally refers to "certain stable attributes of the market that influence the firm's conduct in the marketplace" (Caves 1980:64), or as "characteristics that are inherent to the product or relatively impervious to easy manipulation by policy" (Greer 1984:9). Cohen and Cyert (1975:14) define the term "market structure" as "the number and size of buyers and sellers in the market, the restrictions that may prevent firms and households from entering or leaving particular markets, and the availability of information about potential buyers and sellers." Adelman (1972:78) defines the market structure as "the number and size distribution of suppliers and the degree of vertical integration." Greer's definition is wider than the others. The following discussion will be in line with this wider concept, although most attention will be devoted to the aspects of market structure contained in the definition proposed by Cohen and Cyert.

Changes in these aspects of the international oil market are supposed to constrain the market actors' behavior, but also to make some paths of action more feasible than others. In line with the aim of this study, it is the constraining and enabling of oil-producer cooperation that will be the focus.

The most important aspect of the market structure is the concentration dimension, the extent of monopoly or competition. In this study the concept is employed in a wider sense. The market structure consists of the institutional framework built around a transaction and is decisive for the negotiation (Williamson 1979:239). The market structure has thus both a vertical and a horizontal element.

Vertical Structure

Since the beginning of the oil industry at the end of the nineteenth century, the vertical structure has been important for the concentration of market power. The Rockefeller empire was initially built on control over refining and transportation, not control over production. The market power of the "Seven Sisters"[1] after the Second World War was based on their control over several stages of the production chain. This section briefly describes the key characteristics of the vertical structure of the international oil market. It forms a foundation for the discussion in the following sections of this chapter, and in the rest of the study. The production chain of oil can be divided into five stages:

TABLE 2.1   Proved Reserves at End of 1975, 1985, and 1995 (share of total)

	1975	1985	1995
North America	8.55	13.06	8.52
S. & C. America	3.88	4.93	7.76
Europe	4.29	4.00	1.74
(Former) USSR	12.06	8.60	5.61
Middle East	55.25	56.14	64.85
Africa	9.76	8.00	7.19
Asia & Australia	6.21	5.26	4.34
Total World	100.00	100.00	100.00
Of Which: OECD	12.60	17.03	10.22
OPEC	67.11	66.80	76.53

SOURCE: *BP Statistical Review of World Energy* 1996.

1. exploration
2. production
3. transportation
4. refining
5. distribution

Successful exploration assumes actual presence of oil deposits. Although some advantage can be gained by technology and know-how regarding the discovery and determination of oil fields, the location of low-cost oil deposits is the first determinant of the structure of the oil market. Table 2.1 shows the proved reserves at the end of 1975, 1985, and 1995.

Also at the production stage, the geographical location of the field is the main determinant of the production costs. Offshore drilling increases costs compared with onshore activity, and, for instance, Alaskan or Siberian oil drilling takes place in a far more difficult climate than drilling in the Saudi Arabian desert. Furthermore, there are different crude qualities, as well as differences in the location of deposits and their quantity and quality, which will determine the costs of depletion of individual oil deposits. New drilling techniques have been developed to increase rate of depletion and lower the costs of production. Extraction rates have been improved by horizontal drilling and injection programs. In addition, the areas under consideration for exploration are constantly expanding due to technology enabling companies to produce oil in deeper waters and in harsher climatic conditions.

The transportation of oil can take place both before and after refining. Pipeline transportation often gives rise to what is known as a natural mo-

TABLE 2.2   Refinery Capacity and Throughputs, 1995 Thousands of Barrels Per Day (th. b/d)

	Capacity	Throughputs	Utilization (%)
United States	15,235	13,970	91.70
Canada	1,835	1,560	85.01
Mexico	1,520	1,315	86.51
S. & C.	6,235	4,835	77.55
Europe	16,595	14,395	86.74
former USSR	10,325	4,900	47.46
Middle East	5,315	5,145	96.80
Africa	2,860	2,315	80.94
China	4,015	2,710	67.50
Japan	4,865	4,170	85.71
Others	7,625	7,600	99.67
Total World	76,425	62,915	82.32

SOURCE: *BP Statistical Review of World Energy 1996.*

nopoly. However, most oil transport today is by ship, except for short-distance transportation from producing wells to shipping terminals. At this stage of the production chain, the economics of the oil industry are connected with the shipping industry. Subsequently, the interests of the shipping industry and the political importance this industry plays in some countries might have an important influence on the oil industry.

The refinery industry plays an important role in the oil-production chain. One aspect has been the location of the refineries: "Since the Second World War there has been a steady trend toward locating refineries near consuming centers instead of near the sources of crude-oil production. Whereas in 1939 some 70 percent of refining capacity outside North America and the Communist countries was near the oil fields, this had dropped to about half by 1951 and to about 16 percent in 1965."[2]

Another aspect of the refinery industry is the overall capacity surplus during the last decades. Table 2.2 shows the distribution of capacity and throughputs for some key areas. Since this stage of the production chain is possible to locate anywhere, contrary to the other stages, it is liable to the economic interests of states' national industrial policies. Subsequently, arguments regarding employment, national control over resources, and national economic and industrial development and growth become important political factors in the location and running of the refinery industry.

Unlike the other stages, the last one, distribution (which includes end-user sales), obviously has to take place where the customer is. It is therefore impossible for activities at this stage of the production chain to escape national jurisdiction and control. An international oil company can locate its activities at other stages more or less in a country of its own choice, but this is not so with distribution and sales. Subsequently, these aspects of the oil market are more influenced by particularities of national markets and local governmental regulations.

For the purpose of this study, the different stages of the production chain represent different conditions for the relationship between the actors in the oil market. The main focus of this study is on the crude oil market (i.e., the production stage). However, actors tend to use their power at other stages to influence the development in the crude oil market. A prominent example is the way in which the producers attempt to increase consumption by reducing the crude oil price, which is futile as long as the consuming countries increase taxes on oil consumption (see section 2.5).

Horizontal Structure

As pointed out in the introduction, the horizontal structure has more direct implications for the oil-producer cooperation, as it relates to the structure of the crude oil market as such. Prominent aspects of the structure of the crude oil market are

1. market concentration
2. product differentiation
3. barriers to entry

In Figure 2.1 the market concentration is indicated by the market share of the five, ten, and fifteen largest producer countries in the international oil market.

Figure 2.1 indicates a modest change in market concentration. Although the five largest countries have reduced their market share from 69 percent in 1965 to 46 percent in 1995, the fifteen largest countries have reduced their market share by a more modest 12 percentage points, from 93 to 81 percent. In his taxonomy of markets, William Shepherd uses the term "tight oligopoly" to describe a situation in which the leading four firms have 60 to 100 percent of the market (Shepherd 1990:14). The other aspect of the market structure is the market share of individual producers. Figure 2.2 lists the fifteen largest producing countries in 1965, while Figure 2.3 gives the same list for 1995.

The following trends can be extracted from these figures. First, among the fifteen countries listed in 1995, only two are not on the 1965 list: the United Kingdom and Norway. This indicates a stable pattern of market shares. Second, the differences between the top fifteen countries have de-

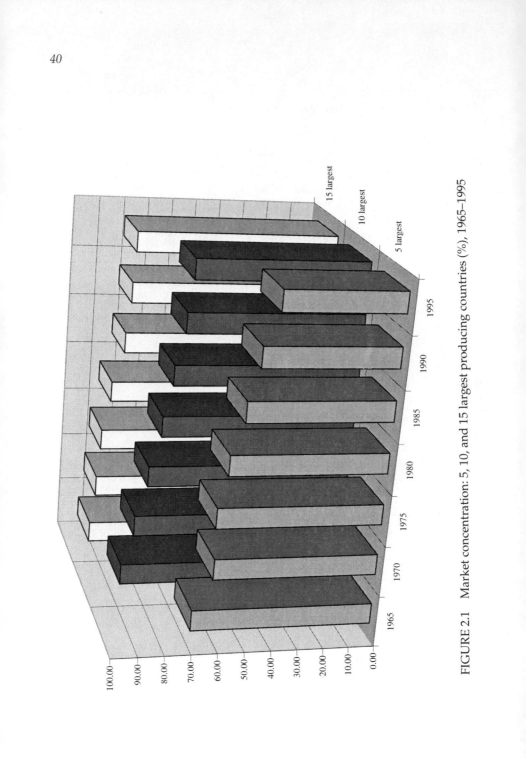

FIGURE 2.1 Market concentration: 5, 10, and 15 largest producing countries (%), 1965–1995

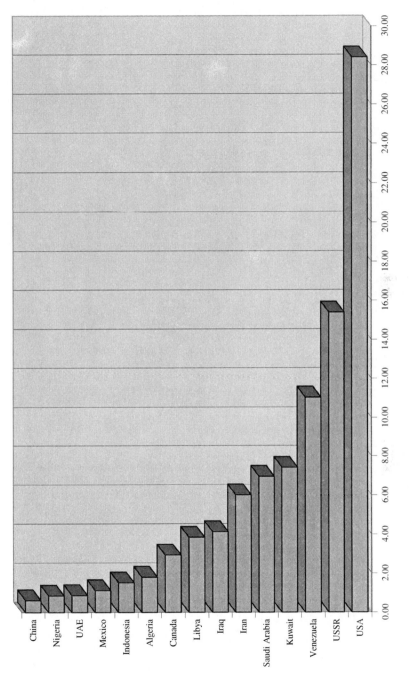

FIGURE 2.2   Market shares, 1955 (%)
SOURCE: Based on data in *BP Statistical Review of World Energy*, various issues.

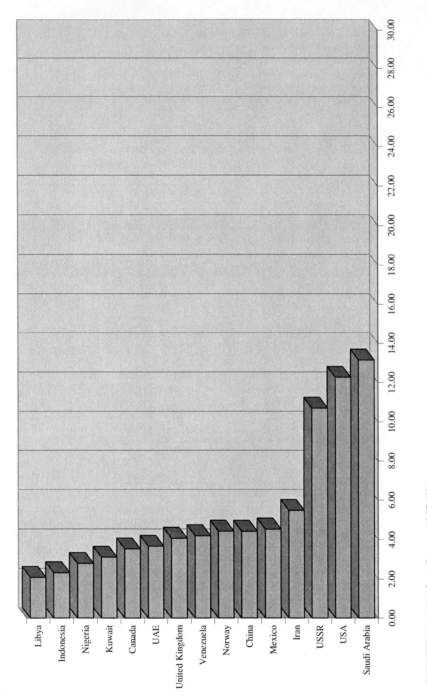

FIGURE 2.3   Market shares, 1995 (%)
SOURCE: Based on data in *BP Statistical Review of World Energy*, various issues.

creased. Third, disregarding the United States and the former USSR, which have substantial domestic consumption, the non-OPEC countries— Mexico, Norway, China, the United Kingdom, and Canada—constitute 21 percent of world production, compared with Canada, Mexico, and China's combined market share of 4.71 percent in 1965. It decreases OPEC's ability to control the market when the main competition is concentrated in a few other countries, rather than having a large number of outsiders taking a substantial share of the market.

Product differentiation in the crude oil market is basically the different oil qualities. These differences are expressed in the price differentials set by the extra costs of refining heavier crude oil. The margins can change somewhat due to differences in demand for different qualities. The simple rule is that the main quality indicator is the API (American Petroleum Institute) gravity—the higher the gravity, the higher the price. But the demand for different qualities changes, seasonally and over time. Also, different sectors of consumption can experience different demand paths, causing the composition of demand for oil qualities to change. More important for the cooperative bargaining between the oil producers is that quality differentials can be an effective way to cover price discounts. If a higher-priced oil quality is discounted, the price can in nominal terms be higher than prices of heavier oil types but still be valued as cheaper by the refiners. It thus imposes pressure on the price of the other oil qualities. Different oil regions have different compositions of oil qualities, making prices vary across regions.

There are few technical barriers to entry in the international oil market. There is, however, one fundamental barrier to entry in the location of resources. This was discussed in section 2.1. There are obviously different levels of technological skills among oil producers. In particular, when oil is first discovered in an area, the countries concerned usually lack the ability to develop the resources on their own. However, in the present situation, with the international oil companies operating globally, the owner of the resource can buy the necessary expertise from them as long as it also provides sound investment condition. As long as oil prices are well above development costs, other producers' behavior has little effect on development decisions of new potential producers. Given the existence of oil resources on their territory, states tend to encourage the development of them.

The concentration of oil production makes the crude market central to the understanding of the total oil industry. "Supply is unlike demand. The amount of the oil demanded results from independent choices of millions of households and firms. . . . a few governments make the most important supply decisions" (Adelman 1993b:1). However, supply-side-created price increases might trigger consumer reactions, such as more efficient use of energy or substitution. As section 2.5 will show, the demand side effects are important for understanding the possible success of oil-producer cooperation.

Market Structure and Oil-Producer Cooperation

The market structure is important both for the market power and for the possible success of oil-producer cooperation as such. The vertical structure described in section 2.2 is an important feature for the changes in market power among the market actors (see section 2.2). It is also important for the development of new trading mechanisms and thus the market power of the producers (see section 2.6). The horizontal market structure influences the market power among the actors—for instance by intensifying competitive pressure on the producer or consumer side. The horizontal structure, demand elasticity, and the number of producers also have a direct effect on the possibility and success of oil-producer cooperation.

The demand elasticity is important for the success of oil-producer cooperation, as it determines the relationship between price and consumed volume. If demand is inelastic, small changes in production create large price changes. If demand is more elastic, the price effect from regulation of production is smaller. Thus, in a situation of demand inelasticity, oil-producer cooperation more easily creates large benefits for the producers than a situation of elastic demand (ceteris paribus). The recent history of the international oil market suggests that demand for crude oil is inelastic in the short run and more elastic in the longer run. The reason for this is the lag between increased oil prices and consumers' adaptation through conservation and substitution. This suggests that oil producers cooperating by limiting output are able to reap substantial benefits in the short term, but the strategy can be less profitable in the longer term.

The number of producers is obviously an important aspect for the possibility of successful cooperation between the producers. The larger the number of oil producers, the harder it becomes to establish a successful cooperation between them (Olson 1965:34–35). The number of producers has increased during the period in question, partly due to the price policy of OPEC, which has made new production areas profitable to develop. The established producers have not been able to set up any barriers to such new entries. This has made successful oil-producer cooperation increasingly difficult.

2.2   Market Power

As mentioned in the introduction, both fundamental economic aspects (as described in the previous section) and other actors' behavior constitute the environment surrounding the oil-producer cooperation. This section deals with the other actors' behavior. The proposition is that oil-producer cooperation is constrained by other actors' behavior. Market power is the basic concept developed to understand the influence of other actors' behavior on the oil producers' freedom of action in the international oil market. Market power is defined as "the ability of a single, or group of buyer(s) or seller(s) to influence the price of the product or service in which it is trading. A perfectly competitive market in equilibrium, ensures the complete absence of market power" (Pearce 1983:274). All the factors discussed in section 2.1 concerning the market structure are important in determining the market power of the sellers. The vertical structure gives rise to actors' strategic positions in controlling other actors' outlet of oil or access to crude oil. The market concentration is the basis for coherent action by a group of actors that leads to the realization of monopoly profit. Barriers to entry ensure this profit against outsiders. And, finally, a high demand elasticity ensures that consumers will continue to buy the product although the price is increased due to the sellers' collecting a monopoly profit. It should be noted that this study concerns the market power of the sellers. The final consumers of oil number in the billions. Even the number of refineries and oil companies around the world is very large. Thus, the events on the supply side of the market are more susceptible to individual or groups of actors' behavior than the demand side, where the large number of actors evens out differences in their behavior. This is not to say that the understanding of oil demand is less important, only that it is more in line with traditional economic models of consumer behavior and less relevant to the core of the research question of this book.

Given the assumption that the different groups of actors that obtain market power in the crude oil market will set the price to their own benefit, the distribution of market power implies the distribution of the monopoly profit. The possible existence of monopoly profit in the industry follows from the definition of market power, as the competitive market is defined as a market without any group of actors having market power. The loss of market power by a group of actors could mean two different things: either that the market has become more competitive, or that another group of actors has increased its market power. Both aspects will be discussed in the empirical sections of this chapter. The market actors can hold tangible power resources like physical control over oil resources or production facilities; ownership of distribution channels or marketing facilities; and concessions to conduct business at the different stages of the production chain where such concessions are necessary. Actors might also hold intangible power resources like information about reserve deposits, production methods, or trading instruments. This emphasizes that market power is exercised in both the vertical and the horizontal market structure.

In the following subsections, it is argued that an understanding of changes in the distribution of market power is the key to understanding changes in the international oil market. This calls for some comments. Given the definition of market power, there is, in a sense, a fixed amount of power at every stage of the vertical production chain. At each step the market actors are in a zero-sum game over the ability to determine the price of the oil traded. It follows that the same must be true for all the stages taken together. One actor's exercising of market power at one stage thus constrains other actors' exercising of their market power at other stages of the production chain. At a given stage, market power is a relative concept. The higher the concentration is on the seller side, and the lower it is at the same time on the buyer side, the higher is the sellers' market power, and vice versa. If there is low concentration on both sides, market power is also low for all actors (see Pearce 1983:274). With a high concentration on both the seller and the buyer side, as for instance in a situation where a monopoly is selling to a monopsony, the monopolist has the advantage if the buyer experiences an inelastic demand. These aspects will be discussed empirically in sections 2.3 to 2.6.

The Trilateral Oligopoly

The actors in the international oil market have been grouped as follows (Adelman 1977; Roncaglia 1985; Mikdashi 1986):

1. oil-consuming countries
2. international private oil firms, upstream and downstream
3. oil-producing countries, including state-run producing firms

Roncaglia (1985) describes the international oil market as a trilateral oligopoly made up of these three groups of actors (Figure 2.4). Inside the groups, in each corner of this triangle, we find attempts to coordinate behavior. The main reason for such cooperation is to strengthen the groups' position in relation to the other actors in the market. One reason for establishing the cooperation between the oil companies was to ensure the strength of the individual company in relation to the authority of producing states.[3] The producers' main reason for establishing OPEC was to counter the market power of the major oil companies. The consumer countries have established the International Energy Agency (IEA) to balance the market power of OPEC. The trilateral oligopoly is characterized by both inter- and intra-group cooperation and conflict.

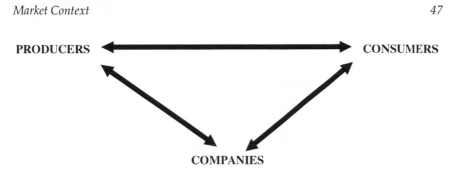

FIGURE 2.4   Trilateral oligopoly

Figure 2.5 highlights the main conflictual aspects of the relations in the trilateral oligopoly. The relationship between consumer and producer countries has a political-ideological dimension, as key oil producers are former colonies of the consumer countries. The main conflict between producers and consumers has been connected with the supply disruptions following political conflicts in the Middle East, and the ideological attacks on OPEC as a cartel disrupting the international free trade liberalism advocated particularly by the United States.

Theoretically, the companies' cooperation with the producers or the consumers would respectively increase or decrease world oil prices. The companies have been attacked by the producers for siding with the consumers. As OPEC gained strength in the early seventies, the first goal was to reduce the companies' influence on the price policy.

On the other hand, in the famous congressional hearing before the subcommittee on multinational corporations, the so-called Church commission, in 1974–1975, representatives of the international companies met senators highly critical of the role of the companies, suggesting that they cooperated among themselves and with the producing countries to drive prices up and thus increase their own profit at the expense of the American consumer.

The cooperative aspects of the inter-group relations highlighted in Figure 2.6 also show how the relations have been perceived by the actors as beneficial. As will be further developed in Chapter 6 on Saudi Arabia, key producers for a long time have sought military support from Western consuming countries in exchange for a somewhat more consumer-friendly oil policy. The exchange between producing countries and the international companies is likewise a combination of both conflictual and cooperative aspects. The consumer-company relationship is rather peripheral to the focus of this book. The relationship was more important in the fifties and sixties than it is today, but this relationship also was char-

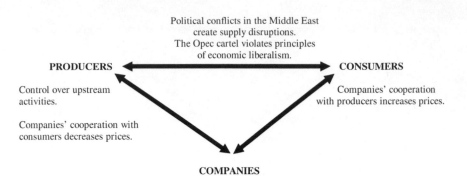

FIGURE 2.5   Conflictual aspects of intergroup relations

acterized by both cooperative and conflictual aspects. The companies to a certain extent benefited from consumer countries' political backing in their operations in the producing countries, and the consumer countries could use the companies as a spearhead in establishing political ties with strategically important countries in the Middle East.

This book is devoted to the study of the intra-group relations between members of one of the groups in the trilateral oligopoly—the producers. Having this aim in mind, it seems fair to confine this empirical outline to the intra-group relations between the producers. In sections 2.3 to 2.6, intra-group aspects regarding consumers and companies will be discussed to the extent that they influence the conditions for producer cooperation. Also on this intra-group level, we find cooperative and conflictual aspects. Three possible explanations of cooperation, or lack of it, will be illustrated:

1.   the presence and role of a hegemon or leader
2.   the constellation of interests
3.   the effect of exogenous shocks

The first aspect is based on the hegemonic stability thesis. Hegemony is loosely defined as a highly asymmetric distribution of power in favor of a single actor. The hegemon is supposed to have interests in line with the collective of actors, and the ability to supply the "collective good." Among the producers, the role of Saudi Arabia in the recent history of the international oil market resembles that of such an actor. The hegemonic stability thesis also implies increased conflict if it should happen that the hegemon is weakened. These aspects are discussed extensively in Chapter 6.

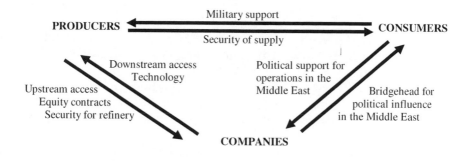

FIGURE 2.6   Cooperative aspects of intergroup relations

The second reason for the emergence of cooperative behavior is the fact that actors have common interests, in other words, the presence of an integrative potential. The question to be asked is what the actors, individually, can gain from cooperation. The relationship between the producers is close to a classic case of the problem of collective action (Malnes 1983). The point of departure for application of the "Prisoner's Dilemma" is that all actors have an interest in limitation of production in order to ensure a high oil price. At the same time, it is in the interests of all actors to sustain their own production volume. In such a case, all actors can gain by cooperating (all reducing production), but individually they can earn more by not cooperating while the others do. These aspects are discussed extensively in Chapter 7. Understanding the oil price as a collective good among the oil producers implies a possibility of free riders. The large non-OPEC exporters—Mexico, China, Norway, and Canada—but also some of the OPEC members acted as free riders during the eighties. These aspects of the relationship between the producers are discussed in Chapter 8, and Chapter 9 is a case study of Norway, emphasizing bargaining problems related to the Norwegian free-rider strategy.

The third aspect of the intra-group cooperation is related to the existence of so-called external shocks—events outside the group that bring them closer together or pull them further apart. The formal producer-cooperative organization, OPEC, was formed in 1960, but not as a result of any crisis. However, in the early eighties, OPEC made decisions that actually restricted the individual member's oil policy by introducing production quotas (see Chapter 5). This decision was a result of the effects of the previous crisis. OPEC had to compensate for the demand decrease and the increase in non-OPEC producers, which had emerged as a result of its own price increases connected with the Iranian revolution and the Iran-Iraq War (see Chapter 3).

Market Power and Oil-Producer Cooperation

The changes of power among the actors in the trilateral oligopoly have implications for the possibility of establishing a successful cooperation between the oil producers. In other words, the relationship between members of one group is influenced by the relationship between the groups. This is the essence of the perspective developed in this section on market power. Three aspects will be given particular attention in the following empirical sections.

First, the concentration on the production side is much higher than the concentration on the consumption side. This gives the actors controlling the oil resources a potential market power over other actors. The transfer of the control over these resources from the international oil companies to the oil-producing states in the first half of the seventies fundamentally changed the basic conditions for any relationship between actors in this market. Although this study is primarily concerned with the oil market after these changes, it is unavoidable as a premise for the discussions presented in most of the study, and in this chapter in particular.

Another aspect to be dealt with in this chapter is the role of different trading mechanisms in the international oil market. The physical cargoes of oil can be traded in different ways, implying different levels of producer control over the price-setting. Long-term bilateral contracts with rigorous price clauses will benefit the seller if prices fall, and the buyer if prices increase. A market characterized by more transparent, market-determined contracts will not create the same asymmetry when prices change, as the actors' adaptation will be more incremental and continuous. The changes in trading mechanisms during the eighties were in themselves not negative for the producers, but since they came at the same time as prices fell, they removed some instruments with which the producers otherwise could have slowed down the price fall. This shows how market power can be exercised in the vertical structure, and has implications for the effectiveness of oil-producer cooperation.

A third aspect related to the market power among a group of actors is the taxation policy of consuming countries. If the producers' cartel policy fails and they attempt to increase the quantities of consumed oil by reducing the price, it is necessary that the reduced crude oil price is passed on to the end-consumers. If instead the consuming countries increase taxes, the end-consumer has no price incentive to increase consumption. This is exactly what has happened in the oil market during the last twenty years. Thus, the oil-consuming countries have increased their market power through this mechanism.

Having outlined the concepts of market structure and market power, and identified the main groups of actors in the international oil market, it is now time to turn to the essence of this chapter—the dynamic interrelationship between market structure, market power, and oil-producer cooperation. The purpose of the following sections is to show how aspects of the market structure created a situation at the beginning of the seventies that made it possible for OPEC to take control over the international oil market. The subsequent behavior of OPEC during the seventies (or, more correctly, until 1981) changed fundamental structural aspects of the market. This once again changed the structural conditions for the successful OPEC cooperation in the late eighties, making it harder and more costly for the producers to pursue a cooperative strategy among themselves—a situation promptly taken advantage of by the other actors in the market. The structural transformation of the oil market since the Second World War has involved a development through three stages: from an integrated market dominated by the large international oil companies, to a market dominated by the oil producers, and finally to a more complex market structure comprising only partially organized groups and division of market power among producers, consumers, and the international companies.

In section 2.3 the empirical discussion is related to how aspects of the market structure and other actors' behavior, in particular that of the international oil companies prior to 1971, were important in forming the oil producers' key desire to gain control over the setting of the oil price. The instrument for achieving this was the cooperation between some OPEC members in a joint strategy against the companies (see section 2.4). This cooperation changed the market structure and the power balance among the market actors (see section 2.5). The OPEC countries did, however, overexploit their position, leaving room for both the return of the companies and an increased position of the consuming countries (see section 2.6).

2.3   The Era of the International Oil Companies

The commercial production of oil started in the United States in 1859, in Titusville, Pennsylvania. Oil demand grew rapidly in the following decades. At the turn of the century, world consumption was twenty-five times the level of that of 1870. Most of this expansion took place in the United States, where the market was soon dominated by the Rockefellers' Standard Oil, whose share of refinery capacity rose from 10 percent in 1870 to some 90 percent ten years later. The near-monopoly situation of Standard Oil in the US market was built on its position in the vertical market structure and thus the establishment of a monopsony position toward producers. It is important to note that the role of Standard Oil was based on a strong position in the downstream segment, not on access and control over resources. For other companies the control of reserves became more important, as did the financial strength to develop such reserves in undeveloped areas. Furthermore, the development of new transportation facilities was also an important means of competition for companies facing Standard Oil in the international oil market.

At the beginning of the twentieth century the focus on the international market intensified among the companies, but not among states:

> The level of government involvement during this period was low due to the fact that oil was mainly seen as an unproblematic commodity, which strategic importance and exhaustibility had not yet been placed on the agenda. ... An exception to the low level of government involvement internationally during this period was the establishment of Anglo-Persian (now BP), where the British government entered as a major shareholder to secure the need for fuel oil for the British navy on the eve of the oncoming War. (Bergesen, Bjørk, and Claes 1989:11–12)

After the First World War the inward-looking attitude of the US government changed. The lack of access to foreign oil supplies was then regarded a "serious international problem facing the United States" (Yergin 1991:194). The same went for the French authorities (Yergin 1991:189).

The area to look for oil was the Middle East. The British made Mesopotamia a British mandate under the League of Nations. In connection with the San Remo agreement, an Anglo-French oil agreement was negotiated.[4] "France would get 25 percent of the oil from Mesopotamia. ... the vehicle for oil development remained the Turkish Petroleum Company ... and the French acquired what had been the German share in it. ... the French gave up their territorial claim to Mosul. Britain, for its part, made absolutely clear that any private company developing the Mesopotamian oil fields would very definitely be under its control" (Yergin 1991:189–190). Access seemed closed to US interests. However, with the breakdown of the Ottoman Empire, the status of the Turkish Petroleum Company concession was unclear, and the companies started a long and bitter fight for influence in the formerly Turkish-dominated area. The US government responded by invoking "the open door policy," which had three elements:

> 1. that the nationals of all nations be subject, in all mandated territories, to equal treatment in law, 2. that no economic concessions in any mandated region be so large as to be exclusive, and 3. that no monopolistic concession relating to any commodity be granted. The United States Government maintained that the war had been won by the Allied and Associated Powers fighting together, and that, consequently, any benefit, whether in oil interests or otherwise, should be available to the nationals of all Allied Powers,

and should not be seized by those of any one particular power. Moreover, the United States asserted that the San Remo agreement discriminated against the rights of American nationals, that no rights in Iraq were vested in the Turkish Petroleum Co., and that no valid concessions could come into existence through the government of the people of the territory. The British point of view was that British nationals had "acquired rights," that these rights must be respected, and that, although the United States had been an Allied Power, this fact gave its nationals no right to trespass upon acquired rights. The term "acquired rights" referred to the rights held by the Turkish Petroleum Co. and the rights promised to that company by the Ottoman Grand Vizier, as evidenced by his letter of June 28, 1914, to the British and German Ambassadors. (Federal Trade Commission (FTC) 1952:51–52)

After yearlong negotiations, the United States, the United Kingdom, and France reached a compromise in 1928. As shown in Table 2.3, the American companies got a fourth of the Iraq Petroleum Company (IPC, formerly the Turkish Petroleum Company) concession. The figure also shows the substantial UK and French governmental stakes in the companies constituting the Turkish Petroleum Company—a situation not likely to be the case for the US authorities.

Furthermore, the companies and authorities also agreed to the so-called self-denying clause of 1914, stating that all parties should work jointly—and only jointly—in the region (Yergin 1991:204). The region included the Arabic peninsula (except Kuwait), Iraq, and Turkey. This was the so-called Red Line Agreement (see Figure 2.7). In the areas inside the red line, the companies would pursue joint concessions. As soon as the US companies mentioned in Table 2.3 were included in the agreement, the open door policy was abandoned and the door was shut to any new company, US-based or not.

By 1928 more than 50 percent of oil production outside the United States was controlled by Exxon, Shell, and British Petroleum (BP). These companies met secretly and worked out a market-sharing deal, the so-called As-is-agreement. This was an agreement to keep the respective percentage market shares of sales in various markets. Another important point in the agreement was the "Gulf plus pricing system," according to which crude was to be priced as if produced in the Mexican Gulf regardless of actual origin. Later the companies also agreed to control production. Most of the other US companies joined the agreement.

The various agreements covered operations in all countries except the United States and the Soviet Union. By the end of the twenties, the companies had set up agreements governing their interrelations in the whole production chain.[5] The scarcity that had made the US companies so eager to get into the Middle East production area soon turned into a giant sur-

TABLE 2.3   The Division of the Turkish Petroleum Company in 1928

Owner	Subsidiary	Share
Anglo-Persian Oil Co., in which the British government held 51%	D'Arcy Exploration Co. Ltd.	23.75
Royal Dutch/Shell (Royal Dutch: 60%; Shell: 40%)	Anglo-Saxon Petroleum Co. Ltd.	23.75
Compagnie Francaise des Pètroles (CFP), in which the French government held 35%		23.75
Standard Oil Co., New Jersey: 25%; Standard Oil Co. of New York: 25%; Gulf Oil Corp.: 16.66%; Atlantic Refining Co.: 16.66%; Pan American Petroleum and Transport Co. (subsidiary of Standard Oil of Indiana): 16.66%	Near Eastern Development Corp.	23.75
C. S. Gulbenkian	Participation and Investments Co.	5.00

SOURCE: Anderson 1981:19.

plus as new discoveries were made both inside and outside the Red Line area. The downward pressure on prices increased.

After the Second World War the international oil market was dominated by seven companies, popularly known as the "Seven Sisters." These companies determined the order of the oil market. The consuming countries were dependent on the companies' position in the upstream sector. This dependency could be exploited, and the consuming countries' authorities have always had an ambivalent attitude toward the integrated oil companies.[6] The Seven Sisters accounted for virtually all the oil produced outside the United States and the Second World. They were integrated in the sense that they controlled the entire production chain right from exploration to sale of the refined products. As of 1953 these companies controlled 95.8 percent of the reserves, 90.2 percent of the production, 75.6 percent of the refining capacity, and 74.3 percent of the product sales.[7] This created a stable structure as long as the oil market did not expand:

> Only a few firms were capable of the risky search for oil in remote often harsh places. In each consuming country, refining and marketing was a small industry, protected by distance and government, making entry diffi-

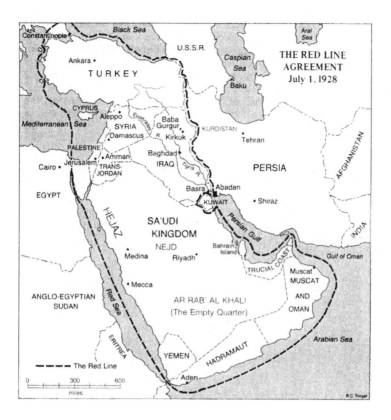

FIGURE 2.7   The Red Line Agreement.
SOURCE: Yergin 1991:205.

cult and unprofitable. Production was too risky without an assured outlet, known as "finding a home for the crude." Refining was too risky without an assured supply of crude. Hence in each country the few sellers were confronted by few buyers, and neither side wished to be at the mercy of the other. The obvious solution was vertical integration. (Adelman 1995:44)

The Sisters also organized their operations in the Middle East through a consortium in which all the major companies were engaged in at least two countries (see Table 2.4). In this way, the Sisters stood stronger against possible regulation by the producing countries, as none of them were totally dependent on the will of one government only. The Middle East oil became increasingly important to the companies as it gradually replaced oil from US domestic sources, which to a greater extent was split

TABLE 2.4   Ownership Shares in Middle East Production Distributed to Companies (%)

Company	Iran	Iraq	Saudi Arabia	Kuwait
Exxon	7	11.875	30	
Texaco	7		30	
SoCal	7		30	
Mobil	7	11.875	10	
Gulf	7			50
BP	40	23.75		50
Shell	14	23.75		
CFP	6	23.75		
Iricon	5			
Gulbenkian		5		

SOURCE: MNC Hearings 1974.

up into several owner interests after American antimonopoly legislation had been enforced against Standard Oil early in the twentieth century. Later, the antitrust laws rendered an extensive cooperation between the Sisters impossible in the United States (Odell 1986:16).

The experiences and military operations of the warring parties during the Second World War established the framework for the political elements of the oil-market structure after the war. Having secured access to foreign petroleum resources as a vital part of their war strategy, the parties did not see the peace settlement as a reason to dissolve their control over these resources. On the contrary, as consumption in industry and consumer markets increased, the companies had substantial economic interest in maintaining control over the international oil market. Without the war the need for governmental involvement was perceived as less immediate. This, together with the overall establishment of a somewhat liberal international trade regime, prompted the most important political actors, the UK and US governments, to withdraw from direct involvement in the international oil market, leaving large room for the international oil companies. In a period with an abundance of oil available at low prices, the political interference in the market disappeared during the fifties and sixties. The next time political actors directly interfered in the international oil market, it was the oil producers who took advantage of changes in the market structure that were in their favor. These changes are the topic of the next section.

As Figure 2.8 shows, the general energy demand increased substantially after the Second World War. Until 1973 there was an unbroken trend in the demand increase. The price increases during the seventies broke this trend (see section 2.4). During the eighties and nineties the increase leveled off (see section 2.5).

The demand for different energy sources also changed in the same period. The main feature of this change was the reduction in the use of coal and the increased consumption of oil (see Figure 2.9). The demand for coal in the OECD area increased by some 15 percent from 1950 to 1987, while the demand for oil increased almost 400 percent in the same period. Natural gas and nuclear power increased, but formed a minor part of energy demand.

As shown in Table 2.1, in 1995 two-thirds of the oil reserves were located in the Middle East. The coal reserves were located in major consuming countries like the United States, the United Kingdom, and Germany. However, in the fast-expanding transportation sector, coal was unusable. The changed fuel composition subsequently also meant that the energy trade increased. This gave the integrated international oil companies a unique position.

Thanks to a combination of rapidly increasing oil consumption and low production costs in the Middle East, the international companies reaped a considerable profit. This profit naturally proved attractive to other private companies as well as national oil-importing companies. There were two strategies open to these companies if they wished to gain entry into the market—they could develop a new area for oil production outside the area controlled by the Sisters, or they could attempt to break the dominance of the "majors" in the Middle East. The French company CFP employed the former strategy, opening production in Algeria in 1959, while the Italian national company ENI (Ente Nazionale Idrocarburi) chose to enter into a joint venture agreement with NIOC (the National Iranian Oil Company) in 1957, providing ENI with access to Iranian offshore territory. A number of similar agreements between exporting countries and smaller oil companies followed (Schneider 1983:79–81). This created steadily increasing competition in the market, which in turn put pressure on prices. Among the main newcomers were companies such as Getty Oil, Phillips, CFP, and Occidental. The last played a crucial role—in 1970 it became the first to yield to Libya's pressure to raise prices and increased tax rates to producer countries (Terzian 1985:120). This forced Shell's independent partners in the Oasis Group to follow suit, and only a month and a half later Shell gave in to Libya's demands.

The developments in the international oil market during the sixties illustrate the general point that, as markets expand, competitive pressure increases. It is easier to be a monopolist in a small market than in a large one. The integrated structure created barriers to entry at the company level, but when the market grew, these barriers became impossible to maintain. Thus, the relations between one group of actors in the trilateral

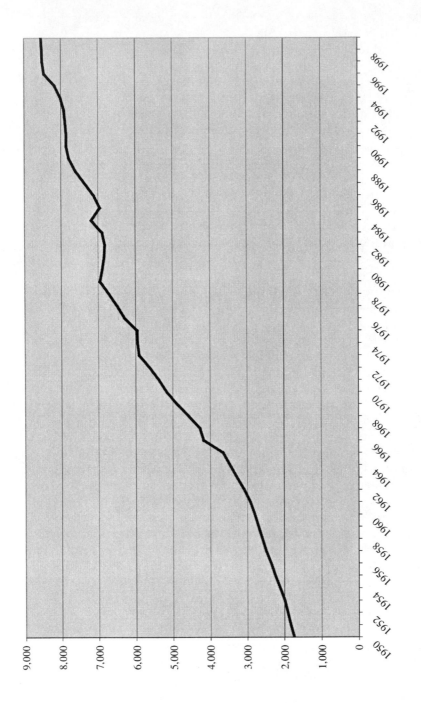

FIGURE 2.8   Energy demand, 1950–1999, million tonnes oil equivalents
SOURCE: Darmstadter et al. 1971:622 and *BP Statistical Review of World Energy.*

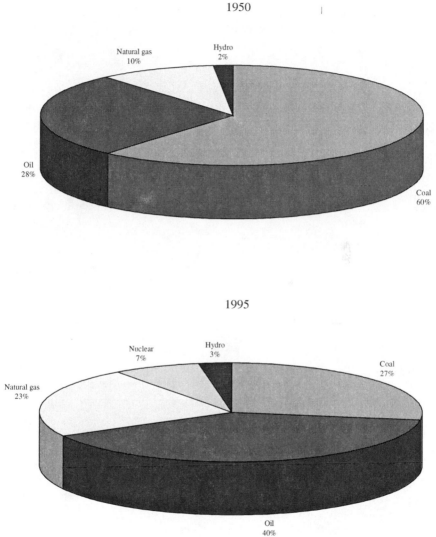

FIGURE 2.9   Primary energy consumption, 1950 and 1995, different fuels (%)
SOURCE: Darmstadter et al. 1971:13 and *BP Statistical Review of World Energy.*

oligopoly, the international companies, changed the conditions for cooperation between the oil producers. The change in favor of OPEC's interests
was enhanced by the continuous increase in oil demand during the sixties. In addition, there were no substitutes for oil in the short term, and
there had been no incentives to conserve energy.

2.4 The OPEC Era

The competition between the companies, between the majors and the
newcomers, weakened their common position in the crude oil market.
The lack of unity, combined with their increased dependency on Middle
East oil, reduced the companies' market power. The companies' position
was to be challenged by the producing countries. In this section, I will
address the importance of this challenge for the oil market. The role of
political events, the institutional creation of OPEC, and the internal bargaining among the oil producers are discussed in the following chapters.

Gaining Market Power

As described in Figure 2.8, the fifties was a time of rapid growth in demand. However, production capacity grew even more rapidly. As there
was nothing holding this oil from the market, the official or "posted"
prices were undermined by competitive discounting, and the saying
went: "only fools and affiliates pay posted prices" (Adelman 1995:54).
This created a dilemma for the companies' relations with the host governments, as it was the posted price that was the basis for the producer
countries' taxes and royalties. Both in 1959 and 1960 the international oil
companies cut the posted prices. This angered the oil-producing governments and triggered the establishment of OPEC in September 1960. "Although the cuts in postings (as finalized in mid-September 1960) were
not rescinded, the formation of a united front by the main oil-exporting
countries ensured that the majors made no future reductions in the unit
revenue of Middle Eastern host governments, regardless of the continuing downward tend in market prices" (Evans 1990:72). "In other words,
the Middle Eastern governments were being kept whole, while the companies absorbed all the effects of the price cuts" (Yergin 1991:515). The
posted price thus became an artificial number unrelated to market prices.
As Adelman (1995:55) concludes: "Many writings on oil markets are
spoiled by reliance on meaningless posted prices."

However, on the political scene, the price cuts by the international oil
companies were to trigger the formation of OPEC (the Organization of the
Petroleum Exporting Countries).[8] Following the production cuts, diplomatic activities were intensified—in particular by Juan Pablo Pérez Al-

fonzo from Venezuela, and Abdallah Tariki from Saudi Arabia, usually regarded as the founding fathers of OPEC. Along with Farman Farmanyan (Iran), S. Nessim (United Arab Emirates), Ahmed El-Sayed Omar (Kuwait), and Mohamed Salman (Arab League), they signed a secret gentlemen's agreement known as the Maadi Pact in Cairo April 1959. The Maadi pact had limited ambitions: "It simply outlined certain principles agreed to by the signatories and proposed a framework for periodic consultation" (Terzian 1985:28). After a new round of price cuts by the companies in August 1960, the producing countries took a further step. On September 14, OPEC was formed in Baghdad.

After the 1956 Suez crisis and the 1967 Arab-Israel War, North African oil exploration was intensified. The North African production held an important advantage over that in the Persian Gulf since the oil did not have to be transported through the conflict area around the Gulf and the Suez Canal. As the Libyan oil contained less sulfur than most Gulf oil qualities, it was cheaper to refine and could therefore be priced higher than the heavier crudes of the Gulf region. "Because of these advantages, Libya received the highest per barrel payments of any Arab government, but most observers still considered Libyan oil underpriced" (Schneider 1983:140). This, together with a new radical regime, meant that the road was open for a confrontation with the oil companies. On September 13, 1969, a coup d'état took place in Libya; two weeks later, Muammar al-Qadhafi became president. After a period of political consolidation, domestically and toward Libya's neighbors, the change in oil policy took form. On January 20, 1970, the new oil minister, Ezzedine Mabrouk, told the oil companies operating in Libya that the government wanted negotiations about a price rise as soon as possible. Algeria and Libya issued a joint statement demanding an immediate increase in the price of oil, and Iraq proclaimed its support for the Libyan action (Terzian 1985:117). The Libyan authorities' strategy was to negotiate with the companies individually, not as a bloc. By playing the independent Occidental and the multinationals against each other, Libya, which had become a major crude exporter, managed to raise posted prices and the government take thereof. Libya was in a somewhat different position than most other OPEC countries. As Table 2.5 shows, Libya was less dependent on the majors, as the newcomers had almost 52 percent of the Libyan oil production.

After the Libyan affair, Iran and Venezuela increased their share of profits and a "game of leapfrog began" (Yergin, 1991:580). After some internal differences, the companies united in a common front and sought to negotiate with OPEC as a whole. When negotiations began on January 19, 1971, the OPEC representatives took the position that they would negotiate only for the Gulf countries and not for the rest of OPEC. While Yergin (1991:582) emphasized the divisions among the OPEC countries, Terzian (1985:130)

TABLE 2.5_ Producing Countries' Dependency on the Majors, 1970 (%)

	Exxon	Mobil	SoCal	Texaco	BP	Gulf	Shell	CFP	Majors	Others
Iran	6.46	6.46	6.46	6.46	37.01	6.46	12.95	5.53	87.77	12.23
Iraq	11.90	11.90	0.00	0.00	23.73	0.00	23.73	23.73	95.00	5.00
Qatar	6.61	6.61	0.00	0.00	12.93	0.00	58.33	12.93	97.41	2.59
Abu Dhabi	7.89	7.89	0.00	0.00	38.00	0.00	15.94	26.89	96.62	3.38
Kuwait	0.00	0.00	0.00	0.00	50.00	50.00	0.00	0.00	100.00	0.00
Saudi Arabia	30.01	9.97	30.01	30.01	0.00	0.00	0.00	0.00	100.00	0.00
Libya	22.72	4.19	6.02	6.02	5.16	0.00	3.96	0.00	48.07	51.93
Algeria	0.00	0.00	0.00	0.00	0.00	0.00	9.08	26.60	35.68	64.32
Nigeria	0.00	0.00	0.00	0.00	31.34	37.31	31.34	0.00	100.00	0.00
Indonesia	2.95	2.95	33.61	33.61	0.00	0.00	16.27	0.00	89.39	10.61
Venezuela	41.65	3.17	1.58	4.84	0.00	10.84	25.92	0.00	88.00	12.00

SOURCE: OPEC Annual Statistical Bulletin.

emphasized the divisions among the companies. Adelman (1995:85–87) emphasized the role of the US government, particularly how representatives of the State Department advocated separate negotiations between the companies and the oil producing countries. Whatever the cause, the companies agreed to conduct two sets of negotiations, one with the Gulf exporters and one with the Mediterranean exporters. It should be noted that the market structure had not changed; there was no scarcity caused by underlying changes in the relationship between supply and demand: "From early 1971 to nearly the end of 1972, prices increased despite continuing substantial excess supply" (Adelman 1995:93).

On February 14, 1971, the so-called Tehran agreement between the international oil companies and the OPEC members exporting through the Persian Gulf was signed. On April 2, 1971, a similar agreement for the OPEC members exporting through the Mediterranean was signed. The agreements covered tax and price increases, inflation compensation, and a fixing of such rates for future years. The effects of the agreements were a 21 percent price increase for Saudi Arabian crude (from $1.80 to $2.18), and an increase in revenue of 38.9 percent. What was more important, however, was the fact that the producer countries had now gained firmer control over the price-setting:[9]

> Even as late as a few months ago, the very idea of the producing countries of the Gulf achieving an across-the-board price increase . . . [as] agreed upon in Tehran on the 14 February would have seemed almost inconceivable. . . . This victory—and victory it certainly was—was mainly due to two factors: firstly the *unprecedented degree of unity* shown by the OPEC member countries; and secondly the great skill and nerve of the three-man ministerial committee which negotiated the deal on behalf of the Gulf states.[10]

The distribution of market power in the international oil market had changed: "Unilateral tax increases were not new. Before Tripoli and Tehran, the OPEC nations had exerted defensive market power. Their excise taxes had put a floor of tax-plus-cost under the price. But raising taxes in concert, to raise the worldwide price floor, was indeed new" (Adelman 1995:80).

Taking the Libyan affair and the Tehran-Tripoli negotiations together, there was a combination of lack of unity among the companies and a new unity among the OPEC members. One could argue that both factors were necessary, but neither of them alone was sufficient to explain the events of 1971. A unified OPEC strategy would not have succeeded unless the companies' unity had begun to crack, as in the Libyan case. The lack of unity among the companies would have meant nothing unless the OPEC members had gained some ability to act in concord.

The relative importance of these factors tends to place more weight on the lack of unity among the companies than on the unity among the oil producers. It is reasonable to argue that with competition for production concessions among the companies, the producer countries would have been able to increase taxes individually, as, in fact, was the case in both Libya and Venezuela. This would not have happened through large negotiations and agreements like the Tehran-Tripoli agreements, but the result would most likely have been very similar. The process started in 1969 and was driven primarily by individual countries. As Terzian (1985:112) notes, in oil circles, the seventies are known as the "'decade of OPEC's offensive'. . . . In fact, the offensive began in 1969, and almost without OPEC realizing what was happening." The focus on the unity of the producer countries at later stages of the negotiations has to be countered by the possibility that the Tehran-Tripoli negotiations might not have commenced at all had the companies played their cards better during the Libyan affair.

Relating to the concepts guiding this chapter, market structure and market power, the conclusion is that there was no structural change in the international oil market in the late 1960s or early 1970s. It was a matter of a change in the balance of power; or, even more accurately, a change in actors' exercise of market power. The international companies would have been able to stop the producing countries from taking control had they kept together. They had the cards but played them poorly, a case of what David Baldwin has named "the paradox of unrealized power" (Baldwin 1979:163). With the international oil companies put on the sideline, the focus turned to what objectives the OPEC countries would pursue, given their achieved market power.

The Oil Weapon[11]

On October 17, the Organization of the Arab Petroleum Exporting Countries (OAPEC) countries[12] announced their intention to reduce production by 5 percent per month until Israel retreated from the occupied territories and the rights of the Palestinians were restored (Blair 1976:264). Oil supplies to the United States and the Netherlands were to be stopped altogether due to their outspoken support of Israel. Saudi Arabia's Sheik Yamani later called the embargo a legitimate political action: "We watched America and learned how they use one's economic power to meet political objectives. We studied this carefully" (Robinson 1988:95). The embargo and the production limitations, however, removed very little oil from the market, and they were short-lived (Blair 1976:266–268). Figure 2.10 shows the production of a selected number of countries' production from September 1973 to April 1974. As the figure shows, Saudi Arabia took a large portion of the cutbacks. However, the Saudi Arabia cutbacks

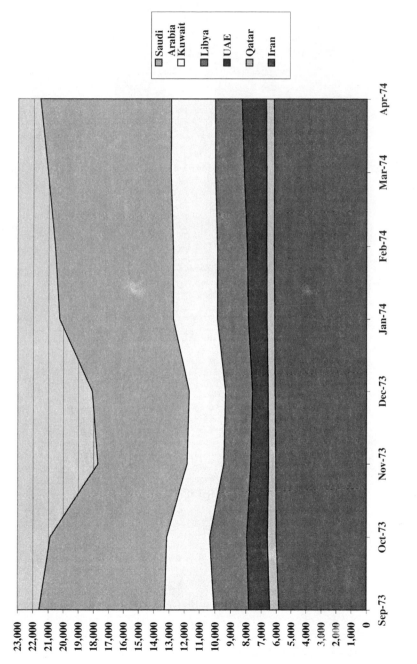

FIGURE 2.10 Selected OPEC countries' production, September 1973 to April 1974 (th. b/d)
SOURCE: Adelman 1995:111.

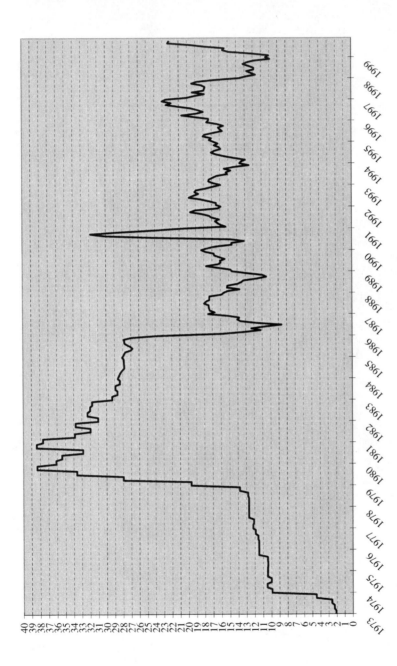

FIGURE 2.11 Monthly oil prices in $/barrel, 1973–2000
SOURCE: *OPEC Bulletin*, various issues.

for December 1973 were canceled, and on December 25, the Arab oil ministers ordered a 10 percent increase in production for January 1974. By January, OPEC production increased again.

No shortage of oil emerged, but expectations that the future might lead to a supply shortage drove up prices: "Nobody knew how long the cutback would last or how much worse it would get" (Adelman 1995:110). Kissinger (1982a:873) finds the embargo "a symbolic gesture of limited practical importance. . . . The true impact of the embargo was psychological. " The uncertainties about the future supply of oil did, however, create a highly favorable environment for price increases. On October 6, the OPEC countries effected a first price increase without the involvement of the companies (Terzian 1985:170), and thus finally buried the Tehran and Tripoli agreements, which had been on their deathbed for several months. The embargo gave the OPEC countries an opportunity to increase prices without suffering from reduction in demand. OPEC increased the government take from $1.77 to $3.05 in October 1973, further to $7.00 from January 1974, and to $10.66 by 1975 (see Figure 2.11).

> The concern of the OPEC nations was to ratchet up the floor to prevent the down-wave from cancelling the up-wave and to make the price increase permanent. Since the OPEC action was anticipated, the price effect came before the cause. In December, Iran auctioned some crude oil at more than $17 per barrel, after exaggerated reports of an imminent unprecedented jump in government take. . . . It became overwhelmingly clear in 1974 how little the market situation explained the price. (Adelman 1995:118)

By 1975 the process of changing the price structure was completed. The average government take had increased from $1.77 per barrel to $10.66, and the posted price had increased from $3.01 per barrel to $11.25 (Adelman 1995:120). Furthermore, the whole concept of posted prices was substituted with the official selling price.

Was the price by 1975 raised too high? Such a question obviously depends on the basis for evaluation. The price of 1970 was "above long-run competitive levels set by investment requirements for continued expansion" (Adelman 1995:133). In competitive market terms, the price increases from 1971 to 1975 seem unsustainable. In 1974, "spare capacity in OPEC was nearly 8 mbd" (Moran 1981:254), so the price increase was incompatible with full capacity utilization. By the second half of 1974, the world economy went into a severe recession. Inflation was running at double digits, thus quickly reducing the real value of the price increases. There was also considerable confusion about whether prices would continue up or fall back. In July 1974, Saudi Arabia announced an auction of about 1.5 mbd to be held in August. Such an auction would have provided a market-based signal of the future price trend. The auction was postponed and subsequently cancelled. Prominent scholars differs on the reason for this, and thus on the role of Saudi Arabia. Morris Adelman argues that Saudi Arabia could have brought the price down single handedly, and that "the public record shows the Saudis leading the price rice. The auction was designed to raise them further. When the hope disappeared, the auction was canceled" (Adelman 1995:127–128). Theodore H. Moran claims that the Saudi Arabians were ready to "accept whatever price the conditions of surplus would produce" (Moran 1981:255). Furthermore, he refers to journals claiming that Yamani, as early as in May 1974, proposed to cut the posted price of Arabian Light to $9 per barrel, and invited Iran to cooperate,[13] and that Yamani in September said that "OPEC's posted crude prices [was] $2/bbl too high."[14] The Saudi Arabian position brought about severe internal tension (Moran 1981:257). Measured against possible effects on demand, the price increases seemed not to be too high. The reduction in oil consumption in the mid–1970s was due to economic recession and slow growth (Adelman 1995:146). In the longer run, effects became substantial.

What, then, were the reactions among the groups of the trilateral oligopoly (see section 2.2), the consuming countries and the companies? In the consuming countries these price increases were seen as a symptom of resource scarcity. It fitted well with a publication from the Club of Rome called *Limits to Growth* published in 1972. "Its arguments were a potent element in the fear and pessimism about impending shortages and resource constraints that became so pervasive in the 1970s, shaping policies and responses of both oil-importing and oil-exporting countries" (Yergin 1991:569). Robert Pindyck (1978:36) refers to a CIA report claiming that "a crisis is likely to occur in the early 1980s as world energy demand exceeds supply, resulting in shortages of energy, rapidly rising prices, and economic contraction in all of the industrialized countries. . . . This view has had an important role in forming the rationale for the Carter administration's energy program." However, there was no shortage; the price increase was a result of OPEC exercising market power, not a lack of available resources. As Pindyck (1978:51) concludes: "The kind of worldwide energy crisis of concern to the CIA and the Carter administration is unlikely to occur."

Concerning the international oil companies, their role in ruling the international oil market was diminished. In 1972 the Iranian state-owned company NIOC took control over Iranian oil production. In Saudi Arabia the oil production was controlled solely by the American companies, organized in the consortium Aramco (Arabian American Oil Co.).[15] Saudi Arabia gradually took control over Aramco in the seventies. However, the company continued to be formally directed from Detroit, and it was not until 1988 that the company elected a Saudi Arabian chairman.[16] Iraq nationalized IPC (the Iraq Petroleum Company) in 1972, and Kuwait was assigned 60 percent of the interests in KOC (the Kuwait Oil Company) in 1974. Qatar and Abu Dhabi followed the Kuwaiti model. The international oil companies thus had to look for oil elsewhere.

With the price increases, the change from posted price to official selling price, and the nationalization of production, the focus turned to the internal OPEC bargaining. "No longer could OPEC governments fix a price floor by fixing per barrel taxes and letting the companies compete freely above the floor. They now had to fix prices in concert and to trust each other not to undermine those prices by trying to hard for additional sales. It was an endless exhausting struggle" (Adelman 1995:143).

Overestimated Market Power

Terzian (1985:235) describes 1975 as a turning point in the history of OPEC—it marked "the end of the 'decade of the offensive' and announced the beginning of the organization's subsequent decline." At a summit meeting in Algiers, some OPEC members attempted to use the organization as a "spearhead of the Third World," something that would involve not only economic but also political and ideological cooperation. These attempts failed, and OPEC remained an "economic" organization. In the years that followed, discord in OPEC increased, particularly concerning the question of price increases. Saudi Arabia was the central opponent of higher prices. This was explained as consideration for the industrialized countries' economies and OPEC's dependence on the growth of these. Other, more curious reasons were also given. Terzian (1985:244) cites a *Der Spiegel* interview in which Yamani said that by limiting the price rise, Saudi Arabia was trying to "prevent the communists seizing power in France and Italy."

In 1977, Iran joined Saudi Arabia in advocating a price freeze. Saudi Arabia and Iran together accounted for a full 48 percent of OPEC's total production. When both opposed price increases, there was little the other countries could do. However, sudden political events were to play havoc with the oil market: The Shah of Iran was overthrown, and the fundamentalist Islamic rule under Ayatollah Ruhollah Khomeini commenced. Despite the fact that the other OPEC countries easily compensated for the disappearance of Iranian oil, demand increased as the buyers wished to secure their access to crude oil in case of a likely future demand surplus. As Figure 2.12 shows, a steep increase in spot prices was followed by increased official prices. From December 1978 to October 1979 the spot price raised from $13.8 per barrel to $38.35.

It was not until 1980 that the market begun to react to the countermeasures of the other OPEC countries and the supply surplus was revealed. But here again, political events undermined stabilization. On September 22, the Iran-Iraq War broke out. However, this time there was a surplus in companies and governments panicked and bought oil to build up stocks at a very high price. We in OPEC took this false demand for real. And we made a mistake: we raised our prices further."[17]

In March 1982, the OPEC members agreed to set their total production output at 18 mbd, and distributed production quotas among the members. Saudi Arabia was not assigned a quota but was to act as a swing producer, and thus vary production to balance the market at the $34/barrel price. Saudi Arabia performed the role of swing producer in the following years by cutting back production. This could not help the price from sliding, albeit slowly, as can be seen in Figure 2.11. The internal OPEC bargaining aspects of this are discussed in detail in Chapter 5. The importance in this chapter is how these actions by the OPEC members helped OPEC maintain its control of the international oil market—a control the organization had gained not by its own merits, but through favorable structural changes, and political events like revolution and war. The Saudi Arabian role as swing producer allowed OPEC to maintain some control of the price level, but from 1983–1984 OPEC's dominance and control over price-setting crumbled (see Chapter 5). This was due to two important developments. In the first place, the growth in demand for oil came to a halt, due partly to higher prices, partly to a general reduction in economic growth that occurred prior to OPEC's price increases, and partly to new energy sources such as natural gas and nuclear energy. Second, competition between oil producers increased, in the same way as it had twenty years earlier between the companies. The new profitability of oil production made fields in non-OPEC countries profitable, and new producers took a larger share of the market. Both factors came as a consequence of the market behavior of the OPEC countries during the seventies. Their behavior during the period 1971–1981 had lasting effects on the structure of the international oil market. The following section tries to capture what effects the price increases of the seventies had regarding both the underlying structural aspects (see section 2.5) and the behavior of the other market actors in the trilateral oligopoly, the consuming countries, and the international oil companies (see section 2.6).

2.5   Structural Effects of the Price Increases

The Leveling Out of Oil Consumption

As pointed out in section 2.3, energy consumption, and in particular oil consumption, rose sharply after the Second World War. Through the fifties the need for gasoline increased due to rapidly expanding private motoring and the growing transport sector in the industrialized countries. The economic growth in the industrialized countries has been an energy-dependent growth. Each increase of one unit in Gross Domestic

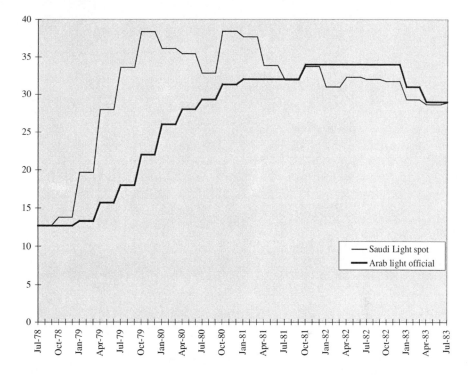

FIGURE 2.12   Spot and official prices, July 1978–July 1983 ($/barrel)
SOURCE: *OPEC Bulletin,* various issues.

the market, possibly as much as 2 million barrels per day (mbd). Iran and Iraq took some 4 mbd from the market, while the remaining 2 mbd were easily supplied by the other OPEC countries, which now had sufficient spare production capacity.

Saudi Arabia refused to cut its production until demand for OPEC oil fell dramatically, which was partly fueled by the oil companies' stock draw-down in the autumn of 1981. This caused Saudi Arabia to perform a volte-face and, quite contrary to its earlier resistance to production regulation, the kingdom now actively supported it. In this way, Saudi Arabia, as the largest producer in OPEC, began to regulate production to create market equilibrium. At this point, the OPEC countries had to prove their ability to function as a cartel and reduce production when demand decreased.

Again, we can raise the question about whether the price was raised too high. With the benefit of hindsight, the 1979–1980 case seems easier to conclude than the 1973–1974 case. In the words of Yamani himself, the price increases were a mistake: "We believe that we made a mistake in 1979/1980 by raising our prices without paying attention to the real sup-ply-demand situation. There was only a false demand, because the oil

72

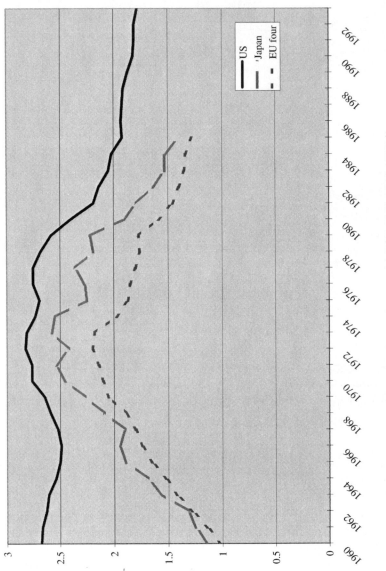

FIGURE 2.13 Oil consumption in barrels per thousand $GDP, 1960–1993 (1980$)
Note: Estimates are based on purchasing power parity indexes obtained from the U.N. International
Comparisons Project. EU-four: France, Germany, Italy, and the United Kingdom.
SOURCE: Adelman 1995:151.

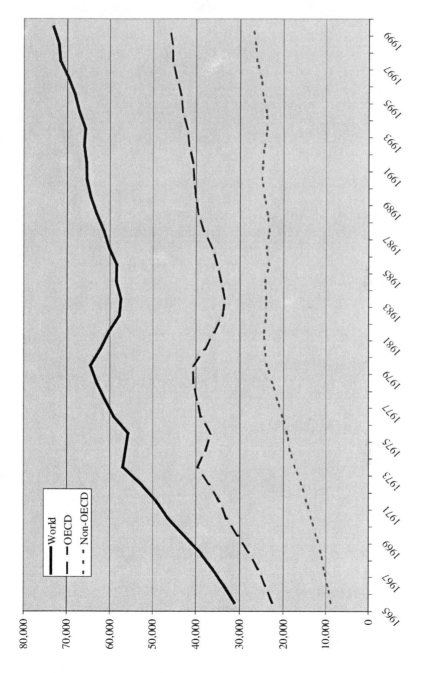

FIGURE 2.14 Oil consumption, 1965–1999 (in th. b/d)
SOURCE: *BP Statistical Review of World Energy,* 1999.

product (GDP) has required a certain number of units' increase in energy consumption; this ratio is the so-called energy intensity (see Figure 2.13).

For oil, this ratio increased until 1973, but has since then fallen. OECD economic growth is less oil-dependent today than ever before. From 1979 to 1995 the economies of the European Union (EU), United States, and Japan grew by 35, 40, and 55 percent, respectively. The oil demand fell marginally in EU and the United States, and grew only marginally in Japan during the same period (see Figure 2.14).

The explanations for this reduction in energy intensity are several. In the first place most industrialized countries today develop in the direction of a postindustrial society. The industrial sector's share of the GDP shrinks. This leads to a reduced need for energy consumption in order to increase GDP. Second, the price rises of the seventies made energy conservation more profitable and other energy sources more competitive.

Since the oil-price fall in 1986 (see Figure 2.11), oil demand has increased only modestly. In fact, in 1993, total world oil demand was at the same level as in 1979, while the price was $17/barrel in 1993 compared with $40/barrel in 1979. The price fall did not stimulate increased demand during the period 1986–1993. Subsequently, the oil producers have not been able to sustain their income level by compensating for the fall in price with increased output.

This lack of demand elasticity can, to a great extent, be ascribed to the consuming countries' use of a rather effective tool, namely, the taxing of energy use. Figure 2.15 illustrates how the product price presented to EU and OECD consumers has increased, while the crude price has decreased. The main explanation for this is a substantial increase in the tax share of the oil product prices shown by the black area in the figure.

When the reduced crude oil price is compensated for by increased taxes, the expected demand increases due to the lowered price will not occur. The consuming countries' governments actually have partial control over a prominent feature of the present market situation—the lack of demand elasticity.

The Increased Number of Non-OPEC Producers

As outlined above, the oil market of the fifties and sixties was dominated by the Seven Sisters (see section 2.3). From 1971 until 1985, OPEC was the dominating actor in the oil market (see section 2.4). However, a number of new oil producers emerged in the course of the seventies and eighties. As described in section 2.4, this development was partly due to OPEC's own price policy, which created a considerable profit margin, and partly to technological advances that rendered feasible oil production in new areas. This undermined OPEC's control over the market development.

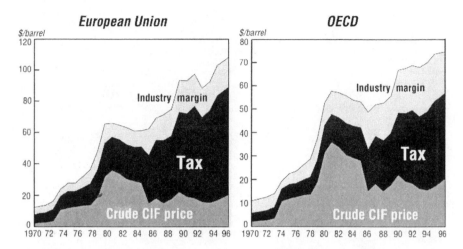

FIGURE 2.15   Trends in taxation of petroleum products
SOURCE: Ghanem (1998:5).

Control of market development thus required coordinated behavior by a larger number of actors than before. Since the beginning of the eighties, OPEC has repeatedly requested non-OPEC producers' cooperation on production regulation in order to strengthen the price. These aspects are discussed further in Chapter 8.

The distribution of market shares among the producers is presented in Figure 2.16. The obvious change since 1973 is that while OPEC and non-OPEC producers shared the market equally then, giving the OPEC countries a substantial market control, OPEC in 1993 controlled only about 40 percent of the market. In the period in between, its market power was substantially lower; in the mid-eighties, the OPEC market share was approximately 30 percent.

The trend is that the production of the traditional non-OPEC producers, like that in Alaska and the North Sea, has been sustained at a high level exceeding the oil industry's forecasts. "Nearly every non-OPEC supply forecast tends to be pessimistic, with a near-term peak" (Lynch 1995:1). In addition, new producing countries are presenting themselves in the international oil market. Several of these are countries that were isolated from the world oil market due to the Cold War or, in some instances, civil wars. The international political changes created economic opportunities for these countries and for the international companies willing to invest in these areas. Prominent examples are Angola, Azerbaijan, Cambodia, Cuba (not open to all companies), Laos, Mozambique, and Vietnam. The

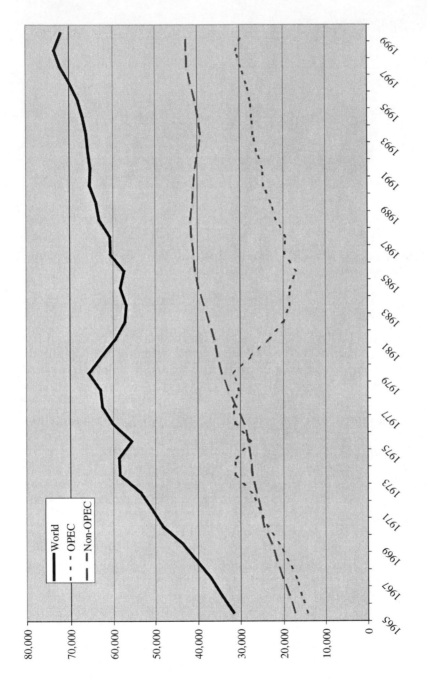

FIGURE 2.16 Market shares, 1965–1999 (in th. b/d)
SOURCE: *BP Statistical Review of World Energy, 1999.*

important question regarding such new oil provinces is how to finance investments in exploration and development. Here lies the role of the international oil companies, which for a long time have been so-called crude short, meaning they have refining capacity that exceeds the crude oil they control. Their financial positions, however, have been remarkably sound, especially those of Exxon and Royal Dutch/Shell.[18]

The reason the international companies sought oil in the North Sea and Alaska in the seventies was a need for alternatives to the Middle East, as the nationalization there made the companies' operation impossible. Alaska and the North Sea were high-cost alternatives to the Middle East. The production costs in the new oil provinces lie between the low-cost Middle East and the high-cost areas such as Alaska and the North Sea. In addition, several of the new oil-producing countries welcome private international oil companies and offer them better tax conditions than the established producer countries. The newcomers among the producing countries might subsequently force the established producers to ease the companies' conditions in traditional producing areas in order to facilitate new investments by the international oil companies.

Structural Changes Redistribute Market Power

The leveling off of the growth in oil consumption, together with the increase in non-OPEC production, totally changed the situation facing OPEC. The high prices achieved during the seventies immediately came under pressure in the eighties. The favorable structural conditions for oil-producer cooperation at the beginning of the seventies had turned into structurally unfavorable conditions by the beginning of the eighties. Chapters 5 to 8 discuss how OPEC met this challenge, and the effects of this structural change on the cooperation between the oil producers.

These changes also affected the relationship between the groups of actors in the trilateral oligopoly, the producers, consumers, and international companies. The reduced market power of the oil producers has improved the position of the companies and the consuming countries. As pointed out in section 2.2, the reduction of one group of actors' market power either makes the market more competitive or increases other actors' market power.

2.6 New Market-Power Relations

The factors discussed above are the so-called fundamentals, factors that directly cause changes in supply and demand. However, other important changes have taken place in the international oil market during the last decades. This section focuses on changes in the vertical market structure (see section 2.1). The actors' behavior in the vertical structure is equally important for the changes of market power among the market actors.

New Trading Mechanisms

The old integrated oil-market structure allowed multinational oil companies to balance world oil demand and supply through a vertically integrated system. OPEC's nationalization of oil-industry assets introduced new market mechanisms, primarily through the system of official selling prices and long-term contracts with a variety of oil companies.

However, throughout the seventies and early eighties, the decline in demand and the appearance of new oil producers outside the cartel made it very difficult for OPEC to enforce its official prices. As a consequence, long-term contracts were gradually phased out. The continuous mismatch between supply and demand created fertile ground for the development of a spot market (a market for single crude cargoes), which is characterized by short-term contracts, a high rate of turnover, and sensitivity to outside events. It is not unusual for a single cargo to be sold dozens of times before it finally arrives at the refinery. This renders it difficult to establish to what extent the transactions should be designated spot or contract sales, since a company may purchase oil from a producer according to a contract formula, only to sell some of this oil in the spot market afterward.[19] The international oil trade subsequently became highly disintegrated. Under increasingly competitive pressure, producers adopted pricing formulas linked to day-to-day fluctuations in spot prices.[20] Under these market conditions individual producers, both OPEC and non-OPEC, had no guarantee concerning the long-term loyalty of their customers. The daily market actors, the traders, obtained an increasingly important position in the market.

From the time OPEC's oil industry was nationalized in the first half of the seventies until 1979, long-term contracts were the dominant form of crude sales. In 1979 the contract market constituted 85 percent of turnover. Sales on the spot market made up the remaining 15 percent (Estrada 1988:9). In the eighties, non-OPEC production increased, and new producers outside OPEC linked their contract prices to the spot market price. The increased production, and the leveling off of demand, pushed the spot price downward (see section 2.5). This created a gap between the spot price and the OPEC official price, a development that prompted more and more buyers to make their purchases on a spot basis (Mossavar-Rahmani 1986:5). This development also gave the spot-related contracts a competitive advantage. In 1984, 70 percent of traded crude was sold either directly or indirectly through the spot market.[21] While the spot price in 1979 and 1980 had pressed the official price upward, it now contributed to the de-

TABLE 2.6   Taxonomy of Trading

Type	Volume	Duration	Price	Physical Condition
Term				
Standard term	Multiple cargoes	Months or years	Government-determined: Official Sales Price (OSP)	Wet
Equity	"	Years	Special arrangements	"
Market-related	"	Months	Adjustable	"
Spot				
Single spot	Single cargo	One-time basis	Set by prevailing market conditions, below or above OSP	"
Daisy chain	"	Multiple transactions of same cargo	"	"
Tertiary	Multiple cargoes	Weeks or months	Discounted below OSP ($1–2/barrel)	"
Netbacks	Multiple cargoes	"	Spot product price-related	"
Forwards	Single cargo	One-time basis	Set by expectations of future market conditions	"
Futures	Less relevant	Less relevant	"	Paper
Derivatives				
Swaps	"	"	Set to reduce price risks	"
Hedging	"	"	"	"

SOURCE: Mossavan-Rahmani et al. 1988:12; Roeber 1993:31–53.

cline of official prices. The companies that signed long-term contracts in the early eighties also suffered, as they had to pay the determined price, while there was plenty of oil available in the spot market at substantially lower prices. The spot market was soon supplemented by the "tertiary market," so called by Mossavar-Rahmani (1986:1), who defines it as a "hodgepodge of somewhat opaque transactions including barter, counter-trade, processing arrangements, crude-crude or crude-product packaging, and outright discounts" (see Table 2.6). This occurred because the OPEC countries, due to the surplus on the market, did not wish to contribute officially to a price collapse, but were at the same time eager to ensure sales of their own crude. By the mid-eighties the tertiary market was being used by several OPEC countries as a method of giving buyers concealed discounts in various ways. Mossavar-Rahmani (1986:12) calculated this to constitute some 50 to 55 percent of all OPEC oil sold, while the contracts covered some 30 to 35 percent, and the traditional spot market only 10 to 15 percent (all 1985 figures). The actual price in this market is difficult to determine, as all agreements between seller and buyer are veiled in secrecy. However, it can be assumed that the price has been somewhere between the spot price and the official price. This reflects the buyers' willingness to pay a little more for ensuring deliveries rather than rely on spot sales alone, though not as much as the official price would indicate:

> With over half of all OPEC crude oils traded on a discounted basis, the pressure on the remaining crude oils grew. Even though the formal OPEC price structure was prevented from collapsing to tertiary market levels, through the end of 1985, official prices became increasingly meaningless as the share of tertiary transactions continued to gain at the expense of term and spot sales. (Mossavar-Rahmani 1986:15)

This caused Saudi Arabia, which previously had strongly opposed discount arrangements,[22] to introduce so-called netback pricing.[23] Netback agreements are "The sale of crude oil with the buyer paying the producer a price which is dependent on the proceeds obtained from the sale of refined products" (Jenkins 1986:423). This method of price-fixing ensures the refineries a profit on oil purchases, as the price is not decided before the refinery has sold the product and is fixed in such a way that the crude price equals the product price minus refining, transport, insurance, loss, and interest costs in processing of the oil (Mossavar-Rahmani 1986:19). The drawback of the netback pricing system was its complexity and the transaction costs connected with negotiating individual agreements to match the circumstances of different refiners (Roeber 1994:262).

A simultaneous development diminished the need for netback agreements. Through communication technology and the frequent publishing of oil-price data (e.g., in *Platt's Oilgram News*, and through Reuters), the spot price transparency increased. This caused the value of the crude oil in the product markets to be reflected in the spot price. The netback pricing was subsequently replaced by market-related pricing. In the market-related pricing system, the other features of the contract between the seller and buyer can vary, at the same time as the price is set according to the different spot crudes. The contract can be a long-term contract or single cargo deal. The important feature of spot-related pricing is that the frequency of price changes is increased compared with the term market. Spot prices are changed almost constantly. The problem of a mismatch between the contracted price and the market price is thus more or less resolved.

During the latter half of the eighties and into the nineties, one of the most prominent features of oil trading has been the increased activity in the paper market or semi-paper market. The forward market is actually a market for spot transactions in which oil is traded for delivery at a future time. So the forward market is a semi-paper market, as it is actual physical crude that is traded. A more genuine paper market is the so-called futures market.[24] Futures contracts are at the outset designed for financial purposes. There was no regular futures trading in the oil market until the seventies, as the major international oil companies had no interest in such a development. The increase in futures trading in the early nineties has been tremendous: "The WTI [Western Texas Intermediate] crude contract was launched by NYMEX [New York Mercantile Exchange] in 1983 and is now [1993] trading at a level equivalent to 100 times WTI production. . . . The Brent contract on the IPE[X] is traded at 40 times Brent production during the first half of 1993" (Roeber 1993:48).

The futures market provides "those in the physical market with the opportunity to offset the inherent risks associated with their business" (Battley 1989:27). The future market might also reduce price uncertainty and thus the possibility of arbitrage (Sykuta 1994:4). Hedging is the prominent instrument for risk reduction in the futures market. An oil producer can buy himself insurance against loss from a fall in the oil price by selling an amount of oil on the futures market, which can be regarded as a promise to supply oil on a future date. When the price for physical oil falls, so does the future price. By buying back the option the producer gains a profit, which could counter his (potential) losses in the physical market.

Sykuta (1994) gives an additional rationale for the futures market by regarding it as an alternative form of contracting in the oil market: "The futures market provides a flexible form of contracting for the commodity which can be used in tandem with, or as a substitute for, forward and spot contracting to add flexibility to the firm's contracting and resource allocation decisions" (Sykuta 1994:5). This role of the futures market reduces buyers' costs of assuring access to the commodity and likewise the producers' access to market outlets.[25]

There are several paper barrels for each wet barrel, and with the price of even long-term contracts related to the price developments of Brent and WTI, the relatively few traders operating in these markets have a disproportional influence on the day-to-day price developments. None of the OPEC countries, and only a few of the companies, are actually involved in futures trading. Thus, they are deprived of information and possibilities to understand the formation of prices. This, of course, makes it more complicated for OPEC and the oil companies to influence the oil-price development. By the end of the eighties the short-term development of the oil price was left in the hands of the oil-market traders. If pessimistic about the OPEC countries' capacity to govern the market, one could argue that the long-term oil price is nothing other than a series of prices of short-term oil deals, wet- or paper-based. It is more fair to say, however, that the new trading mechanisms have introduced a new layer that the oil producers have to penetrate in order to gain control over the oil price. Previously they could make secret deals with consumers, and discriminate among them. Now they have to play the game of convincing the short-term market dealers that they have reason to believe prices will go up in the future, and they should therefore buy more oil in order hedge against the price increase (Claes 1999a).

However, this new oil-trading business has not made the relationship between oil producers and the companies unimportant altogether. In fact, the relationship between the actors moving the physical oil also has undergone fundamental changes during the last decades, changing the actors' position in the vertical structure. This is the theme of the following subsections.

Producers' Downstream Integration

In general, downstream investments have been considered a natural and important step in the industrialization and economic diversification of an oil-producing country. For many, downstream moves were regarded as the way out of underdevelopment and dependence on Western influence:

> Domestic refineries have been regarded as an instrument to increase the value added of the oil produced. As a complement or as an alternative, some oil exporting countries have invested in refineries and distribution networks in the consuming countries. The choice of downstream investments overseas is based not only on technical and financial considerations, but first and foremost on commercial strategy. Thus domestic refineries and international downstream investments must be regarded as strategic choices both at a government and a company level. . . . The ability of an oil producing country to integrate downstream depends on its financial strength, managerial independence from political authorities, downstream experience in domestic markets and qualified personnel with international experience. These factors seem to be more important for the downstream success than the size of the reserves, the volumes of crude oil exported or the prices achieved. (Bergesen, Bjørk, and Claes 1989:27, 29)[26]

Since the early eighties—when the market began to tighten—some of the major oil-exporting countries have made important downstream investments in Western Europe and the United States through a variety of participation agreements. The purpose has been to gain partial or total control over companies that can refine and distribute part of their crude oil exports in the main consuming countries. This should in itself secure outlets for sales and thereby more stable revenues in a volatile market. These exporters have also bought tankers, harbor and storage facilities, and petrochemical plants in consuming countries. In 1987, OPEC exporters accounted for 8.1 percent of the Western European market for oil products (Bergesen, Bjørk, and Claes 1989:28). Among the largest downstream investors are Kuwait, Venezuela, Saudi Arabia, Libya, and Norway. Kuwait and Venezuela have refining capacity (domestic and foreign) covering 90 to 100 percent of their production capacity; the corresponding figure for Saudi Arabia is about 50 percent (Finon 1991:264). Table 2.7 highlights some important foreign downstream acquisitions of oil-exporting countries during the eighties.

The pace of downstream integration has slowed during the nineties (Hamm 1994:186). This might be explained by the weakened financial position of several oil producers. OPEC's total external debt increased from $236.8 billion in 1986 to $343.9 billion in 1992 (Gochenour 1992:977). OPEC countries still would like to secure more outlets, but their financial troubles prohibit further investments in the refining and marketing sectors.

Companies' Return to the Upstream Sector

Turning to the study of the companies' position in the upstream market, two features are particularly important: the financial situation of different companies, and their crude position.

The decline in refining and distribution margins in the late seventies and early eighties led to a wave of closures, modernizations, and takeovers, especially in the United States. During this period of painful restructuring, independents and majors were competing for a limited volume of known reserves that more than tripled the median transaction value for reserves in-place in the United States (Smith et al. 1986). Much of this wave of reserve purchases and oil company mergers and acquisitions was financed through debt. Thus, it came as no surprise that as soon as spot prices began to show the first indications of decline, companies with financial difficulties tried to resell the same reserves bought some years before. Numerous properties changed hands repeatedly in a short period.

In a similar way, refiners who had upgraded their facilities at high costs in the late seventies became caught in an economic squeeze in the mid-eighties. Refinery upgrades were based on the belief that the wide price spread between heavy and light crudes would continue. It actually

TABLE 2.7 Principal Foreign Downstream Acquisitions of Petroleum-Exporting Countries, 1983–1990

Purchaser	Acquired Capacity (b/d)	Country	Seller/Partner	Activity	Share (%)	Date
S. Arabia	600,000	U.S.	Texaco	Ref./dist.	50	1988
Kuwait	75,000	Benelux	Gulf Oil	Ref./dist.	100	1983
	70,000	Den./Swe.	Gulf Oil/BP	Ref./dist.	100	1983, 87
	35,000	Italy	Gulf Oil	Distribution	100	1984
	70,000	UK	Hays/Ultramar Nafta	Distribution	100	1986,87
	100,000	Italy	Mobil	Ref./dist.	100	1990
Venezuela	145,000	Germany	Ruhr/Oel/Veba	Ref./dist.	50	1983, 86
	305,000	U.S.	Citgo/Southland	Ref./dist.	100	1986, 89
	50,000	Sweden	Nynäs	Refining	50	1986
	135,000	U.S.	Champlin/U. Pacific	Ref./dist.	50	1987
	147,000	U.S.	Unocal	Ref./dist.	50	1989
	44,000	U.S.	Sea View	Refining	50	1990
Libya	110,000	Italy	Tamoil/Amoco/Finterm.	Ref./dist.	70	1983, 87
Norway	30,000	Sweden	Exxon	Ref./chem.	100	1985
	45,000	Denmark	Exxon	Ref./dist.	100	1986

SOURCE: Finon 1991:265.

narrowed from $8.5/barrel in 1982 to $4/barrel in 1984. Costly revamping to feed heavy crude proved to be a bad investment in a business already beset by marginal economics.

In several cases banks helped companies resist selling upstream and downstream properties by restructuring loans and advancing some loan forgiveness, but the price decline in 1986 forced many companies to divest in order to fulfill debt obligations. This has reduced the number of oil companies and improved the position of those that were able to react quickly to changes in crude supply and product demand. Upstream, there are similar problems. Between 1985 and 1987 the seven largest majors replaced only 40 percent of US reserves and 59 percent outside the United States through discoveries, extensions, and improved recovery. When revisions of oil reserves and purchases are taken into account, the majors' "replacement" was still 11 percent short compared with production. The majors—primarily Exxon, Shell, and BP—purchased reserves from smaller companies that were either cutting back their oil activity or dropping out of the industry completely, but the majors are still crude short, even if they are better off in this regard than some of their smaller competitors. Also, the late nineties meant restructuring among the large international oil companies. In 1998 British Petroleum agreed to buy Amoco for $48 billion, and a $77 billion merger of Exxon and Mobil was announced. The companies seemed to be preparing for a more competitive environment, where increased size is perceived as necessary in order to take higher risks. The oil price decline that started in 1997 and sent the oil price down to $10 per barrel during 1998 increased the pressure in the oil industry for cutting costs.[27] Another problem facing the international oil companies in the late nineties was their low return on invested capital compared with that of other industries such as information technology: "oil shares have performed worse than any other group of industrial shares over the past decade."[28] Thus, regarding both financial and physical reserves, the nineties resulted in a concentration among the international companies, putting the survivors in a stronger position in the international oil market than would otherwise have been the case. This implies even stronger competition in the years to come, which gives reason to believe that the concentration of resources within few oil companies will continue.

For the OPEC countries the key problem is the ability, or rather lack of ability, to finance the necessary investments in their existing production facilities. Most OPEC countries are currently producing close to capacity (except Iraq, due to UN sanctions). Any increase in production capacity will imply investments. As Figure 2.17 clearly shows, the financial reserves of the OPEC countries are no longer what they were in the heyday of high oil prices. "Virtually all producing countries could use more fi-

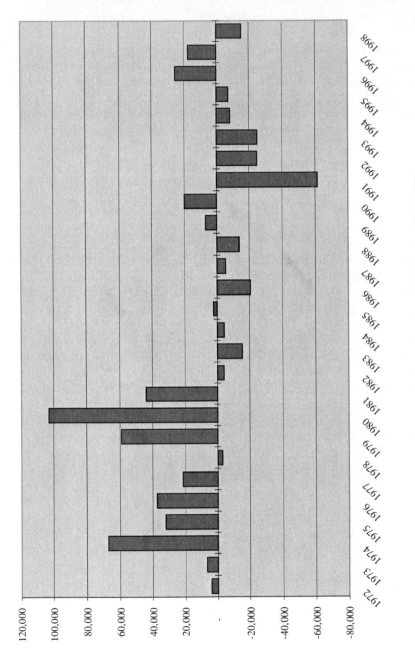

FIGURE 2.17   OPEC member countries' estimated current account balance, 1972–1998
SOURCE: *OPEC Annual Statistical Bulletin.*

nancing, more technology and more organization" (Finon 1991:263). The role of the international companies in OPEC production is on the increase. "Recently [by 1995] . . . many OPEC countries have started to revise their laws and regulations and become more open to production-sharing agreements with foreign firms. Some Members, such as Algeria, Venezuela, Iran and Iraq have now followed Indonesia, Nigeria, the UAE, Libya and Qatar, in opening up to foreign equity sharing. Saudi Arabia and Kuwait may follow suit at a later stage" (Ismail 1995:18).

Vertical Market-Power Relations

This section has focused on the relationship between different market actors along the vertical dimension of the market structure. The factors discussed in the previous sections give rise to the idea of a "New Deal" in the international oil market, whereby previous enemies cooperate and exchange control over different market segments, creating a new, integrated, oil-market order. This new international petroleum order is based on a convergence of interest. On the one hand, the large oil exporters search for secure outlets for their crude oil in order to protect themselves against future market volatility. Downstream integration—in one way or another—is an expression of risk-aversion on their part, which is understandable given their experience in the oil market during the eighties. This fits nicely into the predicaments of the oil industry at present. Companies with financial difficulties need new investments—for example, in their refineries—while crude-short companies are interested in arrangements improving their access to oil reserves. In that way they will also hedge against future uncertainty. In this case the risk is the mirror image of the one the producers face. For the majors, such joint ventures provide protection against future scarcity, which was the companies' nightmare of the seventies. This will open the way for the companies' return to the upstream market, and subsequently partly reverse the structural change of the seventies. Figure 2.18 illustrates this point. Regarding the future outlook for the structure of the international oil industry, Luciani (1995:49) expects

> producing countries to establish new rules under which foreign companies will be allowed direct access to oil reserves under conditions that will guarantee the government's political control. I also expect the oil companies of the producing countries to evolve gradually into integrated international oil companies, with downstream operations increasingly in line with their upstream assets, and reserves located abroad as well as in their country of origin. The process of vertical reintegration will not eliminate the spot and short-term futures markets. . . . As the process develops, the distinction be-

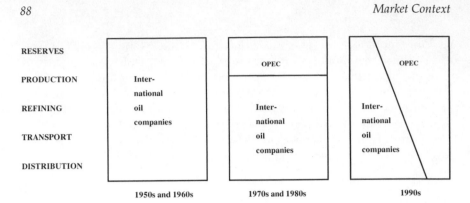

FIGURE 2.18   Changes in control over the vertical production chain

tween the various types of companies—national oil companies of the producing or importing countries, international integrated oil companies, small
nonintegrated companies etc.—will fade out.

While the fifties and sixties were dominated entirely by the major international oil companies, the upstream section of the market in the seventies was taken over by the main oil-producing countries. These were first
of all the OPEC members, but other producing countries also reserved a
large share of the upstream sector for national oil companies, as in Mexico (PEMEX), the United Kingdom (BP), and Norway (Statoil). The main
changes related to reserve control and production.

The new structure that emerged in the nineties has given large exporters control over some downstream outlets, and the major oil companies have gained access and some control upstream (see Figure 2.19).
Such a market structure will give both groups more long-term security.
Commercial freedom to maneuver will be more limited, but it is unlikely
that any company would commit 100 percent of its sales or purchases to
long-term relationships. Within a long-term security arrangement, a margin of flexibility will always be maintained by continued trading on the
spot and futures markets.

2.7 Conclusion

The relationship between actors' behavior and the market structure is dynamic. What actors (producers or others) do at t_1 might change aspects of
the market structure in a way that constrains the actors' behavior at t_2.
Furthermore, the potential for successful producer cooperation (i.e., a sit-

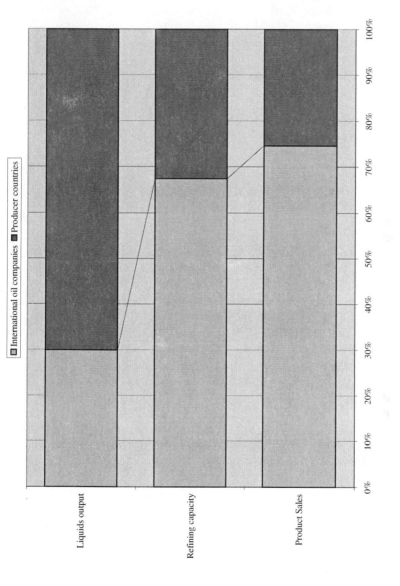

FIGURE 2.19   Interrational oil companies' and producing countries' share of product chain
SOURCE: Luciani: 1995:35–36.

uation where the net income of oil producers is raised due to collective action) is also constrained by the behavior of consumers and companies. Finally, producers present in the market at t_1 may behave in a way that attracts new producers to the market at t_2. All these aspects have been presented above as important in the development of the international oil market since the Second World War. The prime focus of the rest of this book is the period since 1971 and in particular the decade from 1985 to 1995. This concluding section spells out some implications for the producer cooperation, suggesting a less favorable structural environment for successful producer cooperation in this period than in previous decades.

As pointed out in section 1.5, both the theoretical contribution of Hotelling and the notion of scarcity can be argued to be inadequate descriptions of structural forces in the international oil market. Consequently, these factors are of lesser importance also for the oil-producer cooperation. As will be shown later in this study, some countries have tried to use their large proven reserves as a bargaining card in internal OPEC negotiations regarding production quotas. These attempts have usually been futile. However, the production capacity is to some extent based on the actors' reserves, and the production capacity is an important factor in the oil-producer bargaining, as it determines the possibility for an actor to gain, or at least reduce losses, in a price war. This argument is obvious—only producers with spare capacity stand to gain from a price war, as will be examined more deeply in Chapter 7.

Also, the level of production is an important element in the discussion of collective action in Chapter 7. Whether an actor increases its production by some percentage is assumed to have little effect on the politics of that actor, but large and small oil producers are assumed to pursue different policies regarding oil-producer cooperation.

Another important aspect influencing the oil-producer cooperation is downstream integration. Oil producers with large downstream assets are less affected by low crude oil prices. In fact, to some extent the interests of these actors are similar to those of consumer countries, since low input prices in refineries increase the profitability of these assets. The most prominent example is Kuwait, which during the nineties has increased its foreign downstream assets to a level equal to its income from crude oil sales. This enables the country to make money in situations of both high and low oil prices.

The changes in market power among the producers, consumers, and companies presented in sections 2.3 to 2.6 obviously constrain the potential for successful producer cooperation. Before the newcomers broke the Seven Sisters' dominance in the international oil market, there was little room for oil-producer cooperation. As will be underlined in Chapter 3, the oil producers are not a politically homogeneous group. The only factors that hold these countries together are their common interests related to the oil market and, in fact, their opposing interests against the other groups, the international companies, and the consumer countries. The Middle Eastern countries needed the split between the companies (see section 2.4) in order to gain the upper hand in the control of the market. When this was achieved, the oil-producing countries experienced a decade of prosperity, from the beginning of the seventies to the early eighties. Then they had to face the revenge of the market forces and the consumer countries as described in section 2.5. The demand slackened, and importing countries began taxing oil consumption, making the end-user insensitive to changes in crude oil prices. The price decrease during the eighties has subsequently not increased demand, as consumers have been presented with sustained high product prices (see Figure 2.15). The aspects of reintegration in the international oil market (presented in section 2.6) are a way for both crude-short companies and crude-long oil-producing countries to be able to live with both high and low oil prices. For the oil-producer cooperation this also establishes an internal split between the oil producers with and without downstream assets.

The discussion of these changes in market power in this chapter has focused on how the ability of one of these groups to influence price-setting, and to capture the monopoly profit of oil production, has been determined by structural changes and the behavior of the other groups of actors. The empirical analysis has identified a dynamic relationship between the different groups of actors and between actors' behavior and structural effects. The rest of this book is dedicated to the study of the cooperative behavior of one of these groups, the oil producers.

Notes

1. The designation "the Seven Sisters" was first used by the Italian oil man Enrico Mattei, and was later used as the title of Anthony Sampson's book about the seven largest oil companies (Sampson 1975:11). This group included Exxon, Mobil, Standard Oil of California, Texaco, Gulf (all American), BP (British Petroleum; 51 percent of the shares were formerly held by the British government), Royal Dutch/Shell (60 percent Dutch and 40 percent British). CFP (Compagnie Francaise des Pètroles) is sometimes included in this group, despite representing a minimal share of world production (approximately 1.2 percent in 1950) (Schneider 1983:39).

2. W. L. Newton's paper given at a seminar on the international petroleum industry at the School of Oriental and African Studies, University of London, 1967; cited in Penrose (1968:82, fn. 2).

3. It should be noted that the explanations for the companies' involvement and behavior in the Gulf region during the fifties and sixties are mixed and not always strictly commercial.

4. The San Remo agreement was an agreement primarily between France and the United Kingdom on the mandates in the Middle East. France was awarded the mandate for Syria and Lebanon, and the United Kingdom received the mandate for Palestine and Mesopotamia (later, Iraq).

5. Prices came under pressure from discoveries in the United States, in East Texas, and subsequently outside the international petroleum cartel's control.

6. This was the case when US authorities dissolved the Standard Oil Company in 1911, when the FTC investigated the cartel of international oil companies in 1952, and when a US Senate committee conducted hearings on international oil in 1974.

7. The figures refer to markets outside the United States and the Second World, and include CFP (Schneider 1983:40).

8. The members and organizational structure of OPEC are presented in Chapter 4.

9. Terzian (1985:143) refers to an anonymous source in an American oil company's statement to *Platt's Oilgram News*, February 3, 1971: "they (the OPEC countries) could ask for $5–$6 and there is really nothing we could do about it."

10. *Middle East Economic Survey*, February 19, 1971:4, cited in Adelman (1995:80), emphasis added by Adelman. The ministerial committee was made up of representatives Jamshid Amuzegar (Iran), Sadoon Hammadi (Iraq), and Ahmed Zaki Yamani (Saudi Arabia). By a resolution at the Twenty-first OPEC Conference in December 1970, it was established to negotiate on behalf of Abu Dhabi, Iran, Iraq, Kuwait, Qatar, and Saudi Arabia.

11. The implications of the embargo on the internal OPEC relations will be discussed in Chapter 5. Here, the focus is on the market behavior of the OPEC countries collectively.

12. OAPEC is the organization of Arabian petroleum exporting countries. It was formed in 1968 by Kuwait, Libya, and Saudi Arabia. Algeria, Bahrain, Egypt, Iraq, Qatar, Syria, and the United Arab Emirates have subsequently joined the organization (Jenkins 1986:429).

13. *Middle East Economic Survey* May 31, 1974, cited in Moran 1981:254 note 33.

14. *Oil and Gas Journal* June 17, 1974:38, cited in Moran 1981:254 note 33.

15. The original partners in Aramco, established in 1948, were Standard Oil of California (SoCal, subsequently Chevron) (30 percent), Texaco (30 percent), Exxon (30 percent), and Mobil (10 percent). In February 1973, the Saudi Arabian government took over 25 percent of the company, and in 1974 increased its share to 60 percent (Schneider 1983:40, 393, 407).

16. *Financial Times*, April 7, 1988. The company was not regarded as a Saudi Arabian state company, even though the American companies operated only on a contractor basis. The role of Aramco in the Saudi Arabian oil industry has been subject to further changes due to the restructuring of the Saudi Arabian oil sector in the late eighties.

17. *Middle East Economic Survey* July 18, 1983.

18. Exxon's net income in 1995 was $6,470 million; the corresponding figure for Royal Dutch/Shell was $6,918 million (*OPEC Annual Statistical Bulletin 1995*).

19. Central in this marketing of oil is NYMEX (New York Mercantile Exchange) and IPEX (International Petroleum Exchange). However, the market is in no way

bound to these bourses, as state-of-the-art information technology makes possible the sale of these "paper barrels" quite independent of geography.

20. For a discussion of the role of new trading mechanisms, see *Petroleum Intelligence Weekly*, April 22, 1985; Fesharaki and Razavi 1986; and Mabro 1987.

21. *Platt's Oilgram News*, August 29, 1985, article by Bijan Mossavar-Rahmani, Special Supplement, p. 1; *Petroleum Intelligence Weekly*, June 17, 1985, interview with Yamani; and *Petroleum Intelligence Weekly*, April 25, 1985.

22. "I think one of the very few countries that is still selling on term contracts is Saudi Arabia." Interview with Sheik Yamani on June 7; reported June 17, 1985, in *Petroleum Intelligence Weekly*.

23. The concept had been used earlier by other producers (e.g., Nigeria), but not in the same strategic way that Saudi Arabia did in 1985.

24. "It is in some ways helpful to see forward markets as unripe futures markets. There is a logic in the evolutionary sequence that runs from spot to forward, and on to futures" (Roeber 1993:45).

25. Sykuta (1994:47). Sykuta limits his argument to the purchasers' access to the commodity, but as he claims elsewhere the argument "applies equally well to sellers of the commodity" (ibid.:35, fn. 4).

26. It is also worth noting that in every case some type of reorganization of the national oil companies of the exporting countries was necessary before it was possible to adopt a sizable internationalization program. Kuwait's "success" has largely been attributed to its organization, while the Saudi hesitation to invest downstream (in relation to the Texaco deal) indicates that the kingdom had to review its relationships with the Aramco partners. In the case of Mexico, internal problems at Petróleos Mexicanos (PEMEX) have made it very difficult for the commercial managers to adopt an aggressive foreign investment policy. In Venezuela the large investments in foreign refineries have created mounting political opposition to the Petróleos de Venezuela SA (PDVSA) internationalization program (Bergesen, Bjørk and Claes 1989:29).

27. *The Economist*, November 28, 1998.

28. *The Economist*, December 5, 1998.

3

Political Context

The oil-producing countries are, in addition to being actors in the international oil market, also part of the international system of sovereign states. Sovereignty means there is no formal legitimate political authority above the individual state. The international system of states has no central world government and is thus defined as anarchy. This system is a self-help system where the states are individually responsible for upholding their sovereignty, although they might pursue this fundamental goal in concert. By reproducing their sovereignty, or surviving as independent political units, the states also reproduce the anarchic structure (Buzan et al. 1993:132). While the market structure distributes scarce resources, the political structure distributes power. The validity of an integrated notion of the wealth and power is not new to students of international relations.

> 1) Wealth is an absolutely essential means of power, whether for security or for aggression; 2) power is essential or valuable as a means to the acquisition or retention of wealth; 3) wealth and power are each ultimate ends of national policy; 4) there is a long-run harmony between these ends, although in particular circumstances it may be necessary for a time to make economic sacrifices in the interests of military security and therefore also of long-run prosperity. (Viner 1948:10, cited in Keohane 1984:23)

Keohane's comment on the fourth point in this citation is that "in the short run, tradeoffs exist between the pursuit of power and the pursuit of wealth" (Keohane 1984:23). Paraphrasing the citation from Viner (1948), the question to be scrutinized in this chapter is *to what extent security threats constitute "particular circumstances" that force* the oil producers *to make "economic sacrifices in the interests of military security."* An example could be if the US military's support of Saudi Arabia has made Saudi Arabia reluctant to increase the oil price. Another case would be if the Iranian antagonism against Western culture has made their oil industry less efficient than would have been the case if they had been part of the international oil industry.

The relationship between politics and economics has been the subject of considerable debate among political scientists and economists. Particularly, attempts to give one factor primacy before the other have created debate. "Unless definitions of *politics* and *economics* are arranged so that one category necessarily includes all fundamental phenomena, neither economic nor political determinism can explain events successfully" (Bergsten et al. 1975:4). Keohane (1979:97–98) points out: "Even people who accept close linkages between domestic and foreign policies frequently draw a sharp contrast between 'economics' and 'politics.' Thunderous mock battles take place between analysts who believe that political motivations are primary and those who contend that the 'real objectives' of policymakers are economic." The interrelationship between politics and economics is a matter of "how the institutions, fundamental assumptions and 'rules of the game' of political systems support or undermine different patterns of allocation for economic activity, as well as in the converse—how the nature of economic activity affects the political structure" (Keohane and Nye 1973:117).

If politics and economics are totally intertwined, the relationship between them is impossible to detect or discuss. In order to understand the interaction between politics and economics, we need to separate the concepts analytically although we agree on their ontological inseparability. Since this study tries to explain the cooperation among oil producers in the fields of oil, we will limit this conceptual discussion to how political interests might influence the oil-related behavior of the oil-producing states. A concept capturing this process is the term politicization.

3.1 Politicization

Politicization is a concept commonly used, but which few have attempted to give a precise analytical content. According to one definition, politicization is to "transform an activity that seems to have no political connotations, into one that is consciously bent towards political ends" (Scruton 1982). Here, politicization is attached to the objectives of the actor. Secondly, one can examine the action itself, or the type of means the actor employs. In this book, politicization will denote linkage of the economic matters to a political decisionmaking level (Hirsch and Doyle 1977:11–13). Let us start out with the possibility that economic interests are the single cause of market behavior. Figure 3.1a illustrates this situation. Political factors can influence the actors market behavior in two ways. First, politicization occurs when an actor in a given market allows his political aims, *outside* the market concerned, to affect his behavior *in* the market (Figure 3.1b). Secondly, politicization occurs when an actor in a given market employs political means for purposes of achieving objectives in the market (Figure 3.1c). In the first case, politicization can be an unconscious linkage as one's political interests predominate over one's economic interests and behavior in the market. In the second case, politicization will have to be a conscious linkage. Bergesen defines politicization as: "simply the interference of a government in the international oil market" (Bergesen 1988:3). This also agrees with one of Wilson's (1982:10) definitions. If we provide that the state can never have any objectives other than political ones and all other market actors can never have political objectives, this will agree with the first definition. If we provide that the state has only political means and no other actors have any political means, then this agrees with the second definition. However, it seems unreasonable to argue that states by definition cannot act based only on economic interests. It is also possible that a state would like to abandon the politicization strategy. This means that a market behavior previously influenced by political interests are set to be determined by only economic interests. This could be indicated by letting the economic interests determine both the market behavior and the political interests (Figure 3.1d).

There might be an infinite number of political factors behind the market behavior of oil producers. However, for most of the states in question, oil exporting is the dominant economic sector. For some countries the exporting of crude oil accounts for all of their foreign currency earnings, and the state income from taxing the oil production is the sole source of government income. In these cases the economic importance of the petroleum sector makes it an important political issue, and only other political issues of utmost importance will induce a change in what is assumed, by the state leadership, to be the optimal petroleum policy. The survival of the state is a prominent issue of this kind. For religious fundamentalists, religious imperatives might also be regarded as more important than the economic interests of the oil sector (see Noreng 1997). However, the security interest of the regime and the citizens is regarded as a, if not the, prominent political interest of states. "No purpose of government is more central than the protection of its citizens' physical security. Philosophically, many thinkers have held that this, in fact, is the ultimate reason why humankind form governments" (Smoke 1975:247).

The claim in this chapter is that the development of the oil-producer cooperation is best understood by studying the relationship between actors' economic and security interests and behavior. What is important is not that states have a hierarchy of interests, putting security at the top, but that the priority among interests might vary over time and according

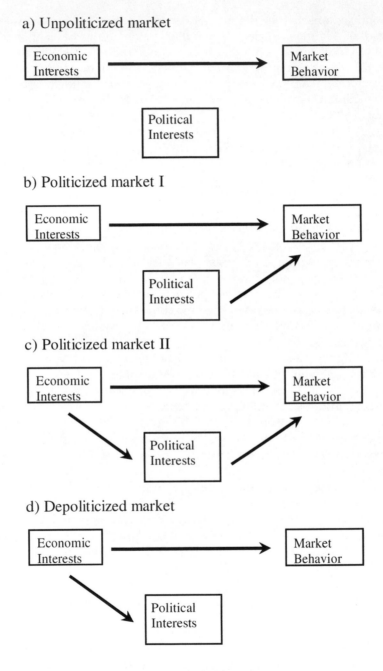

FIGURE 3.1   Categories of politicization

to the actors' perception of the situation surrounding their decisions (see the situational analysis presented in section 1.4). In this chapter possible threats to the security of the regimes governing oil-producing states are regarded as a motive that might change an individual country's oil policy. The empirical discussion is organized along the division between external security threats (sections 3.3 and 3.4) and internal security threats (section 3.5). Section 3.3 discusses the consequences of the Iran-Iraq War for the oil producers' behavior in the oil market and their oil-related cooperation, and section 3.4 follows the same line of argument in relation to the Iraq-Kuwait War. Section 3.5 deals with the internal political stability of oil-producer regimes and the role of oil income in securing these regimes, while section 3.6 highlights some political cooperative aspects of the OPEC relations. First it is necessary to relate the concept of security to the characteristics of the oil-producing states.

3.2   Oil and Security

According to Buzan (1991:8), the concept of security has been dominated by the concept of power in the literature on these aspects of international relations: "reduced to little more than a synonym for power, security had little independent relevance in wider systemic terms." Buzan quotes several definitions that he finds point out important aspects of national security, namely, "the centrality of values, the timing and intensity of threats and the political nature of security as an objective of states" (Buzan 1991:18). Buzan does not seek an overall definition, but instead divides the security concept into five categories, related to the sectors affecting national security, of which three are of particular importance to the discussion in this chapter:[1]

> Generally speaking, military security concerns the two-level interplay of the armed offensive and defensive capabilities of states, and states' perceptions of each other's intentions. Political security concerns the organizational stability of states, systems of government and the ideologies that give them legitimacy. Economic security concerns access to the resources, finance and markets necessary to sustain acceptable levels of welfare and state power. (Buzan 1991:19)

To pursue the fundamental interest of survival, states have to resort to power capabilities. These capabilities can be physical (like oil reserves in the ground), organizational, financial, technological, or purely political (including military forces). Usually, military force, or coercive force, is regarded as an ultimate capability:

If the security dilemma for all states was extremely acute, military force, supported by economic and other resources, would clearly be the dominant source of power. Survival is the primary goal of all states, and in the worst situations, force is ultimately necessary to guarantee survival. Thus military force is always a central component of national power. (Keohane and Nye 1977:27)

As will become evident in this and the next chapter, on the role of Saudi Arabia, states facing security threats have a complex menu of power capabilities; they need not resort to coercive force immediately. In addition to such fundamental resources, states need the skill and will to use their power resources effectively (Baldwin 1979:163). The resources themselves are of no use unless the state is able and willing to use them. For instance, Kuwait in 1990 had no ability to stand up against the Iraqi invasion. Although Kuwait had been attacked before, it did little to build up military deterrence against such attacks. Another problem is the context of power resources: "the capabilities (or potential power) of an actor must be set in the context of a 'policy-contingency-framework' specifying who is trying (or might try) to get whom to do what" (Baldwin 1979:164). Certain types of capabilities might not be effectively applicable in certain issue areas or situations. Baldwin argues that political power resources are relatively low in fungibility, for instance compared with money.

Often it is impossible to distinguish between a country's security and economic interests regarding oil-market-related behavior: "Aside from our military defense, there is no project of more central importance to our national security and indeed our independence as a sovereign nation [than energy saving, import independence, and consumer cooperation]" (Kissinger 1982b:xx). This statement indicates that oil importing at reasonable prices is perceived as a question of national security, not as a matter of economics alone. The discussion of separating the issues quickly becomes one of words, but this is no less important, as the use of words can imply changes in actors' behavior: "By saying 'security' a state-representative moves the particular case into a specific area; claiming a special right to use the means necessary to block this development" (Wæver 1989:5–6, cited in Buzan 1991:17). Since the politicization of market behavior seems obvious if the actor regards the oil market in the same way as Kissinger, it might not be worthwhile to distinguish the economic interests from the security interests. A further restriction of relevant cases to the ones where actors give priority to the security interests is thus necessary. The following section will therefore deal with cases where oil is related to potential or actual threats of intervention or subversion. In such cases it seems reasonable to assume that the security interest of the state takes priority over economic welfare interests.

Most of the states included in the discussion in this chapter are autocratic regimes. The state leaderships perceive threats both from internal opposition and from other states. They themselves are perceived by other political actors, domestic and foreign, as posing threats both toward other states and toward their own citizens.[2] This makes the traditional external security concept too narrow for comprehension of the security issue pertaining to the Middle East oil-producing states. In addition to demanding a more comprehensive conception of security, this reality also loosens the assumption of states as unitary actors, which is a methodological basis for the most of the discussion in this book. In this chapter, the "black box" will be opened in discussing the role of oil in the state-society relations in selected oil-producing countries (see particularly section 3.5). The transcending of the national-international level divide is even more important for the next chapters, which include the case studies of Saudi Arabia and Norway (see Chapters 6 and 9).

The following two sections will focus on the implications for the oil-producer cooperation of two major military conflicts: the war between Iran and Iraq from 1980 to 1988 (section 3.3), and then the war between Iraq and Kuwait from 1990 to 1991 (section 3.4).

3.3   The Iran-Iraq War

Iran and Iraq have been involved in most military conflicts between OPEC countries. This can be shown with data from the data-set Militarized Interstate Disputes (International Consortium of Political Science Research (ICPSR data-file 9044). These data are based on coding procedures similar to those of the Correlates of War data, with two important exceptions. First, the criterion of number of deaths is zero, while for the war data-set the minimum number of deaths is set at 1,000. Second, the war data-set requires some military interaction to have taken place, while in the dispute data-set it is sufficient that military threats of some form have been uttered. A total of forty-six disputes in this data-set involve two or more OPEC countries, on opposite sides. With one exception—a border dispute between Saudi Arabia and Qatar in 1992, killing two border-guards—Iran or Iraq has been involved in all disputes between OPEC members since the Second World War. Iran and Iraq have never been on the same side as any other OPEC member during the same period, except for the Kuwait-Iraq War of 1961 where Iran supported Kuwait. These findings suggest that all militarized conflicts having effect on the OPEC cooperation are related to conflicts involving Iran or Iraq. Most prominent among these conflicts is the war between the two countries from 1980 to 1988.

The factors behind the Iran-Iraq War were many. Traditional conflicts between Sunnite and Shiite Muslims, historical conflicts concerning disputed land and river areas, and expansionist objectives by former leaders had created clashes between the two countries for centuries. Thus, Iraq's declaration of war on Iran on September 22, 1980, was in line with a traditional conflict pattern in this region. Iraqi troops soon made substantial advances into Iran, but then Iraq stopped and offered to negotiate. The Iranians refused, and at the same time gained time to mobilize. At the end of 1981, the Iraqi advances came to a complete halt. In the spring of 1982, the Iranian counterattacks had substantial success, and the temptation to continue into Iraq became irresistible for Tehran. Although the Iranian forces gained some Iraqi territory, the war soon ran into a stalemate; neither of the parties was able to advance forcefully over a longer period. Iran conducted several offensives against Iraq between 1984 and 1987, but none of such a magnitude to decisively end the war. In February 1984, as Iran started the first of these so-called final offensives, the war turned to the Persian Gulf waters, and the tanker war commenced. Iraq attacked ships going into Iranian ports, probably with the aim of provoking an Iranian blockade of the Strait of Hormuz, which in turn would prompt the Western countries to take more severe action against Iran. Iran did not fall for the trap, but launched attacks on tankers serving Kuwaiti and Saudi Arabian ports in order to deter these countries from supporting Iraq. By 1985, the intensity and brutality of the land war had increased again. The use of chemical weapons contributed to a substantial increase in civilian deaths; estimates range between 450,000 and 730,000 on the Iranian side, and 150,000 and 340,000 on the Iraqi side (Cordesman and Wagner 1990:3). Adding the direct and indirect costs of the warfare, estimates have been put at $627 billion for Iran and $561 billion for Iraq.[3] Most important for the oil market was the war in the Persian Gulf initiated in 1984. Three hundred ships were hit from 1984 to 1988. Furthermore, Iraq tried to destroy Iranian oil-loading facilities, particularly on Kharg Island. Although Iraq received laser-guided bombs and navigation equipment from France, the number and small size of loading points at the Kharg installations made the bombing ineffective. The Iranian oil production varied during this period, but on average a substantial level was sustained.

The West did not pay much attention to the conflict until 1984. Not even the Iranian advances into Iraq caused much concern. One reason was that until June 1982 there was virtually no activity at sea. The first sea war efforts were also characterized as small, single attacks and not part of a broader strategy of sea war. The oil production of the two belligerent countries was already low, so this did not change the flow of oil from the Persian Gulf.

While Iran in 1984 started using the "human wave" tactic, Iraq escalated the war into the Gulf waters. This obviously brought the warfare closer to the other Gulf countries' territories, and they were soon directly affected. On May 14, two Kuwaiti tankers were attacked, followed by an attack on a Saudi Arabian tanker on May 17. This development also brought the United States into the conflict, as Washington decided to supply Saudi Arabia with 400 Stinger antiaircraft missiles (Kechichian 1990:100). Thus, Saudi Arabia was set to defend the Gulf waters. On June 5, 1984, a Royal Saudi Air Force jet shot down an Iranian F-4 Phantom fighter-bomber. The kingdom tried not to let this incident broaden the war.[4] However, after this point the other Gulf countries' ability to mediate or end the conflict by other diplomatic means was severely weakened (Kechichian 1990:101). The next major shift in the war directly affecting the other Gulf countries was the change in the Iranian sea war strategy. As Iraq intensified its attacks on Kharg Island and the Iranian shuttle traffic to the more distant islands of Sirri and Larak, the Iranians intensified their attacks on sea traffic to pro-Iraqi countries like Kuwait and Saudi Arabia. Since Iran's air force was insignificant, its light naval forces conducted hit-and-run attacks on tankers, a kind of naval guerrilla warfare. Thus, the ability to actually sink supertankers was limited until Iran was supplied with heavier rockets, particularly by China. By 1986 the Iranian attacks on ships in the Gulf increased, and the attacks became more severe. In January 1987, Kuwait sought US naval protection of its tankers by suggesting that the ships be "re-flagged" to fly the "Stars and Stripes." Kuwait also leased three Soviet tankers, which the Soviet Union agreed to escort. By June, the first ships with US flags and protected by the US Navy entered the Gulf. This led to an increased internationalization of the conflict. Both superpowers were now directly involved in the Gulf War. In spring of 1987, Iranian forces attacked two Soviet tankers. In May, Iraq attacked the US frigate *Stark,* killing thirty-seven mariners. This caused a political crisis in the United States, and Western public attention to the war increased dramatically. When Iran laid out mines that reached Kuwaiti ports, minesweepers were sent to the area, and a joint operation with Saudi Arabia, using Saudi Arabian AWACS surveillance planes, was established. On July 20, 1987, the UN Security Council passed UN Resolution 598, calling for an immediate cease-fire.

Saudi Arabia strengthened its position in the Gulf both as a result of the US presence and through its own military buildup. In particular, the Royal Saudi Air Force became the strongest air power in the region during this period.[5] Saudi Arabia's increased self-confidence also meant that it became more willing to challenge Iran. After the eighth GCC (Gulf Cooperation Council) summit in 1987, the Saudi Arabian foreign minister, Prince Saudi-al-Faysal, stated that "the aim of the GCC countries [was] to end the war and put an end to Iranian attacks against the GCC states" (Kechichian 1990:106). While Kuwait and Saudi Arabia wanted to take a tougher position against Iran, the United Arab Emirates and Oman sought continuous dialogue with Tehran (Kechichian 1990:106). Also, the gunning down of 400 Iranian pilgrims in Mecca on July 31, 1987, must be understood as a result of a more potent and confident Saudi Arabian regime. The war thus influenced the overall power relations between key OPEC members. The next question is what effects the war had on the economic oil-related relations between the affected OPEC countries.

The price effect was short-term, and the lasting importance for the market was the disappearance of the two countries' production capacities. This made the hegemonic role of Saudi Arabia even more prominent, as these two countries, given their installed production capacity prior to the outbreak of the Iranian revolution, were the possible challengers to the Saudi Arabian position (see Chapter 6). The Iranian oil production had been about 6 mbd in September 1978, while Iraq produced about 3.5 mbd in the first half of 1980. With the outbreak of the war, the Iranian production fell from 1.3 mbd in August to 350,000 barrels in October. Iraqi production fell from 3.4 mbd to 500,000 barrels over the same period. Figure 3.2 shows the development of the two countries' production from 1976 until 1989. The figure shows how the Iranian production first dropped due to the Iranian revolution. It was restored at a lower level, but dropped again at the beginning of the Iran-Iraq War. The Iraqi oil production also dropped at the beginning of the Iran-Iraq War.

The problem to be raised in this section is whether the conflict between the two countries created problems for the economic cooperation inside OPEC in the bargaining process. Regarding the OPEC negotiations, a summit of heads of state was scheduled for November 4 in Baghdad to celebrate the twentieth anniversary of the organization in its founding city. Plans were made for a renewal of the organization. The meeting never took place. However, on December 15, 1980, the OPEC Conference met at Bali, with representatives of two belligerent parties. The head of the Iranian delegation, Oil Minister Javad Tondguyan, was in fact a war prisoner captured by Iraqi troops at the beginning of the month. Terzian (1985:286–287) describes how OPEC handled this first meeting after the war broke out:

The Iranian delegation entered solemnly, bearing a portrait of their captured minister . . . installed the photo of Tondguyan on the chair reserved for the head of delegation and took their places behind it. Suharto, the President of Indonesia, arrived next and, after his inaugural speech, launched an appeal for a cessation of hostilities between Iraq and Iran. . . . the Iraqi and Iranian delegations were given the floor. They exchanged endless accusations, each country blaming the other for the war. Finally, when the diatribes were over, the ten other OPEC members adopted a resolution backing the call for peace

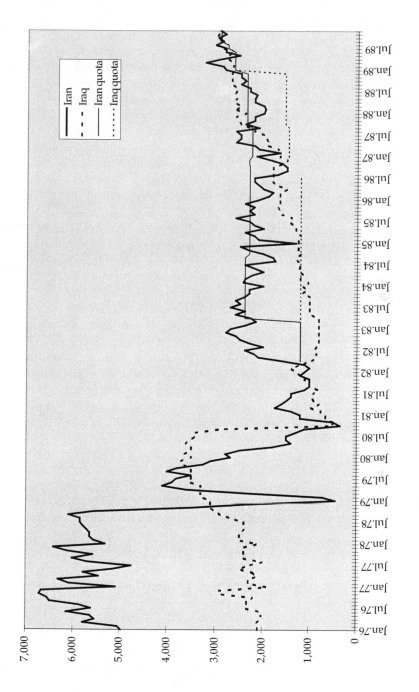

FIGURE 3.2 Iranian and Iraqi production, 1976–1989 (th. b/d)
SOURCE: *Petroleum Economist;* OPEC (1990); *OPEC Bulletin.*

issued by Indonesia. Once all these matters had been settled, the delegates moved on to the other items on the agenda, and it was business as usual.

The official OPEC reaction was expressed in very diplomatic terms: "The Conference endorsed the sincere and honest appeal made by His Excellence the President of the Republic of Indonesia in his inauguration speech to the two Member Countries—Iran and Iraq—who are presently in dispute, to quickly seek the best possible solution to their conflict leading to a peaceful settlement of their differences" (OPEC 1990:192).

Due to the war, Iran became a pure price-taker, maximizing its oil exports. The success of this strategy is clearly illustrated in Figure 3.2. Iranian oil production rose throughout 1982, from 1.1 mbd in March to 2.8 mbd in December. On April 10, 1982, Syria cut off the Iraqi pipeline to the Mediterranean, cutting 400,000 bd of Iraqi export capacity. Also illustrated in Figure 3.2, Iraqi production fell from 1.3 mbd in the first quarter to about 850,000 bd in the second half of 1982. The quotas allocated to the two countries in April 1982 were 1.2 mbd each. At the Sixty-fifth OPEC Conference in July 1982, Iran "demanded a quota of 2.5 m b/d and that its increase should be taken from the Saudi share" (Skeet 1988:188). The boldness of this demand was fueled by the success on the battlefield. In 1982 Iran had stopped the Iraqi advances and was ready for its counterattack, and only weeks after the meeting, Iran invaded Iraq. The resolution of the Sixty-fifth Conference simply states that "the Conference . . . decided to suspend the deliberations of the Conference until further notice" (OPEC 1990:204). As Figure 3.2 shows, Iran did not at all abide by its quota in the following months. On the battlefield the Iranian offensive was soon stopped, and the war became a war of attrition. Saudi Arabia and the other GCC countries became more relaxed, no longer fearing rapid Iranian expansion. They accordingly began to take a tougher stand against Iran, a stand that extended to the OPEC negotiations. A statement from the GCC oil ministers' meeting in Salala on October 14, illustrates this: "The other producers should know that the GCC Ministers expect them to shoulder their responsibilities and if they continue their misguided actions they will not be protected by the member countries from the GCC from the consequences of these actions" (Skeet 1988:189).

In his opening address at the following OPEC meeting, the chairman of the Nigerian delegation, Alhaji Yahaya Dikko, with a clear reference to the above statement, said that "threats are never a basis for cooperation" (Evans 1990:607). The Conference decided that the total quota for 1983 should be 18.5 mbd, but it was unable to agree on the allocation of national quotas. Thus, the 18.5 mbd ceiling was not convincing to the market actors (see Chapter 7 for the criteria for a successful cartel).

The Sixty-seventh Conference was held over twelve days in London, but only the last hours on the last day transformed it into a full conference. The Iranian quota was doubled, from 1.2 to 2.4 mbd. Iraq agreed to keep its 1.2 mbd quota only on the condition that it should be revised upward to parity with that of Iran as soon as its production capacity allowed. Saudi Arabia was not allocated a quota but was officially given the role of "swing producer to supply the balancing quantities to meet market requirements" (OPEC 1990:208). Obviously, the following downswing of Saudi Arabia would have been harder had both Iran and Iraq had their exporting capacity intact. Given these facts, one should expect there to have been a turbulent situation when the war ended in 1988. However, by that time, the price had crashed (in 1986), and the market to some extent had taken into account the production capacity of the warring parties. As the war damage to oil installations was reduced through the US presence in the Gulf and the military buildup of the GCC countries, the production of Iran and Iraq picked up gradually, giving room for a smoother market adaptation.

To conclude the discussion of the implications of the Iran-Iraq War on the OPEC cooperation, it is necessary to distinguish between the effect the war had in changing the power resources of the belligerent parties and the effect on the OPEC negotiations as such. The OPEC negotiations were only modestly influenced by the war. Aside from the incident involving the captured minister, and some exchange of accusations, the negotiations were business as usual. However, the power basis for the different countries' positions in the OPEC discussions was dramatically changed by the war. Both Iran's and Iraq's oil production dropped significantly at the beginning of the war, from above 3 mbd to under 1 mbd each. Iran was able to regain a production level of about 2 mbd, while the Iraqi production remained at about 1 mbd until 1985, and then started to climb slowly (see Figure 3.2). This reduced these two countries' positions in the OPEC bargaining compared with those of other countries like Saudi Arabia and the other Gulf states.

3.4   The Iraq-Kuwait War

At the Arab Cooperation Council meeting in February 1990, Saddam Hussein told King Hussein of Jordan and President Mubarak of Egypt to tell the Gulf states to forgive their loans to Iraq. Saddam perceived the loans as payment for Iraq's defending the Gulf states against Iran. "Let the Gulf regimes know that if they do not give this money to me, I will know how to get it," he said.[6] At the Arab summit meeting in May 1990, Saddam argued that the continued violation of OPEC quotas by some Arab countries was equivalent to a declaration of war against Iraq. In a radio speech in July, his argument was even stronger:

War is fought with soldiers and much harm is done by explosions, killing, and coup attempts—but it is also done by economic means. Therefore, we would ask our brothers who do not mean to wage war on Iraq: this is in fact a kind of war against Iraq. . . . we have reached a point where we can no longer withstand pressure.[7]

In mid-July the buildup of military forces and a diplomatic offensive began. On July 16, the Iraqi foreign minister, Tariq Aziz, delivered a memorandum to the secretary-general of the Arab League, presenting the Iraqi indictment. Among other accusations, Kuwait and the United Arab Emirates were accused of having created a glut in the oil market, bringing prices down with devastating economic impact on the Middle East and Iraq. Furthermore, Kuwait was claimed to have robbed Iraq by setting up oil installations in the southern section of the Iraqi Rumaila oil field (Freedman and Karsh 1993:47–48). The following day, Saddam increased the tension by an address to the nation. He accused Kuwait and the United Arab Emirates of conspiring with world imperialism and Zionism to "cut off the livelihood of the Arab nation," and threatened that "if words fail to afford us protection, then we will have no choice but to resort to effective action to put things right and ensure the restitution of our rights."[8] Kuwait responded by "refuting the Iraqi accusations and expressing strong indignation at Iraq's behavior" (Freedman and Karsh 1993:49).[9] On July 31, representatives from Iraq and Kuwait met in Jeddah for negotiations after Iraq had placed 100,000 men along the Kuwaiti border. The talks ended the next day. The parties disagreed on the reason for the breakdown of the talks.[10]

On August 2, 1990, Iraq invaded and occupied Kuwait. The Iraqi military operation was a success: Kuwait was occupied in twelve hours.[11] Contrary to the Iran-Iraq War, the first phase of this conflict was less characterized by changes on the battlefield and more by those in the political and diplomatic arenas. Two developments made the invasion look less like a success for Saddam. The first was that the international response, condemning the Iraqi action, included most Arab countries. At the meeting of the Arab League on August 10, Egypt proposed a resolution condemning the invasion, imposing economic sanctions on Iraq, and offering military support to Saudi Arabia. Twelve of the twenty delegates supported the resolution, and only Libya, the Palestinian Liberation Organization (PLO), and Iraq voted against it. The other development was the US deployment of military forces in Saudi Arabia. There had never been foreign forces in Saudi Arabia, and the thought that the Custodian of the Two Mosques should be defended by large US forces seemed odd. The United States, the world's largest oil consumer, felt indirectly threatened by the prospect of Iraq, having taken the Kuwaiti oil reserves, being able to put political or military pressure on Saudi Arabia. "President Bush became convinced that the kingdom was vulnerable and that the United States could not afford to see an Iraqi takeover" (Freedman and Karsh 1993:86). When King Fahd agreed to the establishment of US forces on Saudi soil, the Operation Desert Shield started.

Already on the night of August 2, the UN Security Council had passed a unanimous resolution (660) condemning the invasion. On August 6, it decided to introduce economic sanctions against Iraq (Resolution 661),[12] and on August 18, it sanctioned an embargo of Iraq (Resolution 665). By mid-September, the US forces in Saudi Arabia had reached 150,000. The Iraqis were disturbed, and started building up forces in Kuwait and southern Iraq. In early October it seemed President Bush "was becoming impatient and increasingly pessimistic with regard to the effectiveness of [the economic] sanctions" (Freedman and Karsh 1993:203).[13] On October 30, a proposal for the additional forces needed to turn the operation into an offensive one was presented to the president by Colin Powell, chairman of the Joint Chiefs of Staff. "Bush reportedly concurred: 'If that's what you need, we'll do it'" (Freedman and Karsh 1993:208). On November 29, the UN Security Council passed a resolution sanctioning the use of all necessary means unless Iraq did not withdraw from Kuwait by January 15, 1991 (Resolution 678). Hectic international diplomatic activity followed until the last minutes before this deadline. No solution was reached, and on January 17, the air strikes commenced. Operation Desert Storm had begun. On February 24, a ground attack was launched; it lasted for 100 hours.

The embargo of Iraq was set to continue until Iraq complied with all UN sanctions, including the one demanding the destruction of all Iraqi atomic, biological, and chemical weapons. The sanctions have caused substantial suffering among Iraqi citizens, with an increase in diseases and child mortality. Although the embargo did not include food and medicine, without oil exports Iraq had no money to pay for such goods. In spring of 1996, negotiations commenced in order to let Iraq sell some quantities of oil to pay for food and medicine to its suffering citizens.

The UN Security Council boycott resolution of Iraq and the new regime in Kuwait in August 1990 immediately brought to a halt all oil flows from the two countries. The oil price skyrocketed from $18/barrel to almost $30/barrel in a couple of weeks. Other producers, particularly Saudi Arabia, quickly filled the gap. "On 19 August the Saudi Oil Minister, Hisham Nazer, announced that his country would increase production by 2 mbd with or without the blessing of OPEC" (Freedman and Karsh 1993:182). There was no shortage of oil. After a few weeks, the OPEC production was back at almost its prewar level. Some additional barrels from non-OPEC producers made the total market balance, although there were some elements of panic buying (see section 5.3).

After conducting informal consultations among OPEC oil ministers in Vienna from August 26 to 28, 1990, and convening a meeting of the OPEC Ministerial Monitoring Committee in Vienna on Wednesday, August 29, 1990, OPEC issued the following press release:

> After reviewing the trend of the oil market, and being of the opinion that it may well be prolonged, thus increasing the uncertainty of oil supply in the fourth quarter of 1990 and the first quarter of 1991, OPEC, as a body which is fully aware of its mandate and responsibility to help ensure an adequate global energy supply, has independently decided to adopt the following position and interim course of action: To clearly restate to the world that OPEC stands for market stability and regular supply of oil to consumers. . . . That OPEC shall consequently increase production, in accordance with need, in order to maintain the above-stated objectives. . . . Consumers, however, need also to actively participate in the stabilization process, by executing the IEA Oil Sharing Agreement, which was specifically designed to meet eventualities such as the present situation, and also by utilizing the present huge accumulation of stocks owned by the oil companies. . . . This is a temporary arrangement, applicable only until such time as the present crisis is deemed to be over, and this arrangement shall not in any way compromise the provisions of the 1990 resolution, which is still valid. Once the present crisis is considered to be over, the Organization shall return to the July 1990 Resolution. (OPEC 1990:310–311)

Although OPEC wanted the IEA to initiate its sharing agreement, there was harmony between key OPEC members' political interests and the possibility to act "responsibly" by creating stability in the oil market. For Saudi Arabia and other producers with spare capacity, individual short-term economic incentives were satisfied through increased production; for the countries with less spare capacity, a price increase would be more beneficial. Iraq, Iran, and Libya accordingly advocated that OPEC should not increase production but let the price increase. Indonesia, Algeria, and Nigeria favored only moderate production increases. As the adopted resolution hardly put any restriction on the individual countries' increase in production, Saudi Arabia stood to gain the most from the organization's response (see section 6.5).

Before discussing the effects of the war on the oil-producer cooperation, it is necessary to outline briefly the oil-related reasons behind the outbreak and outcome of the Iraq-Kuwait conflict. Two questions arise regarding the relationship between the oil interests and the Gulf War. First, to what extent was the Kuwaiti overproduction (measured against its allocated OPEC quota) an important reason for Saddam Hussein to invade Kuwait? Second, to what extent was the fact that the annexation of

Kuwait gave Saddam control over about 20 percent of world oil reserves an important reason for the United States and Saudi Arabia to try to evict Saddam from Kuwait?

As described above, Saddam, in his political attacks on the Gulf states during spring of 1990, focused on both the repayment of war loans from the Gulf states in connection with the Iran-Iraq War and the low oil price caused by the overproduction by particularly Kuwait and the United Arab Emirates. The Kuwaiti drilling activity in the Rumaila oil field, which crosses the border between Kuwait and Iraq, was also a cause for Iraqi concern. However, the question is not whether these factors were a part of the Iraqi argument in the buildup toward the invasion, but whether Iraq would have abstained from attacking Kuwait had these factors not been present. In other words, were these factors necessary conditions for the outbreak of war?[14] It is obviously problematic to distinguish the economic motives from the political ones, since they, in this instance, pull in the same direction: Both lead to the conclusion that Saddam stood to gain from invading Kuwait. The conclusion offered by Freedman and Karsh (1993:429) on this issue is interesting to note:

> The mistake in the Arab world as well as in the West was not to recognize the desperation of Saddam's situation. Such a recognition should not have led to pressure on Kuwait and the United Arab Emirates to give generously to Iraq, although that would probably have been the result. As the Kuwaitis recognized, if Saddam was rewarded this time he would soon be back for more. They might have been more tactful, especially in the realm of honoring oil quotas or gratuitous snubs to Saddam's pride, but our judgment is that only a very large bribe would have persuaded Saddam to pull back his troops once he had determined on his campaign of intimidation.

The previous support of Iraq in the war against Iran, and the importance of Arab unity, suggested that the other Arab countries would be reluctant to interfere once the Iraqi invasion was completed. Give Iraq's expansionist and imperial ambitions, the attack on Kuwait cannot be ascribed solely to the lack of some billions of dollars in loan remittance. Regarding Kuwait's and the United Arab Emirates' overproduction against their OPEC quotas, one should note that Iraq itself produced substantially above its allocated quota, and in fact did not accept its quotas for most of the eighties (see section 7.4). This argument was part of the rhetorical game connected with the invasion. The economic issues were used to legitimize the invasion rather than the fundamental reason for it. Saddam regarded the international and regional political situation as one in which he could get away with the invasion of Kuwait, and he took advantage of this perceived opportunity. It turned out that either he misread the situation or his opponents changed their minds as they saw the implications of his policy.

This leads to the question about the motives of the United States and the Gulf countries in opposing the invasion. Again, the problem of distinguishing different motives of individual actors appears. For the United States the normative argument of punishing the obvious breach of fundamental international norms of nonaggression, the political argument of securing the sovereignty of an important ally like Saudi Arabia, and the undesired situation of having Saddam in control of one-fifth of world oil reserves all pulled in the same direction. The answer was to eject Saddam from Kuwait. For the other OPEC countries, this was not so. The OPEC advocates of pressing the oil price higher got unexpected help from Saddam, while the low-price advocates (the Gulf countries) focused on the negative effects of another period of oil-market turmoil. This division of the OPEC members' interests was exposed at the OPEC meeting in Vienna in late August 1990, where several non-Gulf countries advocated not increasing production in order to counteract the price rise after the invasion. For the Gulf countries, the security interests were of utmost importance. Although it seemed unlikely that Saddam would push farther into Saudi Arabia, gambling the nations' sovereignty on the rationality of Saddam seemed foolish. Furthermore, with an acceptance of the annexation of Kuwait, Saddam would be in a position to increase the political and economic pressure on the Gulf countries, even without military threats toward them. In the longer run this could have politically undermined the fragile regimes in the Gulf countries and possibly pressed them to change their oil policy according to the interests of Saddam. As suggested in Chapter 6, the security interests of Saudi Arabia have in several instances been important in explaining the kingdom's oil policy. The Saudi Arabian regime found itself in a very tight position with Saddam's army on its northern border, imposing threats in order to change Saudi Arabian oil policy. This leads to the final issue in this section: the implications of the Iraq-Kuwait War for the OPEC cooperation.

After the war, Iraq was subject to an embargo; its oil production was about 500.000 barrels a day until the end of 1996. Accordingly, the production-sharing between the other members was eased. In particular, Saudi Arabia's position had been strengthened. Table 3.1 compares Saudi Arabia's and Iraq's share of OPEC production in July 1990 with the production from 1991 to 1994 (see also Table 5.2 for the nominal figures).

As Table 3.1 shows, the Saudi Arabian share rose from 22.45 percent to 34.22 percent of total OPEC output. The Saudi Arabian position inside OPEC became even stronger than before. The UN sanctions prohibiting Iraqi oil exports made the UN an "acting member of OPEC," exercising production limitation on behalf of Iraq. Another effect of the war was

TABLE 3.1   Saudi Arabian and Iraqi Share of OPEC Production, July 1990 and 1991–1994 (%)

	July 1990	*1991–1994*
Saudi Arabia	22.45	34.22
Iraq	13.51	1.65
Total Share	35.96	35.87

SOURCE: *Petroleum Economist; BP Statistical Review of World Energy.*

that the Iraqi opposition internally in OPEC was modified. The earlier harsh criticism of the Gulf states' oil policy was no longer a viable strategy for Iraq in OPEC. Without any oil exports, its role in the organization was dubious. Threats from the Iraqi leadership to other countries due to their oil policies would rapidly have been met by condemnation and, possibly, sanctions.

At the end of section 3.3 there was a distinction made between the direct effect of the Iran-Iraq War on the OPEC negotiations and the effect on the basis for the belligerent parties' position in OPEC. The result of the Iran-Iraq War was that the position of the parties was weakened, but the OPEC negotiations were conducted in a business as usual fashion. After the Iraq-Kuwait War, the Kuwaiti oil-production capacity was soon recovered, and the country's position in OPEC has been strengthened, particularly because it was given carte blanche to increase oil production above previous quota levels in order to accumulate revenues to recover from war damage. By June 1992, Kuwaiti production passed 1 mbd; in September 1993, it leveled off above 2 mbd. When it comes to Iraq, its production reached 2 mbd in April 1998, and 2.5 mbd by February 1999. According to the UN mandate, Iraq was in 1998 allowed to sell oil worth $5.25 billion. Having set the terms in $-value, the lower the price the more Iraqi oil would be allowed on the market. However, the lack of Iraqi production capacity did not bring the production up to the mandated level in $-value. As for the Iraqi economy in general, the UN embargo following the war has damaged the country's severely. Its position is thus weak and without any basis for economic or political influence in OPEC or in the Middle East region at large. At present it seems unlikely that the sitting regime in Baghdad will be able to regain sufficient confidence among the other OPEC producers or the Arab states to play a major part in regional politics. However, the politics of the Middle East are unpredictable, so one cannot be certain on such issues. Another point is that *if* there should be a new regime in Iraq more friendly toward the Gulf states, it would most likely be supported, financially and politically, both by the GCC countries and by the United States.

3.5   Internal Threats

In the previous sections the state was regarded as a unitary actor, but with two prominent interests: security against external threats, and income from oil exports. This was a fruitful simplification, as the purpose of the previous sections was to study the effect on the oil cooperation of the military interaction between OPEC countries. In this section the state is not viewed as a unitary actor, as the focus will be on the internal threats to the state. Such threats might often be as serious as external threats. Buzan (1991:118–123) distinguishes between political and societal threats, although he notes that they can be hard to disentangle. The political threats are "aimed at the organizational stability of the state" (Buzan 1991:118), while the societal threats "amount to attacks on national identity" (Buzan 1991:122). Although both political and societal threats can be external, the focus in this section will be on the internal types of such threats.

In several oil-producing countries the political legitimacy of the regime is controversial. The societies are polarized along religious, ethnic, or other dimensions, and the regimes are aware of their weak political foundation. The oil income in many cases plays an important role in reinforcing the political basis of these regimes. It is thus appropriate to ask to what extent this influences the oil-related cooperation between such states.[15] First, it is necessary to describe the relevant internal political characteristics of the oil-producing countries in question.

To describe the kind of political regimes that characterize the OPEC countries, I have utilized information from the Polity III database on regime type and political authority, and data from Freedom House on political rights and civil liberties (Kaplan 1996).[16] The Polity III database includes indexes for calculating democracy-autocracy scores for 161 states from 1946 to 1994.[17] Democracy and autocracy are measured on a 21-point scale from +10 (democracy) to –10 (autocracy). The global average of democracy measured in this way was –2.4 in 1977 and climbed to +3 in 1994 (Jaggers and Gurr 1995:477). The Freedom House data are from 1995 and 1996.[18]

Table 3.2 shows the average score on this index for twelve of the OPEC countries from 1970 to 1994 (no data were available on Qatar). Of these twelve countries, only two had a positive democracy score in the period from 1970 to 1994. There are substantial regional differences between the OPEC members. As Figure 3.3 clearly shows, the democratic OPEC countries are located in Asia and South America, while the members located in Africa and the Middle East have on average very high negative scores. The global average on the Polity III index was +3 in 1994; Africa in general was rated at 0, and the Middle East about –5 (Jaggers and Gurr

TABLE 3.2   Democracy Indexes for the OPEC Countries, 1970–1996

Country	Polity III	Freedom House	
	1970–1994	1995	1996
Algeria	-7.58	14	12
Ecuador	4.58	5	5
Gabon	-8.59	9	9
Indonesia	-7.00	13	13
Iran	-7.08	13	13
Iraq	-7.88	14	14
Kuwait	-8.32	10	10
Libya	-7.00	14	14
Nigeria	-3.63	13	14
Saudi Arabia	-10.00	14	14
Qatar	NA	13	13
UAE	-9.58	11	11
Venezuela	8.92	6	6
OPEC Average	-5.26	11.46	11.38

SOURCE: Polity III database; Kaplan 1996.

1995:477). This shows that the level of autocracy is even higher among the OPEC members of these regions than for the regions in general.

Several of the most important oil producers are monarchical authoritarian states. Buzan finds the political vulnerability of such regimes to be very high:

> In a broad sense . . . one might argue that the whole *Zeitgeist* of the twentieth century has posed a political threat to the legitimacy of monarchical rule. The shah of Iran was but the last in a long line of autocratic rulers to be swept away by mass-based political movements of various persuasions. Such events cause no puzzlement, although they may cause considerable surprise. The mystery is how such anachronistic forms of government manage to survive at all when the entire socio-political environment of the times acts to corrode their legitimacy. (Buzan 1991:121)

The proposition that monarchical regimes will break down is supported by Riggs (1993:216). In his test of the fragility of Third World regimes, he finds that twelve of thirty-two monarchical regimes existing in 1920 were still in power in 1985, giving such regimes a survival rate of 38 percent. Of the 111 constitutive regimes, 58, or 53 percent, had survived until 1985.[19] Among the twelve monarchical regimes surviving as of 1985, six were oil-rich states (Bahrain, Brunei, Kuwait, Oman, Saudi Arabia, and the United Arab Emirates). Of the monarchical regimes that lost power

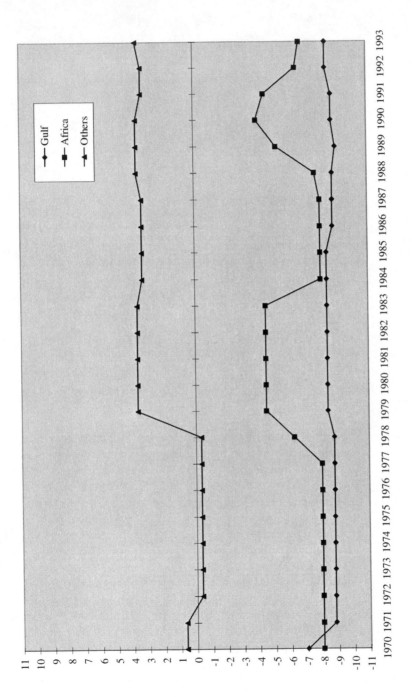

FIGURE 3.3   Democracy index of OPEC members by region, 1970–1993
SOURCE: Polity III database

TABLE 3.3 Classification of the Regimes of OPEC Countries

Regime Type	Regimes in Power as of 1985	Year of Independence	Regimes That Lost Power	Year of Regime Breakdown
Monarchical	Kuwait	1961	Iraq	1958 + 3 subsequent coups
	Qatar	1971	Libya	1969 + 1 subsequent coup
	Saudi Arabia	1932	Iran	1979 revolution
	UAE	1971		
Single party	Algeria	1965		
	Iran	1979*		
Presidentialist			Ecuador	
			Venezuela	
Parliamentary			Nigeria	1966 + 5 subsequent coups

*Year of the Iranian revolution
SOURCE: Riggs 1993: 216–225.

during the same period, we find three oil-rich states: Libya, Iraq, and Iran. As Table 3.3 suggests, several important oil-producing countries are monarchical regimes that have survived decades of instability among Third World regimes in general. Oil plays an important role in sustaining the regimes of these countries.

Autocratic regimes do not need to legitimize their decisions to the population in any kind of election. Oil-rich autocratic regimes do not need the support of the people in order to support themselves in economic terms. Rentier states, those that own capital and derive all or most of their income from it, do not need the economic support of the population through taxation. In the case of oil-rich monarchies like Bahrain, Brunei, Kuwait, Oman, Saudi Arabia, and the United Arab Emirates, the oil income has fundamentally changed the role of the state in the economy. As was described in Chapter 2, the oil industries of these states were run by the international oil companies. When these oil industries were nationalized, the states took on a dominant role in the national economies of the respective oil-producing countries. The capital accumulation derived from the state-owned oil business by far exceeded the income from any other part of the economy. The state thus became a net provider of capital, and did not have to impose any form of taxation on the population. This points to a fundamental aspect of state formation: the way rulers finance the building of the state institutions through taxation.

The role of taxation in state formation was discussed by Schumpeter (1918, 1954). He summarizes his description of the formation of European states by stating that "without financial need the immediate cause for the creation of the modern state would have been absent. . . . Taxes not only helped to create the state. They helped to form it. . . . Tax bill in hand, the state penetrated the private economies and won increasing dominion over them" (Schumpeter [1918] 1954:16–17). This created close links between the monopoly of power and the monopoly of taxation, but it also made the rulers dependent on the citizens in an economic sense. The citizen was regarded as an object of taxation:

> Although the precise political implications of tax levying may vary according to the nature of the tax itself, in most cases the operation requires a large degree of acceptance on the part of the population. . . . This establishes a link between the ability to raise taxes and legitimacy, which is captured in the saying "no taxation without representation." (Luciani 1990:75)

In the oil-rich states this dependency does not exist. The ruling elite derive their income directly by collecting rent from the oil activity on their soil, as described by Jill Crystal:

> In the Gulf, the most important impact of oil and the rentier economy it produced was that it gave rulers direct access to external revenues, revenues generated outside the local economy. Where once these revenues had to be squeezed from the population, through the merchants, who in turn exacted a political price, the rulers now received revenues independently. There are always moments when the state develops a high degree of autonomy from its social bases. . . . But oil-based states are unusual in that their higher degree of autonomy from other social groupings is not the result of a momentary crisis, but part of a structurally determined, ongoing process. This independence is almost uniquely peculiar to oil. Almost any other export—coffee, cotton—involves some accommodation between the rulers and the elite who control the workforce and extract surplus revenues. Oil does not. The elites on whom the ruler depends are not local, but rather multinational oil companies. (Crystal 1990:6–7)

The political implications of the oil wealth for the relationship between elite and society extend further, as oil "gave the regime resources to develop new allies among the national population through distributive policies" (Crystal 1990:10). In several oil-producing countries the state redistributes its oil income not to preserve justice or even out inequalities among societal groups, but to gain support and loyalty from potentially challenging groups in society (Noreng 1997). Maktabi (1993:170) argues that, "judging from the economic programs implemented and the financial rewards distributed in post-war Kuwait, it seems that the rulership persisted buying the allegiance of the citizenry by distributing economic compensations to secure a legitimate basis for its rule." Maktabi describes the way the al-Sabah regime pursued this strategy after the Iraq-Kuwait War: "Immediately after the liberation, an amiri decree announced that all personal bank loans were canceled. Outstanding telephone, electricity and water bills were annulled. . . . All employees in the public sector received back-dated salaries" (Maktabi 1993:170). Cash compensations of about $1,700 were given to all citizens that had endured the war, and $34,500 to those families having suffered losses during the war (Maktabi 1993:170).[20] Although it is reasonable to expect the authorities to make some economic provisions for the population after a war, the extent of the aid in this case gives a clear impression of a true rentier state, reinforcing a "political clientelistic contract" (Maktabi 1993:170) by economic means.[21]

Using oil wealth to gain political support is a double-edged sword as not only the welfare but also the regime's political stability is dependent on the oil-derived income. It may also stand in the way of the development of other instruments of handling the relationship between the elite and the society. This is pointed out by al-Naqeeb (1990), referred to by Crystal (1994:269): "At first the state tried to depoliticize these [opposition] groups by buying them off. When these efforts failed, rulers increasingly resorted to terror, perhaps because owing to oil revenues, they had never before been forced to develop other, more nuanced ways of dealing with opposition." Accordingly, the relationship between economic growth and democratization can very well be negative in oil-rich countries, contrary to traditional assumptions (Rostow 1967; Huntington 1968).

The tendency to use oil income to gain support from influential groups in the society opens the possibility for other groups to claim that the regime fosters inequalities. Noreng (1993:7) points out that this creates a social-democratic feature of the Islamic fundamentalist opposition in the Arab countries, since it is able to protest against the injustice of the regime's distribution of the oil wealth. According to Karawan (1994:448), the Islamic fundamentalists "have been successful in gaining support among a younger generation of the urban poor, and among those segments of the middle class who were afflicted by the costs of economic adjustment programs." When the oil income collapsed in 1986, it was a political as well as an economic challenge to the regimes in the Gulf countries. When they started to run budget deficits due to reduced income, they soon realized that they had to cut spending. This meant less money to distribute in order to gain political support for the regime.

Sørensen (1996:377) argues that, in contrast to the European state-building process, the state formation in the Third World was characterized by decolonization [giving] formal sovereignty, or juridical independence, to states that had very little in terms of substantial statehood. The situation creates a peculiar security dilemma in the weak [Third World] states. . . . they are guaranteed juridical survival by the international society of states, no matter how deficient they are in substantial terms. . . . In earlier days, state elite were compelled to create some substantial legitimacy of rule and thus gain support from their populations to be able to weather perennial external threat. In the absence of substantial external threat, that is no longer necessary; state elites can go to any extreme in terms of violence against their people without paying the ultimate price: termination of the state.[22]

This means that prospects for strong internal democracy movements in the Third World are slim. Existence of political opposition and regime change would not improve the legitimacy of the regime. If one were to propose a general conclusion based on the empirical studies referred above, it would be that there is no general trend. The Third World states differ in terms of important factors influencing the regimes' political legitimacy. This is also true of the states focused on in this book. They have one important aspect in common, their oil revenue, but are highly different along other variables. For instance, the tendency to buy political support is characteristic of wealthy authoritarian countries, such as the members of the GCC.[23] Among the poorer countries, or societies where wealth is more equally distributed, this strategy is not an option. This can have further implications, as the fall in oil prices may increase the divergence between rich and poor oil producers. It may also increase the potential threat of Islamic fundamentalists, as they can use the economic situation to strengthen and broaden internal opposition.

With the lack of need for both political support and financial support, the oil-rentier state is self-supportive in times of high oil prices and thus in no need of the population for political or economic support. Furthermore, the population will to an increasing degree be dependent on the state, as most of the economic goods allocated are financed through the oil revenue generated by the state's position as owner of the oil resources. In economic terms the oil-rentier states are better off than autocracies in general, as they can compensate for lack of democratic legitimacy by selective allocation of economic welfare. When the oil revenue fell dramatically during the eighties, this strategy was impossible to pursue. If the classic hypothesis that discrepancy between the population's expected need satisfaction and actual need satisfaction creates potential for revolts, or at least gives ammunition to political opposition, one should expect an increased instability among these regimes in times of low oil prices (Davies 1962). It further implies that autocratic oil-rentier states should be more stable in times of high oil revenues, and less stable in times of low oil revenues, than autocracies in general. This is because they are both economically and politically dependent on the oil revenue. The reduction in state oil revenues creates political instability in addition to economic instability. Democratic oil producers would not be politically jeopardized to the same degree by lower oil income.[24] It would lead too far astray from the topic of this book to go into any empirical investigation of such hypotheses as those suggested here. The findings do, however, have implications for the argument in this study of the oil-producer cooperation. They point to the importance of bearing in mind that, for some of the world's most important oil producers, the oil income might be perceived as a matter of self-preservation against internal threats. This does not, however, lead to any clear-cut argument regarding their cooperative behavior. As discussed in Chapter 7, actors finding the oil income important might join collective efforts to increase or sustain prices, but might also compensate for falling prices with increased production, the latter being a strategy that undermines the collective efforts of a producer cartel. What can be concluded is that the political importance of oil income to the regimes of these countries will tend to make them place more importance on the oil industry and the international oil market than they otherwise would. They will thus follow whatever strategy they choose, cooperative or competitive, more eagerly and forcefully than regimes with other means to achieve political legitimization. For them, politics and oil are even more intertwined than for other types of oil producers, as oil prices can be perceived as being a matter of regime existence.

Taken together, the external and internal threats discussed so far in this chapter paint a picture of rather conflictual relationships between Middle East oil producers. The question arises as to what extent the oil production also has contributed to the emergence of cooperative political interests among these countries. Aspects discussed in this section suggest a common interest among the rich against the poor, or among the Western-oriented sheikhs against the Islamic fundamentalists. Thus, oil and politics go together in defining some common enemies and hence a primary incentive for the establishment of cooperative structures in the relations between some of the oil-producing Middle East countries. These political cooperative aspects are the topic of the next section.

3.6 Political Cooperation Between the Gulf States

In February 1981, the Gulf monarchies—Saudi Arabia, Kuwait, Qatar, the United Arab Emirates, Bahrain, and Oman—formed the Gulf Cooperation Council (GCC). Both the external and internal threats discussed above motivated this cooperative effort. The establishment of the GCC was triggered by the uprising in Mecca in late 1979 and the Iran-Iraq War. Later, the Iraqi attack on Kuwait identified yet another common security threat to the GCC states.

Let us start out with the external threats. Economically, the Iran-Iraq War obviously was beneficial for all oil producers, as the oil price increased. Later, the reduced production capacity of the belligerent states gave room for increased production from other countries without decreasing the oil price. Politically, the other Gulf countries found the war to be in their interest. The new regime in Iran represented Islamic fundamentalism, which was perceived as a threat to the royal family in Saudi Arabia and the emirs in the other Gulf countries. The Gulf countries provided Iraq with financial assistance (estimates vary between $25 and $65 billion) and sold so-called war-relief oil on behalf of Iraq. The Gulf leaders perceived Iraq as the lesser of two evils, but were "no less concerned over potential Iraqi hegemony in the Gulf region" (Kechichian 1990:92). However, the Gulf countries were primarily concerned with preventing the war from spreading to their territories. In the first two years of the war, the GCC countries pursued a neutral strategy in their official statements. Saudi Arabia and Kuwait provided Iraq with financial support, while the United Arab Emirates tried to preserve "an open and friendly line of communication with Tehran" (Kechichian 1990:95).[25] The neutral strategy was abandoned during 1982: "By November 1982 . . . the council's attention was clearly focused on Iran's persistent intransigence in the war" (Kechichian 1990:97). Also, the rejection of mediation attempts by Iran led to the GCC countries' official support of Iraq. This also meant that they kept a low profile when it was revealed that Iraq used chemical weapons (see section 3.3).

At the beginning of the Iran-Iraq War, the GCC countries were militarily weak. This changed during the war, as the US military guaranty to these countries was strengthened, and the GCC countries' own military power was enhanced. In addition, the GCC as a security organization had developed from nothing into a military alliance with a common defense strategy, weapons programs, and joint military exercises. "For the first time in this century, forces from all six states participated in cooperative military activities aimed at defending their territories. . . . Whereas the Gulf War had initially posed a threat to the GCC states, the end result was a stronger, more unified military structure" (Kechichian 1990:108). The external threat imposed by Iran strengthened the GCC's internal political cohesion.

The Iraqi attack on Kuwait in August 1990 demonstrated the inability of the smaller Gulf states to provide sufficient military resistance against the larger countries in the region. The then-nine-year-old GCC cooperation had not changed this fact. The consequences of the Iraq-Kuwait War were that the GCC cooperative efforts were pushed further: "The second Gulf crisis opened a new era in the GCC interstate relations. The small GCC countries, with the exception of Oman, became more inclined to follow Saudi foreign policy. The GCC states have accepted the Saudi perspective on Gulf security" (al-Alkim 1994:89).

There are, however, political differences between the Gulf countries. Some of these, as long as they remain unresolved, will represent a hindrance to the extension of cooperation between the Gulf states.[26] To some commentators, the cooperation thus looks like one based on common fear rather than genuine common interests: "The only bond holding the Sheikhs together was that their fears of Iran and Iraq were greater than their dislike of each other" (Heikal 1993:125).

Also, the perception of internal threats contributed to the formation of the GCC. The members are all sheikhdoms, with a political front against countries with "revolutionary" leaderships, or socialist or Nasserite ideologies. The pan-Arabic idea was at this point dead: "Divisions in the Arab world were nothing new, but signs of deeper fragmentation emerged in 1980, when the sheikdoms formed what amounted to a club for the rich. The Gulf Cooperation Council" (Heikal 1993:115). This interpretation implies that regional cooperation stands in conflict with broader cooperation. This is not necessarily true, but in this case the GCC underlines deeper societal differences between the Arab countries, between the oil-rich, and mostly small, scarcely populated countries, and the poorer and heavily populated countries.

The other aspect of the internal threats is the threat represented by Islamic fundamentalism, fostered by the regime in Tehran. The Islamic leaders do not need tanks and troops to represent a threat to the Gulf regimes. The possibility of internal fundamentalist groups conducting sabotage or terrorist attacks, or challenging the secular regimes in other ways, is a more likely development. The bomb explosion in Riyadh on November 13, 1995, which killed five American citizens, underlined the seriousness of these threats. Although this was the first terrorist action of this kind in the kingdom, it "suggested an ominous escalation of the conflict between the Saudi royal family and its Islamic opposition."[27]

The two external military threats perceived by the GCC countries—the threat of Iraq and the threat of Iran—are thus linked to the two political and societal threats: the threat of Arab radicalism, represented primarily by Nasser and to some extent Saddam Hussein, and the threat of Islamic fundamentalism, inspired and supported by the regime in Iran. Thus, the external and internal threats are to some extent linked.[28] This points to the complex interstate relations in the Middle East in general.

According to Halliday (1991:230), the Middle East

interstate competition is more complex than anywhere else in the world because it involves not just a bipolar conflict . . . but a set of interlocking con-

flicts—Arab-Israel, Iran-Iraq, Iraq-Syria, Iraq-Saudi Arabia, Saudi-Yemeni.
. . . The history of formal and informal treaty organizations in the region is one of weakness, incompleteness and failure: by the Arab League in the 1940s, by the Baghdad Pact—CENTO (Central Treaty Organization) in the 1950s and 1960s, by the 'Twin Pillar' approach in the Gulf in the 1970s, by the Gulf Cooperation Council and the Arab Cooperation Council.

The development during the period discussed in this study is thus one of deterioration of the political coherence among the Arab oil producers. The oil wealth has not lead to increased political inter- or intrastate unity among this important subgroup of oil producers. The question, then, remains: To what extent do the political issues discussed above influence the oil policy of the Gulf states?

First, the security interests of the Gulf regimes have been given more weight than the economic interests. During intensified conflicts in the region, the economic expenditure on arms, payment for foreign forces, and so on have been carried out regardless of economic costs. Oil has also been used to ensure alliances, such as when Saudi Arabia and Kuwait sold oil from their neutral sector in order to support the Iraqi war against Iran. The economic interests and the security interests have pulled in the same direction. When this is the case, it is harder to establish the relative importance of the different factors.

Second, the warfare in the region has destroyed production capacity in the belligerent countries. Figure 3.4 compares combined Iranian, Iraqi, and Kuwaiti oil production with that of Saudi Arabia from 1978 to 1994. The figure clearly illustrates how the warfare has reduced output from the affected countries. The Iranian production in spring of 1978 of almost 6 mbd has never since been achieved, although the potential oil reserves are present. In spring of 1980, Iraq produced approximately 3.5 mbd; although the production in the first half of 1990 approached this level, the subsequent attack on Kuwait reduced Iraqi production to about 0.5 mbd. The Kuwaiti loss of production has been more short-term. Contrary to what was predicted after the retreating Iraqi forces had set a substantial part of the Kuwaiti oil fields on fire, the country regained its production capacity during 1992, and in 1993 was back to the prewar level.

Third, the wars have made the internal OPEC negotiations over production quotas easier, as other producers have been unable to produce at full capacity due to destruction of belligerent states' production capacity.

Fourth, the political antagonism created between the OPEC members by the warfare seems to have had only short-term effects on the internal negotiations inside OPEC. Both Iran and Iraq, and later Iraq and Kuwait, have accepted the presence of each other's delegations at the OPEC meetings. Apart from some incidents of political confrontation, "business as

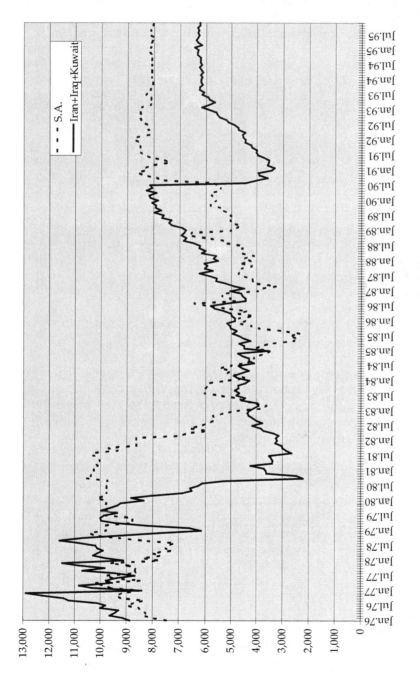

FIGURE 3.4 Iranian, Iraqi, Kuwaiti, and Saudi Arabian oil products, 1976–1995
SOURCE: *Petroleum Economist.*

usual" has been the norm at OPEC meetings conducted during military conflicts between members.

In a longer-term perspective the political cooperation between Arab countries that was prominent in the fifties and sixties, and particularly inspired by Nasser, gave political support to the oil cooperation and the confrontation with the international oil companies. When this political unity fell apart, so did the political basis for the economic and oil-related cooperation.

3.7 Conclusion

The discussion in this chapter has focused on the prominent role of security interests. This is in line with traditional understanding in international relations of the importance of self-preservation in any state leadership. The analysis has been based both on traditional aspects of security, namely, external threats against the intrusion of foreign military forces (sections 3.3 and 3.4), and on the possible threats to state leadership from internal forces (section 3.5).

The findings in this chapter suggest that, in addition to the more direct effects of political interests on the production capacity of belligerent oil producers, warfare has also changed their interests in participation in cooperative efforts among the producers. If the explanation of this is purely political, it will have to be distinguished from the explanation that wars have a tendency to cost money, putting the country more in need of income, and thus making it less able or willing to reduce its production. The security argument implies that states support or counter producer cooperation *for security reasons*. It is highly problematic to reach a definite conclusion about why a state leader did what he or she did in a particular instance. The discussion above does, however, suggest that at least during the Iran-Iraq War and the Iraq-Kuwait War, several Gulf countries allowed security interests to govern their oil-market behavior. Indications of this are the GCC's attempt to lower oil prices in order to hurt Iran, and its strategy to sell oil on behalf of Iraq in order to influence the course of the war. Also, the internal threats to the regimes and the role of oil in supporting the regimes politically are fundamental to understanding the oil-market behavior of the Gulf oil producers. The role of oil in these societies might also be an additional obstacle to possible democratization. This aspect, however, points to questions outside the scope of this study (see Noreng 1997).

The authoritarian characteristics of the regimes of many of the OPEC states might also discourage democratic oil producers from cooperation with OPEC.[29] The general point to be made here is that collective economic interest does not make states disregard the political obstacles to cooperation. This represents a difference between cooperation among states and cooperation among firms. Firms, solely dedicated to profit, can more easily join profitable cooperative arrangements. States, or state leaderships, with political aims such as reelection in mind, will forgo profitable economic relations that might have negative political consequences.

Threats to vulnerable authoritarian regimes can make them behave according to neither the logic of consequence nor the logic of appropriateness (see discussion in section 4.1). Their behavior becomes less predictable and more contradictory compared with theoretical models of states' behavior. Economic models, designed for understanding cooperation between firms, and institutional models, designed for understanding behavior in the light of norms, miss this point when they are applied to the economic cooperation between such states. The answer is a closer, more detailed, more historical, and idiosyncratic perspective—in other words, case studies. This is the approach pursued in Chapters 6 and 9.

The political conflicts between OPEC members discussed in this chapter were assumed to have had a negative effect on the OPEC cooperation. An organization with members in direct conflict is likely to suffer significant setbacks in its cooperative efforts. However, this is not the conclusion regarding OPEC. Some aspects of the ideological and political conflict between Iran and Iraq seeped into the OPEC negotiations, but the general picture is that the oil-related cooperation in OPEC has been only marginally affected by the political conflicts between its members. The organization was to some extent immune to spillover from the military conflicts.

Notes

1. Buzan himself argues that the concept should be defined in view of empirical cases: "Attempts at precise definition are much more suitable directed towards empirical cases where the particular factors in play can be identified." (Buzan 1991:20)

2. The "'orthodox' conception of security cannot comprehend either the threats or state structures or regimes that do not emerge from other states, or the threats that states and regimes can pose to their own citizens and societies" (Krause 1996:320).

3. Kamran Mofid in *The Independent*, July 20, 1988, cited in Hiro 1989:251.

4. "Saudi Arabia's brilliant chief of operations was shunted aside for allowing the intercept and kill of the Iranian F-4 (Cordesman and Wagner 1990:214,n. 7).

5. "Riyadh upgraded its F-15 inspectors and in 1987 placed an order with Britain for 72 Tornado fighter-bombers, thus giving it an almost insurmountable edge in the area. Further, the Saudis not only welcomed four US Air Force AWACS sentry aircraft in 1980 but purchased five of their own, deploying the first in 1986. The AWACS in tandem with the F-15s clearly gave Saudi Arabia,

and presumably the GCC, a credible deterrent capability." (Kechichian 1990:107–108)

6. *The Observer*, October 21, 1990, cited in Freedman and Karsh 1993:45.

7. Baghdad Radio, July 18, 1990, cited in Freedman and Karsh 1993:46.

8. Baghdad Radio, July 18, 1990, cited in Freedman and Karsh 1993:48.

9. The Arab League tried to mediate and chose Hosni Mubarak as mediator. He went to Baghdad on July 24. Saddam Hussein assured Mubarak that the military forces along the border were meant for intimidation, but asked Mubarak not to let the Kuwaitis know: "Brother Husni, do not let the Kuwaitis rest easy before the meeting" (Freedman and Karsh 1993:50). When Mubarak arrived in Kuwait, Iraq announced that the Kuwait issue had not been discussed in Baghdad. Mubarak was annoyed and told the Kuwaitis that Saddam did not intend to invade. "When asked what Saddam wanted the Egyptian leader replied: 'It seems he needs some money'" (ibid.).

10. The Iraqi version is that they asked for $10 billion in compensation for the Rumaila oil field, but the Kuwaitis humiliated them by offering only $9 billion. The Kuwaiti version is that Iraq was not content with $10 billion, but demanded surrender of some disputed territories, as well as oil-pumping rights inside Kuwait (ibid.:59–60).

11. The attack involved about 140,000 men and 1,800 tanks. The 16,000-strong Kuwaiti army was not fully mobilized in order not to provoke Iraq, and was subsequently not able to resist the Iraqi attack. The emir, however, managed to escape to Saudi Arabia with most of the royal family. The Kuwaiti air force had made some attacks on the advancing Iraqi divisions, and some sporadic fighting occurred, particularly around the royal palace.

12. Yemen and Cuba abstained.

13. "Sanctions will take time to have their full intended effect. We shall continue to review all options with our allies, but let it be clear, we will not let this aggression stand. Iraq will not be permitted to annex Kuwait. And that's not a threat, it's not a boast, it's just the way it's going to be" (BBC Radio 4, October 9, 1990, reprinted in Freedman and Karsh 1993:204).

14. An even stronger argument would be that these factors were sufficient to explain the outbreak of the war. Regarding the magnitude of factors influencing the conflictual relations between Middle East countries, it seems unlikely that such aspects should be the overriding cause of this particular conflict.

15. As will be emphasized below, one should be cautious not to generalize about all oil producers' policies on the basis of studies of the politics of Arabian oil-producing countries. Important member countries are located outside the Middle East and have characteristics different from those of the Middle East oil producers.

16. The data are registered as ICPSR 6695, produced by Keith Jaggers, Department of Political Science, University of Colorado, and Ted Robert Gurr, Center for International Development and Conflict Management, University of Maryland.

17. The coding includes scores on five variables: Competitiveness of political participation, from competitive (+3) to suppressed (–2). Regulation of political participation, from factional/restricted (–1) to restricted (–2). Competitiveness of executive recruitment, from election (2) to selection (–2). Openness of executive

recruitment, from election (+1) to closed (−1). Constraints on chief executive, from executive parity or subordination (+4) to unlimited power on executive (−3). See Jaggers and Gurr 1995:472.

18. The data are derived by adding the scores on the Political Rights and Civil Liberties indexes. Each scale goes from 1 to 7, and the combined scale thus goes from 2 to 14, with 14 indicating the least free regime and 2 the most free. Measuring different years and combining different sources are of no consequence to the argument in this section, because the characteristics of political regimes seldom change dramatically, and the arguments in the following subsections are based only on a general picture of the political regimes in the oil-producing states.

19. Among these there were substantial differences, as single-party regimes had a survival rate of 80 percent, parliamentary regimes 69 percent, and presidential regimes 0 percent.

20. The negative economic consequences of the war were reduced by the fact that the Kuwaiti regime derives a large proportion of its income from investments abroad. As pointed out in section 2.6, Kuwait has been one of the most active OPEC countries in using its crude oil income to invest in the oil marketing and refining industry in consuming countries.

21. "Political clientelistic contract" is a phrase borrowed from Maktabi 1993:170.

22. The concept of weak states is taken from Buzan (1991:96–107) and can be summarized as states with low sociopolitical cohesion.

23. The relationship between the ruling elite and Islamic or other kinds of opposition varies from country to country; it is hard to generalize about the implications of it for all Arab OPEC members' oil policies. Some more detailed comments on this issue are provided in Chapter 6, which is a case study of Saudi Arabian oil policy.

24. There are too few cases to make empirical investigations of this hypothesis possible. Also, there have been only a few years of low oil prices since the independence of the Gulf states, reducing the possible significance of a time-series study.

25. This strategy was made somewhat difficult by the fact that Iran occupied parts of the United Arab Emirates (UAE) islands Abu Musa, Greater Tunb, and Lesser Tunb. The island conflict escalated in 1992 when the "Iranian authorities on Abu Musa suddenly demanded that the civilians entering the island to live on the Arab side have Iranian visa stamps in their passports. . . . Although Iran backed down on the visa issue, the dispute continued in the years after 1992 through repeated exchanges of accusations between Tehran and Abu Dhabi. . . . The Iranian statements were often very strong; for example, after the December 1992 GCC summit meeting, Tehran declared that if the UAE tried to take the islands, it would have to 'cross a sea of blood' to do so" (*The New York Times*, December 28, 1992, cited in Rugh 1996:62).

26. "The border dispute that had the most damaging effect on the GCC was the Saudi-Qatari problem. . . . the crisis culminated [in Abu al-Khufs] in an armed clash in August 1992, in which two Qataris and one Saudi were killed" (al-Alkim 1994:81).

27. *The Economist*, November 18, 1995.

28. However, the outcome of the Iraq-Kuwait War reduced the Iraqi threat against the Gulf states. It seems improbable that Iraq will be able to represent a military threat to the Gulf states in the foreseeable future.

29. Arve Johnsen, the director of Statoil in 1986, argued against Norwegian co-operation with OPEC, not for economic reasons, but because of characteristics of the regimes in several OPEC countries. *Aftenposten*, February 6, 1986.

4

OPEC as an International Organization

While the previous chapters discussed the structural conditions for oil-producer cooperation, the aim of this chapter is to examine to what extent institutional factors have contributed to changing the behavior of key OPEC members in a more cooperative direction that would otherwise have been the case (see section 1.4).

The institutional factors are applicable only to OPEC members, contrary to the structural aspects discussed in Chapter 2, which were assumed to influence oil producers in general. Thus, the question to be answered is: What aspects of OPEC as an international organization make the members behave more cooperatively than they would in the absence of the institution?[1]

In the empirical analysis in section 4.3, six aspects of OPEC as an international organization will be discussed. These aspects are based on a combination of different approaches to the study of institutions. These approaches are dealt with in section 4.1. Section 4.2 briefly describes the organizational characteristics of OPEC.

4.1 Institutional Approaches

Rational Choice and Institutional Constraints

In economics the debate between institutional and neoclassical economists is rooted in a fundamental ontological question of what actually motivates individual behavior, and in a methodological question of how to study the behavior of man.[2] The basic problem for the new institutionalists is the assumption made in neoclassical economics about rational behavior:

The objection to the economic man was, or is, not so much his materialism or egoism, but the extent of his knowledge and his virtually unbounded rationality. It is not such an extreme oversimplification that people *want* to maximize, or *aim* at maximizing, *something*—(though of course there are difficulties about defining the maximand). What is extremely oversimplificatory is to assume that people generally *have the knowledge* to maximize. (Hutchinson 1984 1991:38–39)

John Stuart Mill made strong assumptions regarding the importance of the concept of competition: "only through the principle of competition has political economy any pretensions to the characteristics of a science" (Mill 1909:242, cited in Hutchinson [1984] 1991:39). Hutchinson's interpretation of Mill suggests that it was only in a competitive situation that "the assumption about full rationality and correct expectations [could] be assumed to hold" (Mill 1909:242, cited in Hutchinson [1984] 1991:39). Furthermore, the state of perfect competition, should it come into existence, would not function for long, because no actor would have any incentive to invest:

the incentive to invest depends in part on the knowledge of a limited competitive supply from other firms, or the establishment of a belief that others do not possess the information regarding the opportunity that is available to the investor. (Hodgson 1991:186)

In a state of perfect competition, such opportunities do not emerge. This is not to make the obvious point that perfect competition does not arise, but, more importantly, "that it would not be viable if it did" (Hodgson 1991:187). So, the limited rationality, taken together with "the impossibility of perfect competition," makes room for supplement to the orthodox neoclassical economic theory.[3] March and Olsen argue that actors often act on the basis of normative behavioral prescriptions:

In a logic of appropriateness . . . behavior (beliefs as well as actions) are intentional but not willful. They involve fulfilling the obligations of a role in a situation, and so of trying to determine the imperatives of holding a position. Action stems from a conception of necessity, rather than preference. (March and Olsen 1989:161)

One part of this institutional economics is the study of transaction costs. Coase (1960:15) describes transaction costs as follows:

In order to carry out a market transaction it is necessary to discover who it is that one wishes to deal with, to inform people that one wishes to deal and on what terms, to conduct negotiations leading up to a bargain, to draw up the contract, to undertake the inspection needed to make sure that the terms of the contract are being observed, and so on.

Transaction costs thus consist of search and information costs, bargaining and decision costs, and policing and enforcement costs (Dahlman 1979:148). Although Dahlman finds this division unnecessarily elaborate, as all these costs are caused by the lack of information, the division shows the need to identify transaction costs in all parts of a bargaining process—a point highly relevant to the empirical discussion in section 4.3. The transaction costs emerge as a result of bounded rationality and opportunism. Robert Keohane points to the reduction of transaction costs as one prominent reason for the establishment of international organizations incorporated into international economic regimes (Keohane 1984:89–92). As pointed out by Caporaso (1992:610), there are several ways by which international organizations reduce transaction costs:

> They provide administrative help, an ongoing forum in which representatives of different states can meet, and a set of rules and procedures for dealing with problems. In addition, regimes provide valuable informational services that facilitate mutual contact. They collect information, standardize conceptual categories . . . codify rules and practices, and attempt to increase the transparency of both cooperative and defecting moves.

This points directly to the aim of the empirical discussion in section 4.3. By studying how OPEC has reduced transaction costs along the lines pointed out by Caporaso, it is possible to detect the effect of the organization on the cooperative behavior of the member states.

In the sociological institutional approach the mechanism by which the actors make their choices is different from the assumed rationality of the rational, or economic, model:

> Institutional conceptions of action . . . differ from rational models in a more fundamental way. . . . Within an institutional framework, "choice," if it can be called that, is based more on logic of appropriateness than on the logic of consequence that underlies conceptions of rational action. Institutionalized rules, duties, rights, and roles define acts as appropriate (normal, natural, right, good) or inappropriate (uncharacteristic, unnatural, wrong, bad). (March and Olsen 1996:251–252)

Both the rational and the sociological institutionalism pay attention to the problem of incomplete information and the implications for rationality. An effort to combine the institutional perspectives presented above should thus develop this possible "common ground" between economics and sociology (Williamson 1988:161).

Bounded Rationality: The Common Ground

The most persuasive criticism of the rational choice model is based on the information required for actors to choose rationally among possible choices of action. Lack of information creates uncertainty regarding the possible consequences of different choices. Herbert Simon strongly renounces rational action in such cases: "Wherever such uncertainties are present, an enhanced opportunity is provided for unconscious, or only partly conscious, drives and wishes to influence deliberation. . . . where evidence is weak and conflicting, a rationality principle has little independent predictive power" (Simon 1985:302).[4] This lack of information makes bargaining relations subject to manipulation by opponents. Arild Underdal outlines the effects on the bargaining process:

> In an essentially co-operative context, Party would probably try to reduce Opponent's uncertainty . . . by submitting more extensive or more precise information, or by trying to strengthen Opponent's confidence in the information he has. Also in the context of largely distributive bargaining, a Party confident in its own perception of Opponent's uncertainty would probably take measures to reduce that uncertainty, but it is likely to do so by trying to exploit the situation, by transforming it into one of partly inaccurate information, so as to enhance its own bargaining position. In general, a belief that Opponent is, or can feasibly be made, uncertain seems to be a necessary condition for purposively making efforts to mislead. (Underdal 1983:187)

What is important here is that, regardless whether an actor seeks to guide or misguide another actor, the use of language will be important. The lack of certainty or the weakness of the actor's perception might make him or her receptive to rhetorical arguments: "persuasion rests upon the ability to organize the experience of those who are to be persuaded" (Paine 1981:10). The uncertainty not only becomes a basis for satisfaction rather than maximization (Simon 1976) but also increases the actor's uncertainty regarding the sincerity of other actors' utterances. The costs of verifying whether another actor speaks the truth or not is fundamentally different from gaining information about aspects of the substantive world, and such verification might be unobtainable. Furthermore, in some situation one cannot be satisfied with merely probable information about the sincerity of others.[5]

If an actor wants some assurance regarding the truth of another actor's sincerity, this will have to be sought without reference to that actor. Looking at the actor's reputation for truthfulness, or asking third parties about the same actor's truthfulness in other situations, might be a way of improving the information about the other actor's sincerity. One problem is the costs of pursuing this strategy; another problem is the possibility of creating endless regress, as actor A might try to increase the possibility that actor B will believe actor A speaks the truth, although actor A does not. This strategy by actor A will further increase actor B's costs of finding the truth, and so on. The relationship between espionage and counterespionage and contra-counterespionage illustrates this point.

The implication of incomplete information for economic behavior is that "all economic exchange cannot be organized by contracts and market" (Furubotn and Richter 1991:4).[6] At least, the contractors are unable to foresee all possible future events that might change the conditions on which the contract was established. Bounded rationality would not have created problems had all the actors always been trustworthy. The incentive to cheat one another is always present; actors are, "in Williamson's phrase 'self-seeking with guile' . . . and . . . it is . . . very costly to distinguish opportunistic from nonopportunistic actors, ex ante" (Furubotn and Richter 1991:5). The actors can gain advantages by "selective or distorted information disclosure or . . . self-disbelieved promises regarding future conduct" (Williamson 1975:26). Williamson assumes that self-enforcing commitments that would annul the second type of opportunism cannot be secured (Williamson 197526). The basic assumption underlying this approach is as follows:

> Institutional theories . . . assume that action is based on incomplete and possibly biased information. They focus the behavioral and social bases of information. They emphasize the ways in which institutions influence the perception and construction of the reality within which action takes place. Institutional history shapes the definition of alternatives. Institutional capabilities and structures affect the flow of information, the kinds of search undertaken, and the interpretation made of the results. (March and Olsen 1994:251)

Although section 4.3 provides an empirical analysis of the effect of institutional aspects on OPEC members' behavior, let me briefly spell out the relevance of the theoretical discussion above for this particular case. Incomplete information has been a problem for the OPEC cooperation, both regarding the actual prices different countries charged and regarding the actual production volumes placed on the market. Also, factors outside the organization—particularly future demand, the non-OPEC producers' behavior, and the intentional oil companies' stocking policy—cause uncertainties regarding the optimal response (see Chapter 2). This has created problems for the OPEC countries' ability to fine-tune their market operations in order to achieve the desired price. As pointed out above, incomplete information need not create problems for the effectiveness of the cooperation if the parties involved can trust each other and jointly adapt to the changed market situation and the new information. Then, none of the OPEC members would take advantage of the situation and let another member bear a larger burden. However, this has not always been the case among OPEC members. As described in Chapter 3, some members have actually been at war with each other (Iran-Iraq and Iraq-Kuwait). The political regimes in the different countries are very different, including conservative Arabic monarchies, democratic countries, Islamic states, and communist states. The members are spread over three continents, and include some of the poorest and some of the richest countries in the world. Differences, more than similarities, characterize the members of OPEC, except for one point: They are all substantial net exporters of oil and are all to a substantial degree dependent on income from their oil exports. This, however, is not likely to make them fully confident of each other's trustworthiness.

The conclusion of this section is that an actor's behavior can be influenced by utilizing weaknesses in the information and uncertainty of the truth of the language used in the interaction. Given uncertain information, the actor's preferences might be influenced also by the way options are presented and perceived.

Combining Economic and Sociological Institutional Approaches

In the situational model outlined in section 1.4, institutions are a part of the social environment defining the opportunity set of the actors. The importance of institutions in defining the opportunity set of actors' behavior is perfectly consistent with the assumption of rational actors making rational choices inside the opportunity set. When the institutional framework around the actors' decisions changes, they gain new information and form new beliefs that change the calculation of costs and benefits and subsequently make rational actors change their behavior. The question then becomes: What aspect of the actors' choices are influenced by the institutions? It could be the payoff from different choices, the calculation of costs and benefits connected with the different choices, the utility connected with different strategies, the interests, or the identity of the actors. The theory of rational choice would regard the actors' interests or desires as given at the individual level—"the unmoved movers, reflecting Hume's dictum that 'reason is, and ought only to be the slave of the passions' [Hume 1739:415]" (Elster 1989a:4). In this chapter it is argued that institutional factors change actors' interests. The fact that the theory of rational choice regards the actors' interests as given creates no contradiction with such an argument. The theory of rational choice does not include interest formation, and thus it is compatible with other theories explaining the formation of actors' interests, as long as they are consistent.

It is thus possible to combine the rational and sociological perspectives. Starting with the situational model presented in Chapter 1, the institutional perspective of March and Olsen offers two supplements. First, it develops the institutional constraints included in the specification of the *situation*. As pointed out by Hovi and Rasch (1996:74), institutions are part of the social environment included in the situation model. On this point there is no difference between the perspectives. The second point is the argument that actors make their choices not on the basis of rational calculations but on the basis of an abidance of norms created by institutions—that is, the logic of appropriateness. This supplement establishes another mechanism for the actors' choices within the opportunity set. The actors do not seek the best action given desires, but rather the right action according to the norms established. On this point there is a substantial difference between the perspectives.

The next question is to what extent and how these fundamental theories are applied to international institutions.

The Study of International Institutions

Keohane defines institutions as "persistent and connected sets of rules (formal and informal) that prescribe behavioral roles, constrain activity, and shape expectations" (1989:3–4). He then distinguishes between three forms of international institutions:

1. formal intergovernmental or cross-national nongovernmental organizations, which are "purposive entities . . . capable of monitoring activity and reacting to it, and are deliberately set up and designed by states"
2. international regimes, which are "institutions with explicit rules agreed upon by governments"
3. conventions, which are "informal institutions, with implicit rules and understandings"

In this chapter the focus will be on OPEC as a formal intergovernmental organization. It is obvious that informal rules coexist with or within formal organizations. Formal organizations might thus be based on existing conventions or regimes. In the case of OPEC, it can be argued that the formal organization was established prior to the development of informal cooperative ties between the founding members (see section 4.2). In this chapter the informal institutional aspects will be regarded as underlying aspects of OPEC, while the formal organization is the dominant institutional feature of the relationship between the oil producers. Underlying informal aspects will be included without the introduction of the concepts of regimes or conventions. This makes the analytical distinction between the concepts of organization and institution less relevant to the discussion of the role of OPEC in the oil-producer cooperation conducted in this chapter. Chapter 8 provides a more detailed examination of the relationship between oil producers inside and outside OPEC. Another reason for downplaying the discussion of different approaches to explaining international institutions is that the focus of this chapter will be the effects of institutions on states' behavior:

> International institutions are important for states' actions in part because they affect the incentives facing states, even if those states' fundamental interests are defined autonomously. International institutions make it possible for states to take actions that would otherwise be inconceivable. . . . They also affect the costs associated with alternatives that might have existed independently. Institutions may also affect the understandings that leaders of states have of the roles they should play and their assumptions about others' motivations and perceived self-interests. That is, international institutions have constitutive as well as regulative aspects: they help define how interests are defined and how actions are interpreted. (Keohane 1989:5–6)

The study of international organizations has been characterized by two separate traditions, an empirical tradition studying formal international organizations, and a more theoretical one studying the institutionalized cooperation of states. There seems to have been little contact between those studying the international institutions under the regime perspectives and those conducting studies of formal international organizations. Probably the most influential book in the latter tradition is Robert W. Cox and Harold K. Jacobson's *The Anatomy of Influence*, published in 1973. This book hardly mentions the then-emerging tradition established by Keohane and Nye (1972). In his textbook on international organization, Jacobson devotes one paragraph to the perspective developed by Keohane and Nye (Jacobson 1984:386). "Robert Keohane argued for 'questioning traditional conceptions of international organizations as highly institutionalized entities with explicitly developed formal structures'" (Keohane 1975:361, cited in Rochester 1986:794). Two years later, together with Joseph Nye, he argued that "we need to think of international organizations less as institutions than as clusters of intergovernmental and transgovernmental networks associated with the formal institutions" (Keohane and Nye 1977:240). Stokke (1997) shows how the interdependence school, together with the integration theory, formed the basis for the international regime literature but does not include the international organization literature as such a foundation.

As pointed out above, although this study deals with a formal organization—OPEC—aspects of the relationship between the OPEC members and the role of the organization in the international oil market are ascribed to mechanisms related to international regimes. This calls for a combination of the insights generated in the two traditions, but first some fundamental aspects of the two schools will be presented.

A fundamental problem in explaining the implications of a certain institutionalization (formal or informal) is the counterfactual question what would the actors' behavior have been without the present institutions?[7] Answering this question might be easier in this study than elsewhere, as the actors involved would have had to relate to one another in the marketplace anyway. The competitive market might serve as the norm for evaluating the impact of institutionalization. On the other hand, this does not account for the possibility that, without the present institutions, some other kind of institutionalization would have occurred, implying yet another pattern of behavior by the actors. This kind of second-order counterfactuality leads beyond my present imaginative capabilities, and the evaluation of the effects of institutionalization will subsequently be made incrementally over time instead of by comparing the institutional situation with some other imagined situation.

Turning to the relations between the organization theory and the study of formal international organizations, Ness and Brechin (1988:245) state: "The gap between the study of international organizations and the sociology of organizations is deep and persistent. . . . each appears to run its own course, largely uninformed by the other." International organizations are full-fledged organizations similar to the national organizations of ministries, firms, or special-interest groups. Some aspects of bureaucratic theory might even be more relevant in international organizations than in national ones (Claes 1994). Ness and Brechin see a similarity between the sociologists' focus on organizational environment and the study of international regimes: "Defining and identifying variance in environments has proven difficult and illusive. There is . . . a strikingly parallel development in conceptions with the more recent *regime* perspective in international relations" (Ness and Brechin 1988:249).

Describing different theoretical approaches and the relationship between them is of no value unless it improves the analysis conducted. Obviously, the choice between the perspectives outlined above will lead to different foci in the study of OPEC as an institution. The explicit aim of this chapter is to analyze how the institutionalization of the cooperation between the OPEC members has contributed to changing the individual members' behavior and steering it in a more cooperative direction. This analytical focus implies a certain mix of the different theoretical insights gained in the various approaches presented. Studies of international regimes generally have been open to such a variety of theoretical approaches.

Theories of International Regimes

The classic, and now referred to as the consensus definition of international regimes, was put forth by Stephen Krasner in a special issue of the journal *International Organization* in 1982:

> International regimes are defined as principles, norms, rules, and decision-making procedures around which actor expectations converge in a given issue-area. Principles are beliefs of fact, causation, rectitude. Norms are standards of behavior defined in terms of rights and obligations. Rules are specific prescriptions or postscriptions for action. Decision-making procedures are prevailing practices for making and implementing collective choice. (Krasner 1982:186)

Several authors have tried to modify and clarify this definition, giving different interpretations and meanings to the concept international regimes. Helen Milner argues that "even strong proponents of the [regime] concept admit the difficulty in defining it" (1993:493), and that the term "regime" has lost its earlier charm. Some scholars have thus retracted to the language of institutions, or institutionalism (Milner 1993, Keohane 1989); others use concepts like "policy coordination" (Haas 1992:371), or "governance system" (Young 1994). But as Hasenclever, Mayer, and Rittberger state: "the *substantive questions* that define the regime-analytical research agenda—whether couched in terms of 'regimes,' 'institutions' or otherwise—still count among the major foci of International Relations scholarship in both Europe and North America (Hasenclever et al. 1997:1). Relating the concept of regimes to the perspective developed in the previous sections seems to be a matter of labels. International regimes is a subgroup of international institutions, of which international organizations is another more formalized and bureaucratic subclass. If one starts from the regime tradition, one would say that regimes can be accompanied by organizations; if one starts from the international organization tradition, one would tend to say that organizations can include regimes. Such statements need not have different empirical implications, and thus both concepts and different theoretical traditions can contribute to the understanding of OPEC.

Hasenclever et al. (1997) divide the theories of international regimes into three schools: power-based, interest-based, and knowledge-based theories.

- Power-based theories of international regimes can be described as 'realist theories of cooperation.' Not only conflict but also co-operation is explained by power and the distribution of capabilities among states.
- The interest-based theories are the mainstream of regime theories. They "emphasize the role of international regimes in helping states to realize common interests" (Hasenclever et al. 1997:4). The focus is on situations where the constellation of actors' interests is so that they can only achieve beneficial outcomes through institutionalized cooperation.
- The knowledge-based theories stress ideas and knowledge as explanatory variables. The focus is partly on how "causal and normative beliefs *form* perceptions of international problems and thus demand for regimes" (Hasenclever et al. 1997:137).

Almost any theory of international cooperation can be included in these three broad categories. The number of different theoretical topics covered by Hasenclever et al. (1997) clearly indicates the lack of demarcations of what is to be counted as theories of international regimes. The book covers political market failure, situation and problem structures, institutional bargaining, hegemony, distributional conflict, relative gains, ideas, arguments, and social identities. If we relate the substantive definition of regimes as the norm-based convergence of expectations that leads to the production of explicit rules (Stokke 1997:27), this wide scope of theories of international regimes obviously encompasses more than this. Similarly, all theories explaining the existence, persistence, and effects of substantive regimes cannot possibly be counted as theories of international regimes. Obviously there are other explanations for the existence, persistence, and effects of international institutions than what we reasonably would include in the category "theories of international regimes."[8] We thus need to limit the category "theories of international regimes" to explanations that include a normative core. The second aspect of the concept of regimes that needs clarification is thus its underlying normative core. Levy, Young, and Zürn (1995:271) express this when they write: "Given the basic thrust of regime analysis as a tool for understanding international cooperation and the role of norms in the pursuit of cooperation there is a need to go beyond merely routinized or patterned behavior. The principal claim of regime analysis is that states may generate institutions in identifiable issue areas that affect their behavior and foster cooperation, even if short-term interests would dictate deviation." If the observed cooperation is explained by patterns of complementary interests and underlying distribution of power, regimes have no effect and thus, in such cases, theories of international regimes does not contribute to the explanation of cooperation.

The discussion in this chapter will primarily be related to the effects of regimes. It then seems important to distinguish how the regimes improve conditions for cooperation and the "degree to which a regime ameliorates the problem that prompted its creation," to use a phrase by Levy, Young, and Zürn (1995:291). In the case of oil producer cooperation, this would be the difference between how the rules make oil producers cooperate and the extent to which this rule-based cooperation leads to a higher oil price than what would otherwise have been the case.

In the empirical investigation in section 4.3, I will search for institutional effects changing behavior according to both the logic of rationality and the logic of appropriateness. All the factors discussed can be included in the broad definition of theories of international regimes given by Hasenclever et al. (1997). However, the discussion will show that the norms of cooperation inherent in the concept of international regimes are not necessary to explain the institutional role of OPEC on the cooperative behavior of oil-producing states. Before turning to these specific empirical analytical topics, the next section briefly describes the organizational structure of OPEC.

4.2   The Organizational Structure of OPEC

Hovi (1992:230) defines an international organization as "a formal, permanent set of institutional structures, by which a group of sovereign states seeks to regulate or solve certain problems connected with their mutual relations" (my translation). OPEC is an international organization according to this definition. A treaty formally establishing OPEC as a permanent intergovernmental organization was published in September 1960, and after ratification by the signatory countries it was registered at the United Nations in November 1962. OPEC was officially recognized as an international organization by the UN Economic and Social Council in June 1965, and subsequently became a regular participant in meetings of various UN bodies, including the UN Conference on Trade and Development, and in other international forums (Evans 1990:149).

The founding members are Iran, Iraq, Kuwait, Saudi Arabia, and Venezuela.[9] Subsequent members have been Qatar (January 1961), Indonesia, Libya (June 1962), Abu Dhabi (November 1967),[10] Algeria (July 1969), Nigeria (July 1971), Ecuador (associate member June 1973; full member November 1973), and Gabon (associate member November

1973; full member June 1975). Ecuador abandoned its membership in 1992, and Gabon abandoned its membership effectively from 1995. The organization had its headquarters in Geneva from 1961 to August 1965. Since then the headquarters have been located in Vienna.

The principal aim of OPEC is "coordination and unification of the petroleum policies of member countries and the determination of the best means for safeguarding their interests, individually and collectively" (Article 2 of the Statutes, OPEC 1990:32). Interestingly enough, consideration of the interests of the other groups of the trilateral oligopoly, discussed in Chapter 2, is taken into the Statutes: "Due regard shall be given at all times to the interests of the producing nations and to the necessity of securing a steady income to the producing countries; an efficient, economic and regular supply of petroleum to consuming nations; and a fair return on their capital to those investing in the petroleum industry" (Article 2 of the Statutes, OPEC 1990:32). However, individual collusion with these groups by member states is prohibited: "If, as a result of the application of any decision of the Organization, sanctions are employed, directly or indirectly, by any interested company or companies against one or more member countries, no other member shall accept any offer of a beneficial treatment, whether in the form of an increase in oil exports or in an improvement in prices, which may be made to it by such interested company or companies with the intention of discouraging the application of the decision of the Organization" (Article 4 of the Statutes, OPEC 1990:32).

The criteria for membership are defined according to the role of petroleum in the country in question: "Any other country with a substantial net export of crude petroleum, which has fundamentally similar interests to those of member countries, may become a full member of the Organization, if accepted by a majority of three-fourths of full members, including the concurrent vote of all founder members" (Article 7 of the Statutes, OPEC 1990:33).[11]

OPEC has three organs: the Conference, the Board of Governors, and the Secretariat. The Conference is OPEC's supreme authority. It consists of delegations representing the member countries, each of which should be represented at all conferences. However, a quorum of three-quarters of member countries is necessary to hold a conference. Each full member country has one vote. All decisions of the Conference, other than on procedural matters, require the unanimous agreement of the full members (Article 11 of the Statutes, OPEC 1990:34).

The Conference meets twice a year. However, an extraordinary meeting of the Conference may be convened at the request of a member country or by the secretary general, after consultation with the president and approval by a simple majority of the member countries. The

Conference elects a president at the beginning of its meeting. The president holds office for the duration of the meeting of the Conference, and retains the title until the next meeting. As OPEC's supreme authority, the Conference formulates the policy of the organization and decides on all substantial matters: "All matters that are not expressly assigned to other organs of the Organization shall fall within the competence of the Conference" (Article 16 of the Statutes, OPEC 1990:35). The Board of Governors is composed of governors nominated by the member countries and confirmed by the Conference. The Board of Governors directs the management of OPEC affairs and the implementation of the decisions of the Conference; in fact, it runs the organization between the conferences. The Board of Governors' role leaves little authority or autonomy to the Secretariat: "The Secretariat shall carry out the executive functions of the Organization in accordance with the provisions of this Statute under the direction of the Board of Governors. The Secretariat of the Organization shall consist of the Secretary General, the Deputy Secretary General and such staff as may be required. It shall function at the headquarters of the Organization" (Articles 25, 26, OPEC 1990:37). The persons who have served as secretaries-general of OPEC are listed in Table 4.1.

The secretary-general is to some extent able to represent OPEC in external relations: "The Secretary General shall be the legally authorized representative of the Organization. The Secretary General shall be the chief officer of the Secretariat, and in that capacity shall have the authority to direct the affairs of the Organization, in accordance with directions of the Board of Governors (Article 27 of the Statutes, OPEC 1990:37).[12] In addition to the OPEC Conference (twice a year), some important ministerial committees have been established (see Table 4.2). These are constituted of members of the Conference, and report directly to fellow members of the Conference. The committees are important instruments in the development of OPEC's policies.

4.3   Institutional Functions of OPEC

There is little literature applying institutional theory to the study of OPEC. In fact, even authors discussing OPEC's role in the world economy tend to downplay the autonomy of the organization in relation to the interests of the member countries:

> It must be recognized that the character and direction of OPEC is determined not by what OPEC has done or intended to do but failed to do, but by what each member government has done or proposed to do. . . . The history of OPEC is replete both with cases in which OPEC actions were inspired by deci-

TABLE 4.1   Secretaries-General of OPEC

Name	Country	Period of Office
Dr. Fuad Rouhani	Iran	Jan. 1961–April 1964
Abdul Rahman Al- Bazzaz	Iraq	May 1964–April 1965
Ashraf T. Lutfi	Kuwait	May 1965–Dec. 1966
Mohamad Saleh Joukhdar	Saudi Arabia	Jan.–Dec. 1967
Francisco R. Parra	Venezuela	Jan.–Dec. 1968
Dr. Elrich Sanger	Indonesia	Jan.–Dec. 1969
Omar El Badri	Libya	Jan.–Dec. 1970
Dr. Nadim Pachachi	Abu Dhabi	Jan. 1971–Dec. 1972
Dr. Abderrahman Khene	Algeria	Jan. 1973–Dec. 1974
Chief Meshach O. Feyide	Nigeria	Jan. 1975–Dec. 1976
Ali Mohammed Jaidah	Qatar	Jan. 1977–Dec. 1978
Rene G. Ortiz	Ecuador	Jan. 1979–June 1981
Dr. Marc S. Nan Nguema	Gabon	July 1981–June 1983
Dr. Fadhil S. Al-Chalabi	Iraq	July 1983–June 1988
Dr. Subroto	Indonesia	July 1988–June 1994
Abdalla Salem El Badri	Libya	July–Dec. 1994
Dr. Rilwanu Lukman	Nigeria	January 1995–

SOURCE: Evans 1990:150; *OPEC Bulletin*, January 1995.

sions already taken by individual members, as well as by instances in which individual members opted to disregard decisions made by OPEC. . . . The moment the perception exists that an individual country's interests and goals are not served by an OPEC decision . . . the interests of that country can be expected to supersede those of the organization's common objectives. (Alnasrawi 1985:3)

In this chapter it will be argued that there are aspects to the history of OPEC that contradict this statement. The following sections provide an empirical account of the presence of six institutional factors.

The first aspect is the role of the organization in providing an arena for exchange of information. This aspect is grounded in the rational choice tradition of treating states' interests as given. The role of the organization is to influence the cost-benefit calculation of rational actors by being an arena where the members can exchange information and positions and search for new solutions. This aspect only suggests that, without a place where such exchange can take place, cooperation becomes harder to establish. In fact, without any arena for communication, cooperation is impossible.

The second aspect is the role of the organization in providing information about the members' positions and the oil market in general. This as-

TABLE 4.2   Key Ministerial Committees of the OPEC Conference

Ministerial Committee	Formed	Members
Ministerial Committee on long-term strategy	May 1978	Algeria, Iran, Iraq, Kuwait, Saudi Arabia, Venezuela.
Ministerial Committee to monitor the oil market	Mar. 1982	To December 1984: Algeria, Indonesia, UAE, Venezuela. From Jan. 1985: Algeria, Ecuador, Iran, Iraq, Libya, UAE.
Ministerial Committee on price differentials	Oct. 1984	Initial members: Libya, Saudi Arabia, UAE. Additional members in December 1984: Algeria, Kuwait, Nigeria, Qatar.
Ministerial Executive Council on implementation of pricing and production agreement	Dec. 1984	Indonesia, Nigeria, Saudi Arabia, UAE, Venezuela. Open to other members.
Ministerial Committee on price evolution ("Committee of Five")	June 1987	Algeria, Indonesia, Nigeria, Saudi Arabia, Venezuela.
Ministerial Committee to motivate members to comply with the 1986 agreement on quotas ("Committee of Three")	June 1987	Indonesia, Nigeria, Venezuela.
Ministerial Monitoring Committee	Nov. 1988	Algeria, Indonesia, Iran, Iraq, Kuwait, Nigeria, Saudi Arabia, Venezuela. Open to all members and split into two subcommittees in July 1990.

SOURCE: Evans 1990:152–153.

pect also is grounded in the rational choice tradition of treating states' interests as given. The focus is on the role of the secretariat in providing information about solutions and other actors' behavior. The importance of information is connected with the consequences of uncertainty in the relationship between states: "if actors behave purposively given the information available to them, perception—the information that actors possess about others—can be a critical determinant of behavior" (Stein 1990:55). The more information the organization can provide, the less likely are misperception and misunderstanding among the member states. It is, however, an empirical question whether this leads to more or less cooperation. Information can reveal conflictual interests as well as cooperative ones.

The third aspect is the role of the organization in creating decisionmaking rules that affect the subsequent outcome of the OPEC bargaining. Keohane argues the importance of rules as such: "short-run self-interest is affected by constraints imposed on policy choices by agreed-upon rules; long-run conceptions of self-interest may be reshaped as a result, in part, of practices engaged in over a period of time" (Keohane 1990:737). The decisionmaking rules are important as they imply that the decisions, to some extent, are the result of the shared interests of member countries. This is an essential feature of cooperation. The rules regulating the decisionmaking in the organization might also be important for the form and substantial contents of the cooperative decisions reached by its members.

The fourth aspect is the role of the organization in monitoring agreements and verifying accusations regarding situations where countries break agreements. The importance of monitoring and verification, which are also rooted in the economic institutionalism, is based on the study of formal organizations and their role regarding state behavior (see Karns and Mingst 1990). Monitoring the actors' behavior presupposes some administrative capacity. It is furthermore a necessary condition for the solidity of the agreements: "institutional arrangements affect . . . the ability of governments to monitor others' compliance and to implement their own commitments—hence their ability to make credible commitments in the first place" (Keohane 1989:2). The assumption is thus that the more verification there is, the more likely are states' commitments to cooperative agreements.

The fifth aspect is the role of the organization in framing decisions and establishing shared perception among the OPEC members. This point is stressed by Axelrod and Keohane (1986:247): "The significance of perception, including beliefs and cognition, will come as no surprise to students of international politics. Yet it is worth pointing out once again that decision making in ambiguous settings is heavily influenced by the way in which the actors think about their problem." This would mean that the way the bargaining problem is presented to the OPEC members influences their cooperative behavior. Two assumptions will be discussed. First, if the bargaining problem is presented as an internal OPEC problem, the members would be more likely to comply, compared with a situation where the bargaining problem is presented as an oil-producer problem in general. Second, the more uniform the OPEC members' perceptions are, the more likely are their contributions to cooperative efforts.

The final aspect is the role of the organization in establishing a collective identity among OPEC members. Alexander Wendt has claimed that international institutions also may perform a role in the formation of interests and collective identity among states (Wendt 1994). He seeks to study situations where states' interests are not given but are endogenous

to interaction: "through interaction, states might form collective identities and interests, redefining the terms of Olson's problem altogether"
(Wendt 1994:384). Wendt considers it an open empirical question when
states' interests really are exogenous and can be adequately analyzed
through a rationalist approach and when this approach becomes inadequate due to a dynamic relationship between states' interests and action
and the institutional formation of interests and identities.[13]

A Permanent Arena for Negotiations

A fundamental function of an international organization is to provide a
meeting place for the members, a setting for members to exchange views
and opinions on issues related to the aims of the organization. Furthermore, arenas "regulate the access of actors to problems and the access of
problems to decision games. Moreover, they specify the official purpose
as well as the rules, location, and timing of the game" (Underdal
1994b:110–111). The arena is essential for the exchange of opinions and
information. In the case of OPEC, the meetings of the Conference are the
most important arena for exchange of views and opinions.

The importance of OPEC as an arena is thus linked to the frequency of
the meetings of representatives of the member countries. The Conference
convened 100 times in the period from the first meeting in September
1960 until June 1996. The oil ministers, which usually represent the member countries, have met, on average, every fourth or fifth month. The
meetings usually last for two days. In addition are the meetings of the
Board of Governors and those of the different ministerial committees
listed in Table 4.2. This must be regarded as a fairly high frequency of
meetings between representatives of the governments of member countries of an international organization. The participants can thus be expected to be quite familiar with each other and the respective countries'
positions, strategies, and so on. If nothing else, this knowledge can be
based on the behavior (statements, voting, etc.) of the same countries at
the previous Conference, which convened, at the most, six months earlier. In addition, a high frequency of informal contact is likely to follow
from the meetings of the Conference. The oil policies of individual countries are unlikely to change dramatically over the short period between
the conferences, unless dramatic events take place. This is important in
particular for the quota agreements (see Table 7.6). Agreements on individual quotas are made for an explicit future period, usually until the
next Conference. The possibility of renegotiating one's quota reduces the
long-term implications of these decisions for the countries' oil policies.
This should make the countries more cooperative than they otherwise
would be, as it is possible for them to come back and argue for a higher

quota in a few months' time. For the negotiations as such, this means that several aspects of the quota agreements do not have to be dealt with every time. In cases where previous quotas have not been rolled over into the next period (i.e., until the next Conference), a marginal change for all members or individual changes for one or two members have been the usual way of changing the level or distribution of quotas. With other aspects held constant, this has reduced transaction costs (see section 4.1). The existing quotas have been a starting point for the negotiations at the conferences, and thus several aspects of the bargaining between the OPEC members are not discussed at every meeting. The multilateral approach also reduces transaction costs in the setting of quotas. Setting quotas bilaterally among the OPEC members would be an impossible project.

This leads to the aspect of permanency. Robert Axelrod (1984:10) has shown that if the actors are to meet an infinite or unknown number of times, they will have the incentive to choose cooperation.[14] Iterated games provide "multiple opportunities for retaliation" (Underdal 1994b:112). Should one actor give concessions at t_1 on the condition that others do the same, it could always change this strategy at t_2. Every member knows that the quota distribution could become a topic only six months later. Together with reliable information about individual members' production, this provides crucial instruments for subsequent sanctioning of quota violation. These aspects are fully developed in Chapters 5 to 7.

An Information Agency

Hovi (1992:236–238) distinguishes between three different forms of information: factual information about the characteristics of the member countries, information about their behavior, and information that elucidates causal connections, that is, the potential effects of the organization's decisions.

The OPEC Secretariat is an important provider of all these kinds of information. The research department of the Secretariat handles these functions. It has the role of providing the members with information about the international oil market. The reports have also offered information about the different member countries, particularly their oil-pricing and production behavior. The Secretariat provides the representatives at the Conferences and in the different ministerial committees with information about developments in the international oil market.[15] Furthermore, as OPEC is one of the major actors influencing the international oil market, it has been necessary to study the likely effects of the different strategy options available to its members. Information about members' positions and behavior forms an important part of the monitoring functions dealt with below.

Although the Statutes provide for an independent role of the secretary-general, and thereby the Secretariat, "its effectiveness has depended on the quality of its staff rather than any particular structure of the organization" (Skeet 1988:237). In 1963, the first secretary-general, Dr. Fuad Rouhani, actually negotiated with the international oil companies for increased royalties on behalf of the member countries. The negotiations, which were substantially delayed by the companies' tactics, ended with a split organization, as some countries signed agreements with the companies and some did not. The issue was excluded from the Conference's agenda, and the role of the secretary-general was subsequently reduced. Skeet (1988:237) concludes that the removal of Rouhani in 1963 meant an "implicit admission . . . that OPEC and its secretary-general would not act, as had been visualized at its creation, as an operating arm of its members." Some of the subsequent secretaries general have been able to create some room to maneuver through their capacities as politicians or oil experts, but any important role as a mediator between members, or as a negotiator with other actors in the market or a spokesperson to the international community, has either been handled by a key member of the Conference or been clearly mandated to the secretary general by the Conference. The Secretariat has no independent role beyond providing information and carrying out procedural tasks in connection with the conferences. This lack of any permanent, powerful autonomous body weakens the influence of the organization on the behavior of its members.

Decisionmaking Rules

In all international organizations, decisionmaking rules are important:

> The decision rule is clearly an important determinant of the capacity to aggregate diverging preferences; other things being equal, aggregation capacity reaches its maximum in strictly hierarchical structures, and is at its minimum in systems requiring agreement (unanimity). . . . Procedural arrangements may differ . . . with regard to differentiation into subprocesses (committee works vs. plenary sessions), and the amount of discretion vested in committee or conference chairs in, *inter alia*, drafting proposals ("negotiating texts"). (Underdal 1994b:111)

The decisionmaking rule of OPEC is described in Article 11 of the Statutes: "Each Full Member Country shall have one vote. All decisions of the Conference, other than procedural matters, shall require the unanimous agreement of all Full Members" (OPEC 1990:34). Thus, it follows from the quotation from Underdal above that the aggregation capacity is at its minimum. According to the Statutes, the individual state has a veto.

TABLE 4.3   Organizations and State Power

| Power Outside | Power Inside the Organization | |
the Organization	Large	Small
Large	indifferent	reject organizational decisions
Small	prefer organizational decisions	indifferent

Obviously, international organizations where the individual members can veto decisions are less autonomous than organizations where individual members face the possibility of losing a vote. However, the OPEC conferences have had a tendency to work toward consensus and thus avoid voting. As a consequence of this consensus strategy, decisions have been postponed from one meeting to the next. This was the case both with price-increase decisions during the seventies and with aspects of the quota system during the eighties. Subcommittees have been used extensively to deal with specific issues in smaller and more clandestine settings. The veto right and the consensus ambition have, however, not always avoided having conferences end with split decisions, as happened at the important December 1976 meeting in Doha, described in section 5.1.

The formal voting power in OPEC is one country, one vote. It is not related to the market power of the members. This discrepancy between the distribution of power inside and outside the organization may have implications for the members' behavior. The general proposition is that actors with a large or small amount of power both inside and outside the organization tend to be indifferent about whether or not issues are dealt with through the decisionmaking procedures of the organization. In this case, to not include issues in the OPEC deliberations means letting them be decided through individual members' market policies. Countries with little power outside the organization (i.e., with little market power) will tend to favor more policy development through the bodies of OPEC, while countries with greater market power will tend to keep issues away from the organization and possibly ignore decisions made by it. This is illustrated in Table 4.3.

In the case of the quota decisions, the members' ability to produce in excess of the assigned quota represents one possible power resource outside the organization. With a large spare production capacity, a country can undermine the collective decision by overproducing. Saudi Arabia has to some extent pursued such a strategy when dissatisfied with OPEC agreements (see section 5.1). The discrepancy between Saudi Arabia's importance in the international market and its single vote in OPEC has to some extent been compensated for by the inclusion of Saudi Arabia in almost all important ministerial committees (see Table 4.2). The particular role of Saudi Arabia is fully developed in Chapter 6.

Karns and Mingst (1986:467; 1990) have made an interesting contribution to the discussion of the relationship between international organizations and their member states. Their approach is to study the relationship between an intergovernmental organization (IGO) and its members as a combination of the IGO as a source of influence on the member countries' foreign policy and the IGO as an instrument for the member countries' goal achievement. When looking at OPEC as an instrument of states' goal achievement, it is important to note that the decisions made in OPEC relate to problems that the individual countries could in principle handle themselves. The interesting question is to what extent making decisions jointly increases the members' net utility. This calculation might naturally differ from country to country and vary over time. When the room for coherent action in OPEC increased during the seventies as the producing countries nationalized, or gained control over their oil industries through other means, the role of the organization became obsolete—no coordination or institutional arrangement was necessary to serve the members' interests (see section 2.4). Instead of enforcing the strength of OPEC as a cartel, the price increases soon caused severe disagreement inside OPEC (see section 5.1). The seventies was a period when OPEC struggled with internal differences rather than gained control over the market and strengthened its position against the other actors, such as the international companies, the consuming countries, and producers outside the organization.

The rule of unanimity gives the organization little autonomy in relation to the members, but it has also made the members aim at consensus. The differences among OPEC members have made some of the collective decisions vague, and members have tended to disregard the decisions. So far, the analysis suggests that OPEC has been an arena for negotiations between sovereign states. The next three sections will modify this picture to some extent.

Monitoring Functions

An important element in ensuring cooperation is the detection of defectors.[16] An organization may play a role in this by providing administrative staff and technical instruments, or establishing impartial inspection bodies. The reliability of the information gathered is an important aspect of the role of the organization in this respect. The monitoring functions of the organization are meant to deal with the possibility that member states behave opportunistically. As pointed out by Keohane, "some actors, may be dishonest, and enter into agreements that they have no intention of fulfilling" (1989:226). As pointed out above, Williamson (1975:25–26) does not believe it is possible to establish self-enforcing commitments that would annul self-disbelieving promises. Although the organization cannot extinguish opportunistic behavior, it can increase the probability that opportunism will be detected. This should, ceteris paribus, make other actors more willing to enter into agreements with potential opportunists.

OPEC took on a more substantial institutional role in the early eighties. This happened not through an activation of the established institutions or Statutes but through the creation of a new subcommittee, the Market Monitoring Committee, at the Sixty-third OPEC Conference in March 1982. This committee, established to monitor the production quotas initiated at the same time (see section 5.2), held its first meeting on April 21, 1982. At the Sixty-fourth OPEC Conference on May 20 and 21, the production ceiling was maintained, and was to be subject to continued surveillance by the monitoring committee. The Conference discussion was dominated by Iran's noncompliance with its quota, an issue pursued by the monitoring committee after its meeting on July 7:

> Members of the committee expressed some concern about certain member countries' "over-production" relative to their ceiling. . . . The 65th (extraordinary) meeting of the OPEC conference opened in Vienna on July 9 to consider the monitoring committee's recommendations. Differences over the economic issues involved, were, however, sharpened by political tensions, and on July 10 the meeting was suspended after reaching deadlock. . . . Iran claimed that there was wide support at the meeting for the principle of an increase in its quota to 3,000,000 bpd and that this represented a "moral triumph" over Saudi Arabia. (Evans 1990:605–606)

The Seventy-second OPEC Conference in December 1984 called for a system to provide full information on individual members' production exports and prices:

> For this purpose, OPEC will create a Ministerial Executive Council. . . . The Ministerial Executive Council . . . is empowered to take any measures it deems necessary to fulfill its tasks. The Council will be assisted by one or more reputable international auditing firms to provide a check on Member Countries' petroleum sales, tanker nominations, shipments, prices, quantities, etc. The auditing firm will be empowered to send its representatives to Member Countries to check the books, invoices, or any other documents that are deemed necessary by the firm in fulfillment of its tasks. Likewise the

Council may choose any other means of check and control, such as tanker tracking methods, to be undertaken by consulting firms. The Council may also send its representatives to pay visits to the ports and loading terminals of Member Countries to provide check and control, besides the auditing firm's representatives. Member Countries undertake to make available to the auditors, their representatives and the representatives of the Council, all the required documents. They also undertake to send all the information on tanker nominations to the OPEC Secretariat. (OPEC 1990:226)

This unanimous adoption of this resolution was, in jurisdictional terms, dramatic. The Ministerial Executive Council is empowered to apply any measures necessary, and the auditing firms are also given wide authority regarding inspections in the member countries' territories. However, the resolution did not spell out any sanctions to be implemented should members break the agreed production quotas. In a separate meeting on January 27, the Ministerial Executive Council outlined a proposal for the monitoring scheme, and suggested that a Dutch accounting firm, Klynveld Kraayenhof, should be hired to carry out the audits (Evans 1990:658–659). The identities of quota violators were not officially published by the organization, but were raised during the internal bargaining at the conferences, as was reported for instance at the Seventy-second OPEC Conference in December 1984: "Several delegates expressed deep concern about the Organization's diminishing credibility in the marketplace, in which connection there was much blunt criticism of various members' noncompliance with Conference decisions" (Evans 1990:645).

Problems emerged when this resolution was to be implemented. At the Seventy-fourth Conference in August 1985, the

Ministerial Executive Council informed the conference that five OPEC members had declined to co-operate fully with the auditing procedures approved by the 73rd Conference meeting and made various recommendations for improving the effectiveness of these procedures. The five countries concerned (which were not publicly named) agreed to open their books to the auditors in the future and joined the other member countries in approving a strengthening of the Council's monitoring methods. The Conference did not, however, accept a proposal by some member countries that the Council should be empowered to recommend the imposition of sanctions on countries where "malpractices" were revealed as a result of independent audits. (Evans 1990:665)

The monitoring efforts represented important improvements to the cohesion and effectiveness of the production quotas, but the unwillingness to impose threats of sanctions made the organization's efforts half-hearted. The decision made in the second part of the Seventy-eighth Conference in August 1986, illustrates that the quota distribution and the individual members' adherence to it were questions open for discussion. At this meeting, Iraq was released from quota restrictions. This was not only an economic concession but also a political one (see section 3.6). The resolution also contained a formulation of the status of the quota decision: "this temporary measure should not prejudice the discussion in the Conference concerning new national quotas for its Members and OPEC's appropriate and rightful total production" (OPEC 1990:245). In addition to the fact that no sanctions were effected against quota-breakers, the temporality of the quota decisions was underlined.

As the figures of total OPEC production and quotas in Figure 4.1 suggest, the production was reduced below the quota level during the monitoring period. However, by comparing the figures for Saudi Arabia and the other OPEC members it becomes clear that this reduction was entirely due to Saudi Arabia cutting its production. Rather than the effect of international institutions monitoring state behavior, the role of Saudi Arabia should be emphasized. Chapter 6 is entirely devoted to the hegemonic role of Saudi Arabia. Figure 4.1 also demonstrates how the change in the distribution of production quotas in March 1983 was a transfer of quota from Saudi Arabia to the rest of the OPEC members. The internal bargaining over quotas is further discussed in Chapter 5.

Framing of Decision

The situational model presented in section 1.4 distinguished between aspects of the situation surrounding an actor and the actor's actual behavior or choice. An important aspect between these two levels is the actor's perception of the environment surrounding his or her decisions. The organization can influence the actors' perceptions of the situation surrounding their decisions—in other words, the organization can frame member states' decisions. Although this is not necessarily incompatible with the assumptions of the theory of rational choice, it is fully in line with the sociological institutional approach. As pointed out by March and Olsen (1994:251), "institutions influence the perception . . . of the reality within which action takes place."

According to the theory of rational choice, the actors' preferences regarding different alternatives are not taken to be dependent on the way the alternatives are presented. This is the assumption of invariance. Important studies in cognitive and social psychology have shown how the preferences of actors vary according to the presentation of possible choices (Tversky and Kahneman 1986; Quattrone and Tversky 1988;

156

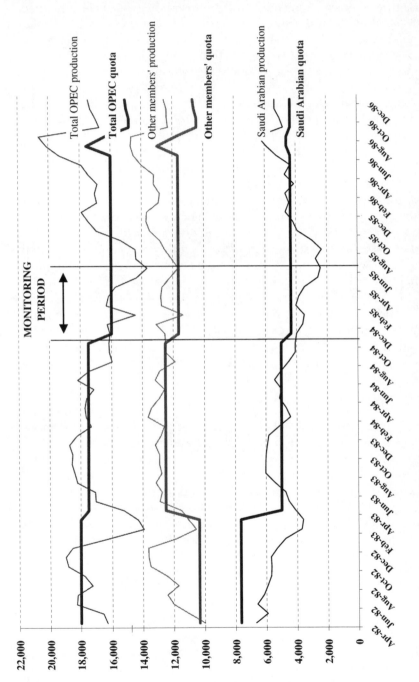

FIGURE 4.1   Production, Quotas, and Monitoring, April 1982–December 1986 (th. b/d).
SOURCE: OPEC 1990 and *Petroleum Economist.*

Tversky, Slovic, and Kahneman 1990).[17] Quattrone and Tversky (1988:735) conclude their article as follows:

> The descriptive failure of normative principles, such as invariance and co-herence, does not mean that people are unintelligent or irrational. The fail-ure merely indicates that judgment and choice—like perception and mem-ory—are prone to distortion and error. The significance of the results stems from the observation that the errors are common and systematic, rather than idiosyncratic or random, hence they cannot be dismissed as noise.

Kenneth Arrow (1983:29) regards this as "the most damning criticism of risk-benefit analysis." Also, March and Olsen (1989:154–155) argue that there are "numerous reasons for lamenting the tendency to treat preferences as given in theories of choice. Where preferences are ambigu-ous and changing endogenously, treating them as consistent, clear, stable, and exogenous leads to predictive theories that are wrong and normative theories that are misleading."

Like uncertain information, undecided preferences will increase the actor's susceptibility to influence from other actors. This is not contrary to the theory of rational choice, as this theory does not pretend to ex-plain why the actor has the preferences he or she has. Richardson (1990:5), however, regards this as a serious weakness of the rational choice theory: "the goals, preferences etc.—remain unexplained. The language of the expected utility offers a reformulation of the explanan-dum not an explanation. . . . The thin theory of rationality, like the syllo-gism, is empty of content, it enters into every explanation, but in and of itself it can explain nothing." Elster (1983:15) describes the dilemma as follows: "to say that truth is necessary for rational beliefs clearly is to re-quire too much; to say that consistency is sufficient, to demand too little . . . for rational desires: the requirement of consistency is too weak, that of ethical goodness too strong."

When regarding framing of decisions, other actors' use of language be-comes an important feature. It seems even more difficult to reveal fram-ing than lies. How should the actor become aware that his or her choice has been framed? It is possible to have the world presented to you in dif-ferent ways, but what should be the norm from which to decide which presentation is the real one?[18]

The strategy of the Market Monitoring Committee in 1983–1984 was a case of framing of decisions. As shown above, the Committee intro-duced the concept of overproduction. The leader of the committee, Dr. Maneh Said al Otaiba, thus tried to establish the perception of the situa-tion as a problem of distribution of production quotas rather than as a question of which relationship between price and total OPEC production would present the best possible outcome for the OPEC countries.[19] By changing the perception of the game structure into one of pure distribution, the individual members' calculations were framed, as one member's overproduction would mean that another member would have to cut back.

The monitoring committee met both in August and September 1983, and decreased its estimated demand for OPEC crude. Its recommendation was subsequently to maintain the 17.5 mbd production ceiling. In July 1984 the role of the Market Monitoring Committee was praised by the president of the Seventieth OPEC Conference:

> The most effective instrument of success was the strict adherence to our agreement and the maintenance of cohesion of the Organization. The work of keeping abreast of oil market developments and Member Countries' performance was facilitated by the Ministerial Monitoring Committee [Market Monitoring Committee][20]. . . . It has continued to maintain a close and vigilant watch on market developments, advising Your Excellencies of the situation at any given point in time and enabling OPEC to take the right decisions. (OPEC 1990:215)

Focusing on overproduction led OPEC into a role as a residual supplier. The Market Monitoring Committee actually initiated the now-widespread way of reading the oil market: First one estimates the total demand; then the non-OPEC supply is taken as given, and account is taken of likely stocking or destocking; the rest of the demand is the so-called call on OPEC. The "call on OPEC" thus neglects the possibility of demand being influenced by the price level, which in turn could be influenced by OPEC's production. It is also assumed that non-OPEC producers produce at full capacity regardless of price (i.e., that they are genuine price-takers). This way to read the market is in line with the dominant firm model (Crémer and Isfahani 1991:42–45). With this perception of OPEC as a residual supplier comes a reduced role of the monopolist in the price-setting. Although OPEC does not become a price-taker in this model, the organization becomes a non-OPEC production-taker. What happened in the market was that the monopolist's (OPEC's) market share decreased as the fringe (non-OPEC) increased its market share—all in line with the dominant firm model. In theory, three strategies are open to the monopolist in such a situation, and OPEC did, to a variable degree, try to pursue all three:

1. cut prices in order to increase demand
2. put pressure on non-OPEC producers in order to include them in the production-limitation program
3. cut one's own production

Since the first failed because of the increased taxation of oil consumption by the governments in oil-consuming countries (see Figure 2.15) and the second failed due to the lack of means to force the non-OPEC producers to comply (see Chapter 8), OPEC came to rely on the third strategy. In the period 1983–1985 the costs were almost entirely borne by Saudi Arabia (see section 6.5).

The role of the monitoring committee during 1982 was that it reduced the room for members to demand a higher total ceiling, although some members obviously advocated this at the conferences. Since more weight was given to the total ceiling, the individual members' claims for higher quotas became an entirely distributional bargaining process, in which one member's increase in production would have to be followed by another member's decreased production. Distributional bargains are for obvious reasons much tougher than bargains with integrative potential. The role of the committee in actually framing the OPEC production decisions as a distributional issue contributed to the subsequent solution in March 1983, when Saudi Arabia reduced its ceiling in exchange for an increase in the Iranian quota (see section 5.2). The committee strengthened the organization—that is, the collective strength of the members—but it simultaneously increased the internal tension.

When the quota system was established, the role of the Market Monitoring Committee was enlarged from providing information about not only the market but also the individual members' quota discipline. According to the head of the committee, UAE Oil Minister Dr. Maneh Said al Otaiba, the compliance was monitored on the basis of a quarterly average (Evans 1990:633). Although the committee improved the information on members' compliance, it was unclear what sanctions could be inflicted on non-abiding members. This was clearly illustrated by the statement made by al Otaiba prior to the Seventieth OPEC Conference in July 1984: "Dr. al Otaiba said at the end of the meeting [the committee meeting before the Conference] that it was necessary for the Conference to 'give confidence to the oil market by *asking* the member countries to abolish quota violations and direct and indirect price discounting'" (Evans 1990:636, italics mine). The Conference decided to send OPEC delegations to visit member countries "with a view to further consolidating Member Countries' commitments to stabilize the market and defend the price structure" (OPEC 1990:216).

The perception of quota violations as overproduction and the market balance to create a residual named the "call on OPEC" both frame the choices of the individual OPEC member. The notion of overproduction makes it harder for individual countries to engage in price wars against non-OPEC suppliers, as a quota violation represents an attempt to gain at the expense of fellow OPEC members. The call on OPEC covers the possible effects on the non-OPEC production from a price fall facilitated by increased OPEC production. The non-OPEC producers are assumed to be price-takers, implying that their total production is also assumed to be insensitive to price declines. This is in line with the institutional approach of March and Olsen (1989:45): "In general, the predictions that can be made depend on the fine detail of the ways an institution organizes contact and experiences. . . . Where meaning develops within such a system, there is a tendency to partition a population of individuals into groups or institutions that share interpretations and preferences within groups but not across groups." Although all oil producers in this respect have similar interests in the oil market, the OPEC members tend to view the non-OPEC producers as having different interests than theirs. Common perception and interpretation of the world are aspects of the institutionalization of cooperation between states that cannot be understood through a purely rationalistic approach. The stressing of the difference between OPEC and non-OPEC producers also has important role in the institutional explanations of the OPEC cooperation, as it contributed to the establishment of a collective identity among the OPEC members.

Establishing Collective Identity

The aim of this section is to discuss the importance of a common identity among the OPEC members for the explanation of their cooperative behavior. Increased cooperative behavior might come about as a result of several different processes of identity formation.

Alexander Wendt (1994:388–391) outlines different causal mechanisms that "promote collective state identities." The mechanisms operate on different levels. The first level is the "intersubjective systemic structures [which] consist of the shared understandings, expectations, and social knowledge embedded in international institutions and threat complexes, in terms of which states define (some of) their identities and interests." The second level is the systemic processes, understood as "dynamics in the external context of state action," which lead to increased interdependence, which can imply both an "increase in the 'dynamic density' of interactions . . . [and] the emergence of a 'common Other.' This reduces the ability to meet corporate needs unilaterally and increases the extent to which actors share a common fate. As the ability to meet corporate needs unilaterally declines, so does the incentive to hang onto the egoistic identities that generate such policies, and as the degree of common fate increases, so does the incentive to identify with others" (Wendt 1994:389). The third level is the strategic practice. Wendt develops two subcategories, the behavioral and the rhetorical. "The behavioral suggests that repeated acts of cooperation will tend to have two effects on identities and interests. First, the symbolic interactionist concept of 'reflected appraisals' suggests that actors form identities by learning, through interaction, to see themselves as others do. . . . Second . . . by engaging in cooperative behavior, an actor will gradually change its own beliefs about who it is, helping to internalize the new identity for itself. . . . repeated interaction can transform an interdependence of outcomes into one of utility" (Wendt 1994:390). The rhetorical practice "may have effects similar to those of behavioral practice but it does so through a different mode of communication, variously enacted as consciousness rising, dialogue . . . discussion and persuasion . . . education, ideological labor . . . political argument . . . symbolic action . . . and so on (Wendt 1994:391).

Here, two aspects will be discussed. First, an image of a common enemy might increase the actors' perception of common interests among themselves, increasing their cooperative behavior, a mechanism Wendt calls the systemic process level (1994:389). Second, an organization perceived as a model for others might itself gain confidence, a mechanism Wendt calls the first type of behavioral and rhetorical strategic practice (1994:390).

Different aspects of collective identity among states or societies have been important for the study of international relations for many decades, in particular in the field of integration theory: "one of the crucial questions in integration theory is the relation of a sense of community to behavioral interdependence" (Nye 1971:26). Jacob and Teune (1964:4–5) argue that "political integration generally implies a relationship of community . . . a feeling of identity and self-awareness." According to Bull (1977:54) there is a relationship between common interests and common identity as a "sense of common interests . . . [that] in some cases . . . may express the ability of the individuals or groups concerned to identify with each other to the extent of treating each other's interests as ends in themselves and not merely as means to an end; that is to say, it may express a sense of common values."

The argument in this subsection is that international organizations can influence states' behavior in a more cooperative direction by contributing to the creation of collective identities.

Forming identity through a perception of a common enemy in this case means that the cooperative behavior of OPEC members is developed as a result of the members' perceiving some kind of threat from other actors (Wendt 1994:389). This threat might change in time and space. Concluding his study "Self and Other in International Relations," Neumann (1996:166–167) argues that "the delineation of a self from an other is an *active* and ongoing part of identity formation. The creation of social boundaries is not a consequence of integration, but one of its necessary *a priori* ingredients." This can be interpreted as meaning something like, "no self without an other." The resolutions adopted at the First OPEC Conference in September 1960 clearly indicate that the organization was established as an instrument in the ongoing fight with the international oil companies. Particularly, the price policy of the companies triggered strong reactions from the oil-producing countries. The first sentence of the first OPEC resolution reads as follows: "The members can no longer remain indifferent to the attitude heretofore adopted by the Oil Companies in effecting price modifications" (OPEC 1990:1). The second resolution adopted established the "permanent Organization of the Petroleum Exporting Countries for regular consultation among its Members with a view to coordinating and unifying the policies of the Members." Later, at the Eighth Conference in 1965, this was established as the principal aim of the organization (OPEC 1990:32). As the organization was established in opposition to the companies and with the aim to unify the policies of the member states, the us versus them relationship was between the producing countries inside OPEC and the foreign, mostly private, international oil companies. During the first half of the seventies most OPEC members nationalized their oil production. This made the relationship to the international companies of lesser importance, or, more correctly, made the international oil companies less important for the developments in the oil market. Consequently, "the other," having been one of the main reasons for the establishment of the organization, was no longer an important factor.

Regarding the relationship with other actors wanting to join the organization, the potential new members were restricted by Article 7c of the Statutes, which provides that "any other country with a substantial net export of crude petroleum which has fundamentally similar interests to those of Member Countries, can become a Full Member of the Organization. . . . No country may be admitted to associate membership which does not fundamentally have interests and aims similar to those of member countries" (OPEC 1990:33). This is an example of what Cox and Jacobson (1973) call a boundary-decision, creating criteria for who can be included in the organization and who cannot. The Statutes suggest that countries with a substantial net export of crude petroleum have some objectives in common. They also set clear criteria regarding what kind of countries OPEC is set to represent. Such statutes obviously create a common identity among the OPEC countries.

Creating common identity by being an example for others means that the members of OPEC might find it harder to leave or obstruct the working of an organization that has become an ideal for other Third World countries seeking to better their position against the industrialized countries through similar collective action.

When OPEC succeeded in raising the price of crude oil, it seemed the beginning of a broader change in the relationship between the raw material producers in the south and the industrialized countries in the north. "After the events in the fall of 1973, OPEC became a model, radically strengthening the belief in the effectiveness of producer-exporter cooperation as a means of promoting the interest of the periphery countries" (Hveem 1977:15). The OPEC summit of heads of state in Algiers in March 1975 was the peak of the role of OPEC as "the shield of the Third World," as the banners in the city proclaimed (Terzian 1985:213). Algerian authorities submitted several "draft resolutions" covering, among other issues, an international conference on raw materials and development, a declaration dealing with the international monetary system, a kind of defense pact between OPEC members, and a project for an OPEC fund for development and international cooperation (Terzian 1985:213–214). The OPEC special fund was set up in 1976, providing "interest-free long-term loans to developing countries" (OPEC 1990:139). The support for the Third World was stated on several occasions, as for instance in the eighteenth anniversary address of Secretary-General Ali M. Jaidah:

> OPEC Member Countries, being themselves developing countries, have always identified themselves with the efforts of the Third World to bring about a new international economic order. In this spirit they have done their utmost to aid their brethren in the other developing countries . . . through steadily increasing financial contributions to alleviation of the latter group's balance of payments problems and to enable them to go ahead with development projects. (OPEC 1990:158)

The role as the shield or spearhead of the Third World obvious built a positive common identity among the OPEC members. Although the substantive effort was moderate, and the role later petered out, it contributed to increasing the perception of commonality against the divergent interests emerging during the latter half of the seventies, particularly regarding the price issue (see section 5.1).

The relationship between the members of OPEC is not like that of a community of states. The bonds between the OPEC members are, in this respect, weak. There is no ambition in the organization to try to develop the cooperation between the members into anything broader than the present specific issue—oil cooperation. However, as this section has shown, there are elements of collective identity formation among the OPEC members. Aspects of the Statutes and the way other countries perceive the OPEC members have contributed to this. Thus, to some extent, the OPEC decisions take place "within a broader framework of rules, roles and identities" (March and Olsen 1994:251).

4.4   Conclusion

The role of the Market Monitoring Committee illustrates a much debated aspect of international institutions—the extent to which such institutions have an autonomous role against the interests of the states constituting the organization. Robert Keohane outlines two important aspects of the significance of institutions: "International institutions are important for states' actions in part because they affect the incentives facing states . . . [and] they help define how interests are defined and how actions are interpreted" (Keohane 1989:5–6). In 1982, the Market Monitoring Committee helped define the problem facing the oil producers as one of internal OPEC distribution of production cutbacks. This leads to a discussion of the likely provision of the collective good, which is the key topic in Chapter 7.

The Market Monitoring Committee actually reduced the size of the relevant group from all oil producers to the members of OPEC. Considering this from a purely economic or game-theoretical approach, there is no reason why reduced production of an OPEC member should have any other effect than reduced production of an oil producer outside the organization. However, the committee created such a notion among the members of OPEC by focusing on their overproduction.[21] This focused the bargaining problem on the internal distribution of production cutbacks. At the same time, non-OPEC production increased steadily, leaving less room in the market for the OPEC members' production. Other external factors also contributed, like the slackening of demand and the increased taxation of imported oil by consuming countries (see section 2.5). Also, rather rigorous measures were taken to persuade the members to comply with the agreed quota arrangements, but no explicit threats of sanctions were introduced. Individual members uttered their intention to increase their own production if others did not comply, but this was not the policy of the organization as such.

Thus, the conclusion is that the implementation of the quota system in 1982 would not have had the effect it had without the institutional mechanism provided by the Market Monitoring Committee in establishing the notion of the interests of OPEC producers as different from those of oil producers as such. The committee put an institutional constraint on the behavior of the OPEC members. The effect of the quota system on members actual production is further discussed in Chapter 7.

Furthermore, the production-monitoring efforts made it harder for the individual members to get away with cheating unnoticed. The decision at the Seventy-fourth OPEC Conference indicates that the cheating countries felt some embarrassment of being marked as non-compliers or not abiding with the monitoring procedures. The combination of strong monitoring applied in accordance with a resolution of the Seventy-third Conference and the lack of willingness to sanction cheaters by the Seventy-fourth Conference clearly illustrates how in this matter OPEC tread on the edge of what an international organization can hope to achieve when confronted with the interests of sovereign states. Figure 4.1 also shows that the reduced overproduction in the monitoring period was almost entirely due to Saudi Arabia reducing its production. Also the situation in 1983, when Saudi Arabia reduced its quota while the others increased theirs, shows that the independent role of the quota system on production was rather limited. These topics are further discussed in Chapters 5 to 8.

The importance of the institutional argument still holds some validity, as the OPEC members have behaved differently from non-OPEC producers, large or small:

> Given that the so-called non-OPEC producers, almost by definition, consistently maintain their output levels at full capacity, it obviously follows that whatever spare capacity there is in the world supply system is located in the group of 12 OPEC producers, and that the vital job of regulating supply in order to defend prices—in other words keeping this spare capacity off the market—inevitably remains the purview of OPEC. (Seymour 1996:3)

Even though OPEC did not facilitate other oil producers' contribution to the collective good, it did help to keep OPEC together. A common enemy increased internal coherence.

Looking back at the introduction to this chapter and the role or function of international organizations, the empirical sections of this chapter clearly show how the international organization—OPEC—provides the members with *information* regarding the market, defines a common *perception* of the members' bargaining problem, helps to establish *rules* for production by setting quotas, contributes to the enforcement of these rules by *monitoring* the individual members' actual production, and has increased the coherence of OPEC by enhancing the perception of a common enemy in the non-OPEC producers. In 1982, the members' perception of the situation was partly formed by the organization; in 1984, a monitoring effort was established and pursued by the organization; and in 1986, the coherence of the members against the other oil producers was strengthened by the organization. On the basis of the discussion in this chapter, it is argued that, at these particular instances, the oil-producer cooperation would not have been the same without the institutional factors underlying the behavior of the organization, which partly contradicted the members' interests. When OPEC was established in 1960, the idea of production-sharing agreements was included in the Statutes, but was not implemented. This can be interpreted as indicating that the institutional basis for the implementation of this instrument was not present in 1960. When production-sharing was introduced in 1982, the common institutional experience of the OPEC members made them more prone to act in concert and implement both the quota system and, in 1984, the monitoring system in order to strengthen the organization at the expense of their individual sovereignty.

The focus of this chapter has been on the explicit effects of institutional factors on states' behavior. Even when discussing the aspects of collective identity, the empirical arguments were based on resolutions and statements by representatives of OPEC or OPEC member states. International organizations like OPEC might, however, influence state behavior without such explicit expression. The possibility of institutional factors influencing state behavior through more implicit mechanisms than those discussed in this chapter is suggested by Rosenau and Czempiel (1992:3): "To presume the presence of governance without government is to conceive of functions that have to be performed in any viable human system irrespective of whether the system has evolved organizations and institutions explicitly charged with performing them."

For the purpose of this study, this argument suggests that states' behavior might be influenced by institutional factors without any explicit action by the organization. Investigating such mechanisms would require other and far more thorough methods than the ones applied in this study. The conclusions reached in this chapter cannot rule out that such implicit effects have influenced the cooperative behavior of the member states of OPEC, in addition to the explicit ones discussed in this chapter. Furthermore, when it is argued in the next chapter that the cooperative, cartel-like behavior of the OPEC members is not a result of institutional factors, it is with the reservation that implicit mechanisms of the kind mentioned here have not been active.

Notes

1. This question is based on the assumption that by institutionalizing the cooperation in a formal organization, the individual actors will tend to behave more cooperatively. Hovi (1992:229) points out that cooperation between states might be perfectly viable without an organization, and the establishment and running of international organizations might be costly. The net gain from institutionalizing cooperation is thus an open empirical question.

2. It should be noted that the term "economic institutionalists" in the following pages refers to the "new" institutionalists. It is an important difference between the old institutionalists as Thorstein Veblen, John Commons, and Wesley Mitchell and the new institutionalists discussed in this chapter. While the aspects of new institutionalism discussed here largely accept the primary role of the individual and thus ascribe to methodological individualism, the old institutionalists rejected this primacy of the individual: "Not only is the individual's conduct hedged about and directed by his habitual relations to his fellows in a group, but these relations, being of an institutional character, vary as the institutional scene varies" (Veblen 1909: 245, cited in Hodgson 1991:209). In the discussion in this subsection such arguments would place Veblen closer to the sociological institutionalism developed below than to the economic institutionalism of this section.

3. Phrase taken from Hodgson 1991:186. This approach suggests a fundamental difference (not only one of degree) between competitive markets and markets with some kind of imperfect competition, such as oligopolies or monopolies.

4. "Rationality implies a complete, and unattainable, knowledge of the exact consequences of each choice. In actuality, the human being never has more than a fragmentary knowledge of the conditions surrounding his action, nor more than a slight insight into the regularities and laws that would permit him to induce future consequences from a knowledge of present circumstances" (Simon 1976:81).

5. Michael Dummett (1973:298, cited in Davidson 1984:266) argues that "there is a general convention whereby the utterance of a sentence, except in special contexts, is understood as being carried out with the intention of uttering a true sentence." Donald Davidson (1984:270), on the contrary, argues that "What is understood is that the speaker, if he has asserted something, has represented himself as believing it—as uttering a sentence he believes true, then. But this is not a convention, it is merely part of the analysis of what assertion is. . . . there cannot be a conventional sign that shows that one is saying what one believes; for every liar would use it. . . . There is no convention of sincerity." According to Ramberg (1989:8), "Davidson's kind of theory is one which would enable us to specify the conditions under which a sentence in a language is true, without telling us anything about when those conditions prevail or how to determine whether they do prevail." In line with Davidson's refusal of conventions regarding the truth of utterances, Robert Jervis (1970:66) claims that "since signals derive their meanings from tacit or explicit agreement among actors, an actor can lie as easily as he can tell the truth. A signal used to convey an accurate message can also convey a misleading one. It is logically impossible to design a signaling system that does not have this attribute." Nothing in the language itself makes it possible to distinguish lies from truth.

6. As indicated above, the possibility of making more profit than your competitors is in a fundamental way based on your knowing something he or she does not know. Thus, assuming perfect information misses the whole point.

7. This question is similar to the questions raised by the students of international regimes concerning regime-effectiveness (see Young 1982, 1994; Underdal 1992; Stokke 1997).

8. An example might illustrate this point. GATT (the General Agreement on Trade and Tariff) is often referred to as a prominent example of an international regime (Levy, Young and Zürn 1995:279). I guess not even the boldest advocate of regime theory would include David Ricardo's theory of comparative advantage as a part of the theories of international regimes, although the mechanism specified by the theory, in itself, both can make states change their behavior and start bilateral trade relations (hardly a regime), but also make them change behavior and agree on common rules for free-trade (as in the case of GATT).

9. The founding members are "those countries which were represented at the 1st Conference, held in Baghdad, and which signed the original agreement of the establishment of the Organization" (OPEC 1990:33).

10. In 1974, Abu Dhabi's membership was transferred to the UAE, of which Abu Dhabi is a member together with Dubai, Ajman, Sharja, Umm al Qaiwain, Ras al Khaima, and Fujaira.

11. "A net petroleum-exporting country which does not qualify for membership under [the above] paragraph . . . may nevertheless be admitted as an associate member by the Conference under such special conditions as may be prescribed by the Conference, if accepted by a majority of three-fourths, including the concurrent vote of all founder members. No country may be admitted to associate membership that does not fundamentally have interests and aims similar to those of member countries" (Article 7 of the Statutes, OPEC 1990:33).

12. As is normal for international governmental organizations, the bureaucracy shall not be representatives of their respective countries: "The staff of the Secretariat are international employees with an exclusively international character. In the performance of their duties, they shall neither seek nor accept instructions from any government or from any other authority outside the Organization. They shall refrain from any action which might reflect on their position as international employees and they shall undertake to carry out their duties with the sole object of bearing the interests of the Organization in mind" (Article 32 of the Statutes, OPEC 1990:39).

13. Wendt defines self-interest and collective interest as effects of the extent to which social identities involve identification with the fate of the other (Wendt 1994:386). His position is between the rationalistic and the holistic, as he regards the importance of collective and egoistic interests as an empirical question: "Thus, I am not suggesting that collective interests replace egoistic ones as exogenously given constants in a rationalist model but, rather, that identities and interests be treated as dependent variables endogenously to interaction" (ibid.:387).

14. This implies that the strategy of noncooperation is not a dominant strategy, if we view all sequences of the game as a whole. The structure is thus different in an iterated prisoner's dilemma than in a one-shot prisoner's dilemma.

15. This might seem an unnecessary task today, when daily market information is readily available through international energy information services around the world. It is important to note that this has not always been the case. Not until the mid-eighties was there transparency in key oil-related economic factors such as prices, production, shipping, refining, and so on. Naturally, some aspects of this are today regarded as industrial secrets by producers and other actors in the market.

16. This could be viewed as a part of the information problem, as it is a question of information about other actors' future compliance with agreements. The fact that it is a question of *future* behavior makes monitoring, for the purposes of this chapter, a different issue from the aspects of information discussed in the subsection above on OPEC as an information agency.

17. Below, an illustration is presented of the respondents' choice between the following political programs, presented in two different, but substantially equal, ways:

Case 1	Unemployment	Inflation	Case 2	Employment	Inflation
Program J	10%	12%	Program J	90%	12%
Program K	5%	17%	Program K	95%	17%

In case 1, 36 percent chose program J and 64 percent program K. In case 2, 54 percent chose program J and 46 percent program K (Quattrone and Tversky 1988:727). In case 1, the difference in unemployment is perceived as increasing costs, while in case 2, the difference in employment is perceived as a reduction in gains.

18. For instance, it is impossible to decide which case is more true in note 17.

19. As will be explained in Chapter 7, this price-production relationship was perceived differently among the OPEC countries because of fundamental differences in their production capacities, reserves, and income needs.

20. As Figure 3.2 shows, since the Ministerial Monitoring Committee was established in 1988, it is obvious that it was the Market Monitoring Committee that the president of the Conference had in mind.

21. "Members of the Committee expressed some concern about certain member countries' 'overproduction' relative to their ceilings, it being made clear by the Venezuelan Minister of Energy and Mines that his country (which had to turn away buyers in order to abide by its own production ceiling) would feel free to disregard that ceiling if such violations continued" (Evans 1990:605).

5

Price and Production Policy of OPEC Countries

The previous three chapters have studied constraints on the oil-related behavior of OPEC members. This chapter focuses on the behavior of states themselves, or, more precisely, on the interaction between oil producers. In line with the multilevel approach outlined in section 1.4, the following four chapters represent studies of the interaction of states.

The following discussion of the price and production policy of the OPEC members are organized into three periods.[1]

1. The first period starts with the TehranTripoli agreements of 1971 and lasts until the eve of the second oil-price shock around 1981. In this period *price-setting* dominated OPEC policy and cooperation (see section 5.1).

2. The second period centers on the *establishment of the quotas* in 1982–83 and the following swing-producer policy of Saudi Arabia until 1985. This period is of crucial importance for understanding both the mistakes of the past and the future behavior of OPEC (see section 5.2).

3. The third period is from 1986 to present. The key problem in this period is the *managing of the quota system*, causing OPEC countries to abandon the ambition to set the oil price (see section 5.3).

As mentioned, the discussion is based on cartel theory, which will be described and related to the case of OPEC in Chapter 7. It should be emphasized that in this chapter only internal aspects of the price decisions are relevant. The aspects of price increase that are connected with the relationship between the oil producers and other market actors were discussed in Chapter 2. Thus, the first oil shock is less relevant to the discussion in this chapter. Aspects relating to the relationship between oil producers inside and outside of OPEC are discussed in Chapter 8.

5.1   The Redundant Cartel: OPEC Price Policy, 1971–1981

The First Oil-Price Shock

The Tehran-Tripoli agreements of 1971 implied a 21 percent price increase for Saudi Arabian crude (from $1.80 to $2.18) and an increase in revenue of 38.9 percent. What was more important, however, was that the producer countries gained control over the price-setting (see section 2.4). In the early seventies there was a desire among radical Arab powers to use oil as a weapon against Israel, particularly through the United States' increased dependence on imported oil from OPEC. This idea was not a new one. As early as 1948, supplies of oil to consumer countries were stopped in connection with the conflict between Israel and the Arab countries. The same happened in 1956 and 1967 (Schneider 1983:212). Foremost among advocates of this policy were Iraq, Algeria, and Libya. The only country in opposition was an important one—Saudi Arabia (see section 6.3).

The decision to increase oil prices after the oil embargo of October 1973 was not an OPEC decision, but one reached by OPEC members individually (and to some extent by the OAPEC countries), or by some kind of tacit cooperation between OPEC members. The organization, OPEC, was not the key instrument for facilitating the price increase. It was probably not even necessary, as the countries most likely would have behaved in the same way without any institutional constraints on their behavior (see Chapter 4). Nor is it necessary to have an institutional arrangement like OPEC to make oil producers increase prices as long as their individual production can be sustained at the same level with the new higher price. "OPEC, therefore, found itself, largely by accident, with a price of $11 instead of $5" (Skeet 1988:150). OPEC did make some reluctant members, particularly Saudi Arabia, follow along, and restrained others, such as Iraq and Algeria, from increasing prices even further.

The Two-Tier Price Structure

Although oil consumption was regarded as inelastic, the market experienced a slowdown in demand after the price increases of 1973–1974. The OPEC countries had to absorb it all, and their production fell by 3.5 mbd from 1974 to 1975. The industrialized economies experienced an economic recession creating high rates of inflation. This reduced the value of the price increase, causing some OPEC members to call for further price increases. Saudi Arabia, which had reluctantly agreed to the 1973 embargo, was strongly opposed to further price increases. "Having devoted much of 1974 to the adjustment of the fiscal relationship between host governments and foreign concession . . . the OPEC countries were faced in 1975 with the need to adjust the official selling prices. . . . Against this background, attention focused on the relative market shares of the different members of the Organization" (Evans 1990:466). In 1975, Saudi Arabia produced above 7 mbd and Iran produced 5.3 mbd. Their combined production constituted more than 40 percent of total OPEC production. At an extraordinary meeting of the OPEC Conference from September 24 to 27, 1975, Iran advocated a price increase of 15 to 20 percent, while Saudi Arabia argued for a price freeze. A 10 percent increase was agreed upon for the next twelve months. When the OPEC members met in May 1976, the organization's Economic Commission had estimated that to compensate for inflation the price would have to be raised by another 20 percent. Eight countries favored a price increase: Iraq, Libya, Nigeria, Iran, Gabon, Qatar, Indonesia, and Ecuador. Three countries proposed a 10 percent increase: Algeria, Kuwait, and Venezuela. Only one country opposed any price increase: Saudi Arabia. The decision was postponed until the meeting in Doha in December 1976. At the Doha meeting Saudi Arabia proposed a 5 percent increase, supported by the United Arab Emirates. The members did not agree, and the other countries increased their oil price by 15 percent, while Saudi Arabia and the United Arab Emirates increased theirs by only 5 percent. A two-tier price structure was thus established. After the meeting Saudi Arabian Oil Minister Sheik Ahmed Zaki Yamani threatened to increase production: "We will remove the production ceiling of 8.5 million barrels a day. We will damp the market—it means the whole structure of price will collapse all over the world" (cited in Terzian 1985:244). Saudi Arabian production did actually increase from 8.5 mbd in 1976 to 9.2 mbd in 1977.

In 1977 Iran, too, advocated a price freeze. When these two countries, which together accounted for a full 48 percent of OPEC's total production, opposed price increases, there was little the other countries could do. However, unexpected events were to play havoc with the oil market.

The Second Oil-Price Shock

The second oil-price revolution connected with OPEC occurred in 1979 and 1980. Again, this had less to do with OPEC than with individual OPEC members and reaction among the other market actors (such as the international oil companies). Moreover, to understand the internal OPEC process leading up to the quota decision in March 1982, one needs to understand the way OPEC handled the so-called second oil shock, that is, the effects on the international oil market of the Iranian revolution and the outbreak of the Iran-Iraq War (see section 3.3).

In January 1978, demonstrations began in the holy city Qom in Iran. In the course of October, 37,000 oil workers went out on strike, reducing Iran's oil production dramatically, from some 6 mbd in August 1978 to approximately 450,000 bd in February 1979. Production rapidly picked up to some 3 mbd, but this still meant a halving of Iran's production. After the shah left Iran in January 1979, the new regime threw out all foreign oil companies and personnel. It had no in-house expertise to handle the loss of pressure that occurred in several oil fields. The former production capacity of well above 6 mbd was not possible to regain without new investments.

Several OPEC countries had at that time a deficit in their trade balance, and pressed for an increase in OPEC's official selling price. Saudi Arabia, not wanting such a development, increased production from 8.4 to 10.4 mbd, a figure that approached or even exceeded sustainable production capacity. Moreover, most other OPEC countries were already producing at almost full capacity. Thus, the other OPEC countries were unable to prevent a further price rise by increased production, even if they had wanted to do so. With the disappearance of Iran's production, stocks increased tremendously as consumers ensured supplies in case of future shortage:[2]

> The rush to build inventories by oil companies, reinforced by consumers, resulted in an additional three million barrels per day of "demand" above actual consumption. When added to the two million barrels per day of net lost supplies, the outcome was a total shortfall of five million barrels per day, which was equivalent to about 10 percent of consumption. (Yergin 1991:687)

This pushed the spot price sky-high. When the Iranians went on strike on October 13, 1978, it took only five days to bring the Iranian oil production to a complete standstill (Terzian 1985:257). However, the National Iranian Oil Company (NIOC) managed to continue selling oil off its stocks on the international market for some months. At the same time, Saudi Arabia and some other OPEC countries increased their sales of oil, filling the gap left by the Iranian shortfall (see Figure 5.1). Therefore, there was no actual physical shortage of crude oil during the rest of 1978. However, the market actors perceived a shortage as the price began to climb already in October 1978. In January 1979, the Iranian oil sales came to an end. Total OPEC production fell accordingly to 28.4 mbd, 3.6 mbd less than in September 1978. The spot market price increased rapidly, as Figure 2.12 shows. The OPEC countries increased their official prices following the increase in the spot price, although not to the same level. The discrepancy between spot and official prices was to some extent filled by different kinds of commissions and "black money" transfers to oil officials or authorities in the different producing countries (Terzian 1985:263–265).

As the events evolved in the first months of 1979, OPEC, on February 21, 1979, summoned an extraordinary meeting of the Conference on March 26.[3] A week later, on February 28, the Secretariat issued another statement: "Conference decisions in setting crude oil prices do not prevent Member Countries from making an upward adjustment in light of their prevailing circumstances. . . . In the present circumstances, the actions of Member Countries in exercising their sovereign rights can not be construed as prejudicing the solidarity and unity of OPEC" (OPEC 1990:163). At the meeting on March 26, the marker crude price was raised from $13.335/barrel to $14.546/barrel from April 1. At this time the spot price was above $20/barrel. But the Conference confirmed the above statement regarding upward price adjustments: "Besides this adjustment [the changed marker crude], it is left for each Member Country to add to its price market premia which it deems justifiable in the light of its own circumstances" (OPEC 1990:164). The Conference also made an appeal to the consuming countries to restrain the international oil companies: "the Conference calls upon all consuming countries to take such measures as to prevent oil companies from charging them prices beyond the price decided upon by the OPEC Conference" (OPEC 1990:164).

This shows that the organization did not have any measures available to curb the upward pressure on the oil price. While the OPEC members were free to add to the agreed prices as they saw fit, the organization called upon the consumers and companies to hold back the price escalation. A working cartel has to be able to counter a price increase with increased production, as well as to cut production when the price falls. The 1979 OPEC decision referred to above shows the organization's inability to handle a situation where the oil price increased rapidly.

Different authors emphasize different factors explaining the severity of the second oil crisis. Terzian (1985:261) suggests that statements by James Schlesinger, the US Energy Secretary, added to and substantially aggravated the crisis. Yergin (1991:686–687) emphasizes the stock-building as an important factor making the crisis more severe: "if companies thought that prices were going to go up, they bought more of today's cheaper barrels so that they would have to buy less of tomorrow's more expensive oil. And that was what happened, with extraordinary vengeance and fury, in the panic of 1979 and 1980." Levy (1982:1000) emphasizes the lack of coherent political action on behalf of the importing countries. Neither nationally nor internationally, through the International Energy Agency (IEA), did the consuming countries' governments try to restrict the price

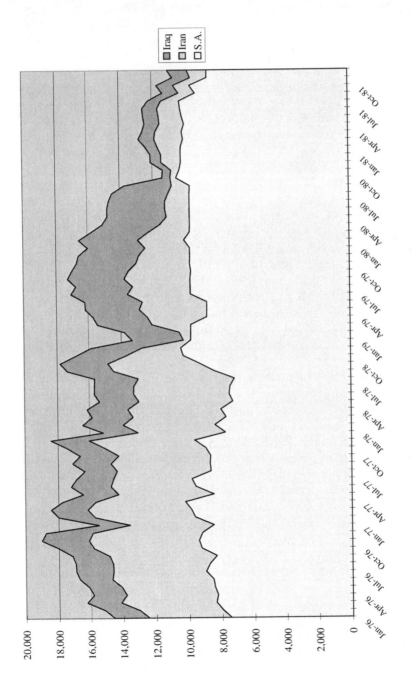

FIGURE 5.1   Iranian, Iraqi, and Saudi Arabian monthly production, 1976–1981 (th. b/d)
SOURCE: *Petroleum Economist*, various issues.

increase or the panic-buying behavior of the oil companies. "While it is, of course, not certain whether any national or international arrangements, had they been made, would have succeeded, in actual fact nothing was even attempted to stem the tide of upward-spiraling prices. It would appear that most of the wounds of 1979 have been self-inflicted" (Levy 1982:1000). Former Saudi Arabian Oil Minister Sheik Ahmed Zaki Yamani, in hindsight, views the events as follows: "Throughout 1979 continued high demand in the west and the peak prices being paid on the spot markets were creating chaos. Oil companies were rushing in to buy. But this was not oil they needed. It was for storage. I asked myself why and the only possible answer was that they thought there could be a total cut-off in oil exports from Iran. . . . So there was all this panic buying" (cited in Robinson 1988:215). He suggests that the solution would have been for the consuming countries' governments to forbid the oil companies to trade in the spot market.

An effective cartel organization would also have been able to prevent the crisis, as it could have prohibited sales at prices higher than what would clear the market. As it turned out, only Saudi Arabia stood firm on official prices and traded mostly in the contract market, but the OPEC Conference did not limit the upward price movement, so the organization did not play any vital part in this respect.

In May 1979, Iran was again selling oil on the international market (see Figure 5.1). The physical shortage had lasted only four months. OPEC met again in June 1979. Although Saudi Arabia had changed its position and was willing to agree to a price adjustment ($18/barrel), the other countries wanted far more. The compromise was the following arrangement:

> In an endeavor to bring some stability to the market, the Conference decided on the following: 1. To adjust the marker crude price from the present level to US$ 18 per barrel. 2. To allow Member Countries to add to the price of their crude a maximum market premium of US$ 2 per barrel over and above their normal differential, if and when such a market premium was necessitated by market conditions. 3. That the maximum prices that can be charged by Member Countries shall not exceed US$ 23.50 per barrel, whether on account of quality and location advantage or market premia. (OPEC 1990:165)

Ian Skeet (1988:160) concludes that "in terms of price management these two meetings of OPEC were an admission that they neither had, nor wished to have, any control. *Carte blanche* was given, or taken, to obtain the highest possible price. The inclusion of a ceiling price in the June communiqué was a weak effort to restrain the worst excesses of price greed, but it had no practical effect." The world obviously looks different to different authors, as Terzian (1985:269) reads the same events as follows: "This 'ceiling price' was quite a development. . . . in this month of June 1979, OPEC was not only not shoring up prices, it was actually holding them down by imposing a 'ceiling.'" It is, however, hard to find any evidence that the ceiling price had any effect whatsoever on OPEC members' behavior. Skeet's interpretation seems more adequate.

In September 1979, the private oil companies increased their stocks, a step that led to a new upward movement of spot prices. This was followed by non-OPEC countries, which increased their contractual prices by adding substantial surcharges to their selling prices (Terzian 1985:271). In October 1979, the OPEC countries started breaking the ceiling of the June meeting, increasing their selling prices. On November 4, the US Embassy in Tehran was occupied, and a hostage-taking crisis evolved, followed by a full US economic boycott of Iran. On November 20, 100 Muslim fundamentalists occupied the Al-Haram al Sharif Mosque in Mecca. It took the Saudi government two weeks to get them out. The stability of the Saudi regime was called into question, adding to the instability of the oil-market situation. The OPEC meeting in Caracas in late December 1979 displayed a conflict between Saudi Arabia and the United Arab Emirates on one side and Iran and the African producers on the other, with Venezuela and Kuwait trying to mediate (Terzian 1985:275). Saudi Arabia would not accept any official price higher than $26/barrel, while Iran would not accept any price lower than $32/barrel. The meeting did not resolve the differences, and the OPEC ministers left without any agreement. Yamani warned that the OPEC production, at that time 3 mbd greater than before the Iranian revolution, was creating a glut in the market. There was no increase in the underlying demand, so the increased production went into building of inventories. When the oil companies felt more secure against future supply disruptions, these barrels would come onstream. Yamani predicted a price fall: "I knew for sure that the oil held in stock would eventually come back onto the market as a source of supply" (cited in Robinson 1988:216). Before leaving Caracas, Yamani declared, "There will be a surplus of oil on the market: the prices will fall" (cited in Terzian 1985:275).

In January 1980, Libya increased its oil price by $4/barrel. Saudi Arabia increased its oil price by $2/barrel to align its price with those of the other OPEC members. This failed, as the others immediately increased their prices by the same $2/barrel (Terzian 1985:275). The same happened in May 1980, bringing the official Saudi Arabian price up to $30/barrel. In the second half of 1980, the increase in spot prices came to a halt. So did the increases in the official prices of the OPEC countries. The ministers met in Vienna in the middle of September. With OPEC's twentieth anniversary coming up, it seemed a good time to standardize prices.

Saudi Arabia once more increased its price by \$2/barrel, and this time the others remained unchanged. A summit of heads of state was scheduled for November 4 in Baghdad, with the prospect of a renewal of the organization. It was never to take place, since, on September 22, 1980, the Iran-Iraq War broke out (see section 3.3).

The outbreak of this war did not affect the oil market in the same manner as did the revolution in Iran. At the time the war broke out, there was a supply surplus in the market of about 2 mbd. The outbreak of war led to a reduction in both countries' production of some 4 mbd, leaving only 2 mbd of actual shortage. This was easily replaced by other OPEC and non-OPEC countries' production increases. The main economic consequence for the oil market was the more lasting disappearance of production capacity of some 3 to 5 mbd (Bjørk 1988).

The exceptionally high oil price accelerated the drop in consumption. This brought OPEC production down (Figure 5.2). On December 15, 1980, the OPEC Conference met in Bali, with representatives of the two warring countries attending. A substantial surplus had emerged in the market, even with Iran and Iraq at war. At the same time, several OPEC countries used the political situation to increase their selling prices. This caused Saudi Arabia to use its idle production capacity as a threat, in order to achieve its long-sought goal of a unified price structure.

A Unified Price Structure

Saudi Arabia, at the time producing above 10 mbd, refused to lower its production unless the other countries lowered their prices. Saudi Arabia was creating the surplus situation to force the other countries to lower their prices. This conflict continued at OPEC's next meeting in Geneva in May 1981. The press release issued after the meeting read as follows: "The Conference . . . decided to maintain the deemed marker crude price at a ceiling of US\$ 36/b with a maximum OPEC price of US\$ 41/b until the end of the year. The majority of Member Countries decided to cut production by a minimum of 10 percent, effective 1st June, 1981" (OPEC 1990:194). Saudi Arabia refused, and Iran and Iraq were excluded from the production cuts as they needed money for their warfare. Although Nigeria, Venezuela, Kuwait, and Qatar cut their production by more than 10 percent, the market was still in a surplus situation. Saudi Arabia continued to produce about 10 mbd, making buyers switch from the more expensive sellers to Saudi Arabia, which, as in past years, kept its prices well below the others. The official selling price of Nigerian oil was at this time \$40/barrel, and the Saudi Arabian price was \$32/barrel. Subsequently, some of the other OPEC members experienced an imposed cut in production, as there were no buyers for

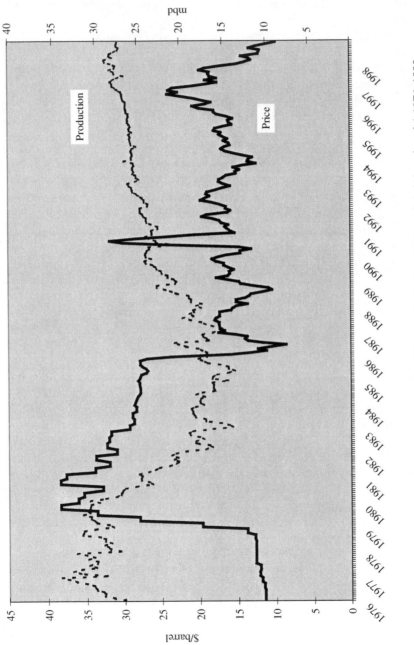

FIGURE 5.2   OPEC production (mbd, right-hand scale) and spot prices ($/barrel, left-hand scale) 1976–1998
SOURCE: *Petroleum Economist; OPEC Bulletin*, various issues.

their crude oil. Terzian (1985:288) puts these forced cuts in production at 30 percent for Algeria, 40 percent for Kuwait, and 50 percent for Nigeria (all 1981 figures).

In August it became known that Nigeria was giving the buyers a $3 discount, and thereby de facto reducing the selling price. The oil ministers were summoned to a consultative meeting in Geneva, August 19 to 21, with the intention to convert the meeting into a full conference if they reached an agreement. A unified price was the obvious goal of the meeting. A compromise of $35/barrel was put on the table, and eleven countries agreed. Iran refused and demanded $36/barrel, while Saudi Arabia insisted on $34/barrel. The meeting ended without any decision. However, the problems got worse. With reduced demand for OPEC oil, and the indecisiveness of the OPEC meeting, the companies foreseeing lower prices started to reduce their stocks of oil. By the same logic when prices increased, there was no reason to keep large stocks in a surplus market with falling prices. The destocking increased the downward pressure on the OPEC official prices. By October even the high-price countries agreed that it was necessary to have a united OPEC. An extraordinary meeting of the Conference, held on October 29, 1981, decided as follows: "The Conference . . . recognizing the necessity to adopt a unified pricing system for OPEC crude . . . has resolved to set the official price of the marker crude at US$ 34 per barrel" (OPEC 1990:199). This decision was exactly the same as the Saudi Arabian proposal in Geneva two months earlier.

This marked the end of this period. At last the Saudi Arabian fight for a unified OPEC price structure had succeeded. However, the reason for the other countries' abidance was not any kind of organizational discipline or the negotiating skills of the Saudis. It was the market forces of reduced demand for OPEC oil, which left the countries with no other options. There was therefore no "role of OPEC" in the process until 1981, in the sense that the states' price and production behavior in the market was a result of institutional factors or collective action. The increase in the oil price in the first half of the seventies was a result of individual countries' utilizing the opportunities the market created (see Chapter 2). The market conditions were such that the actions performed by the members of OPEC would most likely have been the same without the presence of the organization.

The period between 1978 and 1981, when the market changed, created conflict among the OPEC members, and the collective action in 1981 creating a new unified price structure was also a result of the market forces. But by then there was a change in OPEC's role in the international oil market. While the market forces continued to press the price down, the

OPEC countries, having experienced this second oil shock, had to cut back production to sustain prices. This activated the second and third aspects of cartel theory outlined in section 7.2—the determination of a production level for the group and the allocation of output among the members of OPEC.

5.2   The Effective Cartel: OPEC Quota Policy, 1982–1985

The March 1982 Decision

The OPEC decision of October 1981 was not sufficient to keep prices at $34/barrel. As can be seen from Figure 2.12, the spot price then was below the official price and thus pressed prices down, in the same way as the spot market had increased prices during the Iranian revolution just three years earlier. Instead of surcharges, discounts became the order of the day.

At the Arab Energy Conference in Doha on March 6, 1982, Yamani said, "Destocking has reached unprecedented levels: my experts estimate it at 4 million barrels a day. . . . We have to take an initiative. There can be no question of altering the price structure it took us so much trouble to set up again: on the other hand, my country is prepared to make an effort in terms of production" (quoted in Terzian 1985:296).

Two weeks later an extraordinary OPEC conference was held in Vienna. The press release from the Sixty-third OPEC Conference read as follows: "After having examined the current market situation, it was decided by the Conference to reconfirm the price of the Marker Crude, Arabian Light, 34 API, ex-Ras Tanura, at $34 per barrel . . . and to take the necessary measures for stabilizing the market. For this purpose it was decided that, as of April 1, 1982, the total OPEC production will have a ceiling of 18 million b/d. This ceiling will be reviewed at the next Meeting of the Conference in the light of market developments" (OPEC 1990:202). Thus, the price target was kept intact while the production was cut. Saudi Arabia was not given an exact quota, but was to act as a swing producer. Saudi Arabia also unilaterally cut another 500,000 b/d shortly after the meeting "in order to emphasize that this cut—like all Saudi production decisions—was regarded as a sovereign act outside the formal scope of any OPEC agreement" (Evans 1990:601).

Although the international oil companies tried to put pressure on the country they perceived to be the weak link in the chain—Nigeria[4]—the unity of OPEC was more solid than ever before. The trouble was that OPEC perceived the problems to be temporary. Demand continued to be weak. Having to live with temporary production restraints was tolerable, but having to face such quotas for the foreseeable future and simultaneously having to cut prices was very difficult. As Figure 5.2 indicates, although OPEC reduced production substantially in the first half of the eighties, the price did not pick up. On the contrary, it continued to slide. The quota system had come to stay, and reduction of official prices was unavoidable. Several OPEC members had already lived with the situation of being unable to sell all the oil produced, and thus being forced to cut back on production. From their point of view, it would be preferable to let OPEC decide this rather than leave it in the hands of the buyers. The stage was set for a review of the internal OPEC bargaining over production quotas. One could expect the organization to have been instrumental in setting up criteria for the allocation of production quotas. The fact is that the initial quotas of March 1982 were not based on any criteria at all:

> When the production programme was adopted for the first time in 1982, it was not based on a careful study by OPEC, in light of each Member Country's position in the world market and its oil and development potential. Neither was the quota system based on certain objective criteria which could be accepted by all. Subsequent attempts to identify such criteria show that there are hardly any on which Member Countries uniformally [sic] agree. The system was first established as a result of negotiations made more or less on the spur of the moment and influenced, to a great extent, by Member Country production levels which prevailed at the time. (Al-Chalabi 1989:25–26)

Contrary to what Fadhil Al-Chalabi claims, even the criterion of present production was only to some extent determining the first quota distribution. Figure 5.3 shows the previous production and the relationship between it and the initial quotas of March 1982. If there had been an equal percentage cut, the line would be flat; if there had been an understanding that large producers should get a disproportionately larger cut, the line would follow the columns in the figure. No such correlation exists.[5]

At the moment the quotas were established, the allocation was disputed. Iran did not accept the 1.2 mbd quota allocated at the March 1982 meeting. The country had the intention of increasing its oil production to 3 mbd "whatever the cost" (Iranian Oil Minister Mohammed Gharazi, quoted in Terzian 1985:301). The war with Iraq created a need for income, and the National Iranian Oil Company (NIOC) was ordered to sell as much oil as possible, at any price. "Oil was sold on the spot market at prices $4 or $5 below the official price for the equivalent Saudi crude" (Terzian 1985:302). Iraq was hindered from following the same policy, as its production capacity was reduced to about the quota level by Iranian attacks on shipments through the Persian Gulf and because Syria cut off the pipeline to the Mediterranean. Iran was able to increase its production capacity and thus violated the quota agreement.

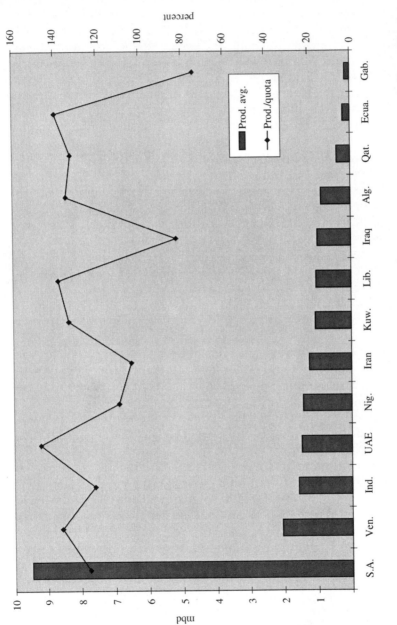

FIGURE 5.3 Average production, January 1981–March 1982 (mbd, left-hand scale), and production over March 1982 quota (percent, right-hand scale)

SOURCE: *Petroleum Economist.*

At the Sixty-fifth OPEC Conference in July 1982, Iran "demanded a quota of 2.5 m b/d and that its increase should be taken from the Saudi share" (Skeet 1988:188). Iran did not abide by its quota in the following months. The statement issued by the GCC countries after the oil ministers' meeting in Salala on October 14 illustrates this: "The producers should know that the GCC Ministers expect them to shoulder their responsibilities and if they continue their misguided actions they will not be protected by the member countries from the GCC from the consequences of these actions" (Skeet 1988:189). In his opening address at the following OPEC meeting, the chairman of the Nigerian delegation, Alhaji Yahaya Dikko, with clear reference to the above statement, said that "threats are never a basis for cooperation" (Evans 1990:607). The Conference decided that the total quota for 1983 should be 18.5 mbd, but the Conference was unable to agree on the allocation of national quotas. Thus, the 18.5 mbd ceiling was not convincing to the market actors.

By the time of the OPEC Conference in December 1982, the market did not have sufficient room for 18.5 mbd of OPEC crude. Several other producing countries had increased their production in the times of high prices, and there was nothing stopping these non-OPEC countries from producing at full capacity. Although the total production was set at 18.5 mbd, adding the individual quota claims at the December 1982 meeting would give a figure of about 23.5 mbd. Iran claimed a quota of 3.2 mbd and called for a cut in Saudi Arabian production to below 5 mbd. Iran also argued that the following criteria should guide the establishment of national production quotas: (i) historical output levels, (ii) size of oil reserves, (iii) size of population, and (iv) extent of current economic and social needs (Evans 1990:607). Venezuela argued for a national quota of "at least 2.1 mbd . . . Libya not less than 1.3" (Terzian 1985:310). Iraq argued for a quota increase equal to whatever Iran obtained (Evans 1990:607) or the historical level of 10 percent of OPEC production, which meant 2.3 mbd (Terzian 1985:310).[6] The United Arab Emirates demanded a quota of 1.35 mbd. The December meeting ended with a decision that "OPEC production for the year 1983 should not exceed 18.5 million b/d. However, an agreement of establishing national quotas for the distribution of that total amount would require further consultations among the respective Governments. . . . every effort should be made by each Member Country to preserve the price structure and to stabilize the market conditions" (OPEC 1990:206). In fact, there was no institutional pressure on the individual member countries to abide by the 18.5 mbd production ceiling; still, the previously agreed price level was sustained. In a declining market, this obviously could not hold for long. The price on the spot market fell, while at the same time OPEC members began to relate contract crude to the spot price (see section 2.6).

The 1983 Revision of the Quota Agreement

At a GCC meeting on January 15, 1983, it was decided to hold a consultative meeting of the OPEC oil ministers in Geneva on January 23 and 24. This meeting was a failure; not even a press release was issued. There was no reason for Yamani or the Saudi Arabians to bear the political costs of pressing for a price reduction, as they were convinced that the market, or, more correctly, the non-OPEC producers, would do it for them in the following months, if not weeks. On February 18, the British National Oil Corporation (BNOC) reduced its price from $33.5/barrel to $30.5/barrel. Nigeria had to follow suit and cut its price to $30; "they also made clear that they would match cent for cent any UK price cut below $30" (Skeet 1988:191). Yamani wanted a $4 cut in the marker crude price from $34 to $30. Now, with the Nigerian oil at $30, the marker would have to go below that level due to the different quality of the oil. "This was the situation when OPEC began a series of consultative meetings in Riyadh, Geneva, Paris, and, finally, London. The London meeting lasted twelve days, with only the last hours on March 14 transformed into an official Extraordinary Conference, OPEC's 67th" (Skeet 1988:191).

The Conference resolved:

1. To set the official price of the Marker crude . . . at US $29 per barrel.
2. To maintain the existing differentials among the various OPEC crudes at the same level as agreed upon at the 63rd (Extraordinary) Meeting . . . with the temporary exception that the differentials for the Nigerian crudes should be US$1 over the price of the Marker Crude.
3. To establish a ceiling for the total OPEC production of 17.5 million barrels per day, within which individual Member Country quotas were allocated. This ceiling is to be observed as an average for the remaining part of 1983. No quota is allocated to the Kingdom of Saudi Arabia which will act as a swing producer to supply the balancing quantities to meet market requirements.
4. The Member Countries shall avoid giving discounts in any form whatsoever and refrain from dumping petroleum products into the world oil market at price which will jeopardize the crude oil pricing structure. The Conference agreed that the recommended oil prices are floor prices and the national production quotas are ceiling figures. (OPEC 1990:208)

As seen in Table 7.6, Iran obtained a doubling of its quota at the March 1983 meeting, while Kuwait, Libya, and Venezuela obtained substantial increases. The March 1983 agreement was to last longer than the March

1982 decision. As the ceiling was an average for the whole of 1983, it is worth noting that during the first half of 1983 the total OPEC production was well below the 17.5 mbd ceiling, while the second half pushed production above this level, as Figure 5.2 indicates. Most OPEC members cheated either on the price floor or on the production quota. This led to new pressure on the agreed price level. The Saudi Arabian buildups of floating stocks especially created downward pressure on prices.[7] The OPEC Market Monitoring Committee tried to impose some discipline on the member countries, but was especially attacked by the Saudi Arabians, who tolerated no interference in their oil policy.

Although the conflict between Iran and Saudi Arabia surfaced at the OPEC meeting in December 1983,[8] the quotas were not changed until the autumn of 1984. At an extraordinary meeting from October 29 to 31, the price floor of $29/barrel was defended, but the total production quota was reduced by 1.5 mbd from November 1 (OPEC 1990:220). Just days before the meeting, Norway had cut its oil price (see section 9.2). The focus was thus more on conflict between outside producers and OPEC than on internal OPEC disagreements (see Chapter 8).

Saudi Arabia: Swinging Low

OPEC's October 1984 decision and Saudi Arabia's actions as a swing producer during 1984 and 1985 created fairly stable prices in this period (see Figure 5.2). However, Saudi Arabia had to cut back on its production to sustain prices. This policy was impossible to maintain indefinitely. The Saudi oil production fell simultaneously with the prices. The loss of market share also gave Saudi Arabia a more marginal role in world politics and in Middle Eastern affairs (see Chapter 6). The characteristic feature of this period was that OPEC was able to counter the downward pressure on prices. There was definitely a "role of OPEC" in this period, as the market outcome would most likely have been different without the organization. However, underlying the organization's role in this period was the willingness of Saudi Arabia to bear the costs of performing as a benevolent hegemon. It was Saudi Arabia that cut its own production to sustain prices. Looking only at the market behavior, it is thus fair to conclude that the "role of OPEC" was to a large extent the role of Saudi Arabia (see section 6.4). This would, however, miss the indirect effect of the organization. Without the institutional framework established within the OPEC organization, it is less likely that Saudi Arabia would have followed the strategy it did. Without any quotas, the role as swing producer would have been meaningless. The fact that the strategy did not succeed for longer than a few years is due to a combination of structural factors (developed in Chapter 2) and the OPEC decisions. The price target of $32

(later, $29) was too high given the increased (long-term) demand elastic-
ity and the increased number of non-OPEC producers following a competitive strategy. We are back to the interaction between market structure
and market behavior emphasized in Chapter 2. It is briefly summarized
by the following contemporary comment:

> The story of the rise and fall of OPEC is starkly illustrated in what has been
> happening to oil prices and to shifting supply and demand in the world
> market. The falling oil cartel, like virtually every cartel before it, committed
> the blunder of setting its monopoly price too high. This simultaneously
> called for vast supplies from outside producers that the cartel could not con-
> trol, and eventually induced conservation by consumers. [9]

In the summer of 1985 there were definite signs that the Saudi Arabians would no longer accept production beyond the quotas by other OPEC
countries, as long as they themselves produced only half their quota.[10] In
October Saudi Arabia shifted policy and increased production by introducing the so-called netback pricing system (see section 2.6). This led to
considerable over-production in the market and heavy pressure on spot
prices, a circumstance several countries tried to compensate for by increasing production. In this atmosphere OPEC gathered for its meeting in
Geneva on 9 December, a meeting that was to change yet again the direction of development in the oil market.

5.3   The Defected Cartel: OPEC
Market-Share Policy, 1986–1998

OPEC Changes Market Strategy, 1985

At the meeting in Geneva in December 1985, OPEC resolved to change its
market strategy from the defense of a high oil price to the defense of the
OPEC countries' market shares. "Having considered the past and likely
future developments in the world oil market and the persistently declining trend of OPEC production, the Conference decided to secure and defend for OPEC a fair share in the world oil market consistent with the necessary income for Member Countries' development."[11]

The OPEC members drew just as much attention to the producers outside OPEC as to those within the organization who were failing to keep to
their quotas. Thus, strong complaints about non-members, and threats of
a price war against them, were expressed: "OPEC still harbors the hope
that other producers will cooperate in trying to maintain prices by curbing their output. But implicit in the communiqué issued yesterday is the
threat of a price war if they do not."[12] A confirmation of this intention

was given in a press release from Yamani some two months later: "When the OPEC member Conference, held in Geneva last December unanimously decided to secure and defend for the Organization a fair oil market share, speculative sales in the market began to push oil prices downward as it became clear to all that if non-OPEC member states did not revise their policies and give up some part of their market shares to OPEC, there would be a production surplus which would lead to a fall in oil prices."[13] The organization now had a twofold task – to ensure internal discipline and to increase the credibility and the perception of the seriousness of the threat posed by other oil producers.[14]

When Saudi Arabia first took on its role as a swing producer in 1982, the need for internal discipline eased. So did the importance of the monitoring committee (see section 4.3). However, as Saudi Arabia changed its market strategy in 1985, and the oil price fell in the spring of 1986, the need for internal discipline and monitoring institutions returned. As Figure 5.4 illustrates, the initial response of the other OPEC members was not to reduce production as a result of the Saudi Arabian threat. On the contrary, the other OPEC countries increased production during the spring of 1986 to compensate for the price fall. Nor did the non-OPEC countries change their policy as a result of the threat.

As described in Chapter 2, the price fell dramatically, and the world oil market was in a situation of a price war between all oil producers. The threat had failed (see Chapter 8 and section 9.3). At the December 1986 meeting of the OPEC Conference, a new accord was agreed upon for the first half of 1987. Now the price issue was resolved by the introduction of the OPEC basket. As the basket included several different OPEC oil qualities, the reference price was that of a composite of OPEC oil, rather than the single marker crude which had been used as a reference in the seventies. Furthermore, the price differentials were fixed, and a system for revision of price policy and monitoring was established. The reintroduction of Iraq to the quota system was discussed, but Iraq would not accept anything less than parity with the Iranian quota of 2.255 mbd as of January 1987. The previous Iraqi quota of October 1984 was 1.2 mbd. The deadlock was resolved when Iran dropped its demand that Iraq be given a binding quota, but Iran "made it clear that it reserved the right to reopen the issue if Iraq failed to respect a new 'deemed' quota" (Evans 1990:704).

Abandoning Quotas During the Iraq-Kuwait War

In July 1990 the Iraqi leader Saddam Hussein accused Kuwait of "stealing" oil from Iraq and demanded repayment, declaring that "Iraqis will never forget the maxim that cutting necks is better than cutting the means of living."[15] The Iraqi foreign minister wrote a letter to the secre-

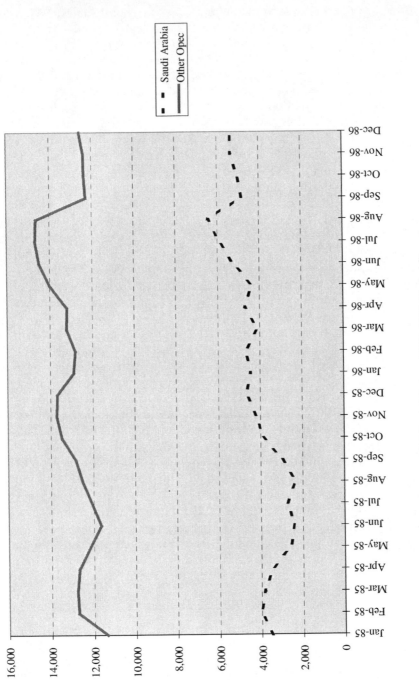

FIGURE 5.4   Saudi Arabian and other OPEC production, 1985–1986 (th. b/d)
SOURCE: Figures taken from *Petroleum Economist*.

TABLE 5.1   Regional Crude Supply Gains and Losses, August 8–October 20, 1990

			Importer			
Sources	*US*	*Europe*	*Japan*	*Asia*	*Other*	*Total*
Kuwait/Iraq (losses)	-1,170	-1,020	-480	-425	-385	-3,480
Others (gains)	+660	+830	+958	+622	+350	+3,420
Balance	-510	-190	+478	+197	-35	-60

SOURCE: *Petroleum Intelligence Weekly*, October 22, 1990.

tary-general of the Arab League, stating that he regarded the stealing as "a direct military attack on Iraq" and declaring the Iraqi "right to return all the money that was stolen from our oil fields."[16] After the Eighty-seventh OPEC Conference in July 1990, Iraq and Kuwait met for negotiations, which immediately broke down. A few days later, on August 2, Iraq invaded Kuwait and subsequently declared a "comprehensive, eternal and inseparable merger" between the two countries.[17] The UN Security Council declared a full boycott of Iraq and the new regime in Kuwait. This immediately brought to a halt all oil flows from the two countries. The oil price skyrocketed from $18/barrel to almost $30/barrel in a couple of days. On August 29, 1990, OPEC issued a press release stating that the organization would "consequently increase production, in accordance with need in order to maintain . . . market stability and regular supply of oil to consumers" (OPEC 1990:310). This implied an abandoning of the quota system until further notice (see section 3.4, where the implications of the Gulf War are discussed in greater detail).

Other producers, particularly Saudi Arabia, quickly filled the gap. There was no shortage of oil. After a few weeks the OPEC production was back at almost the prewar level. Some additional barrels from non-OPEC producers made the total market balance. Once again there was some degree of panic buying. The Japanese oil traders increased their purchases beyond the prewar level, creating a price rise as indicated in Table 5.1.

The disappearance of oil from Kuwait and Iraq eased the pressure on the OPEC quota system, especially the Saudi restraints. The continuous UN blockade of Iraq enabled the other OPEC countries to continue a high production policy without disrupting the oil price. The loss of Iraqi production was almost entirely covered by Saudi Arabia, as Table 5.2 shows.

Although the price fluctuated over the period, with substantial weakening in both 1988 and 1993, there is no obvious trend, neither upward nor downward, in the period from 1986 to 1996. When Saudi Arabia introduced its role as swing producer in 1984, the need to discipline the members through institutional mechanisms was reduced. The Iraq-

TABLE 5.2   Iraqi and Saudi Arabian Production (mbd), July 1990, and Average,
1991–1994.

	Saudi Arabia	Iraq	Total
July 1990	5,435	3,270	8,705
1991–1994	8,224	438	8,662
Change	+2,789	-2,832	

SOURCE: *Petroleum Economist.*

Kuwait War and the subsequent UN embargo against Iraq had the same effect. This gave the other OPEC producers room for increased production without risking a fall in oil prices, as the Iraqi production—3.2 mbd in July 1990—was kept at almost zero.

Muddling Through the 1990s

At the meeting of the Ministerial Monitoring Committee in February 1992, the quota allocations were reestablished, with Kuwait being allowed to produce as much as possible. Iraq was not allocated a quota but was included at its current production level. In January 1993, new quotas were set, including one for Kuwait (see Table 7.6).

The UN sanctions against Iraq continued to block regular Iraqi oil exports. The Security Council of the UN was in effect a part of the OPEC production sharing efforts, and a very abiding one as well, as the UN curbed an increase in Iraqi exports that would otherwise have taken place. In the spring of 1996 the UN and Iraqi authorities worked out an oil-for-food deal. Iraq was to be allowed to sell oil in order to pay for food and medicine under a UN-monitored distribution system. As the implementation of the deal seemed imminent, OPEC included Iraqi oil production of 1.2 mbd in the quota agreement of June 1996 (see Table 7.6). This created an increase in the total quota, as no other country cut back.[18] On December 10, Iraq resumed export of oil under the oil-for-food agreement with the UN. Weather conditions, low levels of stocks, and the fact that traders had anticipated the return of Iraq for several months made the immediate price effects negligible. The return of Iraq with a quota around the Iranian quota of 3.6 mbd would put the OPEC quota agreements under pressure. The reaction from Saudi Arabia would be most important, as it was the country that replaced the Iraqi oil on the market (see Table 5.2).

During the 1990s OPEC also experience two cases of members leaving the organization. In November 1992, the OPEC conference accepted the Ecuadorian suspension of membership effectively from January 1993.[19] In July 1996, the OPEC Conference accepted Gabon's termination of its membership effectively from January 1995.[20] Amuzegar (1999:56) describes the Ecuadorian dilemma as follows: "Facing an increasing need for foreign exchange and having a small crude output, Ecuador regularly exceeded its OPEC quotas, fell behind in its membership fees and finally left the organization as of January 1993."

What would be the reason for any country to leave OPEC? Given the prominent role of the production limitations in the internal OPEC bargains, it can be assumed that countries leaving the organization believe they will be able to increase production further outside OPEC than inside. Comparing the Ecuadorian production increase outside OPEC with the development of OPEC production in the same period, such a strategy seems to have been unsuccessful in that case. While the Ecuadorian production increased with 16.7 percent from 1992 to 1998, the OPEC countries increased their production with 17.9 percent in the same period. In the case of Gabon, which announced its intention to terminate its membership in 1994 a similar pattern can be observed. From 1994 to 1998, Gabon's oil production increased with 6 percent, while the OPEC production in the same period has increased with 13 percent. These two countries were large overproducers inside OPEC; measured in percentage of overproduction above allotted quotas, their small market shares made their lack of compliance a minor problem. These aspects will be discussed extensively in Chapter 7. The fact that most factors influencing the strategic market policies of oil-producing countries are the same for producers outside and inside of OPEC will be discussed in Chapters 8 and 9.

A more dramatic effect on the oil price followed the economic downturn in Asia in the autumn of 1997. The fall in demand following this recession implied a weaker, not stronger, market for OPEC crude. The sensible response would have been to cut production in order to balance the market at a lower level of demand. However, in November 1997, the OPEC countries increased the quotas. The Brent oil price fell from $19.88 per barrel in October 1997 to $13.11 per barrel in March 1998. When OPEC reduced the production ceiling again in March 1998, the new agreed production was not based on the quotas but on reduction from actual production the month before. Mabro (1998:10) argued that "OPEC [had] abandoned its production quota policy." Since the price policy was abandoned back in 1986, there was not much left of the market-governing role of OPEC. Mabro (1998:10) thus concluded that: "OPEC today has neither a price nor a quota policy."

In March 1998, an agreement on production reduction was initiated by Mexico, Venezuela, and Saudi Arabia. It was set to reduce production with more than one million barrels per day. The deal was immediately described as insufficient to bring the market in balance: "It holds out a reasonable promise of shrinking the global surplus of supply over demand . . . what it probably won't do is pull glutted world oil market back into balance overnight."[21] Iran, Indonesia, and Nigeria were not assumed to cut their production. Given its market share and political importance, getting Iran onboard became important. The Iranian foreign minister visited Saudi Arabia and got some concessions. More important was that this was a signal of possible future oil-related cooperation between the two countries.

In June 1998, prices dropped again. This put pressure on the producer cooperation. Now Saudi Arabia took the position than no new cuts should be initiated, unless compliance with the earlier agreement was above 90 percent.[22] In October 1998, a meeting of the so-called producer-consumer dialogue was held in Cape Town. Under the cover of this meeting the major oil exporters discussed further measures to strengthen prices without any concrete measures being taken.

The economic crisis in Asia, which began in the summer of 1997, had severe impact on the oil market. The Asian oil consumption constitutes above 25 percent of total world demand. While the demand of North America and Europe has been fairly stable during the 1980s and 1990s, the Asian demand has increased by more than 40 percent. "In 1998 . . . East Asian oil demand growth, which averaged 5.6% annually between 1990 and 1996, slowed sharply" (EIA 1999a). Instead of continued growth, the Asian demand fell marginally from 1997 to 1998. The economic growth in Asia was seen as "the motor for rising global demand for oil."[23] OPEC, like most analysts, did not foresee the depth and persistence of the Asian economic crisis. However, the decision of the OPEC Conference in November 1997 to increase quotas iced the price slide further. With the benefit of hindsight, it is easy to see that the right answer in late 1997 would have been to cut production, not increase it.

The Phoenix Cartel: 1999–2000

In March 1999, OPEC agreed on substantial cuts in production.[24] This agreement, and the fact that it was negotiated before the meeting blew new life into the organization: "By exceeding most assessments of the reduction required to balance markets, OPEC has clearly shown its determination not to repeat last year's series of cuts, which time again trailed the demand curve."[25] The meeting was over in ten minutes. A new negotiation strategy had been applied. Ministers from Algeria, Iran, Saudi Arabia, Venezuela, and non-OPEC country Mexico met two weeks before the OPEC conference and agreed on a 2 mbd production cut for OPEC and non-OPEC countries. The OPEC Conference was simply a confirmation of this agreement. Also, by June, the implementation of the March 1999 agreement seemed better than ever before. "OPEC's crude oil production figures for May have brought more good news for the producing countries, signaling a rise in the level of compliance with output cutbacks commitments by 10 OPEC member countries (excluding Iraq) to nearly 90% as compared with 87% in April."[26] Another aspect of the developments in 1999 was renewed talks about a firmer price target. In May, the Saudi Arabian Oil Minister Ali Naimi affirmed that Saudi Arabia was ready to defend a price target of $18 to $20 per barrel.[27] Later it was indicated that this strategy was gaining support by several producers, both inside and outside OPEC:

> A senior Gulf official who is familiar with Saudi oil policy has been quoted as affirming that members of OPEC together with some non-OPEC exporters are currently involved in consultations with a view to devising a strategy to stabilize crude oil prices in the range of $18–20 per barrel (for Brent) by intervening in the market whenever prices move outside the targeted band. . . . Saudi Arabia has taken a leading role in discussions with other OPEC and non-OPEC producers on this strategy. . . . OPEC members plus non-OPEC Mexico, Oman and Norway were involved in talks to agree on a mechanism for market intervention.[28]

Both regarding production and prices, the producer cooperation seemed strengthened compared to the bleak prospects in 1998. A long-time commentator on OPEC affairs, Ian Seymour, found the conference to be more "cordial than anything experienced for some years past" and that "there is now a pretty strong consensus . . . that defending prices and revenues is more important . . . than boosting export volumes in an already sated market."[29] Or, in the words of the Algerian Energy Minister Youcef Yousfi, acting president of OPEC: "OPEC is like a 'phoenix risen from the ashes.'"[30]

The renewed efforts in oil-producer cooperation, now including the non-OPEC producers Mexico, Russia, and Norway, paid off. By the summer of 2000, the oil price reached $30 per barrel. It had gone from $10 to $30 in eighteen months (see Figure 5.5).

With such a high price it becomes tempting for the individual producer to sell some extra barrels before the increased production from another producer weakens the market again. We are back at the classical collective action problem, which might be triggered once again among the oil producers. However, by mid-2000, many OPEC members lacked spare capacity. Thus it seemed impossible to increase production in the short run. The only country with substantial spare capacity installed was Saudi Arabia. Thus the underlying strength of the kingdom increased during the price rise of 1999–2000.

In March 2000, OPEC found the price to be too high to ensure a stable market development, and thus reversed the March 1999 production cuts

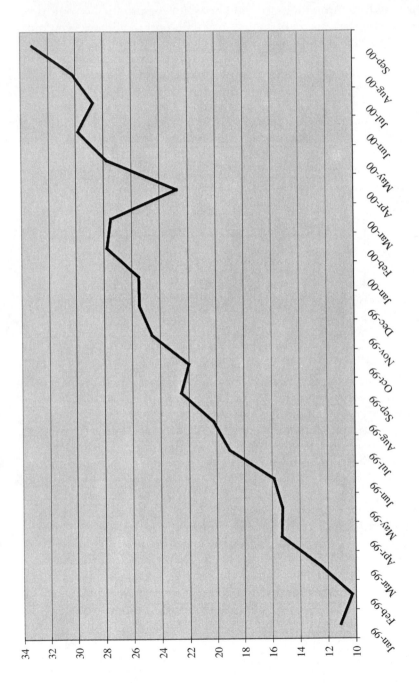

FIGURE 5.5   Brent oil price, January 1999–September 2000
SOURCE: EIA: Weekly Petroleum Status Report

of 1.7 mbd.[31] Iran disassociated itself from the agreement—primarily because the leadership in Tehran disliked the pressure exerted by the US government on the OPEC countries. As Figure 5.5 shows, the production increase had only a temporary effect on the oil price. Thus at the planned but still extraordinary Conference in June 2000, the quotas were raised further by 708,000 barrels per day (see Table 7.6).[32] This Conference also brought Iran formally back into the quota system. Although not explicitly and fully published officially, the two Conferences during the spring of 2000 developed an agreement on a price band mechanism. The agreement sets a target price of $25 per barrel and an obligation to increase production by 500,000 barrels per day if the price rises above $28 for twenty consecutive trading days and likewise decrease production if the price falls below $22 per barrel.[33] In July 2000, the OPEC Secretariat issued a statement in accordance with such an agreement.[34] This could be an instrument for tighter market governance by OPEC, but by the time of this writing (July 2000), it is hard to tell if this is the case. Furthermore, before the Secretariat's statement was published, the dominant OPEC member, Saudi Arabia, had unilaterally announced a 500,000 barrels per day increase of its own production (see section 6.6).

From OPEC's perspective, the world economic outlook by mid-2000 seemed good, as the Asian economies were recovering, and the already unprecedented sustainability of the US growth seemed to go on. These trends might easily turn around and surprise market analysts, as they tend to do. The present agreement among the OPEC members does, however, seem less dependent on increased demand than were previous agreements. The fact that several non-OPEC producers are included in the negotiations also reduces the probability that non-OPEC producers should capture the increased demand. It could be that OPEC is finally coming around to tackle the long-term challenges, as outlined by former Saudi Arabian oil minister Ahmad Zaki Yamani.

> Regarding the longer term, OPEC needs to develop a strategy that keeps oil prices constant in real terms at a level low enough to deter non-OPEC producers from adding to their reserves and keep worldwide oil demand growing at a healthy rate. What this level should be, of course, is open to vigorous debate, but whatever it is it should ensure that the demand for OPEC oil rises steadily to absorb its huge excess capacity—both at present and in the future.[35]

What can be safely concluded is that the political decisions made by the governments of the oil-producing countries regarding their willingness to enter into cooperative arrangements and abide by these agreements will continue to influence the future development of the oil price in the same way as the politics of oil producers have influence the price from 1971 until today. As of September 2000, OPEC will have existed for forty years. The organization has been declared dead or powerless again and again over these years. However, OPEC has always been able to rise from the ashes and recapture its control over the oil market. A primary reason for this is the never-ending ability of a particular country to take the lead. The next chapter is devoted to a case study of the role of this country in oil-producer cooperation.

Notes

1. The problems highlighted in one time period are to some extent present also in a subsequent period. The phases indicate only the time the particular problem was prominent. In the period from 1971 to 1982 the production level was subordinate to the price issue, and vice versa in the subsequent phase from 1982 to the present.

2. Yergin describes how the average gasoline tank of an American car is usually one-quarter full, but that in the days of the Iranian revolution US car drivers increased this figure to three-quarters (Yergin 1991:687).

3. The meeting was intended as a consultative meeting of the oil ministers of OPEC member countries, but was converted into a full conference "in view of the current situation and due to the important developments that have been taking place in the oil industry" (OPEC 1990:162–163).

4. Nigeria exports an oil quality similar to that of North Sea oil, and is thus exposed directly to competition from Britain and Norway. In March 1982, the companies refused to lift oil from Nigeria, referring to the official price as $5.5/barrel above that of the North Sea oil (Terzian 1985:298). After a plea for help from the Nigerian authorities, Yamani reacted, threatening that if the companies did not start lifting oil from Nigeria, they would not get oil from Saudi Arabia, and he persuaded the Kuwaiti minister, Ali Khalifa Al-Sabah, to do the same. The companies gave in after a few weeks.

5. Two countries (Iraq and Gabon) actually gained quotas exceeding their production levels from the previous period. In the case of Iraq, its production level obviously was a result of war damage, and the quota was accepted only on the condition that it would be revised upward to parity with that of Iran as soon as the Iraqi production capacity allowed it.

6. This was more a politically motivated claim, as the production capacity of Iraq was less than the existing quota.

7. In August 1983, Saudi Arabia set up a trading company in Switzerland called Norbec. This company hired oil tankers, filled them up with oil, and sent them to different locations outside the Persian Gulf. This was explained as a precaution if the Strait of Hormuz should be blocked in the ongoing war between Iran and Iraq. However, approximately 60 million barrels stocked at sea led market actors, not surprisingly, to perceive a supply surplus in the market (Terzian 1985:323–324).

8. The Iranian oil minister demanded an explanation of who had benefited from the price reduction of March 1983, and whether Saudi Arabia had conducted its role as swing producer properly (ibid.:325).

9. Leonard Silk, *International Herald Tribune*, March 12–13, 1983.

10. This is expressed particularly clearly in two interviews with Yamani in the Jeddah newspaper *Asharq al Awsat*, quoted in *Middle East Economic Survey*, June 3, 1985, and *Petroleum Intelligence Weekly*, June 17, 1985.

11. Press release from the Seventy-sixth OPEC Conference, quoted in *OPEC Bulletin*, December/January 1986. The resolution promptly triggered a price drop for crude of $3 in three days (*International Herald Tribune*, December 11, 1985). "The market has gone mad," an oil broker told *Aftenposten* (Oslo). "No serious oil expert dares to predict what the oil price will be tomorrow, next week, or in 1986" (*Aftenposten*, December 12, 1985).

12. *Financial Times*, December 10, 1985.

13. Press release from Yamani, cited in *OPEC Bulletin*, March 1986.

14. Some OPEC representatives threaten to retaliate if North Sea producers did not cut production. The only official Norwegian reaction was Oil Minister Kåre Kristiansen's statement to the Norwegian Broadcasting Company that Norway was unable to cut its oil production in the short-term as requested by the organization.

15. *Platt's Week*, July 23.

16. Ibid.

17. *International Herald Tribune*, August 10, 1990.

18. Gabon left the organization in 1996 (formally, from January 1, 1995) and thus was no longer included in the quota distribution.

19. "The Conference regretfully accepted the wish of Ecuador to suspend its full membership in the Organization. However, recognizing the current economic constraints facing that country, the Conference hopes that Ecuador will be able to overcome these difficulties and rejoin the Organization in the not too distant future." Ninety-second Meeting of the Conference press release no. 9/92—Vienna, Austria, November 27, 1992.

20. "The Conference has taken note of the notice submitted by Gabon on 20 December 1994, and considers Gabon's Membership in the Organization terminated as of 1 January 1995, in accordance with Article 8 of the Statute" Resolution No 100.350, July 7, 1996.

21. *Petroleum Intelligence Weekly*, March 30, 1998.

22. *Petroleum Intelligence Weekly*, August 3, 1998.

23. *Petroleum Economist* April 1999:2.

24. Press release from the 107th OPEC Conference, Vienna, March 23, 1999.

25. *Petroleum Intelligence Weekly*, March 29, 1999.

26. *Middle East Economic Survey*, June 14, 1999.

27. *Middle East Economic Survey*, May 17, 1999.

28. *Middle East Economic Survey*, June 14, 1999.

29. *Middle East Economic Survey*, March 29, 1999.

30. *Middle East Economic Survey*, March 29, 1999.

31. Press release from the 109th OPEC Conference, Vienna, March 29, 2000.

32. Press release from the 110th (Extraordinary) OPEC Conference, Vienna, June 21, 2000.

33. *Middle East Economic Survey,* June 26, 2000. *Petroleum Intelligence Weekly,* June 26, 2000, interprets the deal as being more loosely: "if prices go outside the range for 20 consecutive days it will trigger a consultation of members to consider what action to take."

34. The statement has a more subtle formulation as it read: "production would be raised by 500,000 if the average price of the OPEC Reference Basket of crudes remained above a *certain level for a specific period of time*" (my italics). It was furthermore an early warning as it was stated that the certain level and specific period of time was "other things being equal . . . expected . . . [to] happen before the end of the current month" (OPEC press release, July 7, 2000). It did not.

35. Speech by Sheik Ahmed Zaki Yamani, at the Centre for Global Energy Studies and *Oil and Gas Journal* Joint Conference: Oil Price Challenges into the Next Century in Houston, Texas, September 9–10, 1999.

6

Country Case I: Saudi Arabia—
A Hegemonic Power

The aim of this chapter is to answer the following question: To what extent has cooperation between oil producers been achieved by Saudi Arabia's performing as a hegemonic power in the international oil market?

The hegemonic role of Saudi Arabia was one of the most prominent features of the oil-producer cooperation, and thus the oil market, during the seventies and eighties. It is the conventional wisdom that Saudi Arabia holds the key to the success of OPEC and is, in fact, the most influential actor in the oil market. The argument presented in this chapter does not dispute this. However, some qualifications should be made. Two important factors are considered to constrain the Saudi Arabian role as a hegemonic power: changes in the market structure; and the Saudi Arabian regime's preoccupation with security, both internal and external. The underlying features of these aspects were described in Chapters 2 and 3, and will be taken as given in the discussion in this chapter. By focusing on one actor, it is possible to study how oil interests and security interests interact in the formation of a state's policy.

The empirical discussion in this chapter tries to capture the dynamic character of the Saudi Arabian hegemony. Accordingly, four different phases will be outlined:

1. the period from 1973 to 1981, when Saudi Arabia sought to influence the oil policy of the other OPEC members but was unable to do so (see section 6.3)
2. the period from 1981 to 1985, when Saudi Arabia carried a disproportional share of the costs in order to provide the collective good—a higher oil price (see section 6.4)
3. the period from 1985 to the present, when Saudi Arabia first coerced the other OPEC members to change their market strategy in

1985–1986, then took advantage of the UN sanctions against Iraq
to increase its own oil production (see section 6.5)

4. the situation in 1999–2000, when Saudi Arabia used both threats
   and promises in order to establish a new quota agreement (see
   section 6.6)

The fundamental starting point is the thesis regarding the role of a hegemon in international cooperation: "the presence of a single, strongly
dominant actor in international politics leads to collectively desirable
outcomes for *all* states in the international system" (Snidal 1985:579).[1]
The hegemon is perceived to possess some structural power resources,
which are transformed "into bargaining leverage cast in terms appropriate to the issues at stake in specific instances of institutional bargaining"
(Young 1991:288).[2] In applying this to the oil-producer relations, the
point of departure is that all actors have an interest in a collective limitation of production in order to ensure a high oil price. At the same time it
is in the individual actors' interests to sustain their own production volume. In such case, the actors can gain by cooperating (reducing production), but individually they can gain more by not cooperating while the
others do. This is the problem of collective action that will be discussed in
Chapter 7. The argument pursued in this chapter is that the larger the relative size of the individual actor, the stronger the incentive for this actor
to contribute to the provision of the collective good. If one actor is so
large that its consumption of the collective good is so profitable that it
covers the costs of providing the collective good, this actor can be assumed to provide the collective good regardless of whether the other actors contribute or not. Olson states this point as follows:

> One point is immediately evident. If there is some quantity of a collective
> good that can be obtained at a cost sufficiently low in relation to its benefit
> that some one person in the relevant group would gain from providing that
> good all by himself, then there is some presumption that the collective good
> will be provided. (Olson 1965:22)

The starting point in the discussion of the role of a hegemon in establishing cooperation is thus: The larger the size (market share) of an actor, the
stronger the tendency is to contribute to the provision of the collective
good (a higher oil price).

It would, of course, be beneficial for the hegemon to get other actors to
cooperate, even though it would provide the collective good without
such cooperation. This, however, presupposes that the other actors have
insufficient information. If they know that the hegemon will provide the
good regardless of their behavior, nothing would make them contribute.

In such cases, the hegemon would have to change the other actors' cost-benefit calculation by imposing some kind of sanctions on noncontributing actors.

It will become evident in the following discussion of Saudi Arabia that the hegemon has other, noneconomic motivations for providing an economic collective good such as a high oil price. Chapter 3 revealed that the political and security interests of Saudi Arabia caused it to follow a costly cooperative strategy toward the other OPEC members after the Iranian revolution and the outbreak of the Iran-Iraq War. This made the country less sensitive to the economic costs of cooperation. It might even be argued that it was not until this strategy was perceived to have political costs, in addition to the economic ones, that the kingdom changed its oil-market strategy in 1985. This points to the important distinction between a hegemon behaving benevolently and one behaving coercively (Snidal 1985:588):

> In the benevolent leadership model a greater absolute size of the largest actor means it has a greater interest in providing the good. . . . In the coercive leadership model, by contrast, it is relative size that is foremost. The key to centralized provision is the ability to force subordinate states to make contributions, and this ability rests primarily on the relative power of states. . . . The benevolent model focuses primarily on interest, implying that capability follows. . . . the coercive model focuses on capability, implying that interest in providing the public good follows from the distribution of capabilities. (Snidal 1985:588–589)

The two forms of hegemonic power to some extent presume different power resources. In the case of a hegemonic oil producer aiming at sustaining a cartel or a looser producer cooperation, the benevolent strategy assumes the ability to cut back a substantial amount of total oil production in order to increase or sustain prices. The producer must therefore be an initially large producer. A coercive strategy assumes the ability to increase production. In the short-term this means available spare capacity; in the medium-term it means ability to increase production in existing fields from reserves readily developed. The coercive strategy also assumes an ability to survive the assumed low oil price likely to follow from one's own increased production. In other words, the production operating costs must be relatively low compared with those of other producers. This distinction between benevolent and coercive hegemony is important for the following empirical analysis, as it will be shown that Saudi Arabia is characterized by having a large market share, spare capacity, and low operating costs compared with other producers. The kingdom has thus had the capabilities to pursue both the benevolent and the coercive strategy in different periods. The change of strategy over time calls for a dynamic approach to the Saudi Arabian hegemony.

6.1   A Dynamic Approach to Hegemony[3]

Robert Gilpin (1981:10–11) has outlined five assumptions concerning states' behavior leading to what he calls international political change:

1. An international system is stable if no state believes it profitable to attempt to change the system.
2. A state will attempt to change the international system if the expected benefits exceed the expected costs.
3. A state will seek to change the international system until the marginal costs of further change are equal to, or greater than, the marginal benefits.
4. Once an equilibrium between the costs and benefits of further change is reached, the tendency is for the economic costs of maintaining the status quo to rise faster than the economic capacity to support the status quo.
5. If the disequilibrium in the international system is not resolved, then the system will be changed, and a new equilibrium reflecting the redistribution of power will be established.

Gilpin argues that there will be a continuous struggle between "potential hegemons" fighting for dominance. As soon as one of them is in control, it will bring upon itself greater costs relative to the other actors. From the fourth assumption, it follows that the other actors' position will be strengthened the longer the hegemon sits. In the end, the hegemon will fall, and a new one will take its place. Gilpin's line of argument seems rather predetermined, provoking a search for possible alternative courses of action for the hegemon. This is because the hegemon faces more than one type of costs—it is costly to decline as well as to go on as before. Gilpin's fourth assumption, stating that the costs of preserving the system will increase faster than the utility of it, is reasonable. More problematic is the hypothesis that, given this assumption, the hegemon will have to give way to one of the other "potential hegemons."

   The basis for the argument in this section is that changing the system, or letting other potential hegemons get access to the "throne," will imply substantial costs for the hegemon, in addition to the costs of preserving the system. These two cost functions are assumed to be converse in the sense that if one increases, the other decreases. Given that the hegemon wishes to minimize its costs on both dimensions, the question will be how much change is needed to avoid as much as possible of the costs of preserving the system without carrying more than the necessary costs of changing the system. Changing the system could imply that all regulation of actors' behavior is abandoned, or that one or more other actors take the hegemon's place, so that the actors' behavior is still regulated, but by others than the original hegemon.

In relation to the other potential hegemons, the existing hegemon may give concessions to possible rivals in order to conciliate their threats against the hegemon. This can be seen as a way in which the hegemon reduces some of the negative effects of preserving the system by paying the costs of some changes of it. But, there will always have to be an actor taking the hegemonic burdens if the collective goods are to be provided and the system is to be preserved. Despite the hegemon's increasing costs of maintaining an international system, it will be in the hegemon's own interest to carry some of these costs combined with some changes of the system. Thus, the hegemon's strategy options do not constitute a choice between carrying and not carrying the costs; it is rather a question of how to realize the collective goods with minimal costs. This makes the question of where and how the hegemon will find it profitable to adjust an empirical question, not a predetermined one as suggested by Gilpin. This also implies that an essential resource for the hegemon in maintaining a hegemony is the ability to adjust.

The argument above can be illustrated by a formal model. In Figure 6.1, C(W) is the hegemon's costs of changing the system; C(Z) is the hegemon's costs of preserving the system. Change is measured from left to right, and the costs of changing increase the more one changes. Preservation is measured from right to left, and the costs of preservation increase the less one changes. In this case, the costs of preservation are set to be nominally higher than the costs of change; this, of course, is not a necessary condition, as the cost functions are assumed to be additive. The third cost function, C(Z) + C(W), is the sum of the two nominal cost functions. The general assumption can thus be stated as follows: The hegemon will change the system until the sum of the costs of changing *and* preserving the system are minimized. In the model, this is expressed in the point X^0. When $X = X^0$ the hegemon minimizes the combined costs of preservation and change. This minimal cost point is found by fulfilling the follow conditions:

(1) $C'(W) + C'(Z) = 0$, and
(2) $C''(W) + C''(Z) > 0$.

The minimal-cost point is thus equal to the point where the marginal costs of preserving the system equals the marginal costs of changing the system. This argument supplements Gilpin's argument cited above

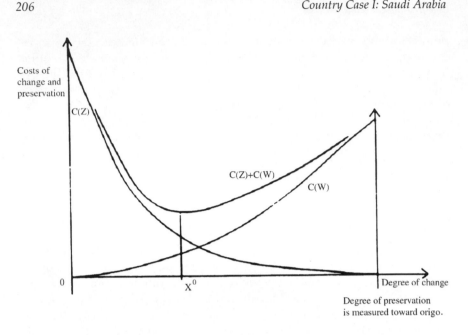

FIGURE 6.1   The hegemonic cost-minimization model
SOURCE: Claes 1986a:44.

(1981:10–11), as it considers the possibility that the hegemon does not seek the equilibrium point of marginal costs and benefits from further change, but the equilibrium point between the costs of preservation and the costs of change (see Gilpin's third assumption above). This might also be more important than the relationship between the economic costs of maintaining the status quo and the capacity to do so (see Gilpin's fourth assumption above). The cost curves in Figure 6.1 can incorporate the hegemon's capacity to sustain the status quo, with the consequence that the slope of the curves will change over time. This puts pressure on the flexibility of the hegemon to adapt to external changes of costs. Given such adaptability, it is the argument of this section that the hegemon can sustain its position, or power, even when costs and capacity change.

The two concepts introduced in the introduction—benevolent and coercive hegemony—point to a change in the hegemon's strategy toward the other actors in the group; in this case, the oil producers. The formal model outlined in this section points to the costs inherent in the role as hegemon, and the consequences for the hegemon's position. In the following sections (6.2 to 6.5) the changes over time of these aspects of Saudi Arabia's role in the cooperation between the oil producers are discussed. The Saudi

Arabian change of strategy from a benevolent one (see section 6.4) to a coercive one (see section 6.5) is an empirical case of a hegemon behaving in accordance with the model outlined in this section. First, Saudi Arabia gained a hegemonic position among the oil producers. Then the country experienced unacceptable costs from having this position, and thus had to change the system. It did, however, counter this loss of hegemony by coercing other producers to cooperate in providing the collective good. Saudi Arabia tried to minimize the costs of change and the costs of preservation at the same time. It sought to obtain the X^0 point in Figure 6.1. These aspects are analyzed empirically in sections 6.4 and 6.5. First, the historical background to Saudi Arabia's position is presented in section 6.2. In section 6.3, the Saudi Arabian policy from 1973 to 1981 is discussed. This period is characterized by Saudi Arabia's seeking a hegemonic position but being incapable of doing so due to the market conditions and the policies of other OPEC members (see Chapters 2 and 5).

6.2   The Making of a Hegemon

This section briefly outlines some aspects of Saudi Arabian history that made the kingdom the most important oil producer in the world. The following modern Saudi saying captures the essence of this development, viewed from the perspective of Saudi Arabia's citizens:

> If you didn't become a Saudi in the days of King Abdulaziz [1932–1953], you will never be a Saudi. If you didn't become rich during the days of King Khalid [1975–1982], you will never be rich. If you didn't become poor during the days of King Fahd [1982–], you will never be poor. (cited in Wilson and Graham 1994:171)

The Formation of the Kingdom of Saudi Arabia

A common perspective on the relationship between Saudi Arabia and Britain in the interwar period is one of imperialism. This is particularly so for political studies focusing on oil as a strategic commodity. A recent example is Bromley (1991), where among others the foundation of Saudi Arabia in 1927 is interpreted as follows:

> This erection of state organizations, and thus the incipient extension of the nation-state system to the region, was in part a particular strategy of territorial control deployed by the British to facilitate both internal pacification by indigenous elite and administrative coherence for operation of oil capital. More generally, it reflected the changes attendant on the consolidation of

formal colonialism under the New Imperialism of the imperialist epoch, without taking a proper colonial form. (Bromley 1991:108)

This argument is not valid regarding Saudi Arabia. The Kingdom of Saudi Arabia was proclaimed an independent state by a decree on September 23, 1932. Contrary to most other states in the Middle East, which were established by colonial powers, it was established by a local force that took control over the territory. However, the relationship between the first king, Abd al-Aziz, and Britain was paramount to the creation of the Kingdom: "Abdulaziz . . . knew he needed British support to succeed in uniting Arabia" (Wilson and Graham 1994:89).

Abd al-Aziz had obvious interests in establishing good relations first with Britain and later with the United States. To understand this, a brief recapitulation of the economic aspects of the founding of Saudi Arabia is necessary. From his first contacts with the British, Abd al-Aziz had emphasized his financial needs. From 1917 until 1924 he was subsidized with £5,000 per month, and some rifles and ammunition (Young 1983:4). The taxation of the pilgrimage to Mecca was the major source of income. Until 1927, as world economy grew, so did the number of pilgrims; however, from 1927 until 1932, the number of pilgrims dropped from 132,000 to 29,500 (Sluglett and Farouk-Sluglett 1982:46). The depression also hit Muslims, and the Saudi Arabian income from the pilgrimage fell dramatically. The position of Abd al-Aziz as ruler of both his traditional area, Najd, and the newly conquered Hijaz also meant increased expenditures. The two areas were different regarding socio-demographic and cultural traditions. Najd was the base area of Wahhabism, while Hijaz, the area where Mecca is located, was a far more cosmopolitan area. The Najd tribes also created the base for the Ikhwan, the military force of Abd al-Aziz. His security interests thus implied that he had to balance his modernization aims with the interests of the more pious and traditional Najd tribes. The Ikhwan rebellion from 1927 to 1930 clearly illustrates the thin line between modernization and traditionalism that Abd al-Aziz had to follow in the first years of his reign. When oil was discovered in Bahrain in June 1932, Abd al-Aziz grasped the possibility to gain political advantages. With the commercial exploitation of oil, "the Saudi ruler was . . . able to purchase armaments and transport and to 'buy' the loyalty of the tribesmen. Thereafter the amir's [prince's] potential to resist him was completely nullified" (Abir 1993:5). Since then, the religious leaders have had only a consultative role in Saudi Arabia, and their influence has been dependent on the king's goodwill. Abir (1993:6) maintains that the Saudi royal family and the ulama have mutual interests in the preservation of their historical alliance. It contributes to "the regime's legitimization, to stability and to national integration. On the

TABLE 6.1 Share of Total Exports, Selected Countries (%), 1950–1965

Country	1950	1955	1960	1965
Venezuela	30.1	26.3	23.6	18.0
Kuwait	6.5	13.1	13.3	11.2
Saudi Arabia	9.9	11.1	10.0	11.2
Neth. Antilles	15.0	9.7	5.7	3.9
United States	5.2	3.7	1.5	0.7
Total of the 5	66.7	63.9	54.1	45.0

SOURCE: Darmstadter et al. 1971:149.

other hand, it helps preserve the Wahhabi character of, and the role of the ulama in, the kingdom."

The Expansion of the Saudi Arabian Oil Industry

After the Second World War the Saudi Arabian oil production grew rapidly. Chevron and Texaco, which held the concessions, agreed to include Mobil and Exxon as additional shareholders in their daughter company conducting the oil production in Saudi Arabia, Aramco. By 1950, Saudi Arabia was exporting approximately 10 percent of the total world oil exports. During the fifties the importance of other producers was reduced, as Table 6.1 indicates. The importance of the Middle East increased, and among the Middle East producers the role of Saudi Arabia increased. In 1950 the enormous oil production in the Middle East area attracted Western companies and governments. The attraction is clearly described in a State Department Policy Paper of September 10, 1950 (reprinted in MNC 1974, part 7:123):

> This area [the Persian Gulf geosyncline] is a uniquely rich section of the earth's crust. Except for some submerged areas under the Persian Gulf, it is completely covered by concessions belonging to US and foreign oil companies. Proven oil reserves, approximately 40 billion barrels, equal those of all the rest of the world combined and are almost double US proven reserves. Only some 500 wells have been drilled in the Persian Gulf as against over one million wells in the US. US wells average 12 barrels per day, Middle East wells 5000 barrels per day. It is further estimated that the Persian Gulf area has an even greater proportion of the "probable" or "possible" oil reserves in the world, i.e., some 150 billion barrels.[4]

The aim of the Saudi Arabian government in the early fifties was to increase the revenues from the Aramco operations. The basis was the model of Venezuela, which had achieved a 50 percent share of companies' net income. Aramco sought to depress the companies' taxable income, but the government's revenue nevertheless rose "from around 28 cents a barrel in 1951 (while the posted price for Gulf exports was $1.75 per barrel) to around 80 cents per barrel in 1956 (posted price $1.93)" (Evans 1990:342). From 1968 the strategy of the Saudi Arabian government changed to seeking state participation in the Aramco upstream operations. Threats of legislative measures unless the government was included in Aramco led to the 1972 agreement in which the state achieved a 25 percent ownership of the company's upstream producing assets. The government put strong pressure on the Aramco partners, achieving 100 percent participation by late 1974. By then, Saudi Arabia's share of total world production was about 14 percent. The resource base for Saudi Arabia's structural leadership or hegemony was thus in place by the early seventies. Saudi Arabia had by far the largest potential oil reserves, its production costs were among the lowest in the world, its production capacity was increasing rapidly, and the political regime was dedicated to modernization—implying increased oil production.

This was not sufficient for Saudi Arabia to determine the future course of the world oil price. As described in section 5.1, the OPEC bargaining in the seventies was primarily centered on the price issue. Until the beginning of the seventies, actual prices for individual cargoes of crude oil were a secret to those other than the buyer and seller of the single cargo. The price transparency was low, and there was room for price discrimination. This price secrecy made it difficult for Saudi Arabia to use a low price as a way to limit exports from other buyers. The publication of OPEC prices, the question of the differentials, and the role of the marker crude all were important factors that enabled Saudi Arabia to play its hegemonic role (see Chapter 5). In the eighties the question changed from price to production, as the transparency problem emerged concerning actual OPEC member production and exports. As discussed in section 4.3, the verification of individual members' exports became a disputed topic. The main cooperative instrument in the eighties obviously was the quota arrangements, by which the individual member was allocated a certain production volume. Saudi Arabia's role as a swing producer made it possible for the country to balance the market with some a priori knowledge about the likely production of other OPEC members.

The State Participation Negotiations

Saudi Arabia was one of the most important countries in the formation of OPEC. It has played an important role, both in the internal negotiations in OPEC and in representing the organization in negotiations with other actors in the international oil market. The reason for this cannot entirely be ascribed to the size of the country's oil reserves, production, or share of OPEC production. This section discusses a case where more intangible aspects of the Saudi Arabian hegemony were prominent.

The formation of OPEC in 1960 is described in section 2.4. Terzian (1985:65) argues that the "founding fathers of OPEC are incontestably the Venezuelan, Juan Pablo Alfonzo and the Saudi Abdallah Tariki." Tariki had become minister of petroleum and mineral resources as a result of the changes in the government following actions by the so-called liberal princes, who in June 1960, inspired by Arab nationalism, demanded constitutional reforms. Being a dedicated nationalist, Tariki wanted more national control over oil production, and OPEC was seen as an instrument to achieve this in alliance with other oil producers.

In 1962 Tariki was replaced as Saudi oil minister by the more pragmatic Sheik Ahmed Zaki Yamani.[5] In the mid-sixties Venezuela pressed for an experimental program for production planning in OPEC. Saudi Arabia made its support for the program conditional on an increase in its own production but failed to gain acceptance for this demand, and withdrew its support for the program. Thus, OPEC's policy during the sixties did not include any joint actions on production or price policy (see Chapter 2).

Through the Tehran-Tripoli agreements of 1971, the OPEC countries gained influence on price-setting at the expense of the international oil companies. The price increases following the two agreements made OPEC cancel further discussions about the production planning program "until such time as the Conference considers it necessary to counteract any element which might lead to instability and deterioration in the oil market" (OPEC 1990:88). In January 1972, negotiations began between OPEC producers in the Persian Gulf and the concessionaire companies on the issue of state participation. The leader of the OPEC delegation was Yamani. In February, Yamani was given a mandate to continue the negotiations at the national level with representatives of Aramco. Aramco was totally opposed to the general principle of state participation but made an exclusive offer to Saudi Arabia that would have given the country a 50 percent stake in the development of unexploited proved oil fields within its concession area. "This proposal was seen by Saudi Arabia as an attempt to undermine its commitment to the Gulf states' collective negotiating position and was accordingly rejected" (Evans 1990:429). Yamani subsequently requested that OPEC hold an extraordinary meeting of the Conference; this request made Aramco accept the principle of 20 percent state participation. The Twenty-seventh OPEC Conference in March 1972 issued a statement threatening sanctions against any company that "may attempt to undermine the solidarity of the Organization by submitting to the demand for participation in some member countries and not in others" (OPEC 1990:98). Yamani was once again mandated to negotiate on behalf of the Gulf OPEC producers.[6] On June 1, 1972, Iraq nationalized the Iraq Petroleum Company, and later that month the OPEC Conference issued a statement in support of the Iraqi government's action. This made Yamani's threats toward the companies more credible when he stated, "participation is our substitute for nationalization" (Robinson 1988:67). Yamani continued his negotiations with the senior oil companies for most of the year. On October 25, the Gulf producers (Abu Dhabi, Kuwait, Qatar, and Saudi Arabia) and the concessionaire companies approved the General Agreement on Participation. The Thirtieth OPEC Conference in October 1972 called the agreement a turning point in oil history and a tribute to the role played by King Faisal in "eliminating many of the obstacles" during the negotiations.

By the end of 1972 the roles of Saudi Arabia, King Faisal, and on the operative stage Sheik Yamani, as leader of OPEC, were established. Yamani's role indicates his skills as an entrepreneurial leader (Young 1991:293). Furthermore, it illustrates Young's argument that the strength of a leader includes the ability to use both its structural position and its entrepreneurial skills (Young 1991:303). It also supports the important argument put forward by, among others, Baldwin (1979) that power resources in international politics have no value unless the actor also possesses the skill and will to use them. The position acquired by Yamani and Saudi Arabia in the negotiations with a (for OPEC) common opponent like the international companies was an important asset when the internal OPEC bargaining got tougher in the second half of the seventies, as it manifested Saudi Arabia's role as the leading country in OPEC. Furthermore, to the outside world, OPEC became identified with Yamani, and his opinions had easier access to international media and attention than those of the other OPEC members.

The "Special Relationship" with the United States

In May 1933, Standard Oil of California was granted a sixty-year concession for oil exploration and production in eastern Saudi Arabia. The company was to lend the government £50,000, which the government was not obliged to repay in full, while Standard Oil could deduct the loan from future governmental revenues from possible oil production. As described above, this income was essential to Abd al-Aziz's financial position at that time. Although the pilgrimage picked up during the late thirties, the Second World War completely halted this source of income. The Second World War also constrained the oil production in Saudi Arabia. The British financial assistance thus constituted a larger part of the

Saudis' income, and this gave the British a clear advantage over US firms. On the political level the United States had not developed a policy toward the region. As late as 1941, President Franklin D. Roosevelt had ruled against any aid to Saudi Arabia. After considering a request from the US companies operating in Saudi Arabia that the US government give financial aid to Abd al-Aziz, Roosevelt instructed one of his aides in July 1941: "will you tell the British . . . I hope they can take care of the King of Saudi Arabia. This is a little far afield for us" (Yergin 1991:394). The US policy changed during the war, partly due to the perception of an increased need for imported oil, and partly due to the perception of the lack of Britain's capacity to secure Western geopolitical interests in the region. To balance the British influence, the US companies operating in Saudi Arabia persuaded the US government in 1943 to extend "lend-lease" aid to Saudi Arabia. This laid the foundation for the political ties between Saudi Arabia and the United States. Roosevelt and Abd al-Aziz met in early 1945, and a US security guarantee to Saudi Arabia was established in 1947.[7] In October 1950, President Harry S. Truman wrote to King Abd-al-Aziz: "I wish to renew to your majesty the assurances which have been made to you several times in the past, that the United States is interested in the preservation of the independence and territorial integrity of Saudi Arabia. No threat to your Kingdom could occur which would not be a matter of immediate concern to the United States."[8] This relationship was subsequently developed both at the political level, through the military guarantee and weapons deliveries, and at the economic level, through the US company Aramco.

Contrary to the argument of Bromley (1991:108) cited above, the preceding discussion shows that the Saudi relations with the United Kingdom and the United States were established on the basis of mutual interests, not on the basis of exploitation in an imperialistic fashion. Furthermore, Abd al-Aziz's political position inside Saudi Arabia was strongly enhanced by the state revenues generated from the oil industry. The oil income not only made the economic modernization of Saudi Arabia possible, it also gave the monarch political freedom of action, as he otherwise would have had to be more subordinate toward the pious religious tribes. This dilemma between traditionalism and modernism is "the most common approach to the analysis of developments in Saudi Arabia" (Niblock 1982:75), and, as argued, the relationship with the United Kingdom and the United States fits right into it.

In section 2.4, the relationship between the international oil companies and the oil-producing states were discussed. The government of the United States played no lesser role in the events surrounding the Tehran and Tripoli agreements of 1971 and the oil embargo of 1973. Based on the experience of Occidental being squeezed by Libya, the oil companies realized they needed to negotiate jointly with the oil-producing states. Such openly coherent market behavior could violate the US antitrust legislation. In January 1971, before the Tehran and Tripoli negotiations began, the oil companies approached the US government and got a so-called business review that, given the information available, the Justice Department would not take criminal action against the companies if they pursued a united negotiation strategy with the oil-producing governments (Church 1974 part 6:224). With this clearance the companies signed the Libyan Producers Agreement, a safety-net agreement that ensured other companies would provide a company with oil if this it was forced by a government to reduce its production (Church 1974 part 6:224–230).

OPEC, at its Twenty-first Conference in December 1970, agreed on a resolution adopting a 55 percent minimum tax rate on oil companies income and a uniform general increase in prices. The resolution demanded negotiations with the companies within thirty-one days. There was thus a time frame for when the negotiations had to commence. On January 16, 1971, the companies was ready to negotiate on all issues, but only jointly, one team from the companies and one from OPEC. The following day Undersecretary of State John N. Irwin met with the shah of Iran. Based on this conversation, Irwin suggested that the State Department urge the companies "to agree to negotiate in Tehran with the Gulf producer" (Church 1974 part 5:167). The US government had in effect hanged its position.

The importance of this change in US government policy has been heavily debated ever since. Morris Adelman (1995:80) claims that: "had the US government not destroyed the new-found solidarity of the companies ... the Persian Gulf producers might have been frustrated. ... The historian can only record that the US government helped the cartel in its hour of greatest need." A key actor in these negotiations was the companies' adviser John J. McCloy. Although he was not "too much impressed ... by the attitude of the US government," he also argues that the US policy "wasn't decisive ... I wasn't disturbed so much by what the Government's position was. I rather took for granted that Mr. MacArthur would side with the Shah" (Church 1974 part 5:266–267). Krasner (1978:265) discusses how the US policy can be explained. He partly attributes it to ignorance, but he also emphasizes the conflicting interests of the US government:

> The fact is that American policy did satisfy the objective of keeping the Shah and Faisal happy, even if it did not keep prices down. American policy-makers acted to preserve the stability of noncommunist regimes even though this strategy meant accepting higher prices and opposing the preferences of the oil companies. It was only after 1973 that prices themselves became a matter of concern. (Krasner 1978:265)

The political relationship between the US and Saudi Arabia had been growing since the Second World War. The US had granted Saudi Arabia substantial aid and loans and supplied military equipment since the Second World War (US Department of State 1993: 754–755). While the international oil companies naturally emphasized the economic relations, the US government had primarily focused on the political relationship, and political in a meaning different from military relations. This is illustrated by the following passage of a letter from the US Ambassador to Saudi Arabia to the State Department in 1959:

> Assistant Secretary Irwin, who appeared exceptionally well briefed, made as his central theme the point that United States Government decisions to train the Saudi military forces and to provide them with arms was basically a political one. Therefore, no matter what our military problems with the Saudis are they should be accepted up to the limit of our national interests. . . . He said one of the worries of Defence was that the Saudis might accuse us of failing to carry out our commitments. . . . I replied I thought Faisal was coming around more to understanding the value of the United States friendship. (US Department of State 1993:743)

In 1970, President Richard M. Nixon stated what became known as the Nixon doctrine:

> Neither the defense nor the development of other nations can be exclusively or primarily an American undertaking. The nations of each part of the world should assume the primary responsibility for their own well-being; and they themselves should determine the terms of that well-being. We shall be faithful to our treaty commitments, but we shall reduce our involvement and our presence in other nations' affairs. (Palmer 1992:87)

According to Palmer (1992:87), the Nixon doctrine had "profound impact on American policy in the Middle East, and its consequences are still being felt in the 1990s." The strategy was to have Iran, not the United States, replace the position of Britain in the region.

By 1973, oil and politics were more mixed than ever before. At a meeting between Faisal and the Aramco partners in May 1973, Faisal, according to transcribed confidential notes, said the following: "Time is running out with respect to US interests in the Middle East, as well as Saudi position in the Arab world. Saudi Arabia is in the danger of being isolated among its Arab friends because of the failure of the US Government to give Saudi Arabia positive support . . . you will lose everything" (Robinson 1988:89). To the companies, "everything" meant the oil concessions;

to the US government, it meant an important political ally in the world's most turbulent and important region.

The 1973 embargo imposed a severe test on the relationship. The Saudi regime did not seek the embargo, but felt pressured by other Arab countries. In fact, the US government and the Saudi Arabian leadership misread each other's situations in connection with the Yom Kippur War and the following oil embargo:

> Washington continued to view the Saudis as Arab moderators who could influence large sections of the Arab world through oil largess. By adopting such a stance, Washington misread Saudi (and Arab) public opinion, and more importantly, the ability of the al-Saud to disregard the strong currents flowing around them. The Saudis committed the same mistake vis-à-vis Washington. Most Americans supported Israel, and would not let it be defeated or destroyed by its Arab enemies; this attitude, in turn, entered into American policy considerations. (Wilson and Graham 1994:100)

By summer 1974, the friendly relationship with the United States was restored. On June 8, 1974, Saudi Arabian Deputy Prime Minister Fahd signed

> an agreement for extensive U.S.–Saudi military and economic cooperation. The agreement was described by Secretary of State Kissinger as "a milestone in U.S. relations with Saudi Arabia and Arab countries in general." It involved massive American assistance to the kingdom in planning and implementing its economic and military development and in return called for Saudi cooperation in meeting the energy needs of the United States and its Western allies. (Golub 1985:22)

The Carter administration's unfortunate handling of the Iranian crisis and the hostage affairs weakened its credibility in the eyes of the Saudi Arabian regime, which could vividly imagine itself in a position similar to that of the shah. The Reagan administration relied more one-sidedly on market forces, and was willing to follow the market even in times of crisis: "In the event of an emergency, preparedness plans call for relying primarily on market forces to allocate energy supplies."[9] The military commitment to Saudi Arabia was, however, maintained. As discussed in Chapter 3, the United States partly intervened in the tanker war during the Iran-Iraq conflict by reflagging Kuwaiti and Saudi Arabian oil tankers and providing protection for these ships in the Gulf area. Also, Vice President George Bush embarked on a trip to Saudi Arabia in 1986 when oil prices plummeted. Being a Texan oil man, Bush saw the producer side of the coin, and did not emphasize the consumer interest in low oil prices:

"on the eve of his trip Bush said that he would 'be selling very hard' to persuade the Saudis 'of our own domestic interest and thus the interest of national security. . . . I think it is essential that we talk about stability and that we not just have a continued free fall like a parachutist jumping out without a parachute.' Bush was clearly saying that market forces had gone too far" (Yergin 1991:756).[10] The incident clearly illustrates the complex domestic interests of the United States regarding oil, including both consumer and producer interests. In addition, oil supply is regarded as a security issue (Bull-Berg 1987:34–56). The oil-price fall of 1986 made oil-producer interests more visible and thus a part of the US foreign policy toward Saudi Arabia.

The next major incident affecting the US–Saudi Arabian relationship was the Iraqi attack on Kuwait in August 1990. This was dealt with in section 3.4. The operation gave Saudi Arabia weapons deliveries and military support on a tremendous scale during 1990–1991, but Operation Desert Storm also created some lasting negative effects on the US–Saudi Arabian relationship. The war and the unsettled situation in Iraq have meant a higher presence of US military personnel in the kingdom. This has provoked Islamic fundamentalists in both Iran and Saudi Arabia. Bomb attacks against US facilities and personnel in Saudi Arabia attest to the level of tension created. It worsens the dilemma of the royal family, between the need for US support against external security threats and the possibility that this support itself increases internal security threats. This illustrates the problem of the internal security of autocratic regimes such as that in Saudi Arabia, as discussed in section 3.5.

This section has pointed out four cornerstones of the Saudi Arabian hegemony. First, Saudi Arabia is the only state in the region that was established by itself and not as a result of imperialistic expansion and subsequent decolonialization. This gives the kingdom a particular position. Second, the size of the Saudi Arabian oil reserves and production gives the kingdom power resources in the international oil market. Third, the negotiation skills of Yamani helped to position Saudi Arabia at the center stage of the political turmoil connected with the oil market during the seventies. Fourth, the close and lasting relationship with the United States provides the kingdom with a military guarantee that strengthens the security of the Saudi Arabian regime against external threats.

It is now time to turn to the dynamic changes in the Saudi Arabian exercise of its hegemonic power in the oil-producer cooperation. Four phases will be discussed: first, the period from 1973 to 1981, when Saudi Arabia was unable to exercise hegemonic power among the oil producers; second, the period from 1982 to 1985, when Saudi Arabia performed the role of benevolent hegemon; third, the period from 1986 to 1996, when the Saudi Arabian hegemonic strategy can be perceived as coer-

cive; and finally the situation in 1999–2000 when Saudi Arabia combined
the two hegemonic strategies.

6.3   The Incapable Hegemon, 1973–1981

The Oil Embargo in 1973

During the Arab-Israeli war of 1967, several Arab countries advocated
the use of oil-export restraints as a political weapon against Western
countries that supported Israel. This strategy failed due to several factors: the main Israeli ally, the United States, imported only 5 percent of its
total consumption from the Arab producers; the exports from non-Arab
countries, like Iran and Venezuela, increased as the Arab producers cut
back. Furthermore, the embargo was not a total volume restraint, and the
international companies were therefore able to swap shipments among
different destinations. The main consequence of the embargo was a loss
of revenue for the Arab producers.

In the early seventies there was a desire among radical Arab powers to
once again use oil as a weapon against Israel, as the United States had experienced an increased dependence on imported oil from OPEC. Foremost
among the advocates of this policy were Iraq, Algeria, and Libya. The
only country in clear opposition to this strategy was Saudi Arabia. This
opposition can be explained by several factors. Schneider (1983:213)
maintains that Saudi Arabia's security interests were particularly important. The Saudi authorities perceived two separate threats to the safety of
their state: (i) Israel's existing and potential expansion; and (ii) Arab radicalism. These were understood as being closely intertwined, as increased
Israeli expansion would strengthen Arab radicalism. US support for Israel
and its lack of support for conservative forces in the Arab world had, in
the eyes of King Faisal, the same effect. Even though an Arab oil boycott
could have solved this question, Saudi Arabia did not wish to confront
the United States, which they considered to be the only possible guarantor of Saudi Arabia's security (see section 6.2). "As late as October 1972,
King Faisal said in an interview, 'It is useless to talk about the use of oil as
an instrument of pressure against the U.S.—it is dangerous even to think
of that'."[11] When it turned out that the United States rejected Saudi Arabia's wish for a more "balanced policy" (Robinson 1988:73), and Egyptian President Anwar Sadat used pressure to obtain the support of Saudi
Arabia in the ongoing conflict with Israel,[12] Faisal changed his mind. On
August 30, 1973, Faisal declared: "We do not wish to place any restrictions on our oil exports to the United States, but America's complete support for Zionism against the Arabs makes it extremely difficult for us to
continue to supply the US petroleum needs and to even maintain our

friendship with the United States."[13] The OAPEC meeting of October 17, 1973, followed a Saudi Arabian proposal and decided to cut oil production by 5 percent and to cut it by a further 5 percent each month until "Israeli forces have completely withdrawn from all Arab territories occupied in June 1967 and the legitimate rights of the Palestinian people are restored" (Evans 1990:440). "However, at a further meeting held on December 24 and 25 the Conference modified its policies after hearing a report by the Saudi Arabian and Algerian Oil Ministers on their recent visits to various Western countries, which had led them to conclude that a more positive attitude should be adopted towards 'friendly' countries" (Evans 1990:442). However, the OAPEC policy from October to December had dramatic effects on the oil price in the spot market. The OPEC members then had the opportunity to raise the official selling prices. At a meeting between the Gulf oil ministers in Tehran in December 1973, Yamani strongly opposed large price increases, arguing that they might drive the industrialized countries' economies into recession. On the other hand, the shah of Iran pressed for maximum exploitation of the market situation, and a price increase as large as possible. To preserve OPEC unity, Yamani agreed to raise the marker posting to $11.651 for 34° crude f.o.b. Ras Tanura. However, he made it clear that this was not the preferred policy of Saudi Arabia, as later confirmed by King Faisal.

Having joined the embargo, Faisal gained prestige among other Arab countries and relieved some of the internal pressure on the regime. However, the oil embargo did not change the US-friendly policy pursued by Faisal and Crown Prince Fahd. Already in June 1974, Fahd made an official visit to Washington, resulting in a comprehensive agreement on economic, technical, and military cooperation (see section 6.2). "Riyadh expressed its readiness to help maintain a regular supply of oil to the market and to curb the rise in oil prices" (Abir 1993:67). In July 1974, Saudi Arabia announced an oil auction of 1.5 mbd, without any minimum price, confident that no one would pay over $11.651/barrel.[14] As demand had slackened, an auction would most likely put the official OPEC prices under pressure. After intense pressure from other OPEC countries, the plan was canceled. However, the stage was set for tense OPEC bargaining over the price issue, which prevailed for the rest of the seventies. In these negotiations Saudi Arabia was to take a different position than most of the other OPEC members. In the following years the most prominent opponent of the Saudi Arabians was the shah of Iran. After the oil auction was called off, "the Shah led the counterattack against Saudi Arabia, insisting that the cartel's principle be that producer revenue should not be allowed to decline (i.e., prices or taxes should rise if volumes dropped)" (Moran 1981:255–256). This confrontation between Saudi Arabia and Iran was the beginning of a lengthy conflict between these two major OPEC producers on the price issue. The Saudi Arabians were not able to dominate the shah's oil policy: "Yamani later insisted that if the United States wanted the kingdom to use its production capacity on behalf of moderation . . . the US government would have to play a more active role in *relieving pressure from Iran*" (Moran 1981:256; italics mine). This was exactly what Jimmy Carter did three years later, in 1977 (see end of the following subsection).

Empty Threats of Price War, 1975–1977

When nationalization or dominant state participation was established in most OPEC countries, the question of tax reference prices and their relationship to posted prices became irrelevant. The new basis for price-setting was the OPEC official selling prices, of which the Saudi Arabian marker crude was to become the key instrument.

According to Stevens (1982:217), the marker crude was a powerful instrument: "Before each OPEC 'price-setting' meeting, Saudi Arabia has decided on the level at which this crude should be set. . . . Thus the Saudis enter the OPEC meeting with the marker price fixed." As this section will show, this is a far too simplistic description. The other countries exercised considerable pressure on the Saudi Arabian control over prices by exploiting the price differentials system, and by 1977 Saudi Arabia actually had to carry out a threat to flood the market, a strategy that caused substantial damage to the Saudi Arabian oil-production facilities.

The marker crude, the above-mentioned Saudi Arabian light 34° API, was in 1973–1974 introduced as a standard crude from which the other OPEC crudes were priced according to formulas based on the differences in gravity, sulfur content, freight advantages, and other quality factors. These factors constitute the differentials, which is the concept that defines the extent of heterogeneity of the different sellers' crude oil. Saudi Arabia took firm control over the setting of the marker crude, leaving less room for the other OPEC countries in their pursuit of an aggressive price policy during the seventies. The differentials caused substantial problems for Saudi Arabia, as the other OPEC countries, in the weak market situation that emerged in 1974–1975, priced their oil just above the Saudi Arabian marker crude. This had the effect that Saudi Arabia lost market share to more "valuable" oil qualities. During 1975 most attention was focused on the narrowing of differentials between Mediterranean and Gulf crudes.

When Faisal died in 1975, he was replaced by Kahled. The strong man in the ruling of Saudi Arabia was, however, the prime minister, Crown Prince Fahd. He restrained Yamani's freedom to maneuver and took complete control over the Saudi Arabian oil policy. Fahd's policy was similar or even tougher than Yamani's. During OPEC's Forty-fifth Conference in September 1975, the Iranian delegation demanded a 20 percent increase in oil prices. Fahd instructed Yamani to prepare a communiqué declaring that Saudi Arabia would disassociate itself from its OPEC partners should they go along with the Iranian demands (Terzian 1985:238).

The Saudi Arabian position within OPEC had by 1975 become exceptional in at least three respects: (i) the country had huge reserves, making it an actor with a long-term perspective on the oil market; (ii) it had spare capacity, allowing it to pose credible threats regarding a price war, as it could compensate for lower prices with higher output; and (iii) it had a population of fewer than 7 million, making the internal economic situation luxurious compared with those of other, more populous OPEC countries.

At the Forty-eighth OPEC Conference in Doha in December 1976, a division between the OPEC members was impossible to avoid. Prior to the meeting, the shah of Iran had announced he would accept nothing less than a 15 percent increase in prices, while Iraq proposed a 26 percent increase (Moran 1981:258). When the Conference opened, Yamani announced that "My government feels that prices should be frozen for a further six months" (Terzian 1985:241). The following day he proposed a 5 percent increase as a sign of great willingness to compromise. The price hawks were unwilling to meet the Saudi demand. Yamani even flew back to Riyadh to consult with Fahd, and returned with the firm position of a 5 percent increase, "take it or leave it." The break of OPEC unity was final; the press release from this Conference states: "Eleven countries, within the Conference, decided to increase the price of $11.51 per barrel . . . to $12.70 per barrel as of January 1st 1977, and to $13.30 as of July 1st 1977. . . . Saudi Arabia and United Arab Emirates decided to raise their prices by five percent only" (OPEC 1990:144). The two-tier price system was a reality. Yamani made the following statement before leaving Doha:

> In the past they used to decide for the Saudi crude oil price and we accepted. Now we refused. So they are deciding for their own crudes and we decide for our own crude. . . . We will remove the production ceiling of 8.5 million barrels a day. We will damp the market—it means the whole structure of prices will collapse all over the world. There will be no structure of prices if they do not accept the price of the Saudi market crude. (Terzian 1985:244)

Both Iraq and Iran reacted strongly to the Saudi Arabian decision. The shah called the planned auction "an act of aggression" against Iran (on French television in January 1977, cited in Moran 1981:258).

The Saudi strategy now was to implement the threat to increase production and thereby bring the prices down. However, "when the Saudi government ordered Aramco to start producing at full capacity in December 1976 'it became evident' that the Company's maximum capacity was only 9.3 million barrels a day, not the 11.8 million that it had boasted of. Fahd was naturally furious" (Terzian 1985:245–246). The company was ordered to do everything possible to increase capacity, and all technical limits were suspended. This made pipelines explode and caused damage to reservoirs as the subsoil pressure dropped and some reservoirs experienced seepage of water. Before the next OPEC conference, "the eleven" had agreed to drop the 5 percent increase of July 1977, while Saudi Arabia and the United Arab Emirates announced a further 5 percent increase in their prices. The OPEC unity was restored. The costs of restoring the pipelines were estimated at $100 million; the damage to the reservoirs was harder to calculate. Saudi Arabia continued to produce above 9 mbd, a policy that increased the glut on the world oil market, reducing the room for further price increases.

The Saudi Arabian threat to flood the market was not credible. As the Saudi Arabian regime was not aware of this, the events of 1977 still prove that Saudi Arabia was willing, although not able, to use its resources to coerce the other OPEC members into compliance with its price strategy. It was to take eight years until the coercive hegemonic strategy was successfully implemented (see section 6.5). The four-year period from the abolition of the anti-US sanctions in July 1974 until the outbreak of the Iranian revolution in the autumn of 1978 nevertheless reveals a high-profile strategy by Saudi Arabia. The willingness to take on the other OPEC members, and to throw OPEC into crisis to avoid price increases, shows that Yamani and the royal family were willing to bear possible political costs in the pursuit of a price policy that they perceived as being in the interest of Saudi Arabia. In economic terms the strategy described above was a risk-aversion strategy. If demand was slack, Saudi Arabia, keeping its prices below those of the other producers, would be the first to sell its oil. If demand was tight, the kingdom would forsake a profit by maintaining lower prices.

In November 1977, the shah of Iran visited President Jimmy Carter in Washington. After this visit the shah changed his price policy and signaled that he would support a price freeze throughout 1978. Saudi Arabia and Iran combined produced 48 percent of OPEC output. Now that they both advocated a price freeze, the other members had little influence. However, during 1978 other political events were to change the situation in the oil market completely.

Security Threats: The Iranian Revolution and the Iran-Iraq War, 1978–1981

Saudi Arabia and the other conservative Arab countries proved unable to restrain the growing Islamic fundamentalism. As pointed out in section

5.1, the Iranian revolution meant a halving of Iran's production, and several OPEC countries pressed for a rise in OPEC's official selling prices. Saudi Arabia did not want a price increase, and countered the loss of Iranian production by increasing production from 8.4 to 10.4 mbd. The Saudi Arabian production thus approached the country's sustainable production capacity. The other OPEC countries were already producing at almost full capacity. As the companies accumulated stocks to ensure supplies in case of future shortage, the spot price increased from $12.8/barrel in September 1978 to $38.35/barrel by October 1979.

The revolution in Iran, contrary to the 1973 crisis, involved no deliberate attempt by the actors to change the course of the oil market by political means, but it did affect their behavior. Yamani expressed it this way: "It had to influence your thinking. This was a major political event. It caused oil consumers to panic, but it did not change the pattern of consumption. And that's what made the price chaos so dangerous" (Robinson 1988:214).

The Iranian revolution also affected the internal political climate in Saudi Arabia. As was pointed out in section 6.2, the leadership in Saudi Arabia has always had to balance traditionalism and modernism, or in this particular respect, fundamentalism and secularism. "The Saudi ruling class was seriously shaken by the collapse of the monarchy and the rise of fundamentalist regime in Iran. . . . a humbled Zaki Yamani accepted a substantial raising of oil prices advocated by OPEC's 'hawks' and Saudi nationalists" (Abir 1993:77). Yamani was pressured not only in the international arena but also on the national political scene, as oil-price hawks and anti-Western interests strengthened their positions due to the Iranian revolution.

The spread of Islamic fundamentalism has always been seen as one of the most severe threats to the position of the House of Saud. The fundamentalism was not only an Iranian phenomenon in the seventies: "As the frustration of the conservatives rapidly grew after the mid 1970s, the wave of 'neo-fundamentalism' began to spread from Al-Madina to the Imam Muhammad ibn Saud Islamic University (Riyadh) and to the theology faculty in Mecca. . . . Many of the 'alims (religious scholars) and the students . . . were openly critical of many of the innovations and Western influences introduced by the government" (Abir 1993:80). On October 19, 1979, 400 to 500 fundamentalists occupied the Mecca mosque, seized the Ka'ba haram, and denounced the corrupt government of the Sauds. It took the regime two weeks to crush the rebellion. The rebels gained little sympathy among the Saudi population, primarily because they had defiled the holiest shrine of Islam, the Mecca mosque. On November 28, an unrelated eruption occurred among Shiites in the Eastern Province, supported by Tehran's calls upon them to rise up against their corrupt rulers in Riyadh. In sum, these incidents confirmed the ruling elite's perception of the Islamic fundamentalism as a major threat to their position.

In the second half of 1980 the increase in spot prices came to a halt, as did the increases in the official prices of the OPEC countries. The ministers met in Vienna in the middle of September. With OPEC's twentieth anniversary coming up, it seemed a good time to standardize prices. Saudi Arabia once more increased its price by $2/barrel, and this time the other members did not change their prices. A summit of heads of state was scheduled for November 4 in Baghdad, with the prospect of a renewal for the organization. It was never to take place; on September 22, 1980, the Iran-Iraq War broke out (see section 3.3).[15]

Saudi Arabia (and Kuwait) supported Iraq financially and contributed to pipeline transmission of Iraqi oil through its own territory to avoid the exposed Gulf area. Saudi Arabia was willing to forgo oil revenues to achieve a lower tension level in the war, or to limit Iran's military potential.

Politically and economically, the period from 1978 to 1981 was highly volatile not only in the oil market but also in the Middle East as such. The security interests dominated the economic interests of several Gulf states in this period. In the case of Saudi Arabia, the developments had a profound impact on the regime and its consciousness regarding its own unstable political foundation. As David Golub states in the introduction to his study, "Saudi decisionmaking has been influenced by a variety of political and economic forces. I will conclude that among these forces, one kind has dominated—concerns about national and regime survival" (Golub 1985:1). The regime was thus pressured both by external forces, as the other militarily potent countries pressed for changes in the Saudi Arabian oil policy, and by internal forces, as the possibility of political unrest increased, inspired by the developments in Iran. "Security first" by now meant oil appeasement with the other OPEC members. At the OPEC Conference in Abu Dhabi in December 1978, the Saudi Arabian strategy was to create a consensus on the price issue. The interpretation of the Saudi Arabian policy differs among writers. Terzian (1985:260–261) emphasizes the perceived imbalance between demand and supply, and the limited production capacity of Saudi Arabia, making the country unable to correct the market. Golub (1985: 28–31) argues that the difference between the Doha meeting in 1976 (where Saudi Arabia induced a split between the OPEC countries) and the Abu Dhabi meeting in December 1978 was politics. The perceived threat had three sources: "Sadat's signing of the Camp David accords on September 17, 1978; the incipient political crisis in Iran; and the announcement of Syrian-Iraqi unity plans on October 26 [1978]" (Golub 1985:29). Siding with Sadat and the United States against Iran, Iraq, and Syria became too much for the Saudi regime. "With the shock of the Shah's departure, Soviet encroachments in South Yemen, and uncertainty about US dependability, Saudi leaders showed extreme reluctance to offend either the new regime in Iran or the newly preeminent Iraq" (Moran 1981:261).

Thus, in 1978 Saudi Arabia took the first step toward a new and more conciliatory OPEC policy. This was seen as a way of reducing internal and external political threats against the regime. As the price of oil skyrocketed during 1979 and 1980, the policy had few short-term costs. Although Golub (1985) shows how Saudi Arabia fueled the crisis, its traditional allies and the consumer countries never blamed Saudi Arabia for the second oil-price shock. Its image as moderator was intact.

As this section has shown, the Saudi Arabian regime wanted to influence OPEC price policy in a more moderate direction. Due to the large and increasing reserve base, and the special relationship with the United States, the long-term economic interests formed the Saudi Arabian preferences regarding the price level. However, the Saudi Arabian regime did not possess the ability to achieve this. The most important factors behind this were the important position of, and the oil policy pursued by, the Shah of Iran. The change in the Iranian oil policy in 1977 was thus an important outside event, strengthening the Saudi Arabian influence in OPEC. However, it lasted only a year and a half, until the Iranian revolution—an event that triggered an increased emphasis on security issues in the Saudi Arabian regime, thus making it harder to pursue the economic interests to a full extent.

6.4 The Benevolent Hegemon: Swing Producer, 1982–1985

In 1982, Saudi Arabia was set to continue its OPEC-friendly policy initiated in 1978, but now the instruments had to change, and the conciliatory role was to become very costly for Saudi Arabia.

After the political crisis was over, Saudi Arabia refused to lower production unless the other countries lowered their prices, and it created a surplus situation to force them to do so. In October 1981, the Saudi Arabian fight for a unified and nonincreasing OPEC price succeeded, as the OPEC members agreed on an official price of the marker crude of $34/barrel (see section 5.1).

However, the OPEC decision of October 1981 was not sufficient to stabilize the oil price. The spot price now was below the official price and thus pressing prices down, in the same way as the spot market had increased prices during the Iranian revolution just three years earlier. Instead of surcharges, discounts became the order of the day. The continuous high production from Saudi Arabia virtually flooded the market. In February 1982, the spot price fell dramatically below the official prices. From the

Saudi Arabian point of view, the unity that had taken so much effort to restore in Geneva in October 1981 already seemed threatened by competitive price reductions. At the Arab Energy Conference in Doha in March 1982, OPEC introduced the quota system (see section 5.2). Saudi Arabia was not given an exact quota but was to act as a swing producer, regulating production up and down in order to stabilize the oil price.

Never before had Saudi Arabia been willing to discuss production levels with the other OPEC members. Now Yamani himself proposed a coordination of OPEC production. This volte-face by Saudi Arabia turned OPEC into a cartel and made the OPEC cooperation more profound than ever before. The problem was that Yamani perceived the problems to be temporary. Once the price was stabilized, the stock drawdown would halt and demand would pick up. This did not happen. In a declining market the combination of an official price of $34/barrel and a production level of 18.5 mbd did not hold for long. There was no institutional pressure on the individual member country to adhere to the established 18.5 mbd ceiling. The price on the spot market fell, while at the same time OPEC members began to relate contract crude to the spot price. Yamani stated: "It was a complete failure. Quite honestly, I don't see a very bright future. In a few days we expect to see the price of North Sea oil come down by $2–3. And that will be the beginning of a chain reaction. . . . We have lost patience with the OPEC members that have chosen a short-term self interest policy in preference to OPEC's and their own long-term interests" (statement cited in Robinson 1988:262).

The Saudi Arabian behavior as swing producer during 1984 and 1985 created fairly stable prices in this period. However, Saudi Arabia had to cut back on its production continually to sustain prices. This policy was impossible to maintain indefinitely. The Saudi oil revenue fell and decreased the Saudi Arabian GDP, as illustrated in Figure 6.2. In 1982, Morris Adelman considered the Saudi Arabian challenge as follows: "Nobody can predict how much the Saudis would be willing to reduce their output; nobody in OPEC wants to find out. But if the current budget is around $88 billion, then there may be trouble if real prices decline below the current $32 and output drops below 7.5 mbd" (Adelman 1982:55). Four years later the price was below $10, and Saudi Arabian output was 4.5 mbd, and had been below 3 mbd.

As Figure 6.2 shows, the increase in Saudi Arabian GDP peaked in 1980; for the other OPEC countries the GDP continued to increase, although at a slower pace. The Saudi Arabian GDP fell 53 percent from 1980 until it reached its lowest point in 1986, while the level of the other OPEC members' GDP was almost sustained in the same period. This was the effect of the swing-producer role, as the lowered oil income during this period was a result of deliberately lowered production. The loss of market share also gave Saudi Arabia a more marginal role in world politics and in Middle Eastern affairs, and lower oil prices meant less political power for the oil producers in general. This was expressed by Yamani on Saudi television:

> In principle, we must draw a line between economics and politics. In other words our political decisions should not affect economic facts and laws. But crude oil is a political power and no one can deny that Arab political power in 1973 was based on oil and that its influence reached its peak in the Western world in 1979 because of oil. At present we are suffering because of the weakness of Arab political power based on oil. These are elementary facts which are known even to the man in the street. (Yergin 1991:747)

The Saudi government budget was severely weakened by these events (see Figure 6.3). In 1983 and 1984 the budgeted deficits were in fact larger than the actual ones. However, in 1985 the Saudi authorities balanced the budget. This was a completely unrealistic maneuver, and King Fahd actually refused to sanction any budget proposal for 1986. A similar non-budget year occurred in 1991 during the Iraq-Kuwait War. The actual figures for these years in Figure 6.3 are International Monetary Fund estimates. Two external factors worked against Saudi Arabia's attempt to balance the market through its role as swing producer: the reduced oil demand and the increased number of producers (see section 2.5). The other OPEC members also contributed to the weakening of the market, as they produced above their quotas.

The power resource necessary for a hegemon to pursue a benevolent strategy is the ability to substantially reduce total output. As Figure 6.4 illustrates, Saudi Arabia cut production substantially from February 1982 to September 1985. As the figure also shows, this did not prevent the oil price from continuing to fall throughout this period. In this respect the benevolent strategy was a failure. It could be argued that the Saudi Arabian behavior prevented an even steeper price fall. The events of the spring of 1986 substantiate such a claim (see section 6.5). On the other hand, the fact that prices were kept high in this period was an important factor behind the development of non-OPEC production capacity in the North Sea and Alaska (see section 2.5). If OPEC had accepted a steeper price decline in the early eighties, it could have prevented the intensified competition in the market and thus strengthened its control over the market. Such counterfactual speculation cannot be empirically substantiated. Furthermore, it is not likely that considerations regarding alternative market effects were the most important for the Saudi decision to abandon the benevolent strategy. Figure 6.3 shows how the actual budget figures for the Saudi Arabian government changed during the first half of

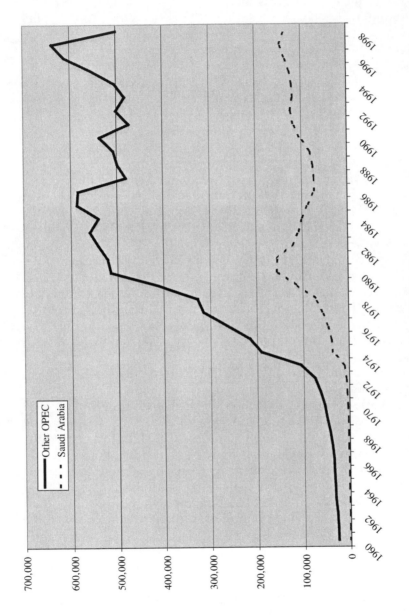

FIGURE 6.2   OPEC and Saudi Arabia GDP, 1960–1998 ($ mill.)
Notes: 1970–1977 GNP.
SOURCE: OPEC *Annual Statistical Bulletin.*

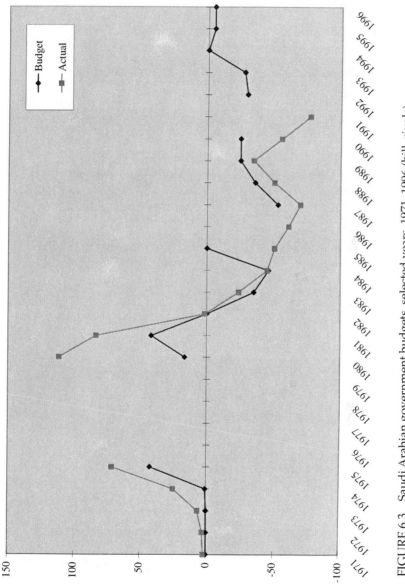

FIGURE 6.3 Saudi Arabian government budgets, selected years, 1971–1996 (bill. riyals)
SOURCE: Ministry of Finance and National Economy, cited in Wilson and Graham 1994:192; and for 1996, Saudi Arabian National Center for Financial and Economic Information.

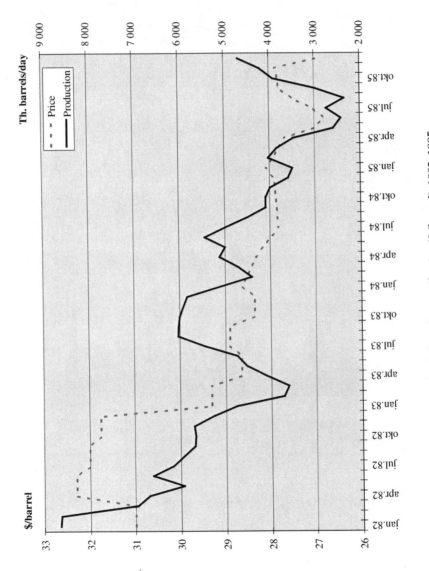

FIGURE 6.4   Saudi production (mbd) and spot oil price ($/barrel), 1982–1985
SOURCE: *OPEC Bulletin; Petroleum Economist.*

the eighties. The government was actually operating at a deficit. Given the argument in section 3.5, this was, in addition to the economic consequences for the royal family, also a political risk. The kingdom's internal security rested on the ability to use the oil revenue to gain political legitimacy. The external threat would also increase with lack of money, as the importance of Saudi Arabia in the eyes of the United States would decrease if the country became an oil exporter on the level of many others and was accordingly without any particular power position in the oil market. Again, oil had security implications for the rulers of Saudi Arabia. The willingness of their ally, the United States, to support the country and its policy was perceived as dependent on their position in the oil market. In the eyes of the Saudi Arabian regime, the benevolent strategy was a proven failure. Oil and politics once again pointed in the same direction: to regain market shares.

6.5 The Coercive Hegemon, 1986–1996

In the summer of 1985 Saudi Arabia no longer accepted production beyond quota by other OPEC countries as long as it produced only half its quota.[16] If we examine the relation between quotas and production in the autumn of 1985, we find that while Saudi Arabia in the third quarter produced 1.85 mbd below full quota, a number of other producers were exceeding their quotas at prices below official sales prices. In October, Saudi Arabia shifted policy and increased production. This led to a considerable overproduction in the market and heavy pressure on spot prices, a situation several countries tried to compensate for by increasing production. At the OPEC Conference in Geneva in December 1985, the member countries resolved to change their market strategy from the defense of a high oil price to the defense of the OPEC countries' market shares (see section 5.3).

As Figure 6.2 indicates, from 1985 the GDP of other OPEC members fell, and from 1987 to 1991 the Saudi Arabian GDP increased while the other OPEC members' GDP on average flattened out.[17] The economic interests of Saudi Arabia took precedence over the need for the swing producer to ensure internal cohesion in OPEC. In some sense it was a depoliticization of the Saudi market behavior (see section 3.1). One possible political reason for coercing the other OPEC members into quota discipline was the need for a hegemonic power to determine the conditions for the minor players' behavior, and not the other way around. The hegemon's costs from maintaining the system increase faster than the hegemon's capacity to support it. The Saudi Arabian oil production increased from 2.6 mbd in 1985 to 5.2 mbd in 1996. This level was sustained until 1990. The spare capacity thus made it to some extent possible to counter the negative effects of the expected price fall following the decision to change market strategy. Saudi Arabia did, however, posses further spare capacity. This was to be utilized as two other large OPEC producers suddenly disappeared from the market.

On August 2, 1990, Iraq invaded Kuwait. The UN Security Council declared a full boycott of Iraq and the new regime in Kuwait. This immediately brought to a halt all oil flows from the two countries. The oil price increased from $18/barrel to almost $30/barrel in a couple of days. Other producers, particularly Saudi Arabia, quickly filled the gap. After a few weeks the OPEC production was back at almost the prewar level.

As described in section 3.4, King Fahd perceived a further attack on Saudi Arabia by Saddam Hussein as possible, particularly when large Iraqi forces in Kuwait were deployed close to the Kuwaiti–Saudi Arabian border. The Iraqi attack on Kuwait had demonstrated that the tacit alliance between Iraq and the Gulf states during the Iran-Iraq War was based on situational conditions that at least Saddam no longer regarded as important. The Saudi Arabian hegemony in the region has never been certain, and both Iran and Iraq have continually challenged the Saudi Arabian oil dictates inside and outside OPEC (see Chapters 3 and 5). The outbreak of the Iraq-Kuwait War proved once again the instability of interstate relations in the region. The security problem of Saudi Arabia again became an urgent concern not only for the Saudi regime but also for its ally, the United States (see section 6.2).

On the oil scene the disappearance of Kuwaiti and Iraqi production eased the pressure on the OPEC quota system, especially the Saudi Arabian restraints. The continuous UN blockade of Iraq enabled the other OPEC countries to continue a high-production policy without disrupting the oil price. Although Saudi Arabia increased the oil revenues through this increase in production, the increase was not at all comparable to what it would have been had the Saudis let the prices go and sustained the prewar production level. As in 1979, they were alone in having substantial spare capacity. However, security interests took precedence. The attack on Kuwait was perceived as a substantial threat to the security of Saudi Arabia itself. The guarantor, the United States, was needed in an immediate military operation—Desert Shield. The Saudis would have found it difficult to secure this help if they had simultaneously squeezed the consuming countries economically by letting oil prices skyrocket. As in 1973 the political interests took precedence, but, contrary to the 1973 events, in favor of the United States' and the consumers' interests.

The prompt action of Saudi Arabia in filling the gap left by Kuwait and Iraq clearly indicates that the country had no intention of being the sucker in the market-share game.

6.6   The Mixed Strategy, 1999–2000

With the reentry of Iraq in the oil market and the demand effects of the Asian crisis, the oil price came under pressure again in 1998. Saudi Arabia did not accept new production cuts unless the other members' compliance with existing agreements was above 90 percent.[18] Again, Saudi Arabia followed a coercive hegemonic strategy.

However, in 1999, Saudi Arabia joined Venezuela and Mexico (a non-OPEC producer) in setting the stage for a renewed producer agreement (see section 5.3). In this case the hegemon used a new instrument, forming a small, more effective, high-level group in order to govern the market. Not surprisingly, the kingdom's political rivals in the Middle East, Iran and Iraq, were not part of the group (see section 6.7). Having designed the policy in advance, and having held a pre-Conference meeting among the largest producers, the deliberations at the One Hundred Seventh OPEC Conference in March 1999 lasted less than ten minutes. The Saudi Arabian strategy on this instance was neither a threat of price war nor acceptance of carrying the burden on behalf of the others. Rather, the Saudi Arabian Oil Minister, Ali al-Naimi, used a strategy of more or less secret negotiations with a few other producers. Announcing a fixed proposal in advance, preempted potential opposition among other OPEC members. It became harder to argue against the proposed deal, since both Venezuela and Mexico were equal partners in the group. When prices went up from $10 to $30 per barrel (see section 5.3), Saudi Arabia strongly argued in favor of increased production. Rather high profile diplomacy by the US Energy Secretary Bill Richardson gave the Saudi Arabian and OPEC decision a political overtone. However, Saudi Arabian long-term economic interests also suggested that an oil price of $30 per barrel was too high, as it could easily dampen demand increases and make consumers substitute oil with other energy sources. Since the price did not come down, further production increases were agreed in June 2000. In July, Saudi Arabia announced an intention to increase production by another 500,000 barrels per day. This was a unilateral decision, although it was said that it would be done in "consultation with other producers."[19] The independent strategy of Saudi Arabia was strongly opposed by other OPEC members, not least the president of OPEC and Venezuela's Minister of Energy and Mines, Alí Rodríguez Araque.

At the time of this writing (July 2000), it is impossible to know if the proposed independent policy has been pursued further. The events of 1999–2000 do, however, illustrate how Saudi Arabia possessed the key ability of a hegemon as argued in the model in section 6.1, namely, the ability to adjust its strategy and be flexible in its relations to other producers both inside and outside the OPEC frame. It thus constitutes a mix of the coercive and benevolent hegemonic power.

While the first half of the eighties saw Saudi Arabia swinging down, the first half of the nineties was marked by Saudi Arabia's swing up, taking the entire room for production left by the UN boycott of Iraq. Obviously, the swinging now was on Saudi Arabian terms. The hegemon had regained strength, although the room to maneuver was more restricted due to factors discussed in section 2.5, in particular the taxation of oil by the consumer countries and the so-far unrestricted development of non-OPEC production capacity.

The period covered in this section shows how Saudi Arabia tried to regain its hegemony among the oil producers through a strong coercive strategy in the autumn of 1985. The benefits to the kingdom from this changed strategy were to a large extent enhanced by the Iraq-Kuwait War and the resulting UN sanctions against Iraq. These factors gave room for increased Saudi Arabian oil revenues: "Saddam Hussein's tanks accomplished in twenty-four hours what Saudi oil policy had failed to achieve during the decade of the 1980s: they boosted prices *and* Saudi oil production" (Wilson and Graham 1994:188). Saudi Arabia took advantage of the situation, and, in line with the model in section 6.1, the fall of the hegemon was countered. Following this the Saudi Arabian position was strengthened as demand increased and made it possible to sustain a high Saudi Arabian oil production even as Iraq came back into the market. But also because the political relations toward Iran and Iraq improved, as is the topic of the next section.

6.7   The Relative Power of the Hegemon

In describing a hegemon's position, it is important to specify the hegemon's relative size, that is, the share of the market. However, this is not sufficient in understanding the potential threats to the hegemon. One also needs to compare the power resources of the hegemon, or leader, with the power resources of other potential hegemonic states (see Nye 1990:174). As outlined theoretically in section 6.1, it is the relative power among the largest states that defines the dynamics of hegemonic cooperation.

In the first (incapable) phase from 1973 to 1981, the Saudi Arabian share of OPEC production was about the same as the Iranian and Iraqi production combined until Iranian oil production dropped due to the revolution in 1978 (see Figure 6.5). Although Saudi Arabia produced above 25 percent of the total OPEC output, the relative difference between Saudi Arabia and Iran was not particularly large. In this respect, the position of Saudi Arabia was not so special. Furthermore, the Saudi Arabian attempt to dominate OPEC was challenged, in particular by the shah of Iran.

The benevolent phase commenced in 1981, when Saudi Arabia produced more than 40 percent of total OPEC production. The potential challengers, Iran and Iraq, were at war with each other, and their oil production had fallen from 25 percent of OPEC production to 10 percent. Iran was no longer a potential hegemon, and posed no threat to the Saudi Arabian position. As pointed out in section 5.2, Saudi Arabia viewed the price pressure of that time to be a short-term problem. Thus, it made sense to take on a benevolent hegemonic role. Figure 6.5 shows the costs of this strategy, expressed as a fall in share of total OPEC output. The Saudi Arabian share fell from above 40 percent to just above 20 percent from 1981 to 1985. In accordance with Gilpin's theory presented in section 6.1, taking on the role as hegemon implied intolerable costs.

The coercive phase commenced in October 1985, when Saudi Arabia changed its market strategy to regain its position (see section 5.2). This caused OPEC to follow suit in December 1985, and the oil price fell dramatically in the spring of 1986. As Figure 6.5 shows, the Saudi share of OPEC production did increase somewhat from 1985 to 1986, but was more or less stable until the Iraq-Kuwait War. Now the reborn hegemon took advantage of the situation and increased production, covering the missing Iraqi and Kuwaiti output. Later on, the UN sanctions made it possible to sustain a high level of Saudi Arabian oil production. At present, the Saudi Arabian policy is a combination of the coercive and the benevolent strategies. When prices come under pressure, as they did in 1998, a coercive hegemon will not reduce output, or will at least force others to contribute substantially to make room for the Iraqi oil. A benevolent hegemon in this situation would cut back its own production, to stabilize the market. Saudi Arabia presently (mid-2000) does both.

This chapter has shown how Saudi Arabia gained its dominance inside and outside OPEC, and the subsequent costs it incurred from this role. The case of Saudi Arabia clearly illustrates Gilpin's argument that "the tendency is for the economic costs of maintaining the status quo to rise faster than the economic capacity to support the status quo" (Gilpin 1981:11). However, the case of Saudi Arabia also substantiates that the response to the rising net costs for the hegemonic power can be offensive, in the sense that the hegemon need not acquiesce and become a state in line with the others, but rather can find ways to regain its position (see Figure 6.1). In the case of Saudi Arabia, this happened through a change from a benevolent to a coercive strategy, and later by combining the two strategies.

In addition to oil-related factors, the political volatility of the internal and external affairs surrounding the Saudi Arabian regime has made it more difficult for the kingdom to utilize its market power. The separation of oil and politics has been the Saudi Arabian policy for most of the pe-

236

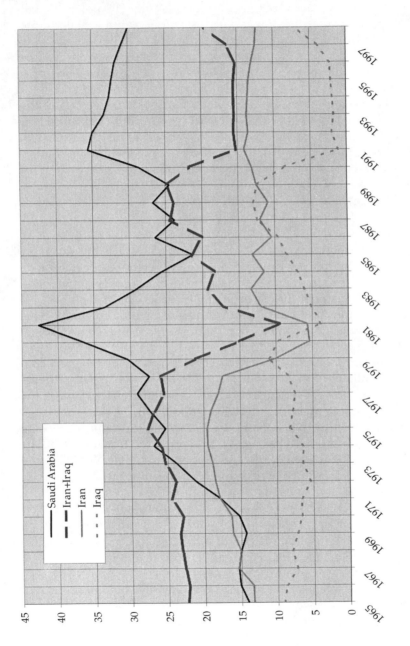

FIGURE 6.5 Share of OPEC production for Saudi Arabia, Iran, and Iraq (percent), 1965–1998

SOURCE: Based on figures from *BP Statistical Review of World Energy*.

riod. This was clearly argued by then-Deputy Oil Minister Saud al-Faisal (now foreign minister) in 1972: "You always hear that you can't separate oil from politics. I simply do not see why not."[20] One notable exception was the 1973 embargo. The problem is that the strategy of separating oil and politics is a viable strategy only as long as other actors accept it. This was not the case with the United States in the sixties, nor with some other OPEC members during the seventies, nor with the internal opposition during the eighties. Thus, the Saudi Arabian regime has continually had to consider the likely political consequences of its oil policy. Today, the consuming countries seem to accept a fairly high price in order to achieve stability in the market. Such a price might also calm internal opposition in Saudi Arabia (see section 3.5). With a more moderate Islamic regime in Tehran, and Baghdad no longer able to pose military threats against Saudi Arabia, the environment is better than ever for depoliticizing the oil-producer cooperation (see section 3.1). Making OPEC a pure economic organization will require political will and skill from the Saudi Arabian regime. On the other hand, the opportunity to do so might never be as good as it is as of this writing. New political issues will most certainly influence the oil market again.

As has been described in this chapter, the behavior of Saudi Arabia is based on the argument put forward in section 3.2. Without including the security considerations of the Saudi Arabian regime, one omits the most important motivation for the oil-related concessions given to other OPEC countries.[21] The seeming weakness of the hegemonic power is due to an understandable preoccupation with security needs. Politics limit the economic options of the world's largest oil exporter.

Notes

1. I will use the term "hegemony" synonymously with "leadership." In fact, hegemony comes from the Greek word for political leadership.

2. See also Underdal's (1994a) argument that the hegemon exercises leadership both through unilateral action and through coercive leadership.

3. This section is based on Claes 1986a.

4. Today the proven oil reserves of the Middle East are 660 billion barrels, compared with the above-mentioned 40 billion barrels in 1950.

5. Sheik Ahmed Zaki Yamani was the Saudi Arabian minister of petroleum and mineral resources from 1962 until 1986. During this period he was the most visible Arab in the international oil industry. He was the most media-wise of the OPEC ministers, making his words more often cited and thus more often read than those of the other representatives of the organization. He also was one of the most media-prominent Saudi Arabians, although not a member of the royal family. Disagreement with the royal family was the reason for his departure from office in 1986.

6. The companies now tried to make the best of the situation and demanded compensation for loss of future income, a demand that was flatly denied by Yamani (Evans 1990:430).

7. *Newsweek*, February 17, 1992:22.

8. FRUS, 1950, vol. 5:1190–1191, cited in Yergin 1991:427–428.

9. Summary of National Energy Policy Plan, US Department of Energy, *Energy Insider*, Washington, D.C., August 3, 1981, p. 3, cited in Lieber 1992:157.

10. The statement of the vice president was in conflict with the official White House policy: "'Poor George,' was the way a senior White House official disparagingly talked about him, adding that Bush's position was not Administration Policy" (Yergin 1991:757).

11. Quoted from the Egyptian magazine *al-Musawwar* in *Middle East Economic Survey*, and subsequently in Golub 1985:9.

12. On August 23, Sadat visited Faisal in Riyadh, and probably informed him of his plans for war with Israel (Schneider 1983:219; Robinson 1988:85–86).

13. Speech on American television, printed in *Petroleum Intelligence Weekly*, September 10, 1973, and referred to in Schneider 1983:220.

14. There are different opinions about who initiated the auction plan. Moran (1981:255) claims that it was US Treasury Secretary William Simon who "got the leadership of Saudi Arabia to announce publicly an auction"; Robinson (1988:137) argues that it was Yamani's idea.

15. The outbreak of war between Iran and Iraq did not affect the oil market in the same manner as did the revolution in Iran. At the time the war broke out, there was a supply surplus in the market of about 2 mbd. The outbreak of war led to a reduction in both countries' production of some 4 mbd, leaving only 2 mbd of actual shortage. This was easily replaced by other OPEC and non-OPEC countries' production increases.

16. This is expressed particularly clearly in two interviews with Yamani in the Jeddah newspaper *Asharq al Awsat*, quoted in *Middle East Economic Survey*, June 3, 1985, and *Petroleum Intelligence Weekly*, June 17, 1985.

17. The volatility in 1990–1991 was due to the dramatic consequences of the Iraq-Kuwait War for the GDP of these two countries.

18. *Petroleum Intelligence Weekly*, August 3, 1998.

19. Statement by the Saudi Arabian Oil Minister Ali al-Naimi by the *Saudi Press Agency* on July 3, 2000, reprinted in *Middle East Economic Survey*, July 10, 2000.

20. *Petroleum Intelligence Weekly*, November 20, 1972, cited in Golub 1985:8.

21. Saudi Arabia's policy in the oil market is taken by more than one observer to be first and foremost decided by internal and external security interests (Golub 1985; Moran 1981; and Bjørk 1988).

7

OPEC: A Successful Cartel?

The question guiding the discussion in this chapter is: To what extent have the individual oil producers behaved cooperatively, and to what extent have the oil-producing countries increased their economic gains through such cooperation?

It is the aim of this chapter to explore the extent that collective action has been a necessary condition for the producers to exercise influence over the international oil market and thereby increase their economic gains. This raises the counterfactual question of what the oil producers' behavior, and thus the oil price, would have been in the absence of cooperation. A competitive international oil market could be taken as the noncooperative outcome. However, empirically this is a second-best assumption. As discussed in Chapter 2, the international oil market has never been a competitive market, with the possible exception of some months in 1986. There is no solid basis for empirically testing how much the oil price has increased due to cooperation among oil producers. Economic models provide figures based on the assumptions entering the calculations. In reality we cannot know what the oil price would have been without oil-producer cooperation. In section 7.5, the difference between the cooperative producers' price setting and income revenue is compared with assumed price and revenue in a competitive market. It is also important to investigate the differences between the OPEC members regarding their contribution to the collective good.[1] The costs and benefits of cooperation can be unevenly distributed among the oil producers. Thus this chapter provides a partial explanation of the price and production policy of the individual member countries discussed in Chapter 5.

The discussion in this chapter will be organized according to some key aspects of cartel theory. The different aspects of cartel theory correspond with the phases of the OPEC cooperation discussed in Chapter 5, which also highlights different aspects of the internal bargaining problem facing the OPEC members. The period from the establishment of OPEC in 1960 un-

TABLE 7.1   Outline of Conditions Affecting the Incidence of Cartelization, Graded on Basis of Feasibility and Necessity

Market Condition or Characteristic	Feasibility: Excellent Need: unnecessary Tacit collusion	Feasibility: Good Need: helpful Cartel	Feasibility: Poor Need: essential Competition
Number of firms	Very few (2–5)	Several (2–25)	Many (30+)
Concentration ratio	Very high	High–medium	Low
Type of product	Standardized	Slightly different	Differentiated
Rate of technological change	None	Slow–moderate	Rapid
Frequency (and size) of sales	Frequent (small)	Often (medium)	Lumpy (large)
Opportunity for secret deals	None	Some	Great
Rate of growth	Slow	Medium	Rapid
Elasticity of demand	Low (less than 0.5)	Medium	High (2)
Production costs across firms	Identical	Similar	Diverse

SOURCE: Greer 1984:277.

til 1971 is of little interest for the question discussed in this chapter, as the OPEC countries had little influence on the oil price during that period. (Some aspects of the OPEC countries' cooperation in this period were discussed in section 2.4.)

7.1   Conditions for Cartels

A cartel can broadly be defined as "an explicit arrangement among, or on behalf of, enterprises in the same line of business that is designed to limit competition among them" (Stocking and Watkins 1948:3, cited in Greer 1984:263). A more precise and specific oil-related definition is presented by Mead (1986:215): a "professional definition of the cartel term—a single seller or a group of sellers operating in unison to reduce output below competitive levels in order to obtain a price above competitive levels."

The factors presented in the model of industrial organization in section 1.5 give certain structural conditions for the feasibility and need for the establishment of a cartel. Table 7.1 evaluates the market conditions affecting cartelization of a market. The fundamental argument is that cartels are easiest to establish when they are least needed.

Some of the aspects outlined in Table 7.1 (e.g., number of producers, frequency of sales, growth rate, and elasticity of demand) are discussed in Chapter 2. To understand the behavior of OPEC members, one needs to combine the effects of the external conditions (Chapters 2 and 3), the role of institutional arrangements (Chapter 4), and the bargaining between members (Chapters 5 and 6).

The concept of tacit collusion produces much the same outcome as cartelization or, in fact, an oligopolistic situation. The point is that with the market conditions spelled out in Table 7.1, there is no need for overt communication or agreement in order to produce high and stable prices. This can be done "solely through a rational calculation by each seller of what the consequences of his price decision would be, taking into account the probable or virtually certain reactions of his competitors" (Turner 1962, cited in Greer 1984:269). Some authors hold this to be the case for OPEC prior to 1982:

> Cartel theory has important implications for analyzing OPEC. It must be applied with care, however, for OPEC is not a true cartel. Members *currently* agree on a common price structure, but they have never reached any kind of formal agreement on sharing of production cutbacks, the hallmark of a full-fledged cartel. (Willett 1979b:584; italics mine)

Applying the insight generated from this general cartel theory to the oil industry suggest that the structural conditions for the cartelization have to various degrees been met in the oil market since OPEC was formed (see Table 7.2).

The number of firms or, more correctly, the number of oil-reserve owners, increased during the period, and the concentration consequently decreased (see Chapter 2). The type of product did not change, although the new producers introduced new oil types or qualities. This, however, does not represent increased variation in the oil differentials, but rather more oil qualities within the same scope or range of oil differentials. There were, of course, changes in the technological development in the oil industry during this period. One important consequence of this was the development of the Norwegian Continental Shelf as an oil province, which would have been impossible in the sixties. The speed of technological change has been relatively slow, although it has been somewhat higher in the nineties. Frequency of sale is an odd factor in the oil market, and in a sense not applicable. If one interprets it more in line with the trading instruments discussed in section 2.6, it illustrates the change from long-term contracts to an increasing amount of spot, or spot-related, sales. It is suggested that the opportunity for secret deals was low in the sixties, greater in the seventies, and low in the eighties. The reason for the

TABLE 7.2 Cartelization of International Oil

	1960s	1970s	1980s and 1990s
Number of firms	Few ("Seven Sisters")	Several (13 OPEC members)	Many (OPEC + incr. number of non-OPEC producers)
Concentration ratio	Very high	High–medium	Low
Type of product	Slightly different	Slightly different	Slightly different
Rate of technological change	Slow– moderate	Slow– moderate	Slow– moderate
Frequency (and size) of sales	Lumpy (large)	Often (medium)	Frequent (small)
Opportunity for secret deals	None	Some	None
Rate of growth	Rapid	Medium	Slow
Elasticity of demand	Low (less than 0.5)	Medium	High (2)
Production costs across firms	Similar	Increasingly diverse	Diverse

low opportunity in the sixties is quite different from the reason for the same result in the eighties. In the sixties most oil was traded by a handful of vertically integrated international oil companies watching each other closely. The terms of trade were accordingly known to the insiders of these companies, and the possibilities to go around this structure were small (see section 2.3). With the OPEC takeover, the actual trading became more concealed, as it became a relation between an oil-producing country and its buyers and, to some extent, the international companies. The relationship between the OPEC producers was not at all as close as that between the companies. Thus, the room for secret deals increased. In the eighties, however, the market situation in this regard changed again. The market became transparent due to a large number of traders independent of producing countries or integrated companies. The international oil press also keeps a close watch on the developments of new trading tactics by the producer countries. The possibility today of closing secret deals and keeping them undiscovered by the market press or the traders is thus rather small. The growth rate has slowed, as discussed in section 2.5. The elasticity of demand was low in the short run, after OPEC's price increases in the early seventies, but has been higher in the long run, manifested by the halt of the growth in consumption during the eighties. The variation of production costs has increased as the number of producers has increased, including producers in very different petroleum regions of the world.

As Table 7.1 suggests, a cartel is easiest to establish when it is least needed. This fits perfectly with the OPEC organization, which in this perspective had little importance in the seventies, as the members were able to increase prices and production without the help of the organization. However, in the eighties this was no longer so, and it became necessary to strengthen the institutional arrangements to achieve higher prices, or, more correctly, avoid price decline. Thus, the need of the producers for a cartel increases simultaneously, as it becomes more difficult to establish and maintain it.

7.2 Cartel Behavior

The structural conditions for the possibility and importance of cartels are, however, not enough to explain the actual existence and "success" of cartelization. The success of a cartel depends on four factors connected with the behavior of the cartel (Crémer and Isfahani 1991:30). A cartel must

1. determine a price for the group as a whole;
2. determine a production level for the group as a whole;
3. allocate output among members; and
4. detect and punish cheaters.

The first two points have to do with the cartel's relations to "the market," while the last two points have to do with internal bargaining problems.

The key problem for OPEC is rooted in an ambition to set both price and production levels at the same time. A cartel that does not control all (or at least almost all) production will work only if it sets a price and defends it by increasing production if the price is above the target and reducing production if the price is below the target. This will discourage other producers from entering the market, as the price will not go substantially above the target price, and it will secure income as production is reduced to keep the price at the target level.[2]

This illustrates the role of the cartel in the market. The internal allocation of production and the subsequent adherence to a set production level create additional problems for the cartel members. As pointed out by Willett (1979b:582), "while all of the oil exporting countries have a mutual economic interest in restricting supply and keeping oil prices well above competitive levels, they have substantial differences of interest concerning just how high prices should be and how great the supply restrictions of each individual producer should be." The following sections address the four factors one by one.

Determining a Price for the Group as a Whole

The first problem, the price, has probably been the most problematic issue in the OPEC bargaining. There are several reasons for this. First, production levels did not genuinely support the official, or fixed, price until 1982. Second, the official OPEC price was discounted by several individual producers when there was a surplus in the market. Third, the increased number of non-OPEC producers reduced OPEC's control over the market price. Of course, the aim for an individual country is not the price in itself, but the income or revenue that a certain price level implies. This is obviously dependent not only on the price level but also on the individual country's production. However, the OPEC cooperation described below shows that OPEC disagreed on the price issue long before the quota debate started. Furthermore, the target price can be seen as a norm for evaluating the actual price in the market, which in itself can be seen as exogenously given. The possible production limits or expansion is thus an answer to discrepancies between the stated target price and the actual market price. The behavior of the OPEC countries from 1978 makes it a reasonable assumption that they perceived the price as a given in the first place, and that their subsequent production limitation was a response to the price decline.

Determining a Production Level for the Group as a Whole

The second problem, the total quota level, is meant to be fixed according to the OPEC production that will realize the price target, at times when such a target has existed. Given an agreed understanding of the target price, the total possible OPEC quota—or, in oil jargon, the "call on OPEC"— (see section 4.3) is a given figure, provided there is accurate information on demand and non-OPEC production.[3] The problem arises when the members disagree on what this level is. Since the quotas were established in March 1982, the market conditions have confronted the OPEC countries with the choice either to cut prices to regain their market shares or to cut production to sustain the price level.[4] When Saudi Arabia increased production in 1985–1986, one of the stated intentions was to make non-OPEC production unprofitable and thereby stop it. This strategy worked well against the US producers, especially the so-called stripper-wells. Here, the investment costs are low, and the variable costs of production are relatively high compared with the fixed costs. In the North Sea, this relationship is reversed. Here, the fixed costs, especially the investment costs, are relatively high compared with the unit costs. Accordingly, production continued even if the profit margin was low or even nonexistent, as it was better for the investor to partially cover investment costs than not at all, which would be the implication if production was stopped. Even fields not onstream, but almost developed, would be put in place; this is especially true of large fields, as was the case in the Norwegian sector of the North Sea. If this strategy by OPEC had been sustained for a longer period, new investments in the North Sea oil sectors would not have been made. The long development time of Norwegian fields suggests that prices would have had to be low for several years. It also follows that Norwegian cooperation with OPEC could consist only of increasing production at a lower pace, not cutting back on the production level, since there was no economically defensible way of stopping already-planned production expansion.

From the late 70s OPEC let non-OPEC producers take their share of the market as competitive price-takers, and its members themselves filled the gap between the non-OPEC production and total demand, acting as swing producers. This, of course, gave OPEC little influence on price, as it was set by the relationship between total demand and the non-OPEC production. As non-OPEC production capacity increased, the OPEC members found themselves supplying less and less oil at lower and lower prices. The quota decision of 1982 was an attempt to change the price problem; the market-share decision of December 1985 was an attempt to handle the production problem.

Allocation of Output Among Members

From the outset, the quotas were disputed. Iran was particularly dissatisfied with its allocated quota. This has led to continual bargaining inside OPEC over the level of total production reduction in the organization and the distribution of quotas. The quota bargaining is special as the actors bargain at two levels: first, over what is to be the level of total quotas; and, second, over what is to be the quota for the individual member. Then, there is the problem of compliance.

If one assumes that the level of total quotas is set to achieve a certain price in the market, this level of total quotas is not negotiable, given the price target and assumed demand. Whether the agreed production level realizes the price target is another matter. The members might disagree about whether the assumptions are correct, and they might disagree on the price target. It follows that the quota-setting bargaining is mostly distributive bargaining—allocating individual quotas within the limit of the total quotas, which is set exogenously.

While the criterion for setting the total level of quotas is rather rigid, the criterion for individual allocation is virtually nonexistent. Obviously, historical production level is important, but production capacity (and spare capacity) might prove to be the most important factor. Also, income requirement, poverty, war costs, and reconstruction programs have been directly or indirectly introduced as arguments for increased quotas. In total, some forty different criteria have been introduced.

Setting the quotas is an example of an iterated game. As pointed out in section 4.3, quotas are seldom set for more than one or two quarters. Thus, agreeing to one quota level at one moment is not formally binding for more than some months. However, agreeing to a "low" quota level at one point in time might make it harder for the country to argue for higher quotas at a later point.

Detection and Punishment of Cheaters

Once the quotas are set, the game changes to one of collective action. If the total quota level is correctly set and thus achieves the decided price level in the market, the OPEC countries find themselves in a traditional prisoner's dilemma situation. This could be analyzed on the basis of a high oil price being a collective good for the oil producers (Malnes 1983).

Applied to the oil-producer relations, the point of departure in the collective good is that all actors have an interest in limitation of production to ensure a high oil price. At the same time, it is in the actors' interests to sustain their own production volume. In such case, the actors can gain by cooperating (reducing production), but individually they can gain more by not cooperating while the others do. The oil price can thus be regarded as a collective good. A collective good is, in this section, understood in accordance with Olson's definition: "If person X_i in a group X_1 ... X_i ... X_n consumes it, it cannot feasibly be withheld from others in the group. In other words, those who do not purchase or pay for any of the public or collective good cannot be excluded or kept from sharing the consumption of the goods, as they can where non-collective goods are concerned" (Olson 1965:14–15).

Olson then distinguishes between exclusive and inclusive goods (Olson 1965:38). Exclusive goods are goods of which one actor's consumption reduces other actors' consumption equally. Inclusive public goods are similar to pure public goods, as defined by Samuelson: "each individual's consumption of such a good leads to no subtraction from any other individual's consumption of that good, so $X_{n+j} = X^i_{n+j}$ simultaneously for each and every i individual and each collective consumption good" (Samuelson 1954:387). Obviously, the price of oil can have a rivalrous effect on the producers, and thus fail to satisfy the definition of inclusive-

TABLE 7.3   OPEC Cartel Strategies, 1973–1999

	Price-Setting	Production Quotas
Dec. 73–Feb. 79	Yes, fixed	No
Feb. 79–May 81	No	No
May 81–March 82	Yes, fixed	No
March 82–Dec. 85	Yes, fixed	Yes
Dec. 85–Nov. 86	No	Yes
Dec. 86–Aug. 90	Target, weak form, not fixed	Yes
Aug. 90–Feb. 92	Target, weak form, not fixed	No, abandoned due to war
Feb. 92–	Target, weak form, not fixed	Yes

ness. The oil price will consequently be regarded as an exclusive collective good for the oil producers.

The following four sections deal with different aspects of the collective action by the OPEC members. Both the price and production behavior of OPEC members are relevant, but most emphasis will be put on the production behavior and its relation to the quota agreements. The final section discusses the OPEC members' economic gains as such.

7.3   OPEC as a Price-Maker

If OPEC should behave in line with cartel theory, it should set a fixed price, based on perceived demand conditions and the assumed production outside the cartel, and then increase production if the price rises above the agreed level, and decrease production if the price falls below the same level. By varying production in this way, OPEC should be able to maintain the agreed price (see above). This implies that the cartel's role in the market is based on two dimensions: price-setting and production quotas.[5] Table 7.3 shows how OPEC has performed along these dimensions. The price-setting since 1986 has been a target price that indicates only at what OPEC should aim; it has not constituted a binding or regulative figure in the OPEC deliberations.

Whether the price was set in a fixed form or the weaker, target form, one should expect a strong positive correlation between changes in price and changes in production. If OPEC behaved like a cartel, it should have increased production when price increased, and vice versa.

Table 7.4 reports the correlation between the individual member countries' production and the oil price from January 1973 to December 1995. The data are presented as time series, where the cases are production and average price in individual months. The data have been divided into four shorter time periods: from January 1973 to December 1978; April 1982 to

TABLE 7.4 Correlation Between Price and Production by Time Periods

	Jan 73–Dec 78			Apr 82–Dec 85			Nov 86–Jul 90			Apr 92–Dec 95			Jan 73–Dec 95		
	r	(n)	P	r	(n)	P	r	(n)	P	r	(n)	P	r	(n)	P
Algeria	0.1681	72	0.158	0.3648	45	0.014	-0.3208	45	0.032	0.6070	45	0.000	-0.3159	276	0.000
Ecuador	0.2751	36	0.104	-0.7649	45	0.000	-0.4555	45	0.002	-0.0022	9	0.995	-0.1018	204	0.148
Gabon	-0.6053	36	0.000	-0.1804	45	0.236	0.0784	45	0.609	0.1275	45	0.404	-0.4553	240	0.000
Indonesia	0.5804	36	0.000	-0.1061	45	0.488	0.2523	45	0.094	0.6530	45	0.000	-0.0026	240	0.968
Iran	-0.2217	72	0.061	0.0779	45	0.611	0.1111	45	0.467	-0.3850	45	0.009	-0.6873	276	0.000
Iraq	0.7004	60	0.000	-0.7444	45	0.000	-0.2048	45	0.177	-0.2230	45	0.141	-0.1169	264	0.058
Kuwait	-0.5381	72	0.000	-0.5812	45	0.000	-0.0670	45	0.662	-0.6407	45	0.000	-0.4655	276	0.000
Libya	-0.2216	72	0.061	0.3511	45	0.018	-0.0386	45	0.801	0.6174	45	0.000	-0.2426	276	0.000
Nigeria	-0.0521	72	0.664	-0.2300	45	0.128	0.0630	45	0.681	-0.3773	45	0.011	-0.3079	276	0.000
Qatar	-0.5384	72	0.000	-0.1196	45	0.434	0.0720	45	0.638	0.2130	45	0.160	-0.3018	276	0.000
S. Arabia	0.3571	72	0.002	0.6921	45	0.000	-0.4366	45	0.003	0.4207	45	0.004	0.0164	276	0.786
UAE	0.5689	72	0.000	-0.0047	45	0.976	-0.0536	45	0.727	0.5778	45	0.000	-0.1640	276	0.006
Venezuela	-0.8343	72	0.000	0.3488	45	0.019	-0.2300	45	0.128	-0.2888	45	0.054	-0.4564	276	0.000
OPEC	0.1728	36	0.314	0.4007	45	0.006	-0.1849	45	0.224	-0.3252	45	0.029	-0.2734	240	0.000

r = correlation coefficient

n = number of observations (i.e., months production)

P = two-tailed significance test

SOURCE: Production data from *Petroleum Economist*; price data from *OPEC Bulletin*.

December 1985; November 1986 to July 1990; and April 1992 to December 1995. These four periods exclude the months during, or in the aftermath of, revolution and war, as well as very volatile periods, such as in 1986 (January 1979–March 1982; January 1986–October 1986; and August 1990–March 1992). The correlations for the period from January 1973 to December 1978 should be read with great care, as the price trend is the same throughout the period. The price dropped between only two of seventy-two months. Thus, the correlation figures for this period do not cover the cartel's ability to reduce production when the price falls. The last column in Table 7.4 reports the correlations for the whole period, including the months excluded in the other columns, when prices changed dramatically. Thus, this column does not constitute the sum of the other columns. As the figures in the last column show, only in the case of Saudi Arabia is there a small, positive, but insignificant correlation between production and price.

According to the criteria for a successful cartel, any price movement, positive or negative, large or small, should be accompanied by similar changes in production. As Table 7.4 shows, no such correlation can be identified for any member for the period as a whole.[6] On the contrary, for several members, there was a strong, negative, and significant correlation between price and production (Gabon, Iran, Kuwait, Libya, Nigeria, Qatar, and Venezuela). This suggests that the relationship between production and price is the opposite of the cartel-theory assumption. The individual producer tries to compensate for falling prices with increased production, and reduces production when prices increase above the target. This argument has been formalized in the economic model called the backward-bending supply curve model (Crémer and Isfahani 1991:45). The point is that the producer would not try to maximize income, but seek a more or less specified target for its revenue; the strategy can be called an income target strategy. The model is based on the Hotelling theorem (Hotelling 1931; see section 1.5). According to this theorem, the oil-exporting country can choose between spending the oil revenues and investing them as a form of equity; the decision is one of weighing the utility of current production against the utility of production at a later date. The producer may find its income so high that production is reduced as prices increase. This argument is, however, influenced by several other distorting factors. First, the producer must anticipate that the oil price will increase more than the existing interest rate. If not, it should instead produce the oil and save the income in other assets. Second, the producer must consider the geological fact that it has a limited amount of oil reserves at its disposal as an actual constraint on its decision. If reserves increase more than production, the idea of the fixed stock becomes less obvious. Third, the producer must

TABLE 7.5   Correlation Between Price and Production by Price Movements

	Decreasing Price			Increasing Price		
	r	(n)	P	r	(n)	P
Algeria	0.1628	87	0.066	0.4634	93	0.000
Ecuador	0.1648	65	0.095	0.0663	62	0.305
Gabon	0.0189	85	0.432	-0.0757	85	0.246
Indonesia	0.0170	85	0.439	0.0664	85	0.273
Iran	0.1106	87	0.154	-0.0496	93	0.319
Iraq	0.3904	87	0.000	-0.3317	89	0.000
Kuwait	0.1175	86	0.141	-0.1640	89	0.062
Libya	0.1805	87	0.047	0.2372	93	0.011
Nigeria	-0.0603	87	0.290	-0.0366	93	0.364
Qatar	0.1305	87	0.114	0.0995	93	0.172
S. Arabia	-0.1768	87	0.051	0.0771	93	0.234
UAE	-0.0741	87	0.248	0.0838	93	0.212
Venezuela	-0.0248	87	0.410	0.0128	93	0.452
OPEC	-0.0385	85	0.363	-0.2695	85	0.007

r = correlation coefficient
n = number of observations (i.e., months production)
P = two-tailed significance test
SOURCE: Production data from *Petroleum Economist*; price data from *OPEC Bulletin*.

not continue production for other reasons, such as beneficial effects on industrial activity or employment.

The first part of the argument above, that producers increase production to compensate for falling prices, is less susceptible to such complicating factors. When prices fall, the individual actor's response is to try to sustain its income level by increasing production. Table 7.5 indicates the relationship between production and price for the period from January 1973 to December 1995, dependent on the price trend. The interpretation of the coefficients is as follows: In the case of decreasing prices, cartel behavior would imply a positive correlation between price and production, as the producers would try to counter the price fall by reducing production. The income target strategy would imply a negative correlation between price and production, as the producers would try to sustain their income level by increasing production. In the case of increasing prices, cartel behavior would imply a positive correlation between price and production, as the cartel members would try to avoid a price increase, and thus increased production by non-cartel members, by increasing production. The income target strategy would imply a negative correlation between price and production, as producers' income would be sustained with lower production. The findings of Table 7.5 do not give any reason for strong conclusions on this point. Very few of the correlations are strong and significant. As suggested, the emphasis should be put on the decreasing price situation. In this column, only the positive correlation for Iraq is highly significant. It suggests that Iraq reduced production when prices fell.[7] For all other producers, the correlations, positive or negative, are weak, and for several countries they are insignificant.

The observed lack of cartel behavior may have been caused by several flaws in the OPEC cartel. As Figure 7.10 shows, prices were anticipated to increase substantially also after 1980. The understanding of demand and non-OPEC supply might have been inaccurate. "To calculate actual elasticities of demand and of non-cartel supply is worth doing, but the results seem too weak and inaccurate for direct application. The cartel will never hear the clang of a market bell: you have raised prices too high, start a retreat!" (Adelman 1982:54). Finally, the lack of cartel behavior may have been a result of lack of adherence to the price agreements; this is the topic of the next section.

The problem after the 1973–1974 price increase was that the agreed posted prices, and later the official prices, were being undermined by individual producers' discounts. Some countries found they had to cut prices to get their crude sold. Figure 7.1 illustrates how dramatic this drop in production was for some countries. Obviously understanding the effects of the price increases, the OPEC countries then adopted a strategy of increasing their share of the profit at the expense of the alleged "excessive margin of profits" by the international oil companies (OPEC 1990:125). The decision at the Forty-first OPEC Conference in September 1974 increased the government take of the marker crude from $9.41 to $9.74, with the explicit stipulation that the adjustment "should not be passed to consumers" (OPEC 1990:125). By October 1975, the government take had increased to $11.18. But secret price-discounting had become widespread among the OPEC members. Several members advocated a higher price at the conferences, but cut prices individually.[8] This situation became more complicated as countries exploited the difference between the quality of the crude oil produced in different regions—the so-called differentials.[9] Lighter crudes were discounted, leaving less room for heavier crudes. The complexity appears as the demand for different qualities varies. The relationship between discounting and increased volumes sold thus became blurred, something that favored the cheaters. Although OPEC's total output between 1974 and 1978 did not increase and the organization had experienced fierce deliberations, described in section 5.1, it "was generally believed in 1978 that OPEC still had unexerted price-raising power" (Adelman 1995:160). As described in Chapter 3, at

252

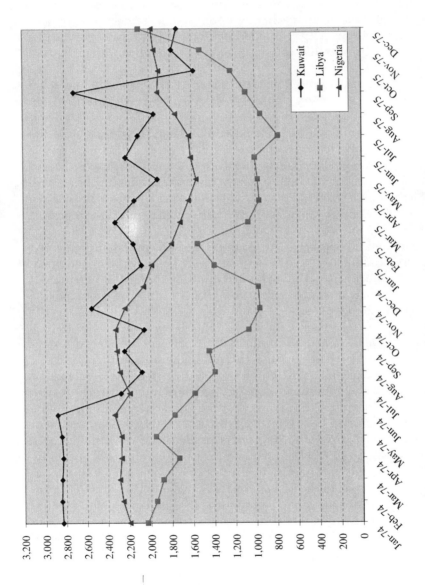

FIGURE 7.1   Kuwaiti, Nigerian, and Libyan oil production, 1974–1975 (th. b/d)
SOURCE: *Petroleum Economist.*

that time factors having little to do with the oil market as such, or the oil-producer cooperation more specifically, created a huge price increase.

From 1980 to 1983, OPEC's dominance and control over price-setting crumbled away. This was due to two important developments. In the first place, the growth in demand for oil came to a halt, due partly to the higher prices for oil, partly to the generally lower economic growth that occurred prior to OPEC's price increases, and partly to new energy sources such as natural gas and nuclear energy. Second, competition between oil producing countries increased, in the same way it had twenty years earlier between the companies. The new profitability of oil production made fields in non-OPEC countries profitable, and these producers took a larger share of the market.

The changes in these factors were discussed in Chapter 2. Figure 7.2 illustrates how they affected the outlook for OPEC production. As the 1977 forecast suggests (Figure 7.2), the production increase of the seventies was anticipated to continue at least during the first half of the eighties. However, five years later, in 1982, this outlook was changed to a slowly declining production volume for OPEC during the eighties and nineties. As the empirical sections above have shown, it took some years before OPEC realized this situation, and even longer before it acted accordingly.

7.4 Quota Compliance[10]

Allocating Output—Assigning Quotas

The initial quota agreement of March 1982 and all subsequent OPEC quota agreements and revisions are shown in Table 7.6. The months indicate the time the agreements came into effect, not the month of the decision. There have also been cases where one decision contained different quotas for different months, as in the autumn of 1986.

As shown in Table 7.6, OPEC made twenty-three changes in the quotas between April 1982 and April 1999. This gives an average life of a quota decision as approximately nine months. The quotas have been a prominent part of the OPEC deliberations since their introduction in 1982. Most of the revisions have been marginal, but for the Gulf countries some revisions have been substantial. In April 1983, the Iranian quota was doubled from 1.2 to 2.4 mbd. In January 1989, the Iraqi quota was increased from 1.540 to 2.640 mbd, creating parity with Iran. The Saudi Arabian quota was discontinued in April 1983, when Saudi Arabia assumed the role of swing producer, and was increased from 5.380 to 7.887 mbd in March 1992, following the disappearance of Kuwaiti and Iraqi production after the Gulf War. The UAE quota was at the same time increased from 1.5 to

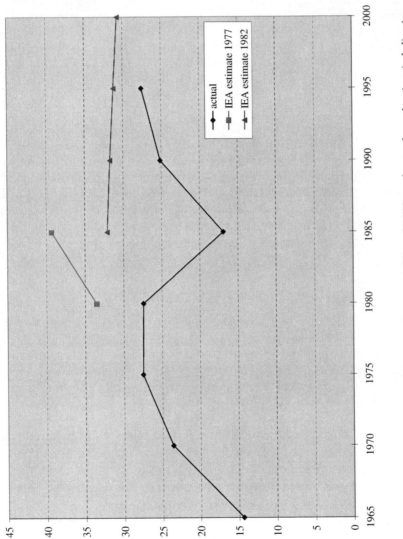

FIGURE 7.2 IEA estimates of OPEC production, 1977 and 1982, and actual production (mbd), nine months average for 2000.
SOURCE: IEA; *BP Statistical Review of World Energy, EIA Weekly Petroleum Status Report.*

2.244 mbd. As pointed out in section 7.2, some forty criteria for distribution of production quotas have been introduced. As argued by Al-Chalabi (1989:25–26), the initial distribution in March 1982 was not based on any objective criteria.

With the quota system, OPEC had proved its ability to formally allocate the agreed production volume. However, the question that immediately emerges is to what extent the quotas have limited production and raised prices so that the net income of the OPEC members have increased.

Changes over Time

Figure 7.3 shows the changes in quotas and production during the period from April 1982 to December 1995. It should be noted that Iraq did not accept its quota between August 1986 and January 1987, nor during 1988. From the Iraqi attack on Kuwait in August 1990 until March 1992, there were no allocated quotas among the members, only an agreed total. As the figure shows, the OPEC countries have produced above the quotas continuously since they were established in April 1982, except for some short periods, mainly accounted for by lack of production capacity due to warfare (see Chapter 3). This does not mean the quota system has not had the effect of limiting production, only that most countries have not abided by the agreed and allocated quotas.

Changes in production are strongly correlated with changes in quotas. The correlation between changes in monthly production and changes in quotas between April 1982 and December 1985 is 0.959. This measure does not tell us which factor causes changes in the other. Lagging the factors, to see if quotas in one month are correlated with production the next month and vice versa, hardly changes the coefficient, although the tendency is that quotas matter more for production than the other way around (see Table 7.7). The differences are small and thus do not rule out the possibility that quotas are set according to production as much as quotas restrain production.

The quota compliance, or lack of such, is demonstrated by the amount of production above quotas (as discussed in section 4.4). It is possible to distinguish between three phases of the OPEC quota bargaining (see Table 7.8). The first period, from April 1982 to December 1985, was characterized by Saudi Arabia's willingness to compensate for the others' overproduction by cutting its own production below its allocated quota. When Saudi Arabia ended this policy, the quota game shifted character. First there was a turbulent period during most of 1986, but when the quotas were more firmly reestablished, a new phase started. This second phase, from late 1986 until the outbreak of the Iraq-Kuwait War in August 1990, was characterized by substantial overproduction also by Saudi Arabia. The quota sys-

TABLE 7.6 OPEC Quota Agreements, April 1982–July 2000 (th. b/d)

	Alg.	Ecua.	Gab.	Ind.	Iran	Iraq	Kuw.	Lib.	Nig.	Qat.	S.A.	UAE	Ven.	Total
Apr 82[1]	650	150	200	1,300	1,200	1,200	800	750	1,300	300	7,650	1,000	1,500	18,000
Apr 83	725	200	150	1,300	2,400	1,200	1,050	1,100	1,300	300	5,000	1,100	1,675	17,500
Oct 84	663	183	137	1,189	2,300	1,200	900	990	1,300	280	4,353	950	1,555	16,000
Aug 86[2]	650	260	190	1,275	2,300		1,250	1,100	1,500	350	4,600	1,250	1,650	16,375
Sep 86	663	183	137	1,189	2,300		900	990	1,300	280	4,353	950	1,555	14,800
Nov 86	669	221	160	1,193	2,317		921	999	1,304	300	4,353	950	1,574	14,961
Dec 86	669	221	160	1,193	2,317		999	999	1,304	300	4,353	950	1,574	15,039
Jan 87	635	210	152	1,133	2,255	1,466	948	948	1,238	285	4,133	902	1,495	15,800
Oct 87	667	221	159	1,190	2,369	1,540	996	996	1,301	299	4,343	948	1,571	16,600
Jan 89	695	230	166	1,240	2,640	2,640	1,037	1,037	1,355	312	4,524	988	1,636	18,500
Jul 89	733	242	175	1,307	2,783	2,783	1,093	1,093	1,428	329	4,769	1,041	1,724	19,500
Sep 90	770	255	184	1,374	2,925	2,925	1,149	1,149	1,502	346	5,013	1,095	1,813	20,500
Jan 90	827	273	197	1,374	3,140	3,140	1,500	1,233	1,611	371	5,380	1,095	1,945	22,086
Jul 90	827	273	197	1,374	3,140	3,140	1,500	1,233	1,611	371	5,380	1,500	1,945	22,491
Apr 91[3]														22,300
Oct 91														23,650
Mar 92	760	273	273	1,374	3,184	505	812	1,395	1,751	377	7,887	2,244	2,147	22,982
Jan 93[4]	764		293	1,374	3,490	500	1,500	1,409	1,857	380	8,395	2,260	2,360	24,582
Mar 93	732		281	1,317	3,340	400	1,600	1,350	1,780	364	8,000	2,161	2,257	23,582
Oct 93	750		287	1,330	3,600	400	2,000	1,390	1,865	378	8,000	2,161	2,359	24,520
Jul 96[5]	750			1,330	3,600	1,200	2,000	1,390	1,865	378	8,000	2,161	2,359	25,033
Jan 98	909			1,456	3,942	1,314	2,190	1,522	2,042	414	8,761	2,366	2,583	27,500
Jul 98[6]	788			1,280	3,318		1,980	1,323	2,033	640	8,023	2,157	2,845	24,387
Apr 99	731			1,187	3,359		1,836	1,22	1,885	593	7,438	2,000	2,720	22,976
Apr 00[7]	788			1,280			1,980	1,323	2,033	640	8,023	2,157	2,845	21,069
Jul 00	811			1,317	3,727		2,037	1,361	2,091	658	8,253	2,219	2,926	25,400

[1] In March 1982 Saudi Arabia was not assigned a quota, but voluntarily limited production by 500 mbd to 7,000 mbd (added 150 mbd in the neutral zone).

[2] Iraq had no quota from August 1986 to January 1987, from January 1988 to December 1988, or from July 1998; figure for March 1992 is actual production.

[3] Following the Iraqi attack on Kuwait in August 1990, the quotas were abandoned until February 1992; figures for 1991 are only agreed total OPEC production.

[4] Ecuador suspended its membership at the 92nd OPEC Conference in November 1992.

[5] The suspension of Gabon's membership was confirmed at the 100th OPEC Conference in July 1996, but was formally effective as of January 1, 1995.

[6] Iran contested its quota of June 1998; it was subsequently changed to 3.623 mbd under the March 1999 agreement, and the official quota of July 1998 changed.

[7] Iran did not agree to the increased quotas and was subsequently not part of the agreement.

SOURCE: OPEC 1990; *OPEC Bulletin*, various issues.

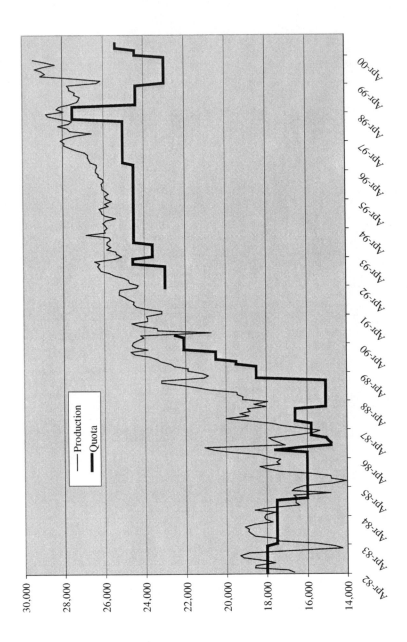

FIGURE 7.3 OPEC production and quotas, April 1982–April 2000 (th. b/d)
SOURCE: OPEC 1990; OPEC Bulletin; Petroleum Economist

TABLE 7.7   Correlation Between Changes in Production and Changes in Quotas

	Production		
Quotas	Base Month	One Month's Lag	Two month's Lag
Base month	.959	.953	.948
One month's lag	.935		
Two month's lag	.912		

TABLE 7.8   OPEC and Saudi Arabian Production, Quotas, and Overproduction During Three Phases from April 1982 to December 1995 (th. b/d)

	Apr. 82–Dec. 85	Nov. 86–July 90	Apr. 92–Dec. 95
OPEC			
Production	17,199	20,752	25,800
Quota	17,167	17,603	24,015
Over-production	33	3,149	1,785
Over-production (%)	0.19	17.89	7.43
Saudi Arabia			
Production	4,667	4,950	8,166
Quota	5,505	4,579	8,004
Over-production	-838	371	162
Over-production (%)	-15.23	8.09	2.03
OPEC			
(excl. Saudi Arabia)			
Production	12,532	15,802	17,634
Quota	11,661	13,023	16,011
Over-production	871	2,779	1,622
Over-production (%)	7.47	21.34	10.13

SOURCE: OPEC 1990; *OPEC Bulletin; Petroleum Economist.*

tem in this period was a failure. After the outbreak of the Iraq-Kuwait War, the quotas were abandoned until April 1992. The following phase, from April 1992 until December 1995, was characterized by the absence of one of the major OPEC producers, namely, Iraq. The UN boycott left more room for the other producers, and this in particular was filled by Saudi Arabia. As Table 7.8 shows, the total quotas in the first and second periods were almost the same, but substantially increased in the third period.

It is hard to determine to what extent the OPEC countries' production was reduced due to the quotas. Several other reasons for changes in production are discussed in this book. From time to time large OPEC producers have neglected their quotas, refused to accept allocated quotas, or simply announced another quota than what was agreed upon at OPEC meetings. On the other hand, OPEC countries' production has been restrained by technical problems, internal political and economical turmoil, and, not least, warfare among members of the organization. The next subsections do, however, indicate a possible explanation for differences in quota compliance among OPEC members.

The Extent of Compliance

Robert Axelrod (1984:10) shows that if the actors meet an infinite or unknown number of times, they will have incentives to choose conditional cooperation because "the shadow of the future" influences the actors' strategic calculations in the game being played. By means of computer-simulated tests, Axelrod shows that the strategy "Tit for Tat" (which involves cooperation in the first round, after which the action the opponent adopted in the previous round is chosen) gives greater discounted utility than the strategy "non-cooperation at all times," which is the strategy when conforming to the orthodox prisoner's dilemma game. Analytically, this is not very helpful because *any* feasible payoff vector can be supported as a Nash equilibrium outcome if there is a sufficient amount of discounting (Friedman 1971 and 1986:103). Furthermore, "in cases where *subsets* of the players find it collectively worthwhile to provide the public good, there arises a quite different strategic problem, which results from some players having an incentive to ensure that the subset which provides the public good does not include themselves" (Taylor 1987:82).

This calls for the inclusion of time as a factor in the study of the OPEC quota-bargaining game. In the following discussion the OPEC quota compliance can thus be seen as n-person prisoner's dilemma iterated an indefinite number of times. The iteration of games opens the possibility for both punishment and forgiveness, and for internal bargains as to who should be allowed a free ride on the others' cooperative efforts. The strategic puzzle facing the individual oil producer is to what extent one's own abidance of quotas is likely to sustain or raise prices, and on the other hand to what extent one's own breaking of quotas is likely to lead to a fall in prices. The answer to this is determined to a great extent by the amount of overproduction, but also by the value of the wide range of contextual factors discussed in Chapter 2. However, it is also highly dependent on the internal strategic question: to what extent one's own quota abidance will make others cooperate, and on the other hand to what extent one's own breaking of quota agreements will make others defect. This is the question to be discussed in this section.

The basic model of an n-person prisoner's dilemma is illustrated in Figure 7.4. Seen from the perspective of player i the x-axis represents the

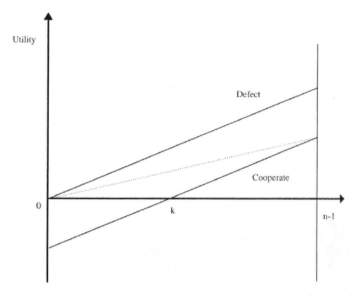

FIGURE 7.4   N-person prisoner's dilemma

number of other actors choosing to cooperate, while the y-axis measures utility.[11] What happens when one moves from a two-person prisoner's dilemma to an n-person prisoner's dilemma is that the so-called k-point can be identified: "there is some number, k, greater than 1, such that if individuals numbering k or more choose their unpreferred alternative and the rest do not, those who do are better off than if they had all chosen their preferred alternatives" (Schelling 1978:218). The critical amount of cooperation (k) illustrates the smallest coalition size that will profit by choosing cooperation rather than a situation where nobody cooperates. It is always better for the individual actor to choose to defect than to cooperate, no matter how many other actors have chosen to cooperate. The value of such defection increases with the number of others that cooperate. This is the so-called free-rider incentive.

From the quotas initiated in April 1982 until September 1999, the average overproduction was above 20 percent. Some members obviously have tried to have a free ride on the others' cooperation. As pointed out by Taylor (1987:82), the aim is not to be part of the group that cooperates. The OPEC members can be assumed to know that their relationship will prevail in the foreseeable future,[12] and that the basis for the collective action, the quotas, can be changed in a few months' time. The quotas are in principle open for renegotiation at every OPEC meeting. In such iterated games, as we have seen, the strategy of noncooperation may no longer be a dominant strategy. Can a situation where *m* members cooperate, while N-*m* does not, form an equilibrium in such a game? The answer is given by the folk theorem: It may for a sufficiently high discount factor. A "trigger strategy" can support such a pattern for a sufficiently high discount factor. In a trigger of this kind, each of the *m* players cooperate in the present round as long as none of the *m* players defected in any previous round.[13]

The higher the discount factor—that is, the more value the players attach to future gains—the lower the subset of cooperators (*m*) is needed in this equilibrium. For a given discount factor, cooperation can be achieved by increasing the number of players choosing cooperation, given others' cooperation. If we assume that ten out of the thirteen OPEC members is sufficient, we will have 286 possible cooperative coalitions.[14] The question of who should constitute the cooperating subset remains open. Based on the discussion in this subsection, two hypotheses about which producers would be likely to cooperate can be put forth: the patient (with the highest discount factor), and the largest (with the highest market share)(Olson 1965).[15] Most of the discussion will be devoted to the latter.

The Role of Patience

A patient producer is one with a low discount rate. Given the discussion above, the lower the discount rate, the more willing the player should be to cooperate by cutting his own production in order to sustain or increase prices. This question then arises: Which producer is likely to be patient? One possible criteria is the relationship between oil reserves and current production.[16] A producer with large reserves compared to present production knows that he will be in the market for a long time. The total income from this producer's oil reserve will thus be stretched out into the future. The producer will have a longer time horizon than a producer with small reserves compared to current production. With a short horizon on the extraction of one's oil reserves, the producer will put little value to the price of oil in the future, since one will not be around as an oil producer at that time.

Figure 7.5 shows the relationship between the reserves/production-ratios of the individual OPEC countries and their overproduction.

The figure shows no clear pattern to the effect that higher R/P-ratios go together with lower overproduction. At least this way of operationalizing patience, or discount rate, does not provide an explanation as to which countries would be more prone to cooperate than others. Let me therefore turn to the other factor: size.

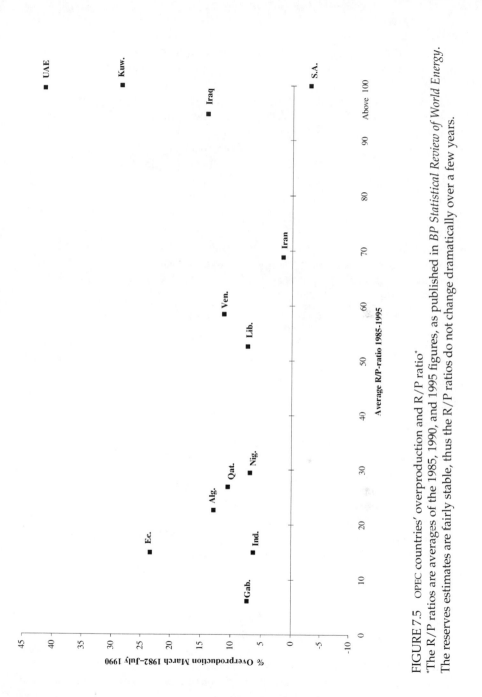

FIGURE 7.5   OPEC countries' overproduction and R/P ratio*

*The R/P ratios are averages of the 1985, 1990, and 1995 figures, as published in *BP Statistical Review of World Energy*. The reserves estimates are fairly stable, thus the R/P ratios do not change dramatically over a few years.

The Role of Size

Olson (1965) emphasizes the size of the group as one, if not the most, important aspect determining the possibility of collective action:

> Even in the smallest groups, however, the collective good will not ordinarily be provided on an optimal scale. . . . This tendency towards suboptimality is due to the fact that a collective good is, by definition, such that other individuals in the group cannot be kept from consuming it once any individual in the group has provided it for himself. Since an individual member thus gets only part of the benefit of any expenditure he makes to obtain more of the collective good, he will discontinue his purchase of the collective good before the optimal amount for the group as a whole has been provided. In addition, the amounts of the collective good that a member of the group receives free from other members will further reduce his incentive to provide more of that good at his own expense. Accordingly, *the larger the group, the farther it will fall short of providing an optimal amount of a collective good.* (Olson 1965:34–35)

In this respect, OPEC is a small organization, with ten to thirteen members during the period studied in this book. However, the OPEC members do not have an equal share of the collective good, understood as a high oil price, as they differ in size; that is, their produced quantity of oil differs. This difference in size of the actors has implications for their willingness to contribute to the collective good. A starting point in the discussion in Chapter 6, on the role of Saudi Arabia, was Olson's argument (1965:22) that the larger the size of an actor (i.e., the market share), the more likely this actor is to contribute to the collective good (i.e., a higher oil price). This is so because the larger the actor is, the larger this actor's relative share is of the collective good if this is provided. Thus, exactly the same argument formulated above by Olson also goes for the size of the individual actor. A small group and a large actor give the same result: a larger share for this individual of the total collective good provided.

Figure 7.6 shows the distribution of the OPEC members' market share and overproduction. Saudi Arabia, the largest producer, is the country least engaged in overproduction. In fact, Saudi Arabia produced less than its allocated quota during the period included in the figure. Among the other countries, the figures are to some extent in accordance with the collective action theory, as the smaller countries, those that most easily would get away with cheating, are less loyal to the agreement than the middle-range countries, albeit with some important exceptions that will be discussed below.

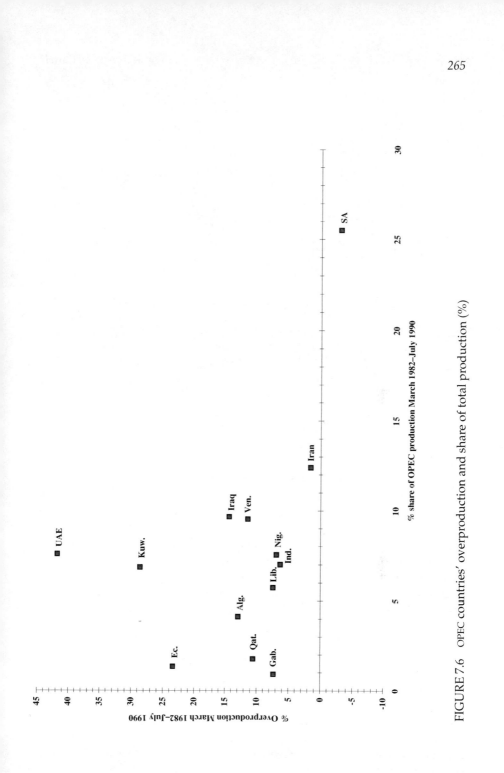

FIGURE 7.6 OPEC countries' overproduction and share of total production (%)

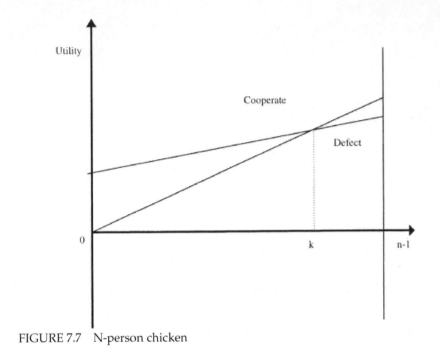

FIGURE 7.7   N-person chicken

As pointed out above, by choosing to cooperate, an actor's utility increases with the number of other actors choosing to cooperate. This implies that the actor's preference for cooperation will increase with its relative share of the total good. For the oil producers, size in this respect is their production, and the relative size is their market share, or, for the OPEC members, their share of total OPEC output. If the actor's production is small, the preference will be never to cooperate (as in the prisoner's dilemma). At a certain size, on the other hand, the individual utility of realization of the collective good will increase, and the actor may regard cooperation as profitable if a number of other actors cooperate. Thus, the larger actor does not have prisoner's dilemma preferences, but preferences represented in the "chicken game" (see Figure 7.7). As pointed out by Hovi (1992:101), if the large actor is sufficiently large, cooperation might even be the dominant strategy; that is, the hegemon will cooperate even if nobody else does (see Chapter 6). The equilibrium point in such a game is that the hegemon provides the collective good, while everybody else defects. In the chicken game it is beneficial for the actor to contribute only if fewer than k actors contribute (see Figure 7.7).

TABLE 7.9   OPEC Members' Overproduction Correlated with Other Members' Overproduction, March 1982–July 1990

Category	Country	Percent Share	Correlation
High	Saudi Arabia	25.50	.335
Middle	Iran	12.41	-.387
	Iraq	9.67	.385
	Venezuela	9.53	-.015
	UAE	7.58	.663
	Nigeria	7.55	.435
	Indonesia	7.01	.244
	Kuwait	6.86	.701
	Libya	5.74	-.110
	Algeria	4.12	.572
Low	Qatar	1.77	.298
	Ecuador	1.34	.005
	Gabon	0.92	.444

Notes: Production is measured as a percentage share of total OPEC production.

The beta-coefficients referred to as "Correlation" in Table 7.9 are calculated as the overproduction of the respective countries in relation to the overproduction of all other OPEC members. A high positive value is interpreted as follows: The more other members overproduce, the more this country overproduces. This would give a crude indication of the countries' tendencies to pursue a prisoner's dilemma strategy or a chicken strategy. A country following a prisoner's dilemma strategy will increase production no matter what others do; a country with chicken preferences will decrease (increase) its own production as others increase (decrease) their production. As Table 7.9 indicates, only Iran and Libya, and to a minor extent, Venezuela, seem to have followed a chicken strategy.

Table 7.10 combines the notion of the three phases of the quota cooperation introduced in Table 7.8 with the three categories of producer size introduced in Table 7.9. The table shows the relationship between others' and own overproduction among the three categories during the three phases.

The coefficients in Table 7.10 clearly demonstrate the change in the Saudi Arabian strategy, from reducing production as others increase theirs to strongly increasing production as other increase theirs. Note that the high-production category consists of only Saudi Arabia. The middle-production category consists of countries with different scores, making the average coefficient almost zero. Some of these countries are discussed individually below, as they represent idiosyncrasies. The low-production category performed as solid prisoner's dilemma actors in the two first

TABLE 7.10   Relationship Between Others' Overproduction and Own
Overproduction

Time Periods	Low	Middle	High	All
Apr. 82–Dec. 85	.2158	-.0565	-.2686	-.1538
Nov. 86–July 90	.3072	.0204	.7185	.0867
Apr. 92–Dec. 95	.0327	-.0474	.6672	-.0209

phases, while the third phase needs further explanation. The number indicated might suggest that the small producers behaved more cooperatively in the third period. The explanation is that Ecuador left OPEC effectively from January 1993, and Gabon left the organization effectively from January 1995. Accordingly, they are not included in the entire third period. Each left the organization stating they would pursue an independent oil-production policy. Their free-rider strategies have thus been even stronger than the others, without this being expressed in Table 7.10.

Some Idiosyncrasies

Apart from the strategic questions discussed, one can propose the hypothesis that the individual actor's quota compliance is determined more by individual characteristics than by considerations about the implications of other members' behavior on one's own interests or of one's own behavior on the other members' interests. To some extent the factors proposed by member countries in the discussion about quota allocation can be used to explain why countries comply or not. Figure 7.6 above demonstrated the relationship between an individual member's production and quota compliance. The findings were mostly in line with the argument that larger producer are more prone to cooperate than small producers.

The most important exception is the United Arab Emirates. Here, there is an idiosyncratic explanation. The UAE consist of several kingdoms joined together in a confederation. The oil policy is not subject to interference from the federal governmental level. There is therefore collective bargaining inside the UAE to allocate the total quota among the kingdoms. The major kingdom, Abu Dhabi, joined OPEC in 1967. After the formation of the UAE in 1971, the Abu Dhabi membership was transferred to the United Arab Emirates. At this time, the other kingdoms were rather small oil producers. In the following years their oil production increased. The other kingdoms did not, however, feel the same obligations toward OPEC as Abu Dhabi. Abu Dhabi is thus subject to pressure from the other kingdoms to make room for their increased oil production under the UAE quota. As a result, the Unites Arab Emirates face a collective action problem internally before the country enters the OPEC negotiations. This actually strengthens the relevance of the collective action problem, as the UAE might more accurately, in this perspective, be included in Figure 7.6 as five small producers with a smaller share of production, but with the same percentage share of overproduction.

Another outlier is Iraq. The Iraqi overproduction is intimately connected with the war between Iran and Iraq. When the quotas were established in March 1982, Iran and Iraq were allocated the same quota. A year later the Iranian quota was doubled from 1.2 to 2.4 mbd. The main reason was that Iran, despite the war with Iraq, had been able to increase its production. This was not the case for Iraq, and the Iraqi quota was therefore not increased. However, the Iraqi government made it clear that it would accept only a quota that was on a par with that of Iran, regardless of what the actual Iraqi production was. Iraq was first able to increase oil output in 1985. Most of the Iraqi overproduction happened between this increase in capacity and the OPEC decision to give Iraq parity with Iran from January 1989. Iraq chose not to comply with a quota the country had not accepted from the outset.

Two other countries can be mentioned here, namely, Kuwait and Venezuela. As discussed in section 2.6, oil producers with large downstream assets stand to gain even if crude oil prices are low, since their income is also derived from refineries and product sales. Kuwait and Venezuela are the oil producers with the largest shares of downstream activities in relation to their crude production. The Kuwaiti revenue is equally divided between crude sales and income from downstream activities. Contrary to the other OPEC members, these producers can increase their downstream income when crude oil prices fall, and thereby make up for the lost income in the crude oil sector. With substantial vertical integration, they also move their own oil downstream and thus operate like multinational companies with internal pricing. This price-setting might exclude some aspects of costs in the different stages of the production chain, in order to make up for fluctuations in the crude oil price. Thus, their cost-benefit calculations are different from those of the other producers, and they also have some freedom of action that the other producers lack. These idiosyncrasies suggest that other considerations might influence the countries' interests connected with cooperating with other producers.

7.5 The Profits of Cooperation

This section will describe the development of revenues to the OPEC countries during the period discussed in this book. How to attribute the profit to the OPEC countries' cooperative behavior is discussed in section 7.6.[17]

Figure 7.8 indicates the movement of price and production and the derived revenue. The vertical axis is the price, the horizontal is the OPEC production, while the iso-revenue curves are drawn to indicate different revenue levels. Income increases diagonally from the origin of coordinates. The line drawn inside the figure is a combination of OPEC production and price, and thus indicates the revenue level.[18] The picture presented in Figure 7.8 clearly shows how the revenue of the OPEC countries increased from 1973 to 1979 (with the exception of 1975), without any reduction in the members' production. Oil demand was virtually price-inelastic in the short-term (a few years). This had less to do with cartel behavior than with the increased oil dependency of the consuming countries, and a psychological notion of scarcity in the industrialized world. As described in section 5.1, most OPEC countries became exhilarated by their success and pushed for further price increases. Furthermore, as is shown in Figure 7.8, after the second oil-price shock in 1979–1980, both OPEC production and price fell until 1985 (see section 5.2). In 1986, the price fell dramatically and OPEC changed its market strategy. During the decade from 1986 to 1996, the oil price fluctuated moderately, but followed a downward trend. OPEC production increased steadily (see section 5.3). This combination left OPEC revenue fairly stable during this ten-year period, with an exception of 1990, when the oil price rose in the autumn as a result of the Iraq-Kuwait War.

Another indication of OPEC's gains is the value of OPEC members' oil exports. Figure 7.9 illustrates how this income has varied substantially, increasing until 1980 and then declining with 1986 as a low point. The argument in this chapter and in Chapter 4, that the organization actually began working as a cartel in 1982 with the introduction of the quota system, means that the cartel has performed poorly in increasing or even in sustaining the revenue or value of exports for its members.

Given an understanding of OPEC as a cartel with a competitive fringe (the non-OPEC producers behaving as price-takers), the key variables determining the future oil price are the total demand, the non-OPEC producers' capacity (as they are assumed to produce at full capacity at all times), and, on the basis of these factors, the "call on OPEC." With the effects of the Iranian revolution and the Iran-Iraq War on oil prices, forecasts followed about the future development of the oil price that were to be proven totally wrong. As was discussed in Chapter 2, the level of consumption had reacted only for a short period to the 1973–1974 price increase. In 1981, consumption was still perceived to be price-inelastic. The non-OPEC producers were perceived to have limited reserves and thus as representing no long-term threat to the position of OPEC. Increased demand and limited supply lead to assumptions of continual sharp price increases (see Figure 7.10).

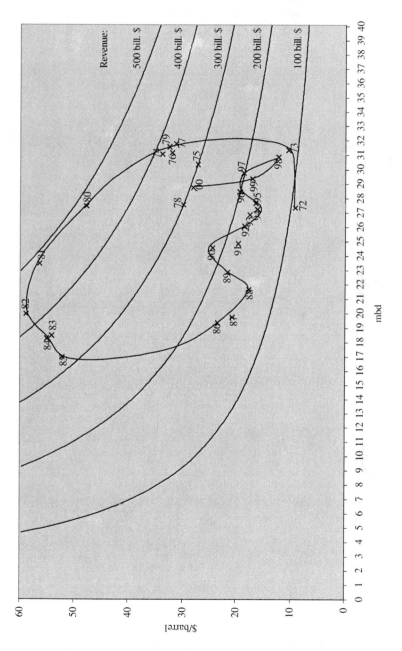

FIGURE 7.8 OPEC revenue (bill. 1998 $), price (1998 $/barrel), and production (mbd), 1972–2000

SOURCE: Author's calculation based on *BP Statistical Review of World Energy 1996* and Mork 1994, and OPEC *Annual Statistical Bulletin*.

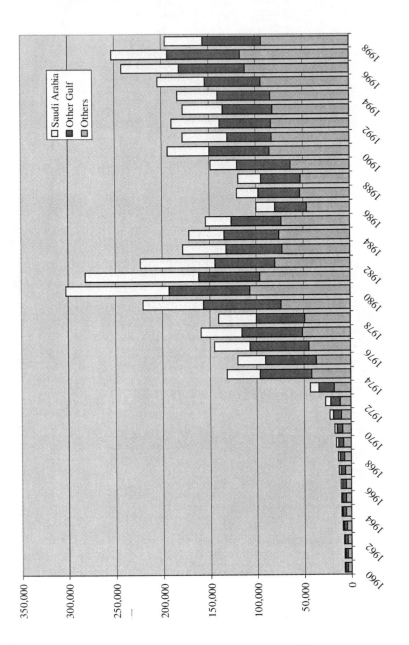

FIGURE 7.9 Value of OPEC members' oil exports, 1960–1998 (mil. $)
SOURCE: *OPEC Annual Statistical Bulletin.*

After 1981, the tables turned. Although the forecasts still predicted higher prices in the longer term, the short-term situation was different. The stock downdraw and surplus production over a demand that was flattening out made the short-term outlook bleak for the OPEC countries. During the first half of the eighties, Saudi Arabia and some of the other OPEC members cut back their production and sustained prices well above the competitive level. This strategy, more in line with that of a cartel, was based on the perception that the weak prices were a short-term problem, caused by the international companies' reduction of stocks. This strategy was understandable, as the message of the 1981 forecasts by almost everybody in the industry was that OPEC, having increased the price of oil from $10 to $50 per barrel, could look forward to $70 per barrel in 1990 and $90 to $100 per barrel in the year 2000 (all figures in 1990 $). There was no reason to believe that the fall in spot prices would continue—it was just a question of riding out the storm (see Figure 7.10). Short-term production cutbacks would ease the pressure on prices. However, as discussed in section 2.5, oil demand did not pick up, and non-OPEC production increased further, beyond all forecasts. The price was additionally pressured, and so were the member countries' revenues.

7.6 A Cartel or a Success?

"OPEC is not the cartel that some of our friends outside like to portray us as; if we acted as a true cartel, prices wouldn't be where they are right now!"[19] "Cartel is by far the most widely used term to describe OPEC. ... However, there is general agreement that the textbook definition of a cartel does not apply to pre-1982 OPEC, and specialists have spent much time identifying the internal features that make OPEC successful despite this fact" (Crémer and Isfahani 1991:31). These quotes highlight the analytical problem of an evaluative chapter like this one: What is the relationship between the cooperative or cartel-like behavior of OPEC and the oil price and thus OPEC members' revenue?

In the introduction to this chapter two questions were put forth concerning the extent of OPEC countries' cooperative behavior and the possible gains from such behavior. The previous section suggests that a nontrivial amount of cooperative behavior has taken place. A more precise measurement is unattainable because we can not know with certainty how these actors would have behaved if they had not cooperated within the framework of OPEC. It is equally hard to determine how much of the revenues that can be attributed to cooperative behavior among the oil producers compared to other factors that increased the producers' profits. As pointed out in the introduction to this chapter, it is difficult to know what the oil revenue of the producers would have been had there been no coop-

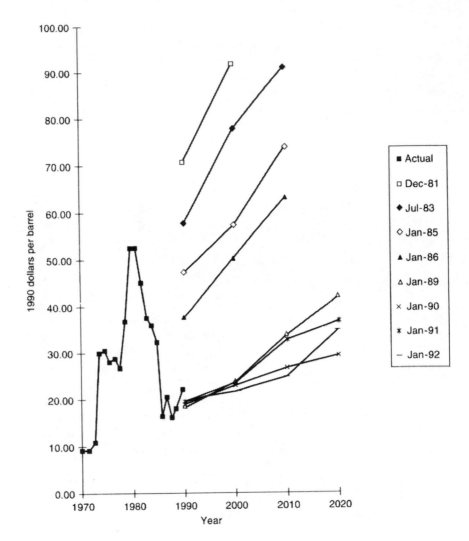

FIGURE 7.10 Crude oil prices, actual and successive International Energy Workshop polls
SOURCE: Adelman 1995:188.

eration between them. In the spring of 1986, when OPEC abandoned the strategy of defending the price level and began pursuing a strategy to protect its market share, the price fell to about $10/barrel (see section 5.3). The same level was reached during the price fall of 1998–1999 (see section 5.3). Since the price only stayed at that level for short periods of time, the actual effect on investments and replacement of reserves was not empirically tested. Adelman (1986) has estimated the competitive price of oil— that is, the price without producer cooperation in some form—in 1986 to be $8 in the short run and $5 in the longer run. He claims that these prices would maintain investments in new reserves and capacity:

> At the high-cost end, it would take a price as low as $4 to produce an immediate shutdown of nearly half of capacity in the United States, and as low as $2 to do the same in the North Sea. . . . At the low-cost end (assuming competition and completely independent decisionmaking) a price of $5 would make it profitable for the OPEC nations to expand their output to over 60 million barrels daily. That price would be sustainable past 1995 at the least. (Adelman 1986:10)

On the other end, one can hardly claim that OPEC has behaved as a full-fledged monopolist, and thus gained the profit of a monopolist. The reason why this monopolist profit has not been reached by a cartel like OPEC is explained by Willett (1979a:55):

> As the members of the cartel raise prices towards the joint profit-maximization level, the expected increase in profits, if the cartel held together, would have to be balanced against the increased risk that the cartel would split apart, reducing profits for all the members. Because of this trade-off between maximum possible profits and the increased likelihood of a breakdown in the restrictive arrangements, the optimal price for a cartel would usually be less than the optimal full monopoly price.

Lack of OPEC cohesion and misreading of the "maximum possible profits" forced prices down. In the seventies they increased the price too much, and in the eighties they cut production too little. They were not at all alone in this misreading (see Figure 7.10).

The conclusion regarding the relationship between cooperation and revenue is thus a mixed one. The stated ambitions of OPEC have not been met, but the revenues obtained have exceeded what would have been obtained in a competitive international oil market. The description of the development of revenue and value of exports clearly shows that the OPEC members gained from the developments of the seventies. But this was not a result of cooperative behavior. In the latter half of the seventies, discounting undermined the official prices. Individual OPEC member countries secretly undercut their own official price. This can hardly be regarded as disciplined cartel behavior, but rather as the use of a competitive tool against other members of the organization. The price increase from 1978 to 1981 was not caused by OPEC but was an effect of revolution and warfare (see Chapter 3).

The picture becomes even more complicated when the argument is taken one step further: How has this market control come about? Has it been provided by deliberative cooperative efforts, or has it been the result of uncoordinated but similar and simultaneous behavior of individual rational actors based on favorable market conditions? As this study has shown, OPEC is not a single headed entity. "Different members of the cartel might prefer different prices because they differed either in their degrees of risk aversion or their expectations about the cohesiveness of the cartel" (Willett 1979a:55).

A solid test of the importance of cooperative behavior is only possible when the individual and the collective rationally diverge. This was not the case during the seventies. One does not need to cooperate with others in order to raise prices when the producer at the same time can sustain the production level. This became apparent during the Iranian revolution in 1978–1979 and with the outbreak of the Iran-Iraq War of 1980–1981. In these situations the restrictions agreed upon at the OPEC Conference were abandoned in favor of a free-for-all price increase. The fact that the price could not be raised without negative consequences for the market outlet for OPEC oil became evident in the beginning of the eighties. When the market-sharing mechanism—the quotas—was introduced, the costs of cooperation followed suit as the free-rider incentive appeared. So, we are back at the argument in the introduction to this chapter: Cartels are least effective when they are most needed. The internal cohesion is the key issue.

> Under competition, market-sharing is automatic. Each operator produces all it can, up to the point where the cost of additional output would exceed the price. But a cartel exists for only one reason: to keep the price above the marginal cost. Thereby, the cartel shuts off the automatic market-sharing mechanism. A joint decision by the members must replace it. But market-sharing is a zero-sum game: any member's gain is another member's loss. (Adelman 1995:6)

This study has, in line with Willett (1979a), emphasized the differences among the OPEC members, and in particular the special role of Saudi Arabia. The costs of cooperation were carried by Saudi Arabia from 1982 until 1985. When Saudi Arabia found this intolerable, the cooperation collapsed. The situation in the first nine months of 1986 is the closest the international oil market has ever been to a competitive market. OPEC's call for help from the non-OPEC producers illustrates how the cartel had lost its previous potential. Political circumstances "helped" the cartel from August 1990—first, as the Iraq-Kuwait War stopped output from these countries and, later, as the UN sanctions prohibited Iraqi exports, leaving room for Saudi Arabia to sustain a higher level of production without causing a deterioration of the oil price. The connection between the market situation and the problem for the internal OPEC cooperation was the starting point of this chapter when it was stated that cartels are easiest to establish when they are least needed. OPEC clearly illustrates this point.

During the seventies, OPEC as an organization played a minor role; the behavior of the OPEC members did, however, cause substantial price increases and, in fact, changed the structure of and market-power relations in the international oil market. During the first half of the eighties, OPEC, or, more accurately, Saudi Arabia, paid the price for having overexploited the market, as demand and non-OPEC supply changed (see section 2.5), with the effect of pressing prices down and leaving less room for OPEC production. Now, the organizational factors made a difference, and the organization actually reduced the freedom of action of the members (see Chapter 4). Since 1982, OPEC has cut production significantly and, in some periods, substantially. This, among other factors, has kept the price above its competitive level. As shown in section 7.5, this gave the OPEC countries increased revenue.

The internal distribution of gains and costs of this cooperative policy has varied over time and among members. Most important in the discussion in this chapter is the tendency to cheat on agreed production levels, that is, the quota compliance. Apart from the important exceptions mentioned in section 7.4, the OPEC producers fit the proposition that smaller countries tend to cheat more than larger countries. This leads back to the role of Saudi Arabia discussed in Chapter 6. Saudi Arabia's role inside OPEC has some similarities with the economic market model called "dominant-firm." This model describes a market with one large producer and several small firms. The core assumption is that "the dominant firm sets the price and allows the minor firms to sell all they can at that price; the dominant firm sells the rest" (Cohen and Cyert 1975:245). This makes the other producers behave competitively, and if the dominant firm's market share becomes very small, the market "reverts to the competitive solution" (Crémer and Isfahani 1991:31). Saudi Arabia performed a role as dominant firm from 1982 to 1985.[20] This made the other producers insensitive to the changes in demand and non-OPEC production (see section 2.5). They had experience with demand regulations. When they had experienced weak demand in the mid–1970s, they had adjusted prices (see section 5.1). When prices had to be defended with reduced production in the early 1980s, Saudi Arabia took the burden. In a way, the problem since then has been to make every OPEC member behave as dominant firms—that is, to constantly consider the right output level in order to support agreed prices target. This price target should be a best estimate of what could be called "sustainable monopoly price." That is the highest price attainable that does not stimulate alternative supplies, conversion into other energy forms, or reduce stable demand tends. If producers do this in concert, we are talking about a cartel, or "cartel-like behavior."

After these four chapters on internal OPEC affairs, the main reason for lack of success (i.e., prices below the sustainable monopoly price) is the individual members' compliance with price and production agreements. Already in the early 1980s the idea of compensating this lack of internal cohesion by increasing the scope of oil-producer cooperation emerged. The next two chapters address this issue.

Notes

1. The phenomenon called collective good is discussed in sections 7.2 and 7.4. A high oil price is regarded as a collective good for the oil producers throughout this chapter.

2. This to some extent assumes stable demand level. The demand also will have to be somewhat inelastic. With an elastic demand, small price changes would necessitate large changes in a production level, which would be costly for the cartel members.

3. Non-OPEC producers here are assumed to behave as price-takers maximizing profit without considering that their production level could influence the world market price.

4. Possibly except for the period during and immediately after the Gulf War between Iraq and Kuwait in 1990–1991.

5. In addition there are two instrumental aspects: allocation of output, and detection and punishment of cheaters (see section 7.2).

6. For some countries there are positive correlations during some of the individual periods.

7. As was discussed in further detail in Chapter 3, the Iranian production is susceptible to factors other than the oil policy and economic interests of the Iranian regime. Warfare and destruction of oil installations have had a detrimental impact on Iran's ability to produce oil.

8. "The 'hawkish' Iraqis, who had demanded a 30 percent price increase in 1975, actually cut prices in 1976 to gain market share" (Adelman 1995:158).

9. "There are two main aspects of crude oil quality which influence the price, the distillate content and the sulphur content . . . light crude oils do command higher prices than the heavier crudes and this may be expressed as a gravity differential" (Jenkins 1986:335).

10. I am indebted to Leif Helland for his comments and suggestions, which strongly improved the game theoretical parts of this section.

11. Let $f(n)$ be the payoff for any player when he chooses cooperation (C) and n others choose C, and $g(n)$ the payoff when he chooses to defect and n others choose C. Then an n-person prisoner's dilemma is defined by: (i) $g(n) > f(n)$ for each value of $n \geq 0$, and (ii) $f(N-1) > g(0)$. (Taylor 1987:83-84).

12. Unless, of course, a member decides to sustain the membership.

13. The discount factor has to satisfy the following condition if defection should not pay off for a member i in m:

$$\delta \geq \frac{g_i(m-1) - f_i(m-1)}{g_i(m-1) - g_i(0)}$$

For example, if we assume that Defect yields 2 utilities more than Cooperation, that is, $g_i(n) = n$ and $f_i(n) = n-2$, and insert the number of OPEC members, we get the following level of discount factor sustaining cooperation:

$$\delta \geq \frac{g_i(13-1) - f_i(13-1)}{g_i(13-1) - g_i(0)} = \frac{12-10}{12} = 0.17$$

14. This number is given by the binomial coefficient:

$$\delta \geq \frac{N!}{m!(N-m)!} = \frac{13!}{10!(3)!} = 286$$

15. Since the OPEC members differ in size, defined by their market share, the actual number is less relevant than the combined market share of the cooperating members.

16. There are of course several other factors influencing a particular producer's patience. Some idiosyncratic factors are discussed below.

17. It should also be noted that I do not address the important question of what the OPEC members have done with the profit. This is a topic recently covered by others (Amuzegar 1999 and Karl 1997).

18. Figure 7.8 includes no estimation of costs. Cost data are inherently uncertain or mostly unavailable. There is no reason to assume that inclusion of cost data would have changed the overall picture presented in the figure, although the shape of the line drawn inside the figure might have been tilted somewhat if costs had changed over time.

19. OPEC's Secretary-General, Rilwanu Lukman, interviewed in *Petroleum Economist* March 1999:8.

20. Willett (1979a:56) predicted this in 1979: "there appears to be a reasonable expectation that over the coming decade the Saudis, perhaps in collaboration with other members of the Organization of Arab Petroleum Exporting Countries (OAPEC) would have to accept a disproportionate share of the group's required cutback in production."

8

Extending the Cooperation: OPEC and the Non-OPEC Producers

The previous four chapters have dealt with the oil-producer cooperation that has taken place inside the organization—OPEC. It is time to turn the focus beyond the borders of this organization. In 1998, 58 percent of world oil production took place outside OPEC. As described in section 2.5, OPEC lost control over prices in the 1980s not only because of reduced oil demand, but also due to increased oil supplies from outside the organization.

> OPEC has lost another 7–8 mbd of marketable oil in favor of these new and numerous producers, who have benefited from the Organization's non-economic pricing system which enabled them to invest directly or through the oil companies in new oilfields. . . . OPEC helped make it easy for non-OPEC countries to invest profitably in oil. (Al-Chalabi 1989:42)

The loss of market share to non-OPEC producers became a pressing problem for OPEC in the beginning of the 1980s. This chapter will describe some of the problems of extending the oil-producer cooperation beyond the organizational borders of OPEC. Although many structural constraints and national interests are the same among producers inside and outside OPEC, the non-OPEC producers as a group are even more heterogeneous than the OPEC members. Likewise, their policies toward oil-producer cooperation vary wildly. A fuller description of a particular bargaining relationship between an OPEC and a non-OPEC producer is presented in section 9.2. Chapter 9 also provides a more thorough explanation of a non-OPEC producer's (Norway's) behavior. Chapter 9 can thus be seen as a case study of the more general issues discussed in both this and the previous chapter.

TABLE 8.1   Categories of Non-OPEC Producers

	Category I	*Category II*	*Category III*
Production (mbd)	Above 2	0.3 to 1	0.1 to 0.3
Share of non-OPEC:			
Reserves	About 70%	Nearly 25%	About 5%
Production	About 60%	Above 20%	Above 5%
Countries	Canada, UK, Norway, US, Mexico, China, Russia	Brazil, Oman, Egypt, Argentina, Angola, Malaysia, India, Syria, Colombia, Australia, Kazakhstan, Yemen, Gabon, Ecuador	Congo, Denmark, Vietnam, Peru, Italy Azerbaijan, Brunei, Romania, Trinidad and Tobago, Turkmenistan, Cameroon

SOURCE: EIA (1999b).

8.1   The Non-OPEC Producers in General

The non-OPEC producers can be categorized according to their production. The U.S. Energy Information Administration (EIA) (1999b) applies three categories that cover all non-negligible producers (see Table 8.1).

In section 3.5 the political heterogeneity of the OPEC countries was underlined. A glance at Table 8.1 proves the heterogeneity of the non-OPEC countries along almost every indicator from political system to economic growth. The previous chapters have discussed the problem of collective action among the now eleven OPEC members. Extending the collective action to include all the thirty-two countries in Table 8.1 seems impossible. The role of these countries in oil-producer cooperation has thus been more as bilateral relations with OPEC or OPEC-countries than as a collective entity. However, there have been exceptions, and informally some of these countries have bilateral relations among themselves concerning oil issues. During the nineties oil ministers from Mexico and Norway have had several bilateral meetings. It should also be noted that the non-OPEC group includes two countries that until 1992 (Ecuador) and 1995 (Gabon) were members of OPEC. In the rest of this subsection I will comment briefly on some characteristics of some of the non-OPEC producers in category I of Table 8.1.

New oil reserves are continuously discovered within and outside of OPEC. However, OPEC still controls over seventy percent of the worlds proven oil reserves. Concerning production, the non-OPEC countries have decreased their share from 66.1 percent in 1988 to 47.9 percent in 1998. These figures conceal an almost halving of the market share of the former Soviet Union. As Figure 8.1 indicates, the other non-OPEC countries have sustained their market share or, in fact, increased it by 1.5 percent, while the increased market share of OPEC has been at the expense of the former Soviet Union.

The political and economic changes in the Soviet Union since 1985 are of course beyond the scope of this study. The fall in oil production was, however, accompanied by an even faster fall in oil consumption. During the 1990s, the (now Russian) export outside the former Soviet Union countries has thus turned around, and increased steadily since 1992 (see Figure 8.2). A paradox then emerged as Russia's role in the international market was strengthened at the same time that its production fell dramatically. Lack of investments during the decade also have made it unlikely that Russia will be able to increase the oil production rapidly. In the longer term, Russia is among the most promising non-OPEC areas for making larger new discoveries. "The former Soviet republics may still offer the best possibilities of developing giant and even super-giant fields outside the Middle East" (Hartshorn 1993:274).

Another large oil producer—in fact, the world's second largest in 1998—the United States has experienced a turbulence when it comes to the relationship between own production and consumption. Figure 8.3 shows the US consumption, production, and import required from 1965 to 1998. The US oil is thus not a part of the day-to-day international oil trade. Changes in US consumption or production, on the other hand, do have substantial impact on the world's overall supply-and-demand balance. The development of US oil consumption during the 1980s and 1990s is also noteworthy. Despite the economic growth and development of two decades, oil consumption as of 1998 was still below the peak of 1978.

The import share has from time to time worried the US government. Increasing imports in times of increasing prices, as was the case of the early seventies, are worse than increasing imports in times of falling prices, as was the case of the late nineties. In November 1973, US President Richard Nixon addressed the nation with the following words: "Let us set as our national goal . . . that by the end of this decade we will have developed the potential to meet our own energy needs without depending on any foreign energy sources. . . . We have an energy crisis, but there is no crisis of the American spirit" (Bull-Berg 1987:3). In 1998, when US oil imports reached an unprecedented high of more than 55 percent, a perception of an energy crisis in the US government was hard to discover.

The two largest non-OPEC producers, Russia and the United States, are both large consumers. The United States is an increasingly large net im-

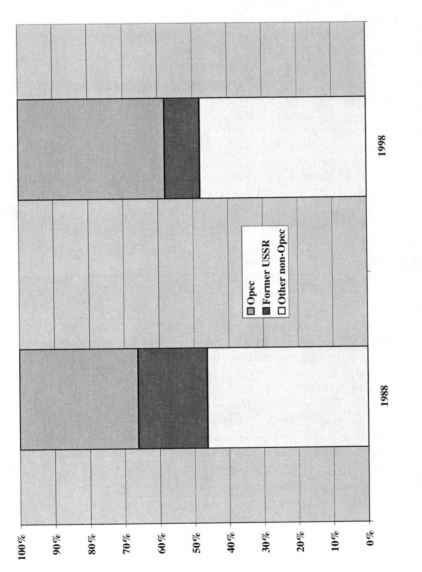

FIGURE 8.1 Market share of OPEC, former Soviet Union, and other non-OPEC, 1988 and 1998 (%)
SOURCE: *BP Statistical Review of World Energy*, 1999.

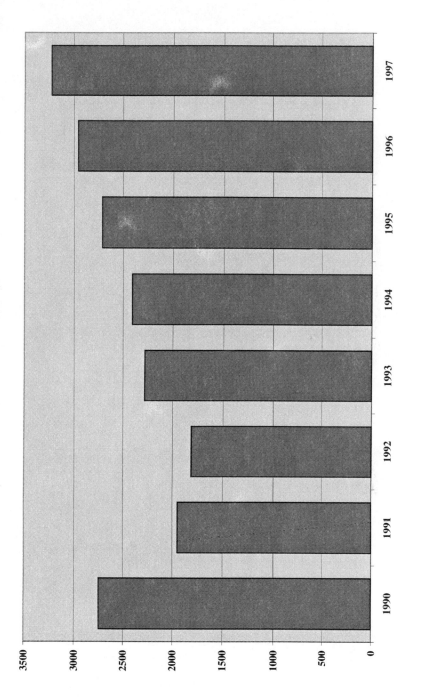

FIGURE 8.2   Russian oil exports outside former Soviet Union, 1990–1997 (th. b/d)
SOURCE: EIA (1998).

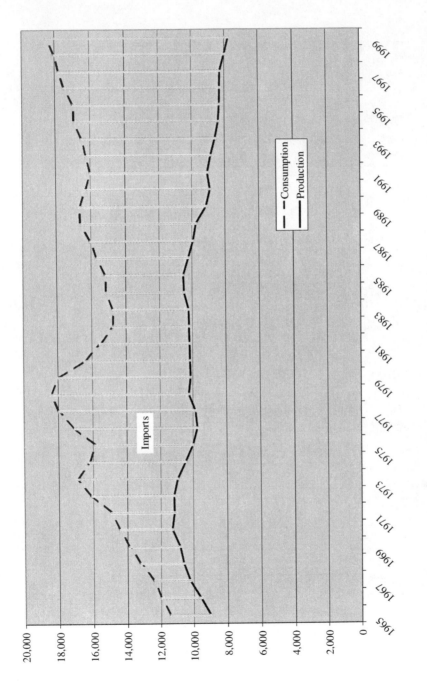

FIGURE 8.3 U.S. oil production, consumption, and imports, 1965–1999 (th. b/d).
SOURCE: *BP Statistical Review of World Energy*.

porter. Russia has contributed to the oil-producer cooperation by stating its intention to cut production in 1986. In 1996, the then Soviet Union increased its production to the OECD the following year (Al-Chalabi 1989:44).

Mexico has been far more willing and active in the dialogue with OPEC (see section 8.2). Having turned into a net importer of oil, a deep-drilling exploration program was launched, leading to large new discoveries in 1972, and by 1974, Mexico was again a net exporter (Yergin 1991:666), thus coinciding with the price increase of the first oil price shock. Adelman (1995:150) argues that all the new Mexican fields of the early 1970s were profitable at pre-1974 prices. Unfortunately, the combination of discoveries and price increases led Mexico to borrow a large amount of money abroad. Adelman (1995:196) is rather harsh in his description of the Mexican oil industry and financial restraints:

> In Mexico, the national oil company Petroleos Mexicanos (Pemex) was a gaudy exemplar of corruption and waste. The belief in ever-raising prices was a national disaster. With roughly 50 billion barrels in reserves and current prices exceeding $30 per barrel, it seemed safe to borrow $60 billion abroad. The result was a national financial crisis and massive disinvestment in oil production. . . . Moreover, many of the wells were uneconomic, drilled to provide local jobs and contracts. . . . The policy was slowly reversed, especially after 1988, but revival and cleaning up the debris of long mismanagement is painful and slow.

Although the Mexican oil reserves have declined during the last decade, the production increased from 2.9 mbd in 1988 to 3.5 in 1998.

Although the production level of Canada and the United Kingdom brings them into the first category in Table 8.1, their net export makes them less significant in the market of internationally traded oil. Thus they will not be commented on further here. China is, in this regard, in the same situation as the United States as a major producer, but also a net importer. The Chinese case is exactly opposite the development in Russia. China has become a net importer due to a strong increase in oil consumption during the last decade (see Figure 8.4).

Taking both market share and net export into consideration, this sketchy description of the largest non-OPEC producers leaves us with three important substantial net-exporters: Russia, Mexico, and Norway. Together with some of the minor non-OPEC producers, these three countries have been the target for OPEC's invitations to cooperation. This will be further discussed in the next section.

288

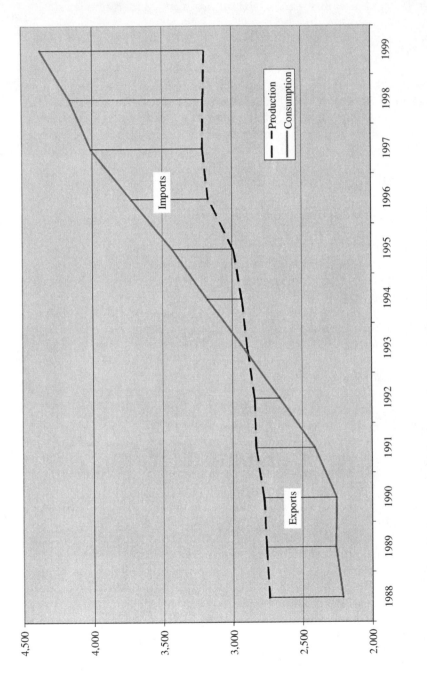

FIGURE 8.4 Chinese oil production and consumption, 1988–1999 (th. b/d)

SOURCE: *BP Statistical Review of World Energy.*

8.2   The OPEC–Non-OPEC Bargaining

In 1965, OPEC had a market share of about 45 percent. In 1998, the share was 42 percent. In between these almost identical figures, OPEC's market share was as high as 53 percent (1973) and as low as 29 percent (1985). With a market share of 53 percent, producers outside the organization were hardly a concern for OPEC at all. With a market share of 29 percent, the non-OPEC producers were almost the only concern.

When OPEC official prices came under pressure in 1981 (see section 5.2), the non-OPEC producers caused problems for OPEC when they led in open price reductions in the years 1982 to 1984. In March 1982, the British oil company BNOC reduced its reference price with $4 to $31, $5.5 below similar Nigerian crude quality. Norway and the Soviet Union followed the British move. Although the price was subsequently increased, the same procedure of reduction happened again in February 1983. In October 1984, Norway took the lead by abandoning the reference price and introducing market-related prices. "Spokesmen for Statoil said, however, that the company's intention was not to lead the market but rather to formalize an existing situation which had been disguised by the use of 'unreal" official prices' (Evans 1991:639; see section 9.3). The North Sea producers' moves were particularly hard to swallow for the weak link in the OPEC chain—Nigeria. A poor African country with high dependency on oil income—and a similar crude quality as the North Sea producers—Nigeria had a hard time placing its crude oil on the market, and had to shadow the price reductions of the North Sea producers. Thus, the market-driven price behavior of the non-OPEC producers had immediate repercussions into the coherence among the OPEC producers. As discussed in section 6.4, Saudi Arabia carried the burden during these years by cutting its production in an attempt to balance the market. When this was impossible to achieve, Saudi Arabia changed its strategy to defend its market share. So did OPEC in December 1985. Then the bargaining game toward the non-OPEC producers also changed character. Now an actual price war commenced. In a press conference held after the December 1985 OPEC Conference, the Saudi Arabian oil minister, Ahmad Zaki Yamani, made a clear warning to the non-OPEC producers when answering a question about the likelihood of a price war: "It all depends on what the non-OPEC producers will do."[1] The Norwegian response is discussed in further detail in section 9.2; here, I shall discuss the general picture regarding the non-OPEC response to the situation that emerged in December 1985.

Table 8.2 lists the most important non-OPEC producers, their production and net exports, and their signaling of a cooperative or noncooperative attitude toward the OPEC invitations to cooperate in 1985. If Norway

TABLE 8.2   Characteristics of Selected Non-OPEC Producers, 1985–1986

	Production	Consumption	Net Exports	Strategy
United Kingdom	2,655	1,630	1,025	nc
Argentina	490	400	90	nc
Canada	1,810	1,490	320	nc
Trinidad	175	NA	175	nc
Norway	815	200	615	nc/c
USSR	12,035	8,360	3,675	c
Mexico	2,910	1,240	1,670	c
Egypt	890	415	475	c
China	2,505	1,810	695	c
Oman	500	NA	500	c
Malaysia	445	195	250	c
Total			9,490	

Note: Production is in th. b/d in 1985, and attitude is denoted by c = cooperative and/or nc = noncooperative

SOURCE: Production and Consumption figures taken from *BP Statistical Review of World Energy*.

is included in the noncooperative group, OPEC received cooperative signals from exporters with production and net exports of 7.2 mbd, with the noncooperative group constituting 2.2 mbd. This suggests that when the non-OPEC producers were confronted with the collective action problem through the OPEC offensive in spring 1986, several of them did consider cooperation rather than continuation of a free-rider strategy. Among the OPEC countries, the larger producers tended to cooperate more than the minor members. This to some extent confirms Olson's general hypothesis that the larger an actor is, the more likely it is that it will cooperate (see section 7.4). This trend is not found among the non-OPEC producers. In 1986, among both smaller and larger non-OPEC producers, there were countries of strategy inclined to cooperate and countries that resisted the invitation from OPEC. The categorizations in Tables 8.2 and 8.3 are based on politically stated intentions regarding cooperation with OPEC. The next question is: How did the non-OPEC producers actually behave?

Table 8.3 compares the cooperative and noncooperative non-OPEC producers' production growth rate from 1985 until 1987. Interestingly, as the figure shows, the growth rate of the cooperative group increased from 0.13 percent in 1984–1985 to 2.10 percent in 1985–1986. The growth rate of the noncooperative group fell from 2.67 to 0.84 percent in the same period. Since Norway subsequently made some concessions to OPEC (see Chapter 9), the table also includes the noncooperative group, excluding Norway. The effect of this is that the noncooperativists actually reduced

TABLE 8.3   Selected Non-OPEC Producers' Production Growth, from Previous Year (%)

	1984-1985	1985-1986	1986-1987
Cooperative group	0.13	2.10	2.72
Noncooperative group including Norway	2.67	0.84	2.50
Noncooperative group excluding Norway	1.88	-0.78	0.00

Cooperative group: USSR, Mexico, Egypt, China, Oman, and Malaysia
Noncooperative group: United Kingdom, Argentina, Canada, and Trinidad
SOURCE: Based on data from *BP Statistical Review of World Energy.*

their production in 1986 compared with 1985. Norway, after stating its cooperative strategy in 1986, increased its production, and the other non-cooperativists kept a flat production profile from 1986 to 1987.

This illustrates the problem of a discrepancy between words and deeds in international cooperation as such. Although it is a matter of correlation and not causality, it is a fact that those non-OPEC producers that signaled their cooperative attitude behaved noncooperatively, and those that signaled a noncooperative attitude actually contributed to OPEC's price-stabilizing efforts.

The most formally institutionalized attempt of collective non-OPEC action was the response to OPEC's call for cooperation from seven non-OPEC countries in 1988. The group of seven included: Angola, China, Colombia, Egypt, Malaysia, Mexico, and Oman. At a meeting in London on March 9, six of the seven countries (Colombia opted out) offered to cut their export by 5 percent, given a proportional response from OPEC (Evans 1990:721). This would have meant some 183,000 barrels per day for the seven non-OPEC countries, and some 700,000 barrels per day for OPEC. The proposal led to a joint meeting in April 1988 of representatives of six OPEC countries, the group of seven, and an observer from Norway. OPEC turned this down, but indicated its willingness to match the non-OPEC proposal barrel for barrel—that is, OPEC, too, would make a reduction of about 200,000 barrels per day.[2] Nevertheless, the meeting was a move in the direction of a broader producer cooperation in the market.[3] The non-OPEC producers continued meeting alone and with OPEC until the outbreak of the Gulf War in August 1990. Then the problem was how to increase production fast enough (see section 3.4). As described in section 5.3, after the Gulf War, OPEC did not apply a particularly coherent market strategy. Thus, the organization did not invite the non-OPEC producers to cooperate further. With Iraq back in the market (see section 3.4), and reduced demand due to economic recession in Asia (see section 5.3), the pressure on prices increased. OPEC had to revitalize its production policy. This also brought to the forefront the issue of cooperation with producers outside the organization. In 1998, the OPEC–non-OPEC relations were reactivated. OPEC approached several non-OPEC producers in order to strengthen the cooperative efforts. This time, Mexico took the lead on the non-OPEC side, initiating diplomatic activities toward other non-OPEC producers like Norway. Thus, in March 1999, four non-OPEC producers (Mexico, Norway, Russia, and Oman) were explicitly included in the OPEC scheme of production cuts.[4] Mexico was particularly instrumental by joining Saudi Arabia and Venezuela in preparing the plan for production cuts before the March 1999 OPEC Conference. Subsequently, the division of producers into OPEC and non-OPEC producers have less importance than before. The bargaining, negotiations, and policy preparation now takes place across the organizational boarder. This implies a higher effectiveness in influencing the market. It might, however, threaten the importance and role of OPEC as an organization. In an interview with *Petroleum Economist*, OPEC's secretary-general rejects that the interaction with outside producers had undermined OPEC:

> On the contrary, Venezuela, Saudi Arabia and Mexico got together on an informal basis to discuss our common problem between OPEC and non-OPEC. After they reached some understanding it was up to OPEC to implement the decisions and they came to us. . . . Consultations are going on all the time, on a formal and informal basis. . . . Mistakenly people have talked about the fact that a new organization is going to emerge from this. . . . The important thing is that we are now getting our friends outside OPEC to cooperate by restraining themselves . . . some of them are cutting. . . . We hope they continue to cooperate . . . the more we cooperate in normal times, the better we will be able to cooperate when times are hard.[5]

8.3   Explaining Non-OPEC Cooperative Behavior

It is of course impossible to go into a discussion of the motives and dispositions for cooperation or lack of such for all or even only the key non-OPEC producers. An entire chapter is devoted to one non-OPEC producer—Norway (see Chapter 9). Here, I can only sketch some general problems of cooperation between an organization like OPEC and individual countries like the non-OPEC producers.

To some extent, the calculation over possible courses of action regarding cooperation with other oil producers is similar for a country outside an organization like OPEC to a country inside OPEC. In the marketplace, OPEC oil is identical to non-OPEC oil. The analysis of non-OPEC behavior conducted in section 8.2 showed the performance of both cooperative and noncooperative behavior among the non-OPEC producers that had stated their intention to cooperate. Chapter 5 showed a similar picture regarding the OPEC countries. The constraining institutional factors that apply to the members of the organization (see Chapter 4) seem insufficient in explaining the variation of cooperative behavior among oil producers. In order to explain oil-producer cooperation, individual studies of all larger oil producers' policies are needed. No single factor is likely to explain all cooperative behaviors among all oil producers. It can be assumed that such a study would reveal a wide variety in the factors leading an individual oil producer to cooperate with other producers. The member countries of the Gulf Cooperation Council (GCC) are building economic cooperation on a wider basis; lack of cooperation on the single most important area for all these countries could be detrimental to the collective efforts for economic growth in this area. For some countries, oil-producer cooperation has from time to time been considered a part of Arab unity. At times, the OPEC cooperation has been interpreted as a spearhead of the Third World's struggle for economic progress.

In general, some countries might join oil producer cooperation from a calculation of potential economic gains, while others might cooperate due to cognition of normative obligations. This points back to the discussion in section 4.1, which was based on two lines of thought, the *homo economicus* and the *homo sociologicus*, where the first is guided by instrumental rationality and the second by social norms. The point is that it is no single norm of cooperation, as pointed out by Elster (1989b:186):

> I shall not assume that there is *a* norm of cooperation, whose presence and operation can be ascertained by the fact that cooperation takes place. Rather I believe that there exists several distinct norms that may, but need not, induce people to cooperate. These include moral norms, derived from utilitarianism, and the social norms of fairness and everyday Kantianism.[6] I do not believe many cases of successful collective action can be explained by stipulating selfish rationality alone. . . . When one is confronted with successful collective action, the task is to identify the precise *mix of motivations*—selfish *and* normative, rational *and* irrational—that produced it.

In economic models of the oil market, the reason for producer cooperation is to increase one's own oil rent. Following the argument above, there might be different reasons, normative or interest-based, for individual states' cooperation. "Within most interest groups there is a range of interest in (or desire for) the collective good. . . . Similarly, group members may differ substantially in resources available to them" (Oliver et al. 1985:528).

In section 7.4, one example of interest heterogeneity—the role of size—was discussed. Based on the classic argument of Mancur Olson (1965), it was argued that small oil producers would be less likely to contribute to the provision of the collective good—a higher oil price. The individual country's dependency on oil income could also influence the willingness to cooperate. The implications of high dependency on oil-generated income is inconclusive, as high dependency might increase the willingness to cooperate but also the temptation to defect if the country thinks it can get away with free riding. Regarding resource heterogeneity, the ability to sustain low oil price politically and economically could explain willingness to cooperate. Such ability is partly determined by variations in cost level and cost structure.

With such "group heterogeneity," the process of extending the cooperation becomes different from the economic calculation of economic gains prominent in economic models. Oliver et al. (1985:527–528) have argued that "many nontechnical discussions assume that each unit of resource contributed 'buys' a constant amount of the collective good, implying that the production function is linear. . . . The more usual assumption of economists . . . is that the production function is S-shaped, third order curve." The production function would then be accelerating at first, and then decelerating as more and more actors contribute to the provision of the collective good. In the accelerating phase, "each contribution moves subsequent decisions to a more favorable part of the curve. Thus, if somehow contributions begin, collective action tends to snowball, involving more and more contributors until the good is provided with certainty. . . . initial contributions lower the interest necessary for subsequent contributions" (Oliver et al. 1985:542–543). At a turning point the s-shaped production function changes from being accelerating to becoming decelerating. Then the free-rider incentive becomes stronger, and further contributions are more likely to be norm-based, as "one should cooperate when others do," or other normative arguments. Such "mix of motivations," to borrow Elster's phrase as quoted above, makes the explanation of cooperation more complex than in the economic models, but also less of an anomaly.

> Much economic analysis—and virtually all game theory—starts with the assumption that people are both rational and selfish. For example, predictions that players will defect in the prisoner's dilemma game and free ride in public goods environments are based on both assumptions. People are assumed to be clever enough to figure out that defection or free riding is the dominant strategy, and are assumed to care nothing for outcomes to other players. The predictions . . . are, however, violated in many familiar contexts. (Dawes and Thaler 1988:187–188)

A mix of individual governments' interests and resources and their individual calculations of own risk aversion and probability of likely success of different strategies determine the potential success of oil-producer cooperation. The next chapter is a case study of the Norwegian policy toward oil-producer cooperation, which tries to provide such a deeper explanation of the behavior of the Norwegian government. In particular, the conflict between economic interests and traditional foreign policy interests dominates the Norwegian case. As for the rest of the non-OPEC countries, I can only advocate more case study–oriented research into those countries' policies toward oil-producer cooperation.

Notes

1. *Middle East Economic Survey,* December 16, 1985.

2. *Petroleum Intelligence Weekly,* May 2, 1988, and *Platt's Oilgram News,* April 26–May 2, 1988.

3. Also present as observers at the meeting were representatives from the oil-rich states of Canada (Alberta) and the United States (Texas). In particular, Kent Hance from the Texas Railroad Commission pointed to the need for production limitations with a view to stabilizing oil prices. *Platt's Oilgram News,* April 28, 1988.

4. *Middle East Economic Survey,* March 29, 1999.

5. *Petroleum Economist,* March 1999.

6. Elster describes social norms as nonconsequentialist and that some moral norms like utilitarianism rest on consequentialist obligations and interdictions (Elster 1989b:101). The term "everyday Kantianism" refers to a norm that says, "one should cooperate if and only if universal cooperation is better for everybody than universal defection" (ibid.:192). This is not exactly in line with Kant's own argument, and thus the term "everyday Kantianism."

9

Country Case II: Norway—
From Free Riding to Cooperation

The aim of this chapter is to describe Norway's role in the cooperation between oil producers, and to explain through a combination of external and internal factors the changes in the Norwegian behavior toward repeated calls for cooperation with the other oil producers, primarily the OPEC countries. The hypothesis is: The increase in production makes it increasingly harder for Norway to ignore the calls for cooperation, in other words, to remain a free rider.

The case of Norway highlights several of the underlying problems related to the oil-producer cooperation in general. During the period discussed in this book, Norway went from a situation with no petroleum resources (the first commercially viable field was discovered in December 1969) to a situation in which it finds itself the world's second-largest oil exporter. Norway has thus experienced most aspects of the *size* (read: market share) dimension emphasized in section 7.4. Contrary to most other non-OPEC producers, Norway has in different phases stated negative and positive attitudes toward cooperation with OPEC. Furthermore, Norway has few traditional political ties with the members of OPEC. Norwegian political relations with these states are entirely "oil-driven." This makes other explanations of the possible political ties between Norway and key OPEC members unlikely.

Norway and OPEC compete for sales of oil and may simultaneously increase prices, provided coordinated production-limitation measures are effected. The asymmetry in the importance of these two actors makes it possible for Norway to avoid actually having to limit production, and at the same time OPEC's production limitations have the effect of realizing the collective good—a high price. However, as far as OPEC is concerned, the growth of producers outside the organization, combined with reduced demand, has rendered it an increasingly costly operation to stabilize the price (see section 2.5). The strategic bargaining problem to be addressed is thus: To what extent can Norway increase its utility by cooperating with OPEC on the limitation of production compared with its utility by pursuing an individual competitive strategy?

It is possible to distinguish different phases in the Norwegian policy toward other oil producers, and particularly the OPEC producers. Prior to 1986, the Norwegian authorities did not consider cooperating with OPEC. In 1986, this attitude changed, and from 1986 to 1990, Norway implemented unilateral measures to support OPEC's policy of stabilizing the oil price. From 1990 until 1998 there were no direct measures in support of OPEC, but the Norwegian authorities have underlined the common interests among oil producers. In 1998, Norway again implemented production limitations in support of OPEC's price stabilizing policy. The initial approach in this chapter is to understand the changes in Norway's behavior as an outcome of a strategic relationship between OPEC and Norway. This, however, cannot fully explain Norway's behavior. Consequently, some aspects of the development of the oil market discussed in Chapter 2 and some particular aspects of the Norwegian economy and foreign policy will supplement the analysis. Concerning the Norwegian economy, the proposition of this chapter is that as the oil sector became more and more important to it, Norway's willingness to cooperate with OPEC increased. The oil market also changed during the eighties, with one of the many implications being that non-OPEC producers, including Norway, gained a larger market share. Thus, Norway's ability to influence the oil price increased. Finally, Norway's change of policy toward OPEC was influenced by the country's traditional political relations with oil consumers. The argument in this chapter is that this played a minor role in the Norwegian decisions related to cooperation with other oil producers.

To understand Norway's behavior, the dominance of the oil sector in the Norwegian economy is important. Since 1979, world oil consumption has increased by about 10 percent; in the same period, Norwegian oil production has increased from 385,000 barrels a day to about 3,000,000 barrels a day. The Norwegian market share has increased from 0.5 percent to 4.5 percent. During the 1990s, Norway became the world's second largest oil exporter. Other actors in the market follow Norwegian oil policy closely, and to some extent change their own policies according to changes in Norwegian policy. Their policies are also to some extent aimed at influencing Norwegian behavior.

This chapter consists of three parts: First, I give a detailed account of the relationship between Norway and OPEC from 1982 to present (see section 9.2). One of the key arguments of this section is that there was a change in the Norwegian interests regarding oil-producer cooperation. Section 9.3 is a game-theoretical discussion of the relationship between OPEC and Norway. When using game theory as a tool of empirical research, it is not sufficient to deduce the actors' interests by observing their behavior, as it is their interests, or preferences, that explain the very same behavior. The change in preferences will have to be deduced from more fundamental changes in the characteristics of the actor. This is done in section 9.4, which discusses the effects on the changes in Norway's role in the international oil market, the Norwegian economy, and internal political deliberations of Norway's willingness to cooperate with OPEC.

These issues highlight the problem of studying international politics separately from domestic politics. It is the aim of this chapter to integrate these two levels. This ambition demands some theoretical clarifications.

9.1   Domestic Factors in International Relations

According to Peter Katzenstein (1985:24), the small European states regard "economic change as a fact of life. . . . they live with change by compensating for it." Norway is obviously a small European country, susceptible to such external forces. However, a perceived linear increase in interdependence has to some extent been countered by an increase in protectionism—but also, and more important to this chapter, by a tendency to create and enforce existing economic alliances between countries and companies. Gilpin (1991:17) argues that such alliances are a widespread phenomenon and that they "are being used to influence and, in some cases, to determine, market relations and economic outcomes." The collapse of the division between state and market is fundamental to this study.

During the 1990s, Norway has become one of the largest oil and gas exporters in the world. At the same time the petroleum sector has become the dominant economic sector in the Norwegian economy. What happens in the petroleum sector has dramatic consequences for the whole Norwegian economy, but to a limited extent Norway is also in a position to influence the development in the international oil market. Having become more dependent on this part of its environment, Norway has also gained some influence on the same environment. This gives Norway a choice other than adaptation to economic changes in the international markets. When international developments impose costs on Norway, the authorities might try to influence these developments to improve the situation instead of rely solely on internal adaptation. This contradicts the assumption of Katzenstein cited above. The empirical argument in this chapter is that the Norwegian foreign petroleum policy during the last ten to fifteen years can be characterized by the Norwegian authorities' use of both domestic and diplomatic instruments to cope with the changes in the most important external determinant for the Norwegian economy: the international oil market. The more analytical argument is that even in determining the importance of external factors for the national economy and the instruments available to the individual governments, it is necessary to disaggregate the national economy by looking at the political economy of the dominant economic sectors in the state in question. It is thus fundamental to this study that the Norwegian petroleum policy is a result of "constraints and opportunities on both the domestic and international boards" (Moravcsik 1993a:17). The Norwegian response to structural changes in the international oil market and the approaches by OPEC is not one of a unitary actor but one of a complex actor in which there are subactors advocating different interests. This calls for an analysis in accordance with the ones developed by Katzenstein (1985) and Gourevitch (1986).

Milner (1997:70) develops a model based on two central hypotheses: "First, the structure of domestic preferences conditions the impact of domestic politics on international relations. . . . Second, the distribution of information domestically has a vital impact on international cooperation." She then discusses the interests and impact of three sets of actors in domestic politics: an executive, a legislature, and societal interest groups. Domestic politics is more hierarchical in autocracies than in democratic political systems. Many of the oil-producing countries discussed in this book are autocracies (see section 3.5). In Norway, the relation to other oil-producing countries has been discussed on the elite level. Societal interest groups have not been important in the development of this aspect of Norwegian foreign policy. As the discussion in the rest of this chapter will show, the conflicts have been as much inside the executive and the legislature as between them. Milner's focus on the game between the legislature and the executive is in this case only part of the picture, since the game between part of the executive and among political parties in the parliament are as important. The explanatory part of this chapter will thus be confined to an empirical discussion of the internal Norwegian policy shifts rather than applying a model of domestic politics. Although Milner's model is not directly applied, her basic argument on the need to capture the "interdependence of domestic and international politics" (Milner 1997:4) underlies the discussion in the rest of this chapter.

Hveem (1994) provides an empirical account of the formation of Norwegian foreign economic policy in different sectors. Both the underlying choice of strategy and the choice of market organization are important parts of the analysis. Regarding the underlying strategy, Hveem regards the Norwegian petroleum sector as a combination of what he calls market adaptation and niche strategy. The sector is a niche sector in accordance with Hveem's notion, as Norway has compensated for its lack of general economic power by gaining a strong position in this particular market (Hveem 1994:28). However, since the oil price has been volatile, the Norwegian vulnerability has increased through this dependency on the oil sector. This has caused the Norwegian authorities to reduce the vulnerability through market adaptation, compensating those groups particularly exposed, and since 1996 by building a buffer through the oil fund.[1] Regarding the Norwegian market organization, a somewhat different strategy has been pursued toward OPEC than toward other international actors.[2] The conflicting interests between political and economic allies have made the Norwegian strategy regarding oil-producer cooperation, in Hveem's terms, a development from a free-market strategy to a "contractual-relation" strategy. By contractual relationship, Hveem implies that actors strike bargains about market shares, prices, or other aspects, unlike free-competition or restricted protectionism (Hveem 1994:40). These initial remarks underline that the relationship to OPEC is part of a broader Norwegian petroleum policy. The policy toward OPEC might have been affected by other issues. It is now time to turn to the historical description of the bargaining process between OPEC and Norway.

9.2 The Bargaining Process

The focus in this section will be the bargaining process between OPEC and Norway. If we are to characterize a bargaining process in relation to other decisionmaking processes, the following criteria can serve as guidelines. First, a bargaining process demands some degree of agreement to reach a decision or outcome. As we shall see, there is no requirement for the counterparts to be in complete agreement (their highest preference), but neither can they be in complete disagreement (their lowest preference) in order to achieve a cooperative outcome. Second, bargaining requires communication. The counterpart must be made aware that a proposal has been put forward. However, explicit communication is no prerequisite. One way of showing how explicit communication differs from tacit communication is to refer to the difference between the notion of "negotiations" in its narrow sense—that is, formal and actual negotiations—in contrast with the notion of "bargaining," which expresses a broader meaning including more subtle and indirect forms of communication. Third, the parties must have both conflicting interests and common interests. This condition was presented by Iklâe (1964).[3] Finally, at one point or another in the bargaining process, there ought to be some movement in at least one of the actors' positions. Without any movement in positions, one can hardly claim to have studied a bargaining process, but rather a static bargaining relationship.

The relationship between OPEC and Norway goes far toward satisfying these requirements. There is no formal agreement between the parties, but one can interpret the moves made by the actors to mean that a cooperative outcome is desirable. Second, communication has taken place, even in the absence of direct negotiations. Third, OPEC and Norway have common as well as conflicting interests. And finally, both actors have changed their positions in the course of the period with which we are dealing.

This section will be organized into five phases. The first phase focuses on the moves made by Norway during the period 1982 to 1985, which are characterized by the relationship being interpreted as one of conflict. The second phase centers on OPEC's change in market strategy in December 1985 (see also section 5.3). The third phase correspondingly centers on the Norwegian decision in 1986 to limit production in support of OPEC, and the subsequent implementation of this strategy from 1986 to 1990. The fourth phase is the period from June 1990, when the production limitations were abolished, until June 1995, when OPEC again approached Norway regarding production limitations. In this phase, there was low intensity in the bargaining relationship compared with the previous phases. The last phase covers the renewed producer cooperation from 1999.

Norwegian Conflict Behavior, 1982–1985

OPEC, and particularly Saudi Arabia, found stabilizing the market an increasingly costly matter in the first half of the eighties. In March 1982, the organization initiated the quota-sharing system among its members (see section 5.2). At the OPEC meeting in March 1982, Saudi Arabia took a surprising position in favor of production regulation. In the wake of this OPEC meeting, the first moves were played against Norway and Britain to help limit oil supplies: "OPEC will now seek contact with countries such as Norway and Britain, and of course Mexico too, to arrange cooperation on the oil prices."[4]

In November 1982, OPEC Secretary-General Nan Nguema was invited to Oslo. OPEC seemed interested in some sort of consultations with certain members of the International Energy Agency (IEA).[5] OPEC convened several times in the spring of 1983 for the purpose of stabilizing the market through production limitations. On February 11, 1983, Saudi Arabian Oil Minister Sheik Yamani stated, "Saudi Arabia will no longer play the role of defending the benchmark price and will let others bear the responsibility for their own mistakes" (Terzian 1985:314). Yamani later admitted that OPEC had not understood in 1980 that oil was over-priced: "But when OPEC supplies started to decline sharply in 1981 and 1982, as a result of the fall in demand and the rise in non-OPEC supplies, we recognized too late that oil was overpriced" (Yamani 1986:11–12). On February 19, 1983, the British National Oil Company, BNOC, reduced the oil price by $3 to $3.5/barrel. Norway and Nigeria followed suit— the price decline had now really set in. OPEC production had declined to 14 mbd. The result of the extraordinary OPEC meeting in March 1983 was that OPEC's official reference price was lowered from $34 to $29/barrel, and the production ceiling was fixed at 17.5 mbd (OPEC 1990:208). This price was sustained for about eighteen months, while Saudi Arabia continued to swing down production. Concurrently, British and Norwegian production continued to increase in 1983, to the annoyance of OPEC:

> Maghur [Libya's oil minister at that time] pointed out that the majority of oil producing countries outside OPEC have been unwilling to support OPEC's efforts to avert a collapse of the oil market and a dramatic drop in price in a practical manner. Instead, many of these countries have increased their production, Maghur said, and he emphasized that production in Norway and Britain in the five first months of this year was 13.5 per cent higher than in the corresponding period last year.[6]

Into 1984 the North Sea producers continued to increase production. The pressure on prices intensified as more and more oil was offered on the market.

This behavior must be regarded as conflict behavior. Despite repeated appeals by OPEC, Norway showed no signs of considering production limitations. The Norwegian government tried rather to establish commitment to the planned production level by statements such as that made after representatives of Venezuela's state oil company, PDVSA, visited Norway in February 1983: "They [Venezuela's representatives] showed understanding of the quite special situation Norway and Great Britain find themselves in, with such large production costs it is impossible to organize a variable production for purposes of regulating the prices."[7] The Norwegian decisionmakers were obviously aware of the common interests with OPEC, a fact expressed in a statement made by the prime minister's personal adviser, Terje Osmundsen: "We have coinciding interests with OPEC in maintaining a steady oil price development. For that reason we would do well also in future to continue to develop the price cooperation with the organization on an informal basis."[8] He emphasized, however, that there was no reason to enter into a production cooperation with the OPEC countries. But again, the self-commitment is evident in Os-mundsen's statement: "Not least the heavy costs connected with North Sea exploitation indicate that Norway will never be able to become a swing producer."[9]

In August 1984, Saudi Arabia's production had declined to just above 4 mbd, while OPEC total production was around 16.5 mbd. The general perception in OPEC circles was that when the oil companies started their usual stockpiling for the coming winter, the market would tighten up. While OPEC prepared an extraordinary meeting on October 28–29, 1984, Norway entered the international oil political arena and created a new crisis in the oil market: "a crisis nobody had expected, not even those who triggered it off, the directors of the Norwegian state oil company Statoil. The OPEC conference that had been called to raise the organization's production ceiling was in fact forced to lower it by 1.5 million barrels a day, in a desperate attempt to save oil prices from the North Sea turmoil" (Terzian 1985:329).[10] Statoil offered an official reduction in price of about a dollar and a half.[11]

The immediate reaction in OPEC to this news was strong. "Norway received rough treatment in Friday's UAE newspapers. Gulf News writes that the Norwegian decision to reduce the price of North Sea oil is extremely difficult to understand."[12] On October 26, 1984, Yamani came to Norway. He had talks with Prime Minister Kåre Willoch and Minister of Oil and Energy Kåre Kristiansen. Yamani was assured that the Norwegian step constituted an adjustment to the market and certainly not an attempt to undermine OPEC's market-stabilization measures. "The Norwegian role in the oil market in October thus appears to be a consequence of the general price and marketing policy and no break away from it. When the principle of not being a price leader was not set aside and Norway was not subjected to criticism from OPEC earlier, it has mainly to do with the market development. When demand slackens the inconsistency in Norwegian policy in this issue area emerges and forces a balancing of the various principles" (Sydnes 1984:29). At the same time, Kristiansen gave assurances to Yamani that Norwegian production in 1985 would not exceed that of 1984.[13] This turned out not to hold true, and considerable irritation arose in OPEC when further Norwegian production increases became a reality.[14] At the OPEC meeting in Geneva in October three days later, OPEC's concern regarding the Norwegian policy was expressed: "The Conference reviewed with great concern the recent developments in the world oil market following the price cuts undertaken by Statoil of Norway and the British National Oil Corporation (BNOC) of the United Kingdom, as well as by Member Country Nigeria" (OPEC 1990:220). The Saudi Arabian weekly magazine *Iqraa* ran an article in the November 15 issue entitled "The Latest Oil Price Crisis: A Saudi View." As pointed out in *Middle East Economic Survey,* which printed a translation, the article was "billed as having been written by a 'neutral international oil expert'—but the article clearly reflects an insider's viewpoint."[15] Probably the views were those of Yamani. The article states that demand was picking up in the last quarter of 1984, until the

> big surprise—Norway's decision to reduce its price by $1.35/b. . . . 10 days before Norway's decision, the prevailing Norwegian view was that the price of oil would begin to rise in November and December as demand increased and that there would be no problems on prices or production until March or April. Therefore the Norwegian decision was based on non-economic considerations. Normally Norway does not take the initiative on pricing but follows the British lead. It is remarkable that in this case the smaller producer took the initiative. . . . Some people believe that internal reasons were behind the Norwegian decision, since the President of . . . Statoil belongs to the opposition political party and wanted to embarrass the present government. . . . There are also those who say that there was American pressure on Norway.[16]

This gives an indication of how the Saudi Arabian oil administration viewed the Norwegian oil-production policy in October 1984. Although this article was also part of the bargaining game between OPEC and Norway, it shows how dramatic the Norwegian decision was perceived to be by other important actors. The general opinion regarding the market situation was that the OPEC measures had stabilized the market, demand would soon increase, and everything would recover. Yamani said oil prices would rise sharply in the coming months due to greater demand and because the importing companies were draining their stocks: "I don't care about what Norway will do. The situation will right itself when demand increases and the market improves."[17] He was to be proved wrong.

The conclusion that can be drawn from the October crisis is that Norwegian innocence in the political game of international oil was gone. The argument that Norway was a marginal producer with high production costs, and thus exerted no influence on the international oil market, became less convincing. Norway had shown that it could, in certain situations, actually influence market developments. On the other hand, the high production costs continued to be an applicable argument for self-commitment. To a great extent, bargaining power involves depriving oneself of alternatives of action (Schelling 1980:22), and at the same time ensuring that the opponent perceives the deprivation. The first event in this bargaining process was precisely that Norway revealed it could influence the market. This drew other actors' attention to Norway's position, thereby arousing their interest in exerting influence on Norway's behavior. The next step was for OPEC to challenge this by putting pressure on Norway to limit production.

OPEC *Changes Market Strategy, 1985*

For the OPEC countries, developments now gathered momentum. The consequences of low demand and reduced market share hit hard as the dollar exchange value dropped in 1985. The pressure on Saudi Arabia increased steadily when other member countries attempted to compensate for reduced income by increasing production above quotas. In the course of spring 1985, Saudi production fell toward 2 mbd, keeping the price at a level between $26 and $30/barrel. Few moves were made by the Norwegian side. In March 1985, Kristiansen visited Saudi Arabia for talks with Yamani. This meeting was described as "idyllic" compared with the meeting in October 1984. Kristiansen again gave assurances that Norwegian production would not rise beyond the present level in the next years. At the meeting, both actors seemed to regard the market as stable, and perhaps tending to rise. Yamani desired Norwegian production limitations, though he did not express this directly. Kristiansen made it clear "that Norwegian oil production cannot be reduced due to the high level of investment on the continental shelf and the long-term development projects." Kristiansen said also that informal channels had been established from the Norwegian authorities and from Statoil to OPEC, and especially to Saudi Arabia, for the purposes of directly communicating reasons for particular market behavior if circumstances should demand it.[18]

As discussed in section 6.5, by the summer of 1985, the Saudi Arabians no longer accepted production beyond quota by other OPEC countries, as long as they themselves produced only half their quota. At the OPEC meeting in Geneva on December 9, the members agreed to change their market strategy from the defense of a high oil price to the defense of the OPEC countries' market shares. The resolution promptly triggered a price drop for crude of $3 in three days.[19] "The market has gone mad," an oil broker told *Aftenposten*. "No serious oil expert dares to predict what the oil price will be tomorrow, next week, or in 1986."[20]

The rhetorical game around this resolution had the objective of drawing attention just as much to the producers outside OPEC as to those within the organization who were failing to keep to their quotas. Thus, strong complaints and threats concerning a price war were expressed: "OPEC still harbors the hope that other producers will cooperate in trying to maintain prices by curbing their output. But implicit in the communiqué issued yesterday is the threat of a price war if they do not."[21] Some OPEC representatives made threats of retaliation unless North Sea producers cut production.[22] The only official Norwegian reaction was a statement by Kristiansen to the Norwegian Broadcasting Company saying that Norway was unable to cut its oil production in the short term as requested by the organization.

The first question concerning the bargaining relationship in this phase is whether Norway interpreted the move as a direct and open threat to enforce sanctions if Norway failed to limit production. Statements made by Kristiansen indicate that Norwegian authorities did not interpret OPEC's action as directed toward Norway: "There is no doubt that the main reason for the price drop is the strong production increase by Saudi Arabia and other OPEC countries. When before it has been indicated that Norway ought to reduce production, the point has been precisely to avoid the price drop that has just occurred. No motive any longer exists for Norway to lower production. I fail to see what we can do today."[23] In hindsight, the situation has been interpreted as the main objective of Saudi Arabia's policy of being a threat to those OPEC countries not sticking to their quotas:

> It was clear, however, to the Norwegian authorities that the collapse of the oil price was wanted. Saudi Arabia wished both to achieve a larger share of oil sales for herself by forcing other OPEC countries to accept lower quotas and to reverse the general decline in OPEC's joint share of the market by means of a generally lower price level. It was clear that any early steps taken by Norway would be contrary to Saudi Arabia's policy—they would be meaningless, because they would not help to achieve the desired objective: a higher and stable oil price. (Udgaard 1989:65)
>
> However, the point for the government was not Norway's high or low volumes of production but rather their realization that not much importance would be attached to Norwegian policy because the internal conditions of OPEC could be considered as decisive. (Ramm 1989:57)

Ramm (1989) also places weight on the self-commitment contained in maintaining that national authorities could not involve themselves in production on the shelf, even under the new section 20 of the Petroleum Act.[24]

The second question is whether OPEC was aware of the break-even price on the Norwegian oil fields. A substantial part of production on the Norwegian shelf had been running production costs of less than $10/barrel. Thus it can safely be concluded that a price war would not have had the effect of lowering Norwegian production before the prices had fallen to around this level. On the other hand, Saudi Arabia could, in such a situation, count on a considerable increase in output by altering its market strategy. This would be of no help to the other OPEC countries, because only Saudi Arabia had sufficient spare capacity to compensate for the price fall with increased production. Another factor was Norway's small share of world production, which in 1986 was 1.5 percent. Thus, for instance, a 10 percent reduction of Norwegian production would in itself have had little effect of clearing the market.

The third question is the solidity of the Norwegian self-commitment. The content of section 20 of the Petroleum Act gave the necessary legal provisions for the authorities to regulate production. It must have been obvious to OPEC that, should the Norwegian authorities have wished to limit production, they had the means of doing so. Thus, there was every reason for OPEC to continue to exert pressure on Norway. It soon turned out that the latter started to yield.

Norwegian Cooperative Behavior, 1986–1990

The Norwegian government steered a somewhat unsteady course in the domestic political landscape in the spring of 1986, a circumstance that also affected relations with OPEC. The various statements made by the Ministry of Oil and Energy regarding possible cooperation with OPEC illustrate this point.

On January 23, 1986, a press release was issued from the Norwegian Ministry of Oil and Energy: "As far as OPEC is concerned, measures taken by Norway are only conceivable in a situation where OPEC is willing and able to regulate production in an effective manner."[25] *Platt's Oilgram News*, a daily oil industry news sheet, wrote as follows: "A flurry of fact and rumor surrounding potential moves toward a united OPEC/non-OPEC producer front kept oil and financial markets on edge today. Norwegian Petroleum Minister Kaare Kristiansen made the biggest splash by suggesting that his government would go along if Britain and other non-OPEC producers reach agreement with OPEC to cut output. Kåre Kristiansen's spokesman quoted him as telling this to a conference in Sandefjord, Norway: "There can be a stable oil price only if there's a high degree of agreement between oil producing countries inside and outside OPEC."[26]

The following day, *Platt's* reported: "Yamani praised Norwegian Oil Minister Kaare Kristiansen's statement yesterday indicating that his country would be willing to cut crude production." A few paragraphs farther down, another news story reads as follows: "Norwegian Oil Minister Kristiansen, who won Yamani's praise for his earlier comments, took back much of the support he implied yesterday for such a pact. Yamani had no sooner set forth his statement than Kristiansen issued a counter statement largely rescinding his remarks of the day before. Today's version of the Norwegian position defined it as 'up to Saudi Arabia' to do something about prices and production. Kristiansen added, 'I can't see any reason for the Norwegian government to impose on companies a reduction in production.'"

A year later, Kristiansen described the situation thus: "I recall an odd episode. Now, it was not my mistake, but a press release went out from the Ministry concerning an address I was to hold at a seminar in Sandefjord just after OPEC had caused the dramatic oil price drop in the winter of 1986. A secretary wrote in the press release something quite different from what I said—namely, that Norway was willing to cooperate with OPEC on certain conditions. But that was not what I said in Sandefjord" (Lindøe 1987:102–103, my translation). On the question that he had gotten cold feet and deleted the paragraph before his speech, Kristiansen adds: "No, the paragraph was part of an earlier draft, but we had discussed the speech in the Ministry and decided to deleted it. However, it became part of the press release" (Lindøe 1987:102–103, my translation).

This episode may have been due to failure in communication between the minister and the civil service, but it soon appeared that the government had altered the political course to some extent. "It was gradually made clear that Norway 'would not work against' any measures OPEC might reach agreement on. This was one of several factors the Government took into account when it debated a proposal early in 1986 to step up the development of the Gullfaks field and finally decided against such a course" (Udgaard 1989:66). However, this did not constitute the official explanation for turning down faster development of Gullfaks. The official explanation was consideration for the investment pace on the shelf. There is reason to believe that the signal was interpreted by OPEC as a positive cooperative measure. On February 9, Kristiansen met with Venezuela's oil minister, OPEC President Arturo Hernandez Grisanti. The meeting was described by both parties as useful, despite the lack of tangible results. Kristiansen expressed willingness to cultivate diplomatic contact with OPEC countries. "I have personally given very high priority to contact with representatives of these [OPEC] countries."[27] In spring 1986, the unanimous attitude toward OPEC among Norwegian politicians had disappeared.[28] After talks in Egypt in April 1986, Foreign Office State Secretary Torbjørn Frøysnes said, "We will not be the ones to take the first step. However, if the OPEC countries, especially Saudi Arabia, make concrete moves with the objective of raising the oil price to a higher level, it has been the Government's view that we on the Norwegian side have been obliged to consider our own moves."[29] This had also been the content of Frøysnes's talks in Egypt.

That the Norwegian argument about the country's irrelevance in the oil market was weakened is apparent from the following statement made by State Secretary Morten Udgaard: "There has never been any doubt that the Government's attitude has been that Norway has a role and a responsibility [in the oil market] relative to our oil production, which is modest in scope viewed internationally, but which nevertheless involves a certain share of responsibility."[30] Although Norwegian authorities still did not consider supporting OPEC actively by means of production-limitation measures, the traditional free-rider attitude had undergone a change. Furthermore, at this juncture the decisionmaking process itself appears to have been somewhat labile. Several actors, both politicians and civil servants, made statements increasing the confusion regarding the Norwegian position (see Engesland 1989). For instance, at a press conference on March 19, 1986, in connection with a meeting between the OPEC ministers and representatives from Egypt, Mexico, Malaysia, Angola, and Oman, President Grisanti stated that "signals have been received to the effect that countries outside OPEC, which until the present have consistently said no to cooperation, may perhaps cooperate after all."[31] This statement may refer to those made by the director of the Norwegian Central Bank, Hermod Skånland, a few days earlier, when he expressed the idea of limiting Norwegian oil production purely out of Norwegian self-interest.[32] In connection with the revised national budget dealt with in the Storting at the end of April, a government crisis developed over the proposal put forward by the Willoch government. The outcome led to the appointment of Gro Harlem Brundtland as prime minister of Norway. In the Brundtland government's inaugural address, it was stated that "If the OPEC countries agree on measures capable of stabilizing the oil prices at a reasonable level, the Government will contribute to such stabilization, which may in turn ensure future supplies of oil and gas."[33]

Out of consideration for opposition at home as well as abroad, the government had to put its policy into practice with caution. It was pointed out that it was a matter of limiting actual production growth only, not the total produced volume. The Norwegian measures would be dependent on OPEC itself enforcing measures inclined to stabilize prices. The new policy was probably not quite clearly formulated yet. For instance, Finance Minister Gunnar Berge at this point stated, "We must act jointly with Britain,"[34] and Statoil director Arve Johnsen, influential in Labor Party oil policy, strongly criticized cooperation with OPEC.[35] Through the spring of 1986, Norwegian measures remained somewhat unclear. Oil Minister Arne Øien explained this situation as follows: "This [the form the measures would take] has not yet been clarified. Even when this has been decided, there would be no point in publicly unfolding such a strategy because we may find ourselves in something resembling a negotiatory position towards OPEC."[36]

In June 1986, Yamani and Øien met for the first time, in Venice. The atmosphere pervading this meeting provides insight into the type of bargaining relationship the parties entered into. In accordance with Yamani's security routine,[37] the Norwegian representatives were informed only of the time of the meeting, not the place. It proved to be the Hotel Daniel, the very hotel the Norwegian representatives had checked into the previous evening.[38] There is reason to believe the first part of the meeting was characterized by strong invective from Yamani, prompted by the Norwegians' lack of will to actively limit production. *Aftenposten* wrote, "Yamani put forward requirements that were turned down by his colleague."[39] He is said to have used consideration for the poor OPEC countries' dependence on oil revenues to feed their people as an argument for Norwegian production limitations. This must be assumed to have created a highly tense atmosphere. Yamani's refusal to comment on the meeting or meet photographers after it (he allowed himself to be photographed after meetings with Kristiansen) was also a sign of tough discussions. At this juncture, the Norwegian strategy toward OPEC was clarified, and the delegation was probably prepared for just this kind of confrontation. The Norwegians made it quite clear that Norway could limit only the growth of production, and that any measures would be conditional on OPEC's own policy. Moreover, the resolution would be a unilateral one and would not be a result of pressure or threats from OPEC.[40] Here again the Norwegian representatives employed a self-commitment strategy, consistently referring to the existing parliamentary situation in Norway. With a minority government, there is an obvious limit to what the government can do if it is to avoid jeopardizing its own position. The alternative would have been a less pro-OPEC government. Thus, any measures beyond those indicated were not to be considered. Furthermore, there was a need for Norway to receive unambiguous positive signals expressing OPEC's satisfaction with Norwegian policy so that the policy could be "sold" at home. This was also explicitly conveyed to OPEC. This strategy created a commitment on the part of OPEC, as speaking of Norway in laudatory terms made it more difficult for OPEC at a later date to demand further measures from Norway. As long as there are other non-OPEC producers who have failed to make any limitations, new attempts to exert pressure on Norway would appear dubious. In this specific bargaining situation, Norway possessed the aces. The Norwegian self-commitment was perceived as credible. The sharp invective from Yamani can be regarded as an attempt to put Øien to the test, to determine whether he could be induced to yield. Toward the end of the meeting, Yamani is said to have adopted a more conciliatory attitude.[41] The follow-up to the Venice meeting consisted of the establishment of regular contact between the OPEC Secretariat and the Ministry of Oil and Energy in Norway. This channel has later been used to clear up misunderstandings and clarify positions.

At the OPEC Conference in Brioni in June 1986, which took place immediately after the meeting between Yamani and Øien in Venice, the retiring president, Grisanti, said in his opening address: "A noteworthy development was the policy position taken recently by the new Norwegian Government and its declared intention to open its doors to dialogue with OPEC with a view to contributing to the Organization's efforts towards market stabilization. This position by a major industrialized oil-producing exporting country could open the way for a concerted all-oil-producers' effort to stabilize the market in face of a possible price disaster."[42] The new president, Rilwanu Lukman, expressed the same opinion. On the other hand, Iraq's oil minister, Qassim Taki al-Oraibi, thought the measures described by Norway were completely inadequate and pointed out how unprofitable Norwegian oil production was, considering the price level of the day.[43] The Brioni meeting failed to provide "the clarification necessary for the Norwegian government to assess national measures as a contribution to the stabilization of the oil price."[44] The OPEC discussion continued in Geneva on July 28. On August 5, OPEC established new production quotas, and the market reacted spontaneously with a price increase.[45] Norway's reaction was positive; the resolution was regarded as "an important step in the direction of stabilizing the market."[46] A Norwegian move was promised before the entry into force of the OPEC resolution on September 12, 1986. On September 10, the Ministry of Oil and Energy issued a press release stating that "the Government has formed a plan to limit growth in Norwegian oil export. In the fourth quarter of 1986 the authorities will do this by refining and building permanent emergency stocks of Government revenue oil that is today sold in the market. This will make it possible to reduce the net export of crude by around 10% in November and December."[47] The resolution resulted in some 70,000 to 80,000 barrels per day being removed from the international market. The following official statement was promptly made by OPEC's President Lukman: "We are pleased about Norway's action. It is extremely encouraging, and we hope that other North Sea producers will follow the good example [Norway has] set."[48] On September 13, Yamani came to Norway for a short meeting with Øien at the Park Royal Hotel at Fornebu Airport. Once more, the meeting was held behind closed doors. This time no invective was heard against the Norwegian position. The whole meeting was held in a highly conciliatory atmosphere and proceeded amicably.[49] Yamani granted an interview to the Norwegian Broadcasting Corporation and praised the Norwegian measures.[50]

At the OPEC meeting in October, Norway was again referred to in highly positive terms. Toward the end of October, Øien and OPEC representatives held two meetings. These were regarded more as courtesy visits, and a confirmation that cooperative relations had been established. The tug-of-war aspect of the relationship prominent at the Venice meeting in June had disappeared altogether. The cooperative relationship had been established and was to be cultivated; the joint interests were stressed. Moreover, Norway indicated that follow-up of the measures subsequent to January 1987 was to take place.[51] This was, in fact, effected by Norway on January 13, 1987: "The Government aims at reducing Norwegian oil production in the first half of 1987 by some 80,000 b/d commensurate with the approved production framework."[52] The measures were subsequently extended, at first to the end of 1987, in approximately the same form. The Norwegian Labor government held office until 1989. The Norwegian production limitation was sustained throughout this period.

Peaceful Coexistence, 1990–1997[53]

When the conservative coalition assumed government after the election in 1989, rumor held that the regulation was to be abolished. For the first half of 1990 the production limitation was cut from 7.5 percent to 5 percent. The decision to cut back on the limitation was a compromise between the conservative government and the Labor Party, which wanted to uphold it. In June 1990, the Norwegian government decided to abolish production-limitation measures altogether. In the spring of 1990 some OPEC countries produced well above their quotas, and several approached their production capacity level.

In this situation further Norwegian production limitation seemed unreasonable. In an interview a few days before the decision, the Norwegian oil minister, Eivind Reiten, stated that political considerations (such as human rights in the OPEC countries) had no place in the discussion of Norwegian support for OPEC. In fact, the Norwegian measures were not to be regarded as cooperation with OPEC at all, and he claimed that "this production regulation has not triggered off any contacts with OPEC countries which we would not have had as an oil producer anyway."[54] This contradicts the statements of the representatives of the government that introduced the regulation. The argument that there would no longer be any need for production limitations seems a more plausible defense for the Norwegian decision. OPEC did in fact pass the Norwegian decision without any official criticism; on the contrary, OPEC Secretary-General Subroto sympathized with the Norwegian decision.[55]

The main explanation behind the Norwegian decision and the lack of criticism is the fact that the oversupply in the market had turned into a perceived demand pressure. By the summer of 1990, demand for oil had picked up substantially, and the midterm outlook indicated an upward price pressure, making producer cooperation to keep prices up superfluous. Due to the Iraq-Kuwait War, the price increased from $16.88/barrel in July 1990 to $34.55/barrel in September. The other oil producers compensated for the loss of Iraqi and Kuwaiti oil, and the oil price returned to an average of $20.05/barrel in 1991 and $19.37/barrel in 1992. In the second half of 1993 the oil price started to fall (see Figure 9.4). This caused OPEC once again to approach Norway to obtain Norwegian production limitations. In late December 1993, when Oil Minister Said Bin Ahmed al-Shanfari of Oman visited Norway, the Norwegian refusal to limit production was clearly stated by Minister of Industry and Energy Jens Stoltenberg.[56] In an article in the newspaper *Dagens Næringsliv* on April 27 of the following year, he wrote, "In order to impose such production limitations we must at least be fairly certain that it actually leads to a more stable market situation." The Labor Party (Arbeiderpartiet) did not rule out Norwegian cooperation with OPEC in the future, if the probability of success was higher.[57] The relationship with OPEC had also created some political discussions in the Storting (the Norwegian parliament). In the final budget debate on December 17, 1993, the Socialist Left Party requested that the government, through international cooperation with OPEC among others, take the initiative to increase the oil price in the short and long term through reduced oil production.[58] The minister of finance during the debate flatly rejected such proposals.[59] In January 1995, Stoltenberg visited Qatar, and Qatari Oil Minster Abdullah bin Hamad al-Attiah launched a strong attack on the Norwegian planned increases in oil production. The attitude of Saudi Arabian Oil Minister Hisham Nazer, whom Stoltenberg also visited on the same trip, was more conciliatory.[60] Another attempt to persuade Norwegian authorities to limit oil production was the statement by the acting oil minister of the United Arab Emirates, which indicated the "possibility of a price war unless non-OPEC producers, particularly Norway, were willing to cooperate on production output."[61] Except for these individual verbal statements, no unanimous OPEC attack on the Norwegian position was officially declared during this phase.[62]

The most dominant feature of this period is the changed situation of the internal OPEC bargaining (see Chapter 5). After the Gulf War, Iraq was sanctioned by the United Nations. This implies, inter alia, that Iraq was prohibited from exporting oil. This made the situation for the remaining OPEC countries, and particularly Saudi Arabia, much easier. Almost all OPEC countries had produced near full capacity, and had thus not been deprived of any income due to the quota agreement. The argument that Norway should reduce production was therefore more problematic to defend. Furthermore, most OPEC countries also stood to lose in a price war, as only producers with spare capacity could possibly gain from a price war.

Renewed Cooperation, 1998–2000

In the 1997 election, the Labor Party lost power to a center-coalition government. Marit Arnstad became the new Norwegian oil minister, representing the Center Party. The Center Party had advocated political initiatives in order to reduce Norwegian oil production, both in short term, by restraining output from existing production facilities, and in the longer term, by reducing the announcement of new concessions.[63] The Center Party's perspective of Norwegian oil policy as a matter of resource management was clearly demonstrated by the interpellation by the party leader in the Parliament in February 1997: "We [the Center party] find it absolutely necessary to reduce the level of production, and govern [the oil sector] in accordance with overriding goals. . . . The present output level creates fundamental unbalance in the Norwegian economy. In the long run this will amplify the tendency to increasing differences among people and regions."[64] When the new government took office, the oil price was above $19 per barrel; less than six months later, the price had fallen to just above $13 per barrel. When OPEC approached the new Norwegian oil minister during their March 1998 deliberations (see section 5.3), the Norwegian government decided, after some rounds of consultation with the opposition in Parliament (see section 9.4), to reduce Norwegian oil production by approximately 100,000 barrels per day, from May and throughout 1998.[65] The reduction was later extended to the end of June 1999.[66] At the end of 1998 the oil price dropped further, below $10 per barrel.

In March 1999, OPEC and other non-OPEC countries agreed on further production cuts in order to reduce the oversupply of oil in the international market, and subsequently stabilize prices (see section 5.3). Norway joined these new and more committed efforts by adding another 100,000 barrels a day to the existing production cuts. The Norwegian cuts were, as in 1986, not cuts from existing production level, but from future planned production. In 1998, Norwegian production had come down from a record level of 3.360 mbd in 1997 to 3.215 mbd. Technical problems during the initial phases of several new oil fields postponed a planned increase in oil production during 1999. By June of that year, the projected production for the coming year 2000 was around 3.5 mbd, as a number of new fields were set to come onstream.[67] The reason for not cutting production from an existing level but based on planned production was explained by the Norwegian oil minister in an interview with *Middle East Economic Survey*:

> We cannot operate with the concept of a quota. The Norwegian oil industry is a private business. The current level of production is not decided by any ministry or even the state itself. That is why we always use the figures that the companies provide each autumn based on their budgets, for what will be the assumed production for next year.[68]

In the same interview she indicated that Norway was participating in informal consultations with other oil producers, and that she found such dialogues positive. In January 2000, Arnstad visited Saudi Arabia, solidifying the relationship between the two largest oil exporters. In March, Norway changed governments. The new Labor government continued the nonformal support of OPEC. When OPEC increased its production in March and June 2000, Norway in two steps abandoned its production limitations.[69] As was the case with the production limitations of 1986, the cuts were set against planned future production. In the 1986–1990 production limitation case, the problem was that the actual production exceeded the planned production, so that even the "limited" production level implied increased production (see section 9.3). In the 1998–2000 production limitation case, the problem was the opposite. Now actual production never reached the expected level, and at the same time as the expected level constantly was revised down.[70] Thus the Norwegian production was limited, but as a result of technical problems rather than policy, which delayed the upstart of new fields and strikes.[71] The comment in the EIA *Monthly Oil Report* after having reported the Norwegian decision to end the production restraint was: "no immediate impact on output is expected."[72]

For OPEC, the number of physical barrels not produced might not be important. The psychological effect of Norwegian "paper cuts" might be of equal value. For Norway, OPEC's efforts to raise prices is of immense national economic importance. If informal consultations by Norwegian authorities can contribute to the success of OPEC's efforts, they are worthwhile conducting. At the time of this writing, it is impossible to know whether these consultations could lead Norway into a more open and formal cooperation with OPEC and other non-OPEC producers.

After this empirical description, it is time to try to explain the changes of the actors' behavior. The changes in the behavior of OPEC and the key OPEC members have been the focus of several preceding chapters. The following sections will therefore concentrate on the Norwegian side, although aspects of OPEC's behavior will be included in section 9.3 on the bargaining game between OPEC and Norway. Section 9.4 is dedicated to understanding the changes in the Norwegian cooperative behavior toward OPEC on the basis of changes in Norway's position in the oil market, as well as domestic economic and political factors.

9.3   The Bargaining Game Between OPEC and Norway

This section will illustrate some aspects of the bargaining relationship between OPEC and Norway on the basis of two game-theoretical concepts: threats and promises. The Norwegian concession to OPEC from 1986 to 1991 is discussed in a separate subsection.

The OPEC *Threat*

We can regard OPEC's altered market strategy, from defending the market price to defending market shares, as a threat to Norway (inter alia) that it had to alter its policy by limiting production or else the OPEC countries would increase their production and thus trigger a fall in the oil price (Claes 1986b).[73] OPEC changed its strategy from defending the price to defending market shares in December 1985 (see section 5.3). As pointed out by an editorial in Petroleum Economist, this involved "a threat of a price war against outside producers, specifically against North Sea Oil."[74] In the model suggested here, OPEC's aim was to get Norway to limit or reduce its production. Such a threat can be game-theoretically described, as in Figure 9.1.

On the basis of the empirical discussion in section 9.2 regarding the Norwegian preferences, and in Chapter 5 regarding OPEC's preferences, the preferences of the two actors in the autumn of 1985 are assumed to be as follows:

Threatened (Norway) $y > z > x$
Threatener (OPEC) $r > p > q$

Hovi (1996:4–9) argues that five conditions must be fulfilled for a threat to be effective:

1. *relevance*, which implies inter alia that the threatened has an incentive to act contrary to the threatener's desires
2. *severity*, the target must prefer to comply, rather than to have the threat executed
3. *credibility*, the extent to which the target believes that the threat will be carried out if it does not comply
4. *completeness*, the extent to which the target believes that the threat will not be carried out if it complies
5. *clarity*, it must be clear to the threatened what the threatener wants, and the consequences of not complying

If we insert the conditions in Figure 9.1, the threat is

relevant	if	$y > z$,
severe	if	$z > x$,
credible	if	$p > q$,
complete	if	$r > p$.

If we insert the preferences described above, it follows that OPEC's threat is relevant, severe, complete, and credible. In a study of the OPEC-Norwe-

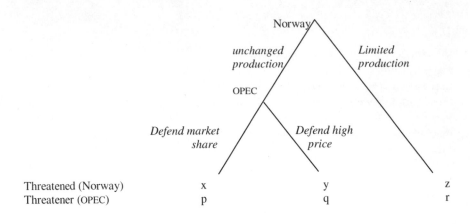

FIGURE 9.1   The threat game-tree

gian bargaining relationship, I carried out an events analysis of moves made by the government in Norway and central leaders within OPEC (Claes 1990:80–95).[75] The findings of that analysis empirically substantiate the game-theoretical argument above. Table 9.1 shows the level of pressure exerted on Norway by OPEC. As the table shows, OPEC increased the level of pressure in 1985. Until the change of Norwegian government in May 1986, OPEC's statements were dominated by appeals for action or threats of sanctions (89 percent in 1985 and 75 percent from January to May 1986). After the change of government in Norway, OPEC's statements changed and became conciliatory, or even laudatory of the Norwegian behavior.[76] It is fair to conclude that, in the eyes of OPEC, Norway had changed its position in a favorable direction.

The effectiveness of a threat depends on the actors' preferences with regard to the various outcomes: to remain firm or to yield. However, credibility also plays a part: the probability of the threat actually being implemented should the opponent fail to yield. As Schelling puts it, "We are back again at the commitment. How can one commit oneself in advance to an act that he would in fact prefer not to carry out in the event, in order that his commitment may deter the other party?" (Schelling 1980:36). During the spring of 1986, the price fell below $10/barrel. The international oil market in this period can be considered a competitive market. In the context of this chapter, OPEC was in fact carrying out what it had threatened. In particular, Saudi Arabia increased its production; the total supply of oil increased, and the price plummeted. On examining the threatened actor, we find that Norway for a long time maintained that Norwegian oil production involved very high production costs, rendering any reduction in production an immediate danger to profitability. The investments in the Norwegian continental shelf demanded, for operations-management reasons, running at full production regardless of price. Moreover, it was said that Norwegian production constituted such a minute part of total world production that a reduction would fail to have any effect on the market. As explained in section 9.2, this argument was weakened by Statoil's price reduction in October 1984.

Two aspects of incomplete information influenced the subsequent bargaining process. On the Norwegian side, the threat seems not to have been clear enough. Several market analysts interpreted the move as the editor of *Petroleum Economist* did as cited above. However, the comments of Norwegian Minister of Oil and Energy, Kåre Kristiansen, and Nils Morten Udgaard, cited in section 9.2, indicate that the Norwegian authorities perceived the threat as an act of Saudi Arabia aimed at the other OPEC members that did not adhere to their quotas. The Norwegian authorities may actually have perceived the threat as not directed toward them.

OPEC, on the other hand, misjudged the cost structure of the North Sea producers and thought they would stop production when the price fell to $10/barrel. However, due to the large relative share of investment costs in this production area, production continued (see section 9.2). Furthermore, few non-OPEC countries are as dependent on oil income as the OPEC countries. For non-OPEC oil producers, other sectors of their economies benefited from the fall in oil prices. OPEC soon realized that the cost of carrying out the threat was larger than assumed initially, and the preferences changed to q > p (see Figure 9.1). Thus, the threat also lost its credibility.[77]

The Norwegian Promise

In the autumn of 1985, the Norwegian authorities probably perceived the situation as one in which OPEC would defend the price regardless of what Norway did. The Labor government that took over in May 1986 found itself in a somewhat different situation. The price was about a third of what it had been in 1985, and the Norwegian economy was suffering. The Norwegian authorities did not immediately yield to OPEC's threat when the Labor government came to power. Instead, they turned the tables and tried to influence the main game—the one inside OPEC (see section 7.4). The new government's inauguration speech included a conditional assertion of cooperation: "If the OPEC countries agree on measures capable of stabilizing the oil prices at a reasonable level, the government will contribute to such stabilization."[78]

TABLE 9.1 Pressure Exerted on Norway by OPEC, 1983–1987, Percent (number of events)

Year	1983	1984	1985	1986 to May	1986 from May	1987	Total Category
Government	Conservative	Conservative	Conservative	Conservative	Labor	Labor	
Threats of sanctions			33 (3)	8 (1)			7 (4)
Appeal for action	100 (2)	50 (4)	56 (5)	67 (8)	13 (3)		39 (22)
No pressure		50 (4)	11 (1)	17 (2)	22 (5)	50 (1)	23 (13)
Verbal reward				8 (1)	65 (15)	50 (1)	30 (17)
Total Year	100 (2)	100 (8)	100 (9)	100 (12)	100 (23)	100 (2)	100 (56)

SOURCE: Claes 1990:90.

TABLE 9.2 Norway's Accommodation to OPEC, 1983–1987, Percent (number of events)

Year	1983	1984	1985	1986 to May	1986 from May	1987	Total Category
Government	Conservative	Conservative	Conservative	Conservative	Labor	Labor	
Support OPEC	100 (2)	88 (7)	22 (2)	32 (6)	93 (42)	92 (24)	68 (74)
No measures		13 (1)	78 (7)	68 (13)	7 (3)	4 (1)	30 (33)
Oppose OPEC						4 (1)	2 (2)
Total Year	100 (2)	100 (8)	100 (19)	100 (19)	100 (45)	100 (26)	100 (109)

SOURCE: Claes 1990:91.

Table 9.2 sums up the Norwegian government's statements concerning cooperative measures or support for OPEC. As the figure shows, the tendency in the statements shifts from a complete lack of will to take any measures at all to an increased willingness to support OPEC in 1986. There is a marked difference between the two governments, but the conservative government's statements, as they are expressed here, show an increased will to support OPEC before the change of government in 1986. At the same time, it is worth noting that the conservative government only to a slight degree stipulated conditions for its partly altered view. This is shown in Table 9.3.

The Norwegian position, to the effect that Norway would contribute to the stabilization of the market on the condition OPEC itself would implement effective measures, may be regarded as a kind of promise. "A promise is a commitment to the second party in the bargain and is required whenever the final action of one or of each is outside the other's control. It is required whenever an agreement leaves any incentive to cheat" (Schelling 1980:43). The attachment of conditions was expressed on several occasions, as reported in Table 9.3. As we see from this figure, the Labor government was the first to attach substantial conditions to Norway's contribution. When the conservative government in 1986 considered support for OPEC, it was of a more unconditional nature than the later Labor government policy, which explicitly attached conditions to its future market actions. The explanation might be that the conservative government had no intention of employing economic measures to support OPEC. There was thus no necessity to attach conditions to the verbal support expressed.

The new Norwegian government's strategy became clear in the course of the spring and summer of 1986. If OPEC arrived at measures that would effectively stabilize the price of oil, Norway was willing to employ independent measures that would support OPEC's attempt to stabilize the market (see section 9.2). At the OPEC meeting in August, OPEC arrived at measures that were satisfactory in Norwegian eyes, and in the middle of September, Norway followed up by removing 10 percent of Norwegian exports from the market. The Norwegian promise and the subsequent implementation of production limitations can be explained in line with the analysis of quota compliance presented in section 7.4. The essence of that discussion was that one important element of such cooperative bargaining is the establishment of a sufficiently large group of actors willing to cooperate on the condition that others do, the so-called *k*-group. Such a group could, under certain conditions benefit from cooperation compared to a situation where none of the actors cooperate. The size of this group, defined as combined market share, was found in section 7.4 found to be a key to potential success of the oil producer cooperation. From

TABLE 9.3 Norwegian Conditions for Cooperation, 1983–1987, Percent (number of events)

Year	1983	1984	1985	1986 to May	1986 from May	1987	Total Category
Government	Conservative	Conservative	Conservative	Conservative	Labor	Labor	
Do more				21 (4)	53 (24)	4 (1)	27 (29)
Status quo					33 (15)	86 (23)	35 (38)
Do less						4 (1)	1 (1)
No conditions	100 (2)	100 (8)	100 (9)	79 (15)	13 (6)	4 (1)	38 (41)
Total Year	100 (2)	100 (8)	100 (9)	100 (19)	100 (45)	100 (26)	100 (109)

SOURCE: Claes 1990:93.

1977 to 1985 the market share covered by the OPEC members fell from 50 to 30 percent (see section 2.5). This led OPEC members to search beyond the organizational borders to gain support for their cooperative efforts. The same fact also led some non-OPEC producers to change their strategy from free riding to conditional cooperation. Among these was Norway.

The market situation was perceived as having dramatic consequences for the Norwegian economy. Any gains in increased prices would help the economy, and possible costly cooperative measures most likely would be outweighed. The official but still conditional verbal support in the inaugural speech and the following meetings during the spring and summer of 1986 had no direct costs attached, but could have positive effects on the internal OPEC bargains. When it came to implementing the cooperative strategy by cutting production, we can interpret the Norwegian authorities' perception of the situation as one of an actor believing that one's own cooperation is, if not pivotal, at least important for others to choose to cooperate. This interpretation is reasonable as the Norwegian authorities themselves emphasized the importance of the cooperation of a substantial number of OPEC members for their own decision to cooperate.

In game-theoretical terms, the Norwegian authorities perceived themselves as being the $k+1$ actor in the n-person prisoner's dilemma game. Such an actor believes that "if I don't cooperate, no one else will." The free-rider strategy is not perceived as a viable option. The government thus had to weight the potential benefits from cooperation against what costs such a strategy would incur. As described above, the potential gains from cooperation if the price increased were perceived as high. The next subsection will show that the actual costs of cooperation soon became negligible.

The Substance of the Norwegian Compliance

The Norwegian production limitations during the autumn of 1986 and spring of 1987 removed only a marginal quantum of oil from the international oil market. Furthermore, the policy was designed in a way that made it increasingly difficult to verify. The limitation was a reduction compared to the planned increase; as new fields came onstream, the exact figure of what would have been produced without the measures became unclear. Thus, the actual impact on Norwegian output from the government's policy was soon (summer/autumn 1987) obscured. The way the companies implemented the restrictions also indicates that the policy was hollow. As the measures were to be monitored monthly, the companies usually produced at full capacity for most of the month and then stopped pumping completely for a few days. This is also normal procedure in order to allow time for maintenance work on the platforms. The distinction between maintenance halts and halts due to implementation of the production-limitation policy became unclear. Figure 9.2 shows the planned production presented by the Norwegian Ministry of Oil and Energy in the spring of 1987, the effect of the Norwegian production limitations, and the actual production from 1986 to 1991. As the figure clearly illustrates, the reductions would have removed very little oil from the international market. Given the subsequent actual development of Norwegian oil production, the limitations seem to have been an illusion.

It can safely be concluded that the Norwegian policy did not have any long-term effects on the Norwegian production level, let alone the international oil market. The Norwegian action was, however, received with great enthusiasm by OPEC Conference President Lukman in his opening address to the Seventy-ninth OPEC Conference in Geneva in October 1986:

So far the measures taken by some non-OPEC producers would constitute an encouraging first step in an all oil-producers' effort to stabilize the market. The Government of Norway's positive and encouraging measures in directly intervening in the country's oil exports with the singular objective of reducing total oil available in the market, deserves special mention. The country is not only a major oil exporter but also an industrialized one. Even OPEC detractors who see Norway's action as "insignificant in the larger scheme of worldwide oil production," were quick to concede that that action had a "psychological impact" on the market and helped OPEC's measures which led to raising prices and creating stable market conditions. But even more important than any psychological impact Norway's action has had, is the fact that an industrialized country has thought it wise, proper and justified to regulate the supply of oil in the market. This is very significant, coming as it did at a time when other industrialized country oil-producers are spreading ideological-oriented concepts of the so-called free market being the best tool to achieve equilibrium in supply and demand in world oil. (OPEC 1990: 247)

The statement identifies both a psychological effect and an ideological effect. The psychological effect might have made other actors, both inside and outside OPEC, more willing to contribute to stabilizing the market by cutting their own production. The ideological effect was that the Norwegian attitude legitimized the fundamental idea behind the founding of OPEC as such, namely, the oil producers' cooperation to sustain fairly high oil prices. Norway to some extent represented the Western countries, although its interests in oil-related matters diverged from those of its traditional Western allies. The Norwegian policy in itself, disregarding the implementation of it, might have made it a bit easier to achieve the internal

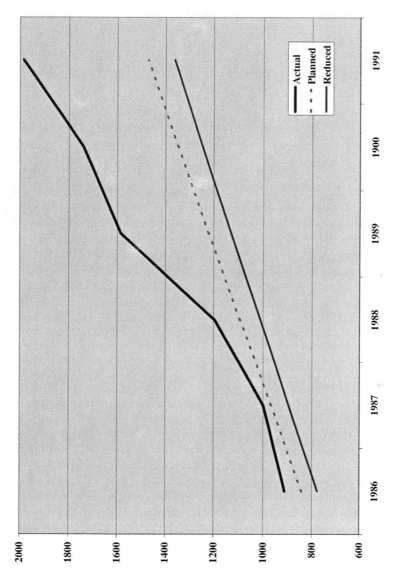

FIGURE 9.2   Actual planned and reduced Norwegian oil production, 1986–1991 (th. b/d).
SOURCE: Official Report to the Storting, St. meld. 46 (1986–87):21–22 and *BP Statistical Review of World Energy*, various issues.

OPEC accord of autumn 1986, as the Norwegian policy strengthened the position of the advocates of quota coherence. These aspects constitute the indirect effects of the Norwegian policy on the oil-producer cooperation, those not detected by looking at the Norwegian market share and reduction of produced volumes.

To conclude this section, it is important to note that Norway employed self-commitment to technological and economic aspects of the investments on the shelf for the purpose of opposing threats and pressure from OPEC to reduce production. As far as OPEC was concerned, considerations for revenue to the OPEC countries were stated as the reason for the change in market strategy in December 1985. The change in the market situation made this measure a necessity for OPEC to ensure a minimum of revenue to these countries, which are heavily dependent on oil exports for their economies. The problem for OPEC was, of course, that until December 1985 it had been able to defend the price, and it was thus difficult to credibly claim an inability to continue to do so after December 1985. Thus, it must be assumed that the Norwegian self-commitment was originally stronger than that of OPEC. This implies that an actual change in Norwegian interests preceded the policy change in May 1986. The policy change can thus not be ascribed solely to bargaining tactics. To fully understand the Norwegian behavior, we need to supplement the strategic model with factors related to the specific Norwegian economic and political interests in the period in question. These are the themes of the next section.

9.4 Explaining the Norwegian Policy Change

This section will discuss different aspects of Norway as a producing country and how these aspects influence the Norwegian authorities' behavior toward the producer cooperation in the international oil market. The argument put forward is that the interests directly connected with the bargaining between OPEC and non-OPEC producers are insufficient in understanding the Norwegian behavior. There are more fundamental aspects of the Norwegian role as an oil exporter that are important in explaining the bargaining behavior of Norway.

Chapter 2 outlined the changes in the international oil-market structure. The next sections will discuss the economic and political aspects of the Norwegian response to changes in the oil market and the implications for Norway's attitude toward oil-producer cooperation. The factors highlighted are parallel to the explanatory approaches presented by Gourevitch (1986:55–68). The first factors discussed are the economic consequences for the Norwegian economy of the oil-price fall in 1986. The hypothesis is that the perceived dramatic effect caused the subsequent change of policy toward OPEC but also changed the national economic policy in general. The second question relates to the consequences for the internal political debate. In particular, the pattern of cooperation and conflict in the Storting will be taken as an indicator of the changed petro-political debate during the eighties. The hypothesis, taken from Gourevitch (1986:19), is that economic crises lead to domestic political conflicts. The third aspect is the bureaucratic rivalry, in particular between the Ministry of Oil and Energy and the Foreign Ministry, regarding the Norwegian foreign petroleum policy. The hypothesis is that as the role of the sector ministry—in this case, the Ministry of Oil and Energy—increases, so does the conciliatory attitude toward OPEC; the Ministry of Oil and Energy did not emphasize the traditional foreign relations between Norway and its military allies, which are also the largest oil-consuming countries, primarily the United States. Finally, the diplomatic consequences of Norway's new attitude toward oil-producer cooperation in the oil market is discussed. The hypothesis is based on Sæter's (1987) claim that the United States and the United Kingdom put pressure on Norwegian authorities in order to block Norwegian cooperation with OPEC.

Norwegian Petroleum Economy

Oil production on the Norwegian continental shelf commenced with the Phillips Group's production at Ekofisk from June 9, 1971. The development in Norwegian oil production is shown in Figure 9.3. Norwegian production constituted 4.3 percent of world production in 1999.[79] Norway has a somewhat larger share in the export market. The Norwegian oil reserves are estimated at some 11.5 thousand million barrels. This represents one percent of total world oil reserves.[80] As indicated in Figure 9.5, the oil industry has become a major part of the Norwegian economy.

It has been established prudence in Norwegian oil policy that the exploitation pace in the North Sea is determined by technological and economic considerations only. It has been maintained that due to the considerable investment involved in the North Sea, it will always be necessary to produce at full capacity in the individual fields. This axiom has rendered Norway a price-taker in the oil market, with no or marginal supply elasticity. The crucial point when it comes to profitability on the Norwegian shelf is the relationship between investment costs and variable costs. In the North Sea, investment costs are high and variable costs are relatively low. On this point the North Sea differs from production in the United States and the Middle East. In the United States this ratio is the reverse, and in the Middle East both types of costs are low. Taking our point of departure as Norway as a price-taker, the short-term supply will be inflexible while the long-term supply will be dependent on the profitability of new investments. In the North Sea, the investments in and the

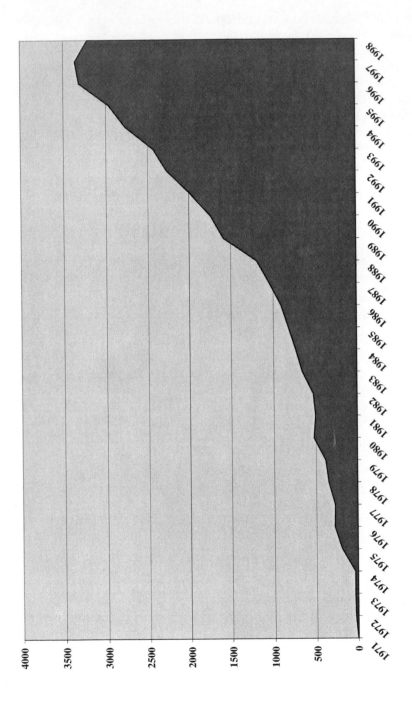

FIGURE 9.3   Norwegian oil production, 1971–1998 (th. b/d)
SOURCE: *BP Statistical Review of World Energy*, various issues.

development of new fields are what are sensitive to price changes, and the immediate production is sustained even with very low prices, as the variable costs are relatively low. It looks as though OPEC in the autumn of 1985 failed to take this into consideration.[81] Investment, on the other hand, is decided by the expected price at the time the field comes onstream. The construction period in the North Sea has been lengthy compared with that of the Middle East. From five to ten years have traditionally elapsed from the time a decision is made to develop a field until it comes onstream. This creates considerable uncertainty regarding the profitability of the various fields, especially at times when price forecasts fail to hold true, or diverge widely, as is the tendency when the current price fluctuates. One cannot fail to notice that oil price prognoses are highly dependent on the price at the time the forecast is made, even if the price at that moment seems to be caused by a short-term disruption of some kind.

As discussed in section 2.5, OPEC's market share fell from about 50 percent in 1979 to approximately 30 percent in 1985. OPEC's argument that non-OPEC producers also had to cooperate in order to stabilize the oil price seems valid. At the same time, the oil price had a downward trend. Furthermore, the oil producers' income from oil exports was propped up by the increase in the dollar exchange rate in the first half of the eighties. When the dollar value fell in 1985, it hit the oil exporters' incomes hard (Claes 1990:31). This is illustrated in Figure 9.4, where the interesting period from 1980 to 1985 shows an increasing oil price in Norwegian kroner and a decreasing one in US dollars.

When the oil price and the dollar fell simultaneously in 1985–1986, the oil price in Norwegian kroner was halved. Thus, the market situation changed dramatically for Norway from December 1985 to May 1986. As pointed out in section 2.5, there was no sign of increase in oil consumption.

With the oil price collapse in spring 1986, the Norwegian economy was severely weakened. The value of the exports of oil and natural gas fell by 32.3 billion NOK from 1985 to 1986. Figure 9.6 shows the taxes paid in 1996 from the petroleum sector. Since taxes are calculated several months after production takes place, the effect of the price fall on the state's income was somewhat delayed, but the coming situation was obvious to Norwegian authorities in spring 1986.

When the economic situation changed so radically, the pressure for drastic political action increased. In the national arena, strong measures were implemented. The Norwegian krone was devalued by 12 percent. The fall in oil prices created a deficit on the current account of 33 billion NOK in 1986.[82] After the devaluation, the Central Bank advocated increased interest rate differential and a fixed exchange rate in order to fi-

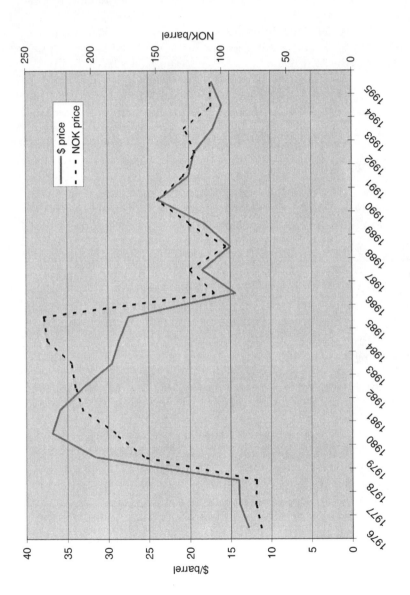

FIGURE 9.4 Brent Blend oil price, 1976–1995 ($ and NOK)

SOURCE: *BP Statistical Review of World Energy 1996*; Statistics Norway, *Statistical Yearbook of Norway 1984, 1993, and 1996*; from 1976 to 1992, average exchange rates; from 1993, rates noted at Oslo Børs (stock exchange).

nance the current account deficit through the private sector. This policy, implemented in 1987, fundamentally changed the Norwegian economic policy, which since 1976 had been characterized by governmental support of the Norwegian export industry through technical or explicit devaluation of the Norwegian krone (Tranøy 1993:238–239). The governmental expenditure was reduced by the equivalent of 4 percent of GNP. On top of this, the high interest rates reduced aggregate demand by about the same amount (Skånland 1988:9).

The Norwegian government introduced harsh measures in the country's macroeconomic policy. If the Norwegian government could increase the oil price, the need for the restrictive economic policy would be reduced. Accordingly, the government's indulgence toward OPEC was motivated by the economic situation that the oil-price fall had caused at home. In a rational cost-benefit calculation, the situation might have been perceived as follows: A policy of holding back some oil production in support of OPEC might have some costs for individual oil companies, but negligible costs for Norway as such. Even small increases in the oil price could have beneficial consequences for the Norwegian economic situation. If Norwegian support—verbal or through small production limitations—could increase the probability that other oil producers inside or outside OPEC also would contribute, the possible gains from an increased oil price would outweigh the Norwegian economic costs. In economic terms, a cooperation with OPEC along the lines described in section 9.2 could be profitable.

The share of the Norwegian economy represented by the oil sector (see Figure 9.5) is low compared with the economies of the OPEC countries. Norway should thus be expected to be more willing than OPEC to limit production. On the other hand, production costs are far higher in Norway, a factor pulling in the opposite direction. Norwegian oil reserves correspond to those of a medium-sized OPEC country. This indicates that saving the oil in the ground and awaiting higher prices can be a possible policy for Norway.[83] Norway, too, is adversely affected by a lack of spare capacity in a price war, and should therefore prefer cooperation rather than provoke such an outcome. Only countries with spare capacity can compensate for a fall in the oil price with increased production.

When the oil price fell again in early 1998, a strong pressure on the Norwegian krone followed during the spring of 1998. The Norwegian Central Bank tried to defend the fall of the krone by increasing the overnight lending rate from 5.75 to 10 percent between May and August of 1998. The demand deposit rate went from 3.75 to 8 percent in the same period. During the first half of 1999, the increased oil price had contributed to a strengthening of the Norwegian krone, and the interest rate was slowly reduced. The events of 1998–1999 demonstrated how actors in the financial market regard Norwegian economy as highly dependent on the oil sector. By mid 2000, the Norwegian government had saved in the so-called Petroleum Fund 304 billion Norwegian kroner ($321 billion or 45 percent of total governmental income in 2001). These assets were placed in foreign equities and bonds, and thus should to some extent counterweigh the oil dependency of the Norwegian public finances. As shown in Figure 9.5, the oil sector continues to constitute an important element in Norwegian economy, expressed by share of GDP and total exports. Figure 9.6 shows the total paid in taxes from the petroleum sector.

In addition to this there is the political advantage Norway can enjoy over OPEC with regard to proximity to the consumer countries. Melvin Conant states "there is a point that Statoil (Norway), Petroven (Venezuela), ENI (Italy), etc. do not represent the kind of risk that would be associated today with a Gulf producer."[84] Here, Norway will be able to exploit the linkage between marketing of its own oil and political affinity with consumer countries. However, this will depend on the consumer countries' judgment of the market situation. In a market with a supply surplus (as in the 1980s), such a linkage would be difficult to establish. However, it would probably be easier to achieve a breakthrough if the consumers were pressured by excess demand. More important is the fact that pressure can be exerted in the opposite direction. To take care of the interests of the consumer countries with a certain supply at an acceptable price, the consumer countries can pressure Norway in the political arena to put a stop to its collaborating with other producers. First it is necessary to discuss the two internal political aspects of the Norwegian cooperation with other oil producers.

Petroleum and Party Politics

According to Gourevitch, "economic crisis leads to policy debate and political controversy; out of conflict, policies emerge" (1986:19). One way to trace the political controversy over the Norwegian oil policy is to study the parliamentary debates. Voting behavior in the Storting is one way to reveal differences of opinion among the political parties. However, voting behavior does not reveal the substance of the parties' positions. I have based my analysis of the political differences on the remarks the different parties have formulated in committee propositions on the different reports presented by the government to the Storting.[85]

Taking the period from 1970 to 1994 as a whole, the pattern of conflict between the parties is similar to the traditional conflict pattern, with one exception: Labor has a higher rate of agreement with the Christian Party (KrF) than with the Center Party (Senterpartiet). The Christian Party is at

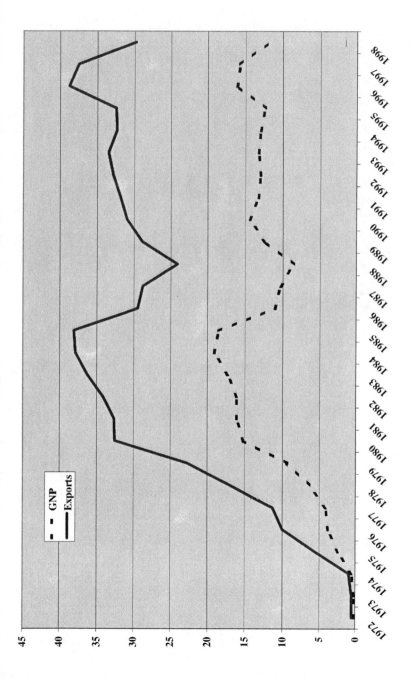

FIGURE 9.5 The petroleum sector share of GDP and total exports, 1972–1998 (%)
SOURCE: Norwegian Ministry of Petroleum and Energy, *Fact Sheet*, various issues.

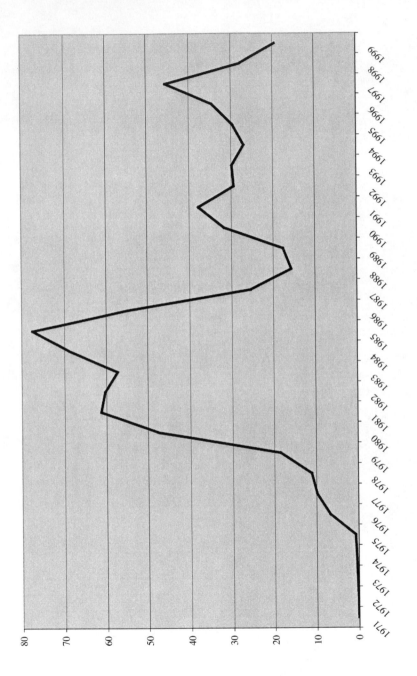

FIGURE 9.6   Paid taxes from the petroleum sector, 1971–1999 (bill. 1999 NOK)
SOURCE: Norwegian Ministry of Petroleum and Energy, *Fact Sheet*, various issues.

TABLE 9.4 Correlation Between Positions by Major Parties in Committee Recommendations to Parliamentary Propositions on Petroleum-Related Issues, 1970–1994

	Labor	*Conservative*	*Christian*	*Center*
Labor	1.0000	.0643 (p = .054)	.2394 (p = .000)	.0691 (p = .039)
Conservative		1.0000	.5259 (p = .000)	.3044 (p = .000)
Christian			1.0000	.6801 (p = .000)
Center				1.0000

Notes: Correlation are persons r, and two-tailed significance.
SOURCE: NSD.

the same time closer to the Conservative Party (Høyre) than to the Center Party. This is indicated by Table 9.4.

Most striking in the data are the changes from 1985 to 1986. The number of petroleum-related reports presented to the Storting in the period 1981 to 1985 was forty-one, compared with sixty-six in the election period from 1985 to 1989. During the same period the number of committee remarks fell from 153 to 79, with a minimum in 1986 of only 6. Table 9.5 shows the agreement between the two major parties, the Labor Party and the Conservative Party, regarding petroleum-related reports to the Storting from 1982 to 1994. As Table 9.5 illustrates, the period from 1984 to 1990 was turbulent. The crisis of spring 1986 clearly increased the agreement between these two traditionally opposed parties. Although the number of cases in 1986 alone is too small (N = 6) to draw any conclusions, the rate of agreement in the nineties is substantially higher than during the eighties. As shown in Figure 9.7, the turbulence in the last half of the eighties was not present when considering all issues. It is thus fair to assume that the turbulence regarding petroleum issues had something to do with petroleum-related controversies, rather than being part of a general political conflict pattern.

The domestic political consequence of the dramatic price fall in the spring of 1986 was not, as suggested by Gourevitch (1986), a political confrontation, but rather an increased political agreement on petroleum-related issues. The crisis period increased the cooperation between Labor and the Conservative Party.[86] The perceived external threat increased the internal cohesion.

What, then, were the consequences for the Norwegian position regarding oil-producer cooperation? The external turbulence represented by the price fall silenced the political opposition. This gave the new Labor government that took office in May 1986 freedom of action in formulating its foreign petroleum policy (Claes 1995). The political parties were in agreement on the need to take political action in order to handle the dramatic

TABLE 9.5   Common Positions Between Labor and the Conservative Party on Petroleum-Related Issues in Parliamentary Committees

Year	Disagree (%)	Agree (%)	N
1982	73.17	26.83	41
1983	50.00	50.00	22
1984	93.62	6.38	47
1985	100.00	0.00	19
1986	0.00	100.00	6
1987	44.44	55.56	9
1988	80.00	20.00	40
1989	97.14	2.86	35
1990	38.75	61.25	80
1991	23.26	76.74	43
1992	28.13	71.88	96
1993	30.56	69.44	36
1994	27.78	72.22	18

SOURCE: NSD.

economic situation. The new Labor government introduced a cooperative strategy toward OPEC during the autumn of 1986 as part of a strategy to handle the economic situation, as such a cooperation was aimed at stabilizing the oil price. Given the circumstances, the other parties could not strongly oppose such a policy.

Another case of party political disputes regarding the relationship to OPEC was when in March 1998, Oil Minister Marit Arnstad announced a press conference expected to consist of an announcement of Norwegian production cuts in support of OPEC. This increased the Brent oil price with more than half a dollar. At the press conference it became clear that Arnstad did not have the necessary support in the parliament's standing committee on foreign affairs. This caused the price to fall back to its previous level. The problem was that Arnstad had not consulted the opposition parties. To the opposition the issue was thus perceived as a fait accompli when they understood that a press conference was announced before they had been given an opportunity to voice their opinions. Although Arnstad at the press conference denied it had been a problematic meeting, and called it a "first consultation with the parliament," she would hardly have summoned a press conference to tell only this. She said to *Dagsavisen* the next day that she had not anticipated the reactions in the parliament. Arnstad had obviously planned to announce a cut in the Norwegian oil production at the following press conference, but did not get the support of the parliament's standing committee on foreign affairs, and had to smooth the embarrassing situation by calling it a first

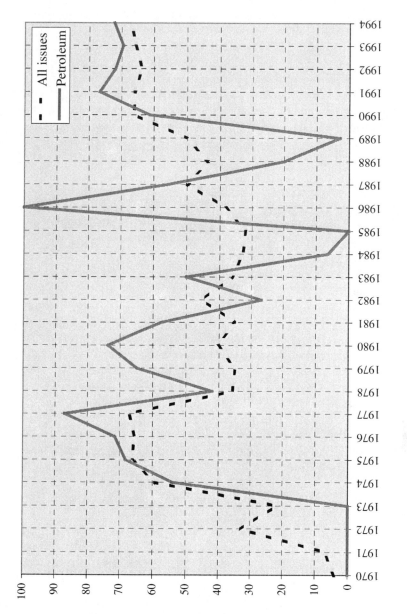

FIGURE 9.7   Agreement in parliamentary committee remarks between Labor and the Conservative Party regarding petroleum issues and all issues (percent), 1970–1994
SOURCE: NSD.

consultation with the parliament. It should be noted that a compromise, cutting the production by 100,000 barrels per day, was agreed upon between the government and the Labor Party the very next day. When the measures where renewed in December, the government consulted the parliament and thus avoided a similar embarrassment.

Given the rather small parliamentary basis for the government—42 out of 165 seats—and the lack of informal consultations, the majority in parliament exercised a role as veto-players. The difference in opinion regarding the oil policy between the government and the Labor Party was not large, but the government's lack of humility toward the parliament provoked the opposition. It thus shows the importance of norms and codes of conduct in the relationship between the government and the parliament.

Bureaucratic Conflicts over Oil Issues

The Norwegian petroleum adventure started with Phillips Petroleum approaching the Norwegian Foreign Ministry in 1962. During the following years the Foreign Ministry tried to transfer the more detailed legislative issues regarding the continental shelf to the Ministry of Justice and other issues to the Ministry of Industry. However, these ministries obviously preferred to have the petroleum issues remain in the Foreign Ministry (Hanisch and Nerheim 1992). In November 1963, the so-called Continental Shelf Committee was appointed and placed under the Ministry of Industry. Both the committee leader, Jens Evensen, and its secretary, Leif Terje Løddesøl, were recruited from the Foreign Ministry. Due to Evensen's special relationship with both Minster of Industry Trygve Lie and the Cabinet as such, the committee had a special position in the ministry, with Evensen operating outside the normal hierarchical structure. The first civil servant in charge of petroleum affairs in the Ministry of Industry, Nils Gulnes, was appointed in 1965. The Continental Shelf Committee laid down the legislative foundation for the first concessions on the shelf. Evensen was also appointed leader of the government's Oil Committee (Statens Oljeråd) in 1965. In this initial phase of the Norwegian oil adventure, governance was entirely left to a small group of people. In addition to the three names mentioned, Carl August Fleischer was an important assistant to Evensen, and these four people defined the Norwegian oil policy during most of the sixties. Evensen and his men had to outline policy in a totally unfamiliar terrain, gathering information and making decisions regarding issues they hardly knew anything about in advance. In the terminology of Charles F. Hermann's model, the situation was an "innovative situation," as the issues were regarded by the decisionmakers as important, the decision time was extended, and the issues were unfamiliar. Such situations will "receive the attention of the most able men available and, similarly, . . . considerable energy will be devoted to investigating the problem" (Hermann 1969:417). The institutional structure for handling the oil issues was established outside the ministerial structure, and the ministries seemed to some extent unwilling to include the issues in their traditional organizational structure. One reason for this was that as long as there were no oil discoveries, the importance of oil issues might be short-lived. Hanisch and Nerheim (1992:22–33) also emphasize the importance of the Kings Bay accident in 1962 and its political consequences, which made the Ministry of Industry unwilling to assume the responsibility for another large-scale governmental industrial project. Furthermore, Evensen's position made the committee's work unfit to be included in established hierarchical structures.[87]

When oil was discovered at Ekofisk in December 1969, the institutional issues had to be settled. The bureaucratic structure was split into three parts in 1972: the Ministry of Industry handled principles, legislation, and concessions; the Oil Directorate handled daily administration, exploration, and control; and a state oil company was in charge of the government's business interests. As the important issues turned from juridical relations toward other states and the international companies to the industrial development of the continental shelf, so did the departmental structure. Control over oil issues thus shifted to the Ministry of Industry. In 1978, the Ministry of Oil and Energy was established. As the Norwegian oil income increased, so did the importance of the question of political governance of the oil sector. The petroleum sector's share of GDP increased from 6.8 percent in 1978 to 16 percent in 1981 (see Figure 9.5). In the same period the sector's contribution to the state income increased from 10.78 billion to 57.63 billion in 1996 NOK (see Figure 9.6). Most of this effect was price-driven, as the increase in production was marginal in this period (see Figure 9.3). The Norwegian economy changed into an oil-based economy. The state revenue increased rapidly in this period, taking most actors by surprise. The increased economic importance of the petroleum sector increased its political importance. In particular, the role of Statoil became a disputed political issue during the first half of the eighties. At the same time the increased oil prices made the relationship between oil consumers and oil producers more confrontational. This created a dilemma for the Norwegian political authorities in charge of the foreign petroleum policy. If the relations with their traditional allies among the Western countries were emphasized, they would risk weakening the common interests with other petroleum producers, and vice versa. As the United States in particular perceived the oil market as a security issue, the Norwegian behavior in this market became politicized.

This external dilemma also created an internal dilemma, as the Foreign Ministry advocated the traditional security interests, while the Ministry of Oil and Energy emphasized the petroleum economic interests. In the first half of the eighties this meant that the Norwegian foreign petroleum policy became less coherent. Sydnes (1985) conducted a thorough analysis of the ministries involved in four petroleum-related issues:

1. the Norwegian attitude toward an energy-dialogue between producers and consumers
2. the Norwegian attitude toward IEA
3. the attitude toward OPEC
4. the price and marketing strategy

She concluded that the Foreign Ministry had a monopoly on the first issue, dominated the second, and was insignificant in the handling of the fourth (Sydnes 1985:162–165).[88] This development, whereby the Ministry of Oil and Energy has taken over the foreign petroleum relations, illustrates a trend that is not restricted to the oil issues. East and Salomonsen assume that "regardless of whether or not the foreign ministry has received resources adequate to meet the increasing demands placed upon it by interdependence, the effects of that interdependence threaten and undermine the government's ability to control and coordinate its foreign policy" (East and Salomonsen 1981:169). Other ministries increased their international activities at the expense of the Ministry of Foreign Affairs. Also, the third issue area, the relationship toward OPEC, was after a while handled by the Ministry of Oil and Energy (Engesland 1989:152). According to interviews with officials in the Ministry of Oil and Energy, the decisionmaking process regarding the policy toward OPEC was governed by that ministry: "the role of the Ministry of Foreign Affairs is not particularly interesting" (Engesland 1989:121–122).

With the Foreign Ministry traditionally handling the relationship with Norway's military allies, it was natural that this ministry also handled the relationship with these countries in the IEA setting. Since the relationship with the OPEC countries was perceived as an economic issue, it was natural that these relations were handled by the Ministry of Oil and Energy. As the importance of the oil sector for the Norwegian economy grew, so did the strength of the Ministry of Oil and Energy in the Norwegian bureaucracy. When these areas of Norway's foreign relations came into conflict, the economic interests represented by the Ministry of Oil and Energy took precedence. This might not have happened had the opposition from Norway's traditional allies been stronger than what it was. This is discussed in the next section.

Foreign Policy Implications of the OPEC Connection

The traditional political allies of Norway are identical with the major oil-consuming countries. In the oil market these have opposing interests with producer countries such as Norway. Hence, we are up against an apparent dilemma between Norwegian foreign policy and oil policy. If weight is placed on the positive Norwegian relationship with the West, the result will be a negative relationship with OPEC. If weight is placed on the positive relationship with OPEC, the result will be a negative relationship with traditional Western allies. Norway has sought to avoid such a linkage, as this constrains freedom of action in the oil market.

Norway's policy toward the IEA illustrates this dilemma. On joining the IEA through an associated agreement, Foreign Minister Frydenlund placed weight on the following factors: "decisive for the government's viewpoint, however, have been considerations of a foreign policy nature. In this connection it is a matter of cooperating with countries with whom we cooperate also in virtually all other areas."[89] The fact that Norway chose to be an associate member of the IEA may be a manifestation of the wish to give some concessions in the opposite direction, that is, toward the oil-producing countries (Sydnes 1985:126). This demonstrates how relations with Western countries in general influenced Norway's behavior in the oil market, as Norway as a net oil exporter became associated with an organization of oil-importing countries. There is reason to believe that relations with the IEA have been important in shaping Norwegian market policy, not least in Norway's approach to OPEC.

The United States, Norway's most important military ally, strongly opposed OPEC during the seventies and eighties. Bull-Berg (1987) points out that the American policy has varied, depending on which interests were dominant; such interests, in turn, have been partially decided by political security interests, consumer interests, and internal producer interests. Regarding the Norwegian conciliatory policy toward OPEC in 1986, "it was the US government who spoke out most strongly against any political intervention in the market, also to Norway" (Udgaard 1989:66). This was in part due to ideological reasons. The oil-price fall in the spring of 1986 was welcomed in the United States and in Western Europe. In the short term this served the interests of the consumer countries. However, in the longer term a price drop could create an unstable situation in the market, and weaken the basis for oil production in the OECD countries. Hence, the United States' strategic desire for supply independence, and consideration for the domestic oil industry, indicated a stable, middle-path oil price. That security motives were behind the US attitude can be deduced from Kissinger's (1982b:xx) statements: "Aside from our military defense, there is no project of more central importance to our national security and indeed our independence as a sovereign nation" than energy saving, import independence, and consumer cooperation. Norwegian politicians also linked developments in the oil market to security policy. Frydenlund said in a statement to the Storting that "the energy problem is one of the international community's most serious challenges today, perhaps indeed the most important. I ask you to recall former energy minister Schlesinger's statement in his farewell speech that the way this problem is handled can be decisive for the political future of the human race."[90] For Norway this meant that as long as one's traditional allies regarded a lower oil price as desirable, entering into overt cooperation with OPEC for purposes of stabilizing the price could imply political problems in the relations with those allies. Considerations of traditional alliances constricted Norway's behavior in the oil market.

Norway has on several occasions sought to act as bridge-builder in international relations. So, too, has it acted in the oil market. After the oil crisis in 1973, considerable antagonism simmered between producers and consumers in the oil market. Frydenlund pointed out in 1975 that "we can ask ourselves whether the conflicts of interest between producers and consumers are so considerable and the cards are so overwhelmingly in the hands of the exporting countries, that the negotiations at present cannot produce results."[91] Four years later Norway took the initiative with the express objective of establishing negotiations between producers and consumers in the oil market with a view to a "global energy order" (Bergesen 1982:112). Prime Minister Odvar Nordli maintained that a greater degree of price prediction could be achieved only "by improving the dialogue between producing and consuming nations, based on recognition of common interest".[92] The motives underlying the initiative may have been several. Norway may have wanted to ensure growth of the Western economies by contributing to stability in the oil market. It must be borne in mind that this move was made at a time when oil prices were rising steeply. Moreover, there *may* have been a genuine North-South commitment behind it. However, the initiative crumbled—a working group's[93] assessment of the response from the various quarters was that there was insufficient political basis internationally for Norway to promote any major engagement (Sydnes 1985:92). Nevertheless, in the wake of the Norwegian approach to OPEC in 1986, the same theme emerged once more. In 1987, Prime Minister Brundtland claimed that "Norway is in a position to make endeavors to bring about the discussions between oil importing and oil exporting countries which are necessary if stable and predictable conditions in the oil market are to be secured."[94] The move was followed up in a number of forums, such as the IEA and the UN. The idea of a dialogue between oil producers and oil consumers was also on the agenda of the World Commission on Environment and Development, headed by Brundtland.

Thus, on several occasions Norway experienced a dilemma in balancing between its traditional allies, the oil-consuming countries, and its economic allies, the oil producers. This dilemma influenced the change of strategy toward oil-producer cooperation. The traditional Norwegian perception of the Western allies' attitude was that they preferred low oil prices. However, in the spring of 1986 it became clear that their attitude was more complex. Sæter claims that the Norwegian change of strategy was implemented "in spite of relatively strong opposition from, among others, officials representing the US and the UK" (Sæter 1987:5; my translation). Since Sæter nowhere in his article gives any references for his claim that the United States and the United Kingdom officially and strongly opposed the Norwegian behavior, it is impossible to evaluate the empirical validity of his statements. However, the issue has been discussed by both Dyrdal (1990) and Engesland (1989). They both find the American reaction to be moderate, and their presentations are substantiated by the interviews they conducted. Dyrdal bases his analysis on interviews with senior US officials in, among others, the State Department and the Department of Energy, while Engesland conducted extensive interviews with Norwegian officials in several ministries. Dyrdal argues that "there is little in the available material to indicate that the American reaction was particularly strong" (Dyrdal 1990:55; my translation). He quotes US Secretary of Energy John Herrington as having said, "Although we don't necessarily agree with it [the Norwegian decision to limit oil exports in September 1986], we respect that decision. And we have a wait-and-see attitude on how it comes out."[95] Both Vice President George Bush and Foreign Secretary George Schultz were of the opinion that too-low oil prices were undesirable (Yergin 1991:757). In March 1986, Prime Minister Kåre Willoch had discussions with both Schultz and European Commission President Jacques Delors. Delors was worried that a low oil price would stimulate increased consumption, reduce the incentives to save energy, increase the industrial countries' energy dependency, and increase the possibility of future price increases.[96] At a press conference on April 1, 1986, Vice President Bush indicated that he would appeal for price stabilization during an upcoming visit to Saudi Arabia. This was, however, disclaimed as a formal US policy by the White House (Dyrdal 1990:109). The ambiguous statements from the US government indicated there were differences of opinion inside the government (see section 6.2).[97]

Although this is not a study of US petroleum policy, it is important to note that the US policy in the oil market has been a result of internal conflicting interests. With a low oil price, in the area of $10/barrel, the producer interests tend to dominate the US policy, indicating no further price decline. With an oil price above \$30/barrel, oil-consumer interests tend to dominate, indicating no further price increase. In between these figures, the price would be perceived to be at a "reasonable" level, in which case the US government is unlikely to have a strong interest in changing the price in any direction (Dyrdal 1990:112). At least after Willoch's discussions with Schultz in Stockholm in March 1986, the Norwegian authorities must have been aware of the US position, and thus able to disregard possible US reactions to Norwegian cooperative moves toward OPEC.

According to Sæter (1987), the United Kingdom also voiced strong opposition toward the Norwegian change of strategy. Relations with the United Kingdom have been crucial in the shaping of Norwegian oil policy. The oil reserves in British and Norwegian sectors of the North Sea were mapped at about the same time. While Norway chose a moderate exploitation rate, the United Kingdom opted for a faster rate in its oil exploitation. The two countries produce oil from the same geographical area—in some cases, from the same fields[98]—and they produce oil of about the same grade. There also exist traditional, strong bonds between the two countries. These factors have led to a coordination of their respective oil policies, both officially and unofficially.

There has been extensive exchange of views between the two countries, and their price-setting practices have followed the same pattern. Thus, when Statoil in October 1984 reduced its price by \$1.50/barrel, BNOC (the British National Oil Company) chose to follow suit, reducing its price by \$1.35/barrel.[99] It was also clear that when the Norwegian decisionmakers decided to change their policy toward OPEC, the British attitude was important; even after the Norwegian Labor Party's inaugural declaration announced the new policy, the British attitude was not ignored. Minister of Finance Gunnar Berge stated that the government had shown signs of a will to cooperate with OPEC. Berge emphasized, however, that it was "necessary for the North Sea oil producers to cooperate in such a situation."[100] And when the resolutions were to be implemented, consideration was duly paid to Britain, since about 16 percent of the Statfjord field is on the British side of the North Sea boundary. If Norway unilaterally chose to reduce production in the field, the percentage share of the United Kingdom would involve a larger nominal extraction. However, this was solved by means of an agreement involving return of the field to Norway when it approached depletion.

The responses from the two North Sea producers to OPEC's move were very different, despite their previous cooperation. While Norway gradually adjusted to OPEC's political pressure, the United Kingdom rejected them.[101] The reason might be that the Norwegian oil production was on the increase, while the British production was expected to decline rapidly in the course of the next few years. Furthermore, the comparative weight of the oil sector in Britain's economy is less than what it is for Norway. While oil production in 1985 constituted 5 percent of GDP, 7 percent of exports, and 10 percent of state revenues in Britain, the corresponding figures for Norway were 20, 36, and 20 percent, respectively.[102] Although the United Kingdom did not at all consider cooperation with OPEC, there is little evidence that it in any way tried to change the Norwegian cooperative policy.

The Norwegian political dilemma between producer and consumer interests in the oil market was obviously present when the call for cooperation with OPEC emerged in 1986. However, the resistance from the traditional allies, the United States and the United Kingdom, was not particularly strong. US Secretary of Energy John Herrington was correct when he stated that the Norwegian change of strategy was an economic decision.[103] In January 1987, the US State Department sent a démarche (a diplomatic note) warning Norway against supporting OPEC and pointing out the possible negative implications for the oil market of a strengthened OPEC (Dyrdal 1990:107). This was the strongest reaction from the United States. It caused concern in the Norwegian Foreign Ministry, while the Ministry of Oil and Energy regarded the negative reactions as less than expected and easily bearable (Engesland 1989:142).

It is fair to conclude that the political costs connected with the Norwegian change of strategy in 1986 were minimal. One official protest from the United States and some statements by representatives of the US administration cannot be regarded as strong opposition, contrary to Sæter's (1987) argument. Given that representatives of the US government also advocated some stabilization of the oil price (e.g., the statement made by Bush, cited previously), considerations regarding the reactions by the traditional allies have to be regarded as an element of little importance in a cost-benefit analysis of the Norwegian decision. Furthermore, there were some certain political gains from a cooperation with OPEC, in addition to the possible economic benefits. An increased flow of information from the OPEC countries to the Norwegian authorities regarding their views of the oil market and related aspects was an immediate effect of the 1986 decision. Frequent meetings with representatives of the OPEC countries have led to the development of closer relations with these countries. Although there are differences of opinion regarding future Norwegian cooperation with OPEC, the information and meetings are important in order to avoid political or economic conflicts with other oil producers. Such relationships can also be useful for Norwegian authorities in areas other than the oil market. Thus, it can be argued that the Norwegian leeway in international affairs has been somewhat increased by this new political oil strategy. In sum, the change of strategy can be evaluated from the Norwegian side as having had minimal political and economic costs, a short-term economic gain as the Norwegian behavior contributed to a rise in the oil price, and probably some longer-term political benefits as Norway gained an opportunity to develop beneficial political relations with a new group of countries.

9.5 Conclusion

Chapter 2 outlined the fundamental changes in the structure of the international oil market from 1971 to the 1990s. OPEC's "freedom of action" became constrained during this period. In the seventies, OPEC dominated the market and was in a position to increase both price and production at the same time. This changed in the eighties. Subsequently, the need for OPEC to include other producers in the effort to control the oil price increased. For Norway, the country's market share increased substantially during the same period, making it harder to hide behind a notion of insignificance in the international market. This became all too clear in October 1984, when the Statoil price decision triggered an international oil-market crisis. The main argument is that, as the actors' preferences change, so does the outcome of the strategic game. In this particular interaction, this was so because the effect of the OPEC threat and the subsequent Norwegian promise provided an opportunity for the actors to increase their utility simultaneously by effecting a cooperative outcome. The game-theoretical argument in this chapter is trivial, but it highlights the strategic aspects of the interaction between Norway and OPEC in this particularly intensive phase of the relationship. However, a question arises as to why the Norwegian authorities changed strategy toward oil-producer cooperation in 1986. An underlying phenomenon is that Norway's market share increased during the period discussed in this book, and therefore Norway's interests might have changed according to the discussion of collective action in Chapter 7. This argument does not consider characteristics of the individual actors, except for their share of the collective good. In this chapter, four factors have been added in order to grasp the Norwegian policy toward oil-producer cooperation.

First, there was the macroeconomic impact of the 1986 price fall. The second oil shock in 1979–1980 increased the Norwegian government's revenues from the oil sector fivefold. This happened with only slightly increased production. However, the Norwegian economy became oil-dependent in this period. When the oil price collapsed in 1986, it all seemed to be a case of easy come, easy go. The subsequent macroeconomic tightening was designed to handle continuously low oil prices and virtually no increase in state oil revenues. In 1986, the coming substantial increase in Norwegian oil production (see Figure 9.3) was not apparent to either Norwegian politicians or to the oil companies operating in Norway. The situation was perceived as one of severe economic crisis. Any measure that could ease the situation would have been attractive to any government, regardless of political stripe.

Second, the political situation created leverage for changing this part of the Norwegian foreign policy. The conservative government was considering abandoning its ideologically based resistance to cooperation with OPEC, if it could improve the Norwegian economic situation. Obviously, it is easier for a new government to change policy when it comes to power than for a sitting government to disclaim its previous statements and change its policy toward other actors. Therefore, even though the conservative government in spring 1986 might have considered supporting OPEC, it was easier for the new Labor government to make this policy official. Thus, the change of government in spring 1986 made it easier for Norway to cooperate with OPEC.

Third, the fact that the Ministry of Oil and Energy had greater bureaucratic strength than the Foreign Ministry on oil issues made it easier to follow economic considerations rather than anticipated political reactions from traditional allied countries. This is connected with the fourth argument concerning US and UK reactions.

Fourth, the claimed external political pressure from the United States and the United Kingdom played a minor role in the Norwegian change of strategy toward OPEC. When the support of OPEC was initiated, some possible political costs were anticipated, as the Norwegian government could not be sure of the US reactions. These reactions turned out to be mild and did not outweigh the perceived economic benefits from the OPEC cooperation. The empirical discussion on this point also reveals the different attitudes of different US presidential administrations. The Nixon-Kissinger administration saw the price increases of the OPEC countries as a security issue, and fought them accordingly. The Ronald Reagan administration saw them as a purely economic issue and confronted the OPEC countries for interfering in the working of the free market. George Bush had a background in the US oil industry and was responsive to its interest in a somewhat higher and more stable oil price. At the same time, the superpower conflict was over, and the alliance with some of the Gulf countries was strengthened by the US involvement in the Iraq-Kuwait War. This also influenced the US attitude toward Norway. With better relations between the United States and the Gulf oil producers, it was of less political importance to the United States what kind of relations Norway established with the same countries.

Notes

1. The idea to invest the oil income outside the Norwegian economy has been a part of the Norwegian petroleum political debate since the seventies. During 1996 approximately 45 billion Norwegian kroner (NOK) was placed in the fund. In mid 2000 the fund constituted 304 billion NOK ($32 billion).

2. For instance, the relationship between Norway and the international oil companies (IOC) has been determined by the Norwegian authorities' decision to include the IOC in the development of the Norwegian oil industry. This strategy was quite in contrast to the ones followed by the OPEC countries during the seventies. Although the Norwegian and governmental share of concessions increased during the seventies, the IOC have an important role in the Norwegian oil industry.

3. Underdal (1987:171) has pointed out that negotiations may be necessary also in cases where only coinciding interests are present: "even in situations characterized by perfect identity of interests policy coordination can be required to *ensure* Pareto-optimal outcomes." However, this is not the case in the bargaining between OPEC and Norway.

4. *Stavanger Aftenblad*, March 22, 1982. All translations of quotations from Norwegian-language publications are mine.

5. *Stavanger Aftenblad*, November 3, 1982.

6. *Aftenposten*, July 11, 1984.

7. Statement by Oil and Energy Minister Vidkun Hveding in *Stavanger Aftenblad*, February 26, 1983.

8. *Aftenposten*, September 13, 1984.

9. Ibid.

10. This episode has given rise to considerable debate on the organization of Norwegian petroleum policy and on the role of Statoil in general. These are aspects of the price reduction that fall outside the framework of this study. Similarly, I will leave aside the question that has probably occupied the most newspaper column space, namely, whether or not the Ministry of Oil and Energy and the government were informed. What is interesting for our purposes is the fact that the opponent, whether deliberately or truly, failed to perceive any difference between a Statoil resolution and a resolution made by Norwegian authorities. It was therefore difficult for the Norwegian authorities to dissociate themselves from Statoil's actions, whether or not they were informed.

11. "Norway yesterday announced measures amounting to a unilateral cut in the official price of its North Sea crude oil of $1.50 a barrel." *Financial Times*, October 16, 1984.

12. *Stavanger Aftenblad*, October 20, 1984.

13. *Aftenposten*, October 27, 1984.

14. Yamani has subsequently been asked about his impression of Arne Øien and described him as able and sympathetic. To the question of his impression of Kåre Kristiansen, he is reported to have said, "Oh, he is a politician" (Lindøe 1987:104).

15. *Middle East Economic Survey*, December 3, 1984.

16. Ibid.

17. *Stavanger Aftenblad*, November 29, 1984.

18. *Aftenposten*, March 19, 1984.

19. *International Herald Tribune*, December 11, 1985.

20. *Aftenposten*, December 12, 1985.

21. *Financial Times*, December 10, 1985. A confirmation of this intention was given in a press release from Yamani some two months later: "When the OPEC member Conference, held in Geneva last December, unanimously decided to secure and defend for the Organization a fair oil market share, speculative sales in the market began to push oil prices downwards as it became clear to all that if non-OPEC member states did not revise their policies and give up some part of their market shares to OPEC, there would be a production surplus which would lead to a fall in oil prices" (cited in *OPEC Bulletin*, March 1986).

22. Iran's oil minister, Hussein Kazimpur Ardebili, as quoted in *Stavanger Aftenblad*, January 27, 1986.

23. *Aftenposten*, January 22, 1986.

24. "When weighty social considerations render it necessary, the King in Council can establish other production rates than those already established or approved pursuant to the above provisions." Section 20.5 of Chapter III of the Petroleum Act, March 22, 1985.

25. Ministry of Oil and Energy, press release, January 21, 1986.

26. *Platt's Oilgram News*, January 23, 1986.

27. *Aftenposten*, February 17, 1986.

28. Norwegian debate on the shaping of policy toward OPEC was now heating up in earnest. A number of actors entered the arena, including the companies, state agencies, and various other parties. However, this discussion falls outside the scope of this study, and has been discussed by others in greater detail, particularly by Engesland (1989).

29. *Stavanger Aftenblad*, May 3, 1986.

30. *Arbeiderbladet*, January 21, 1986.

31. *Aftenposten*, March 20, 1986.

32. Skånland's reasoning was that under the assumption that the price will actually rise in future, it may be rational, at any rate from an economic point of view, to simply allow the oil to remain in the ground while awaiting a price rise. *Aftenposten*, March 13, 1986.

33. The government's inaugural speech to the Storting, May 13, 1986.

34. *Aftenposten*, May 15, 1986.

35. *Aftenposten*, February 6, 1986.

36. *Aftenposten*, May 23, 1986.

37. These were established after Yamani was kidnapped by Venezuelan terrorist Illitch Ramirez Sanchez, alias Carlos Martinez, alias the Jackal (Terzian 1985:219–234).

38. *Aftenposten*, June 24, 1986.

39. *Aftenposten*, June 23, 1986.

40. *Arbeiderbladet*, June 24, 1986.

41. A spaghetti meal, not appearing on the program, was served in the hotel restaurant. The talks became more relaxed, with the probable aim on the part of Yamani to build up trustful relations between the two parties.

42. *OPEC Bulletin*, July/August 1986.

43. *Aftenposten*, June 30, 1986.

44. Press release from the Ministry of Oil and Energy, July 1, 1986. The government's view was explained by Øien in *Aftenposten* (July 5, 1986) and elaborated on in a reply to Kristiansen in *Aftenposten* (July 24, 1986).

45. The agreement was the result of a proposal put forward by Iran's oil minister, Gholamreza Aghazadeh, to the effect that a return should be made to the 1984 quotas, and acceptance that Iraq should be exempted from the quota arrangement.

46. Press release from the Ministry of Oil and Energy, August 6, 1986.

47. Press release from the Ministry of Oil and Energy, September 10, 1986.

48. *Stavanger Aftenblad*, September 12, 1986.

49. Yamani arrived with gifts (sweetmeats and dates) for the Norwegian representatives.

50. This reportedly occurred at the request of the Norwegian representatives, who needed this as a means for domestic opinion-making.

51. *Aftenposten*, October 27, 1986, and *Arbeiderbladet*, December 8, 1986.

52. Press release from the Ministry of Oil and Energy, January 13, 1987.

53. The term "peaceful coexistence" is adopted to indicate that the relationship between OPEC and Norway in this period was antagonistic, but that the direct confrontations were few and of low intensity.

54. *Aftenposten*, June 23, 1990.

55. *Aftenposten*, July 26, 1990.

56. *Dagens Næringsliv*, December 29, 1993.

57. Committee recommendation to the Storting (Innst.S.) no: 251(1995–1996).

58. Official report of the proceedings of the Storting (1993–1994):1844.

59. Official report of the proceedings of the Storting (1993–1994):1795.

60. *Dagens Næringsliv*, January 12 and 16, 1995.

61. *NTB-AP*, June 25, 1995.

62. *Dagens Næringsliv* assumes that to consider production limitation, the Norwegian authorities at least need to see a direct approach from the larger OPEC countries, particularly Saudi Arabia. *Dagens Næringsliv*, January 16, 1995.

63. Committee recommendations to the Storting (Innst.S.) no: 180(1993–1994) and no: 251(1995–1996).

64. Interpellation by Anne Enger Lahnstein, in the Parliament on February 19, 1997.

65. Press release from the Ministry of Oil and Energy, March 29, 1998.

66. Press release from the Ministry of Oil and Energy, December 4, 1999.

67. News brief from the Ministry of Oil and Energy, June 30, 1999.

68. *Middle East Economic Survey*, February 8, 1999.

69. Press release from the Norwegian Ministry of Oil and Energy, June 26, 2000.

70. Press release from the Norwegian Ministry of Oil and Energy, March 29, 1998.

71. *Aftenposten* (Oslo) Internet edition, July 4, 2000.

72. IEA *Monthly Oil Market Report*, July 11, 2000:18.

73. A "threat" is here defined according to Schelling (1980:123) as an action whereby "one asserts that he will do, in a contingency, what he would manifestly

prefer not to do if the contingency occurred, the contingency being governed by the second party's behavior."

74. *Petroleum Economist,* January 1986:2.

75. The methodical point of departure for this analysis is a much simplified and adjusted design based on CREON methods (see Hermann et al. 1973 and Callahan et al. 1982). Only events that are directed directly or indirectly toward the other and that affect the cooperation between the parties in the oil market have been coded. The time horizon is 1983 to 1987. By events, I mean here verbal expressions (words) and actions (deeds). Altogether, 165 events have been registered. The statements come from several sources—public organs (press releases) as well as professional periodicals (e.g., *Platt's Oilgram News*) and newspapers.

76. The total number of events is low, so the numbers indicate only change in the strength of the OPEC pressure.

77. Thus, the rational response was not to cooperate. This logic could be extended to all smaller producers in the oil market, as the Saudi Arabian strategy from October 1985 would probably not have been sustainable indefinitely. The overproduction by the other OPEC members in the period 1986 to 1990 was about twice as much as their overproduction in the period 1991 to 1995.

78. The government's inaugural speech to the Storting, May 13, 1986.

79. *BP Statistical Review of World Energy 2000.*

80. Ibid.

81. See Yamani's statements after the OPEC extraordinary meeting on April 22, 1986, reported in *OPEC Bulletin,* May 1986:4–8.

82. National Budget 1991, Report to the Storting: St.m. nr.1(1990–1991):146.

83. The notion of "saving" oil in the earth has been proposed by Skånland as one option: "If we expect a higher oil price in the 1990s, it should be a wise policy to limit production now in order to take out more for higher prices later on. . . . Only as long as we feel reasonably certain that [the price] will not rise can it be a wise policy to increase production, and of course this policy is to be recommended even more if we believe the long-term trend to be falling" *Aftenposten,* March 13, 1986.

84. *Geopolitics of Energy,* April 1988.

85. The Norwegian Social Science Data Services (NSD) has compiled data on all parliamentary committee remarks made in the Storting since 1945 (Otterå 1982). I have extracted the committee remarks relevant to the petroleum sector.

86. It is more difficult to decide whether it had any effect on the relationship inside the conservative bloc, as these parties were in and out of coalition governments during the eighties. The variation in conservative cohesion in the Storting is to a large extent explained by the internal coordination in the coalition government. The positions in the parliamentary committees will therefore not disclose possible differences of opinion among these parties.

87. This interpretation is the opposite of that given by Johan P. Olsen (1989:33–35). Olsen claims that the oil issues were included in established routines for handling governmental industrial activities, and that the Ministry of Industry rapidly took responsibility for the oil issues. The correspondence be-

tween the ministries provided by Hanisch and Nerheim (1992:23) weakens Olsen's argument.

88. The third issue, the relationship toward OPEC, exploded in 1985–1986. The important developments relevant to this issue were naturally not a part of Sydnes's study, published in October 1985.

89. Frydenlund's account in the Storting, May 28, 1976, referred to in Sydnes 1985:125.

90. Frydenlund's account in the Storting, October 25, 1979, UD-Informasjon, 25, October 26, 1979.

91. Frydenlund, UD-Informasjon 10, February 26, 1975, referred to in Sydnes 1985:87.

92. Nordli's speech at the opening of the Offshore North Sea Conference and Exhibition, August 26, 1980, UD-Informasjon 29, September 4, 1980.

93. Appointed by Nordli to illuminate various aspects of the initiative. The group was composed of State Secretary Olav Bucher-Johannesen, Office of the Prime Minister; State Secretary Harald Norvik, Ministry of Oil and Energy; State Secretary Johan Jørgen Holst, Ministry of Foreign Affairs; Director Einar Magnussen, Norwegian Export Council and chairman of the Oil Price Committee; in addition to other representatives from the Ministry of Foreign Affairs and the Ministry of Oil and Energy (Sydnes 1985:199).

94. Brundtland's address at Harvard University (US), September 18, 1987.

95. Statement made at a press briefing in Oslo, September 16, quoted in Dyrdal 1990:54.

96. *Aftenposten*, March 17, 1986.

97. Dyrdal (1990) especially underlines the differences between the State Department and the Department of Energy.

98. Statfjord is owned 84.09 percent by Norway and 15.91 percent by the UK (Norwegian Ministry of Oil and Energy, *Fact Sheet* 1988).

99. *Financial Times*, October 16, 1984, and Sydnes 1985:144.

100. *Arbeiderbladet*, May 16, 1986.

101. Vetlesen (1989), in his more detailed treatment of the relations between OPEC and Britain, also has pointed to this discord between Norway and Britain.

102. *The German Tribune*, No. 1219, February 16, 1986; Norwegian Ministry of Oil and Energy, *Fact Sheet 1986*; and *NOS: Oil Activity 1984*.

103. Statement made at a press briefing in Oslo, September 16, quoted in Dyrdal 1990:54.

10

Oil-Producer Cooperation and the Study of International Political Economy

What determines the cooperative behavior among the oil-producing countries? That was the research question spelled out at the beginning of this study. The answer provided over the pages between the introduction and this conclusion is a complex story, as many factors influence the co-operation between the oil producers. The conclusions drawn in the different chapters have been conditional, as variables discussed in other chapters have been taken as constants. This chapter aims at drawing the findings of the different chapters together, and relate them to the study of International Political Economy (IPE).

10.1 Empirical Findings

Chapter 2 introduced the concepts "market structure" and "market power." The structure was defined as having a horizontal and a vertical dimension, while market power was defined as the ability of a group of market actors to influence the oil price or conditions for price-setting. The distribution of market power in the international oil market was related to three groups of actors: the international oil companies, the consuming countries, and the oil producers. The relationship between actors' behavior and the market structure was perceived as dynamic, since what actors do at t_1 may change aspects of the market structure in a way that constrains the actors' behavior at t_2. The argument in Chapter 2 was that the structure, the other actors' behavior, and the dynamic relationship between market structure and market behavior constrained the possibility of establishing successful cooperation between the oil producers.[1] The dynamics between oil-producer cooperation and such structural changes is further developed below.

Three changes in the power balance between the producers, consumers, and companies were identified. These changes created different
prospects for oil-producer cooperation. Before the newcomers broke the
Seven Sisters' dominance in the international oil market, there was little
room for oil-producer cooperation, as the Sisters controlled almost all
transport, refining, and distribution of oil, and thus could resist the producers' demand for price increases. The Middle East countries needed
the split between the companies in order to gain the upper hand in the
control of the market. When this was achieved, the oil-producing countries experienced a decade of prosperity from the beginning of the seventies to the early eighties. Then they had to face the revenge of the market
forces and the consumer countries. The demand slackened, and importing countries began taxing oil consumption, making the end-user price
less sensitive to changes in crude oil prices. The price decrease during the
eighties has not increased demand, as consumers have been presented
with continuously high product prices. The reintegration of the international oil market was a way for both crude-short companies and crude-
long oil-producing countries, to be able to live with both high and low oil
prices. It also had a negative implication for the oil-producer cooperation, as it established an internal split between the oil producers with and
without downstream assets.

Chapter 3 dealt with the effect on the oil-producer cooperation of the
fact that several of the OPEC members have been involved in military conflicts with one another. In addition to the direct effects on the production
capacity of belligerent oil producers, the warfare has also changed their
interests in participation in oil-related cooperative efforts among the producers. If the explanation of this is to be purely political, it will have to be
distinguished from the explanation that wars have a tendency to cost
money, making countries more in need of income and thus less able or
willing to reduce their production. The security argument will have to
imply that states for security reasons support or counter producer cooperation. The discussion in Chapter 3 suggested that, at least during the
Iran-Iraq War and the Iraq-Kuwait War, several Gulf countries had security interests govern their oil-market behavior. Evidence of this included
the attempt by the Gulf Cooperative Council (GCC) to lower oil prices in
order to hurt Iran, to sell oil on behalf of Iraq in order to influence the
course of the war, and so on. Also, the internal threats to the regimes and
the role of oil are fundamental aspects for understanding the oil-market
behavior of the Gulf oil producers. The role of oil in securing autocratic
regimes in the Gulf area was another aspect discussed in Chapter 3. The
implications for the oil-producer cooperation were indecisive, as the domestic political importance of oil exports can either enhance or reduce a
particular regime's interest in cooperation with other producers. The

general point to be made here is that economic common interest does not make states disregard the political obstacles to cooperation. This represents an important difference between cooperation among states and cooperation among firms. Firms, solely dedicated to profit, can more easily join profitable cooperative arrangements. States, or state leaderships, which have political aims in mind, will forgo profitable economic relations that might have negative political consequences. The internal threats to vulnerable authoritarian regimes can easily make these regimes behave according to neither a logic of consequence nor a logic of appropriateness (see Chapter 4). Economic models, designed for understanding cooperation between firms, and institutional models, designed for understanding behavior in the light of norms, miss this point when applied to the economic cooperation between such states.

In Chapter 4, the focus turned to the internal organization of the oil producers. To strengthen their position against the other actors, a group of oil producers established an international organization—OPEC—as early as 1960. The organization had no direct influence on the members' market behavior until the seventies, and, as argued in Chapter 5, no substantial effect until the eighties. Chapter 4 dealt with the functions of OPEC, which provides the members with *information* regarding the market, defines a common *perception* of the members' bargaining problems, helps to establish *rules* for production policies by setting quotas, contributes to the enforcement of these rules by *monitoring* the individual members' actual production, and increases the coherence of OPEC by enhancing the picture of a common enemy. The general conclusion is that the organization formally lacks autonomy. However, at certain instances in the period discussed, the oil-producer cooperation was influenced by institutional factors.

The institutionalization of the oil-producer cooperation influences the outcome of the cooperation in at least four ways. First, with the institutionalization of the decisionmaking in certain policy areas, the procedures and routines of decisionmaking become harder to change, even when individual members find it in their interests to do so. Robust routines can create a common understanding of the issues at hand and how the members should deal with them. Second, institutions can affect the interests of the actors, as they might find it hard to pursue a policy that would jeopardize the existence of the institutions created. The risk of being blamed for destroying OPEC became a concern that has to be weighed against the possible gains from pursuing one's economic interests, should they contradict the collective interests of the OPEC members. The preservation of OPEC becomes a goal in itself for the members. Third, the Secretariat or representatives of the organization provides independent input into the deliberations by providing information or suggesting solutions. They also "amplify outputs" through monitoring compliance, thereby enhancing the cooperative behavior of the members. Fourth, institutionalization has increased the time horizon, as the members know they will meet again. In combination with monitoring, this opens the possibility of punishment of noncooperative behavior. The traditional way of measuring the impact of international organizations, solely based on the decisionmaking rules or the member countries' ability to control the organization's bureaucracy, misses these points.

Chapters 5 and 7 analyzed the price and production policies of the OPEC members from a perspective combining cartel theory and the theory of collective action. In strict economic terms, the OPEC countries have behaved cooperatively since 1971 to the present, as the price has been substantially above its competitive level. Some degree of market control has been exercised, and it has been beneficial to the oil producers. Cartels are easiest to establish when they are least needed. OPEC clearly illustrates this point: During the seventies, OPEC as an organization played a minor role; however, the behavior of the OPEC members did cause substantial price increases and, in fact, changed the structure and market-power relations in the international oil market. Between 1982 and 1985, Saudi Arabia performed the role of swing producer, carrying the burden of reduced production to sustain the price. After some months with a competitive market in 1986, OPEC reestablished the quota system, but Saudi Arabia no longer had the role of swing producer. Since the war between Iraq and Kuwait, UN sanctions have kept Iraq out of the market, making the production-sharing easier among the rest of the OPEC members. The price has been above its competitive level, and this has given the OPEC countries an increase in revenue compared with the low point in 1986. The conclusion regarding this temporal aspect was that the benefits from cooperation have varied substantially over time. Regarding the burden-sharing among the OPEC members, it was a solid finding that Saudi Arabia has borne a disproportionate share of the costs of sustaining high oil prices. This is in accordance with the theory of collective action (Olson 1965).

Chapters 6 and 9 were designed as case studies of Saudi Arabia and Norway, respectively. The reason for including the two case studies was the possibility to conduct a deeper investigation of the policy of an important individual country in the oil market (the case of Saudi Arabia) and to include a study of the importance of domestic factors in an oil producer's policy concerning oil-producer cooperation (the case of Norway). The countries were not randomly picked; they represent countries with different positions in the market. Saudi Arabia has been a dominant actor in the oil market since the sixties. Norway has changed position from being insignificant to becoming an important producer. As the chapters showed, they have both changed their strategies toward oil-producer cooperation during the period covered in this study. It was thus fruitful to study these countries with the dynamic approach presented in Chapter 1. In addition, the countries also have different political systems and political orientations. As they differ along several dimensions, it was not possible to conduct a stringent comparative analysis of the policies of the two countries. Nor was this the intention, as the individual case studies were designed with the purpose of shedding light on different aspects of individual countries' cooperative behavior.

Chapter 6 was a case study of Saudi Arabia. In the discussion in Chapter 5 it became evident that Saudi Arabia had performed a particularly important role in the OPEC cooperation. The case study thus discussed the extent and instruments of Saudi Arabia's role as a hegemonic power in the oil-producer cooperation. The structural element of power represented by its production capacity, substantially larger than that of any other member of OPEC, emerged during the late seventies. In 1982, Saudi Arabia took on a "benevolent hegemony strategy," characterized by behavior as a swing producer, leaving room for the smaller members to exploit the big one. The weakening of the market, that is, reduced consumption and increased production by non-OPEC producers, made the hegemonic role increasingly costly. This caused Saudi Arabia to change its market strategy in 1985 in order to regain market share. Subsequently, the Saudi strategy became more coercive, its behavior more like that of the other price-takers, and oil more like other commodities. However, Saudi Arabia did not disappear as a hegemon. It soon regained the leading position inside OPEC, although its position in the global market remained limited. The room in the market created by the Iraq-Kuwait War and the following UN sanctions was rapidly filled by Saudi Arabia.

Chapter 9 was a case study of Norway's role in the oil-producer cooperation. The case of Norway is interesting in the context of this book for three reasons: First, it is a country whose position in the market has grown from nothing to the world's second-largest oil producer. Second, Norway is not a member of OPEC, and thus its cooperative behavior cannot be ascribed to the institutional factors related to such membership. Third, at least for me, a study of Norway made it possible to include domestic factors in the explanation of an oil producer's behavior in the international oil market in general and toward the oil-producer cooperation specifically. One of the findings of Chapter 2 was that the "freedom of action" open to OPEC became constrained during the eighties. Thus OPEC needed to include other producers in its effort to control the oil price. For Norway, the country's market share increased substantially during the same period, making it harder to hide behind a notion of insignificance in the international market. Furthermore, the Norwegian economy rapidly became an oil-dependent economy. The second oil shock in 1979–1980 increased the government revenues from the oil sector fivefold from 1978 to 1981, with only minor increases in production. When the oil price collapsed in 1986, it all seemed to be a case of "easy come, easy go." The subsequent macroeconomic tightening was designed to handle continuous low oil prices and virtually no increase in state oil revenues. In 1986, the coming substantial increase in Norwegian oil production was not apparent to either Norwegian politicians or to the oil companies. The situation was perceived as one of severe economic crisis. Any measure that could ease the situation would have been attractive to any government, regardless of political stripe. Although there existed a bargaining-like relationship between Norway and OPEC, the Norwegian macroeconomic consequences of the oil-price fall in 1986, the following policy response, and the changes of government are important factors for a more complete understanding of the change in the Norwegian behavior in the oil market in general and toward oil-producer cooperation specifically.

As pointed out in the introduction to this chapter, the explanation of oil-producer cooperation is complex. Thus, the conclusions of the different chapters cannot simply be added together. Combining different aspects of the study illuminates elements that are hidden if the chapters are viewed individually. This section will discuss four such combinational conclusions.

The first combination of different chapters is the relationship between the discussion of the market structure in Chapter 2 and the rest of the chapters. The relaxed oil demand (far below predicted), and the increased non-OPEC production (far above predicted) influenced both the oil producers' utility of the noncooperative outcome and the potential utility from cooperation. This fed into the argument of Chapter 7. Derived from cartel theory, the hypothesis was that cartels are most feasible to establish when they are least needed. When there are few producers and low elasticity of demand, a cartel can easily be established, but the producers can easily control the market without such an organization. When there are many producers and the elasticity of demand increases, a cartel is needed for the producers to control the market, but in this situation the establishment of such an organization is much harder to achieve. In empirical terms this means that the influence of OPEC on the increase in the oil price has been constrained by the feature of the market structure (see Chapter 4).

The relationship between the market structure and the Saudi Arabian hegemony, presented in Chapter 6, is largely the same as the relationship between the market structure and the collective action of the oil producers. During the seventies the increasing demand for oil made the authorities of most oil-producing countries, and most oil-market experts, perceive that it was possible for the producers to increase prices without cutting back on production. The Saudi Arabian strategy of collective price restraint was thus hard to implement. Saudi Arabia did not have the power to implement its policy in such a market environment. During the eighties these conditions changed, but by 1985 the Saudi Arabian hegemonic strategy had become too costly due to structural changes in the demand for oil and the presence of new oil producers in the marketplace. In a sense Norway is part of the structural change, as the country is a non-OPEC producer that increased its market share during the period discussed in this study. However, the change in demand and the subsequent price fall of 1986 had no less effect on Norway. The core of the argument presented in Chapter 9 was that changes in market structure caused a change in Norway's market behavior and its policy toward oil-producer cooperation.

Regarding the importance of the market structure in underlying the role of political factors in the oil market, it could be argued that the oil producers' increased control over the oil price both made the oil fields in the Middle East region something worth fighting for and gave the oil producers financial resources to do so. The discussion in Chapter 3 did not discuss such aspects, as the focus of the chapter was the effect of security interests, not their cause.

As this brief summary shows, changes in market structure have influenced the effect on oil-producer cooperation of the other factors discussed in this book. These factors represent intermediate variables between the market structure and the cooperative behavior of the oil producers; their explanatory power is constrained by the changes in the market structure.

The second combination is the role of OPEC, discussed in Chapter 4, and the military conflicts examined in Chapter 3. In Chapter 4 it was argued that although OPEC can be regarded as an organization with little autonomy in relation to its members, it did contribute to the oil-producer cooperation by constraining the free-riding incentives of its members at certain crucial points in time. This role of the organization is strengthened when the military conflicts between the OPEC members are taken into consideration. The conclusion of Chapter 3 was twofold. First, it was concluded that the political conflicts in the Persian Gulf region had little impact on the relationship between the belligerent parties in the OPEC negotiations. Second, it was concluded that the same military conflicts had increased the cooperation between some countries, in particular the members of the GCC, and that this had strengthened these countries' cooperative efforts in the OPEC negotiations. The first part of this conclusion is interesting in combination with the conclusion from Chapter 4 mentioned above. Although it was shown in Chapter 4 that OPEC was an organization with little autonomy, it still was able to sustain its unity while members of the organization were at war with one another or when one country had actually occupied another. In addition to these large-scale conflicts, several countries in the Gulf region have been involved in minor conflicts with one another without any effects on the countries' relations in OPEC. This demonstrates the importance of the oil sector for the economic and political existence of these countries, discussed in Chapters 3 and 4. Given the importance of this policy area compared with others, the international organization that carries out the collective policy in this area enhances its position. Although lacking formal autonomy, OPEC has gained an insulated position, which protects the organization from being substantially affected by the members' behavior in other policy areas. In this way the organization has actually achieved a kind of autonomy, as the member countries do not change their behavior in OPEC due to changes in interests other than the oil-specific ones. This autonomy does not guard OPEC from changes in the oil policies of powerful individual members, as illustrated by the case of Saudi Arabia's change of policy in 1985.

A third combination of conclusions is related to the problem of collective action discussed in Chapters 5 and 7, on the oil-producer cartel, and in Chapter 6, on the Saudi Arabian hegemony. The findings of Chapter 7 concluded that OPEC has been unable to fully meet the criteria of an effective cartel. This can be summarized as a lacking ability to coherently perform the role of swing producer by increasing production as prices increase and cutting production as prices fall. The findings of Chapter 6 concluded that the Saudi Arabian attempt to perform a swing-producer role was unsustainable for more than a few years, as Saudi Arabia had to cut back on its production to an unacceptable degree. The combination of these findings suggests that the OPEC members not only were unable to perform the role of swing producer jointly but also took advantage of the situation when one of the members attempted to perform such a role unilaterally. This implies that the free-rider incentives in this particular bargaining relationship were strong. The collective action of the OPEC members has thus had to be based on the aim of increasing the individual benefits by behaving collectively. Other mechanisms, for instance the establishment of collective identities pointed to in Chapter 4, have only marginally and in certain instances been able to counter the economic motives of the individual OPEC members to increase their own revenues at the expense of others. The case of OPEC is a "hard case" for collective action, as the benefit to the individual member of pursuing a strategy of defection is high. This is further complicated by the fact that this value of the noncooperative outcome changed in the period discussed in this study. In other words, the "hardness" of the problem has not been constant (see Chapter 2). Therefore, the lack of collective action should to some extent be ascribed to characteristics of the problem rather than the efforts of the actors involved.

A fourth combination is that of the bargaining aspects of the oil-producer cooperation, presented in Chapter 7, and the role of domestic factors, partly argued in Chapters 5 and 6 but more deeply developed in the case study of Norway in Chapter 9. The basic point of departure in this argument is the tendency of many oil producers, outside and inside OPEC, to pursue a free-rider strategy. As described in Chapter 7, the position in the market can be shown to largely explain the variation among the oil producers regarding application of free-riding strategy. However, it also depends partly on domestic factors. Domestic factors like the need for income (Nigeria), governmental overspending (Iran under the Shah), rebuilding after war damage (Iran and Iraq), and internal collective action problems (United Arab Emirates) have all caused OPEC members to pursue a noncooperative strategy. Some of these aspects have been connected with security interests of states rather than rational economic calculations (see Chapter 3). In the case study of Norway, such aspects were more thoroughly developed. Also in that case study the change in the actor's position in the market was the most important explanation for the increased willingness to cooperate with other producers, but several other factors were important in forming the Norwegian policy toward oil-producer cooperation. The macroeconomic consequences of the 1986 oil-price fall gave the Norwegian minority government freedom of action, as steps that could aid the recovery of the Norwegian economy were most likely to gain political acceptance in the parliament. In a state of perceived economic crisis, political conflicts on petroleum issues were temporarily put aside. Furthermore, the perception of negligible negative reactions from traditional allies encouraged a cooperative policy toward oil-producer cooperation. Thus, domestic factors matter, and they can explain variation across countries regarding their choice between cooperative and non-cooperative behavior.

10.2   The Explanatory Model Revisited

Let me return to the explanatory model in Chapter 1 and try to provide an answer to the question put forward at the beginning of this book. Let me start with the dependent variable. The cooperation among the oil-producing countries can be characterized along four dimensions: substantive scope, depth, effectiveness, and costs.

The *substantive scope* of the cooperation focuses how the oil producers' collective price and production policy created economic benefits for them. By setting prices in collusion, and to some extent carrying out a united production policy, the oil producers have increased the price of oil above its competitive level. The cooperation has had little influence on other aspects of the relationship between the oil producers. There have been few spin-offs to other policy areas, and there has not been increased societal integration among them as a result of their common interests as oil producers. Attempts to use the oil-producer cooperation as a model for Third World unity in confrontation with the industrialized countries during the seventies were rapidly stopped by the Persian Gulf members of OPEC. *The cooperation has been oil-specific, based on the countries' common interests in the oil market, without having had strong effects on other aspects of the policies of the oil producers.*

The *depth* of cooperation has varied substantially during the time period discussed in this book. This depth is a question of the strength and autonomy of the collective institutions compared to the sovereignty of the individual producer in the formation and implementation of price and production policy. As pointed out above, this is not only a matter of a formal decisionmaking structure but also a matter of how the institutionalization of the cooperation influences procedures and interests of the authorities of the oil-producing states. OPEC provided an arena for collective action, provided information about the market and the members' position, created decisionmaking rules, and monitored agreements. At particular points in time, OPEC also framed the bargaining between the members and increased the collective identity among them. These functions of OPEC make the members behave in accordance with their collective interests. *The institutionalization of the cooperation has influenced the outcome of the cooperation by facilitating more disciplined collective action than would have been taken with less institutionalized cooperation.*

The *effectiveness* focuses on the benefits of cooperation. The question is to what extent the cooperation has produced the intended effects. This raises the question of the criteria that should be used to measure the success of oil-producer cooperation. The income of the oil producers increased strongly in 1973–1974 and in 1978–1980. This is not a sufficient indication, as the oil price might change due to factors other than cooperation between the oil producers. The problem is determining what the income would have been without cooperation. An indication of this is the empirically calculated competitive price of oil of $8 in the short run and $5 in the longer run (Adelman 1993a:188). In 1986, when the cooperation between the oil producers was abandoned, the oil price fell almost to this level. The oil-producer cooperation contributed to the oil-price increases in the seventies, and to some extent to sustaining the price level in the eighties. *The oil-producer cooperation has been effective in the sense that the oil price has been higher than its competitive level, and thus has increased the income of the oil producers.*

The conclusion regarding the *costs* of cooperation focuses both the transaction costs of conducting the cooperation and the opportunity costs to the individual members from their cooperative behavior. The oil producers' behavior in the seventies made their cooperation more costly in the eighties, due to changes in the market structure. The quota system introduced in 1982 and the subsequent efforts to make OPEC members adhere to these quotas substantially strengthened the cooperation. *The costs of "conducting" the cooperation decreased in the eighties, compared with the seventies, while on the other hand the "sacrifices" that the oil producers had to make increased in the same period.*

It is also important to view the costs and benefits of cooperation between the oil producing countries jointly. In the seventies the costs of cooperation were small, but the effect on the oil market was strong. During the first half of eighties the cooperative efforts increased, but the oil producers' control over the international oil market diminished. This can be explained only by understanding the dynamics of the relationship between the oil producers' behavior and the structure of the international oil market (see Chapter 2). The behavior of the oil producers in the seventies was profitable in the short term, but it made their position even harder in the eighties. The result was that a higher amount of cooperation, and thus higher costs in the eighties, did not increase the benefits of the cooperating parties.

Let me then turn to the explanatory factors presented in Figure 1.1. Changes in the market context were argued as constraining the possibility of establishing and maintaining a successful oil-producer cooperation. The effect of the market context on the cooperation has, in addition to a direct effect on the cooperative behavior of oil producers, had an indirect effect through the intermediate variables like the institutional aspects of OPEC (Chapter 4), the collective action of the oil producers (Chapter 5), the hegemonic power of Saudi Arabia (Chapter 6), and the cooperative behavior of a traditional free rider like Norway (Chapter 9). The direct effect of the market context has been strong, as the cooperative policies of several important oil producers have changed according to structural changes in the market. In addition, the market context has influenced the intermediate variables. The effect of the market structure on the costs of establishing the cartel was found to be particularly important (see Chapter 2).

The possibility to exploit the lack of competitors and the inelastic demand were the prime causes of the OPEC price increases of the seventies. These price increases represented a huge increase in the income and thus national wealth of the oil producers. The increased elasticity of demand

and the increased number of oil producers were also the main explanatory factors behind the changes in the oil-producer cooperation during the eighties.

The market context also conditioned the degree of institutionalization of the cooperation and the effects of this institutionalization on the cooperative behavior of the OPEC members. In situations with favorable structural conditions, the OPEC members were more inclined to let price and production decisions be made at the OPEC level, while in more unfavorable structural conditions, countries sought other arenas, or even left the organization.

The institutionalization of the oil-producer cooperation did, however, have an independent effect on the behavior of the OPEC members. As shown in Chapter 4, OPEC provided an arena for collective action, provided information about the market and the members' position, created decisionmaking rules, and monitored agreements. These functions made it harder for individual members to disassociate themselves from the collective aim of OPEC and follow other procedures in forming their price and production policies, or, at least to some extent, made it harder to cheat on decided prices or production quotas. In addition, in some instances, OPEC also framed the bargaining between the members and created a collective identity among them, particularly against the non-OPEC producers.

The effect of the political context, defined as security interests of the members' states (see the introduction in Chapter 3), on the institutional functions of OPEC was found to be negative but rather weak. Even in situations when oil producers were at war with one another, they still found themselves in joint action as members of OPEC (see Chapter 3). Some confrontations were unavoidable, but the general picture is one of "business as usual." The organization thus displayed a certain amount of immunity, as it could withstand belligerent parties and still function as an influential organization in the international oil market.

This also goes for the importance of individual oil producers' political interests for the cooperation between them. This effect, however, was double-edged, as the military conflicts between some oil producers created military alliances between others. In particular, the GCC cooperation was created as a response to the Iran-Iraq War, but also drew the Gulf countries closer on other issues. Thus, a positive side effect on the OPEC cooperation was possible as an indirect result of the negative effect on the same cooperation from the Iran-Iraq War. The net effect of the security interests on the oil producers' cooperative behavior is thus ambiguous.

The relationship between the cooperative behavior of the oil producers and the outcome of the cooperation raises the analytical problem of how to determine whether and to what extent an identification of increased income of the oil producers can be related to their cooperative behavior.

The findings in the study give reasons for making this connection. It has been a fundamental assumption underlying this book that increased co-operative behavior among the oil producers produces a more favorable outcome for them. This assumption is not trivial, as cooperative behavior does not necessarily create beneficial outcomes. In this study it has not been the intention to evaluate the oil-producer cooperation according to an objective optimum like the maximization of oil income, although it is reasonable to assume that the income of the producers could have been even higher had they cooperated even more. The income level of the oil producers has, however, been substantially higher than the assumed level of income in the noncooperative situation. It is thus fair to conclude that there has been a strong, positive relationship between the coopera-tive behavior of the oil producers and the outcome defined as an in-creased income level for them.

Finally, this study has included an understanding of the relationship between the structure of the international oil market and the behavior of the market actors, including the cooperation between the oil produc-ers, as a dynamic relationship. The structure of the market at t_1 con-strains the actors' behavior at t_2; the actors' behavior at t_2 influences the structure at t_3; and so on. The actors' behavior changes the structure in which the same actors behave. In this study the extension of time and inclusion of dynamic aspects provide a framework for the empirical un-derstanding of the relationship between structure and agents in the particular case of oil-producer cooperation. The price increases result-ing from the behavior of the oil producers during the seventies created incentives for new producers and reduced the demand at the beginning of the eighties, thus making it necessary for the oil producers to strengthen their cooperative efforts. This was a nonsustainable strategy in the long run. It was viable only as long as Saudi Arabia carried the costs. This became an unacceptable burden to the kingdom, and when Saudi Arabia changed its market strategy in 1985, prices fell dramati-cally. Since then an increased adaptiveness among market actors and new trading instruments have narrowed the room for individual actors to change the market structure.

The empirical analysis in this study has been a complex one, trying to include explanatory factors of market mechanisms, cartel theory, foreign policy, institutional theory, and domestic economic and political processes. The aim of this section has been to draw these different lines of explanation together. It has not been the intention to construct a rigor-ous, definite model of oil-producer behavior, but rather to present and apply a framework for an understanding of how different aspects of oil producers' environment, interests, and behavior support and contradict one another, creating an understanding of the complex political processes that characterize the turbulent thirty-year history of oil-producer cooperation.

10.3   The Value of Combining
Political Science and Economics

In Chapter 1 two aspects of the approach chosen in this study were particularly emphasized.

First, it was argued that the economic models of the oil market needed to be supplemented with an approach that could handle the fact that, since the beginning of the seventies, the oil producers have been states and not companies. The reason for this argument was that states have a different and more complex set of interests than firms, and that they are more complex and multifaceted social constructs than firms. This led to the claim that analysis combining approaches derived from theories of economics and political science would yield a better understanding of the oil-producer cooperation. As expressed by Susan Strange (1988:191), "what is needed . . . is some analytical framework for relating the impact of states' actions on the markets for various sources of energy, with the impact of these markets on the policies and actions, and indeed the economic development and national security of the states."

Second, it was argued that the multilevel model, combining explanatory factors at different levels of analysis, would increase the validity of the conclusions. This led to the application of a model more complex and more heterogeneous than most economic models of the oil market. This approach was based on an argument by James Rosenau (1990:23): "Virtually by definition, parsimonious theories are compelled to ignore the multiple macro and micro levels at which the sources of turbulence stir and gather momentum." It was also stated that the risk of choosing such an approach was the danger of incoherence and indefinite conclusions. Thus, this study has supplemented economic studies of the oil market both by studying the dynamics of the relations between states' actions and markets, and by applying a broader theoretical framework than is applied in most economic studies of the oil market.

This study has developed such a supplement along four dimensions. First, theories of institutions have been applied to the role of OPEC. The traditional economic approaches to OPEC have been different variants of theories on monopolies, dominant firms, or cartels. The institutional theories suggested in Chapter 4 supplement the economic theory of cartels. Second, the theory of collective action applied in Chapter 7 widens the scope of understanding regarding the bargaining between the oil producers, compared with theories of competition between firms. The economic cooperation of states differs from the cooperation between firms. Third, a, if not the most, prominent concern of states—security—is hard to include in economic models. In theories of international politics, it is hard not to include it. The key to supplementing the economic models of the international oil market along this dimension is not to conduct studies of the security policies of oil producers, but to study the oil-related behavior of these states' authorities in the light of their security interests. In Chapter 3, this was done on a general level, while the case study of Saudi Arabia in Chapter 6 captured these issues more specifically by relating them to one actor's handling of conflicting political and economic interests. Finally, oil producers' behavior in the international oil market is to some extent also a result of domestic economic and political processes. States are heterogeneous entities. As pointed out above, they have a complex set of interests, but the complexity goes further. States also consist of different subnational actors, a fact that makes foreign economic policy decisions a result of complex bargaining processes. One way to contribute to the understanding of the international oil market is to study such domestic economic and political processes leading up to individual actors' market behavior. Chapter 9 provides such a case study of an important producer in the international oil market—Norway.

The discussions conducted in this study are also interesting with reference to a general notion about the oil market during the last thirty-year period. The oil market is usually regarded as having been politicized during the seventies but not the eighties. Yergin (1991:721), commenting on the events of the first half of the eighties, states that "oil was becoming 'just another commodity.'" This, however, was the perspective of the consuming side of the market. As Yergin goes on to state, "In a complete reversal of the 1970s, producers now had to worry about their access to markets, rather than consumers about their access to supplies" (Yergin 1991:721). Viewed from the producer side, the situation in the seventies was commercial, as the oil "sold itself." There were no political arrangements by the oil producers that created the price increases of the seventies; it was simply a group of producers taking advantage of an inelastic demand. They did so jointly, but that was probably not necessary. The cartel was redundant in the seventies (see section 5.1). The consuming countries' perception of this was of political interference in the market, because the price rose. In the eighties, the price fell, and the consuming side perceived the cause to be a more competitive market. For the producers the eighties meant the introduction of more politics in order to sell their oil. They now had to tighten the cartel, introduce production restrictions, and monitor one another's behavior. With the aim of sustaining the price level created during the seventies, the producers had to resort to political means, understood as deeper cooperation between states, and repeated attempts to broaden the cooperation by getting non-OPEC producers to limit their production. Thus, the conclusion is that what is economics for one actor in a market might be politics for another.

Let us now evaluate to what extent the combination of political and economic theories and the application of a multilevel approach has yielded a better understanding of the cooperation between the oil producers than would have been gained with other approaches?[2]

Most economic models of the oil market and economic studies that explain the cooperative behavior of the oil-producing states end up with a large residual category called political factors. In this study, the oil-producing countries' economic behavior has been explained as a political phenomenon. This has several implications.

First, the assumptions regarding optimal behavior have not been as strict as they would have been using an economic model. Although the oil producers have naturally set out to increase income from oil exports, they have had other goals, such as increasing their control over resources or outlets, realizing gains from occupation of one another, resisting internal political opposition, and, in the case of Saudi Arabia, preserving its alliance with the United States. Forsaking oil-market interests is not irrational if other national interests are served. Such trade-offs are seldom included in economic models of the oil producers' behavior, and they are explicitly refuted by oil economists like Morris Adelman (1993b:17), as discussed in Chapter 1.

Second, the usual prerequisite in economic theory that actors have the necessary information to behave rationally in the international oil market has not been applied in this book. The problem of information has been important for several aspects discussed here. It has been important for the consequences of the oil producers' price increases during the seventies, for the price and production agreements and subsequent cheating by the OPEC members, for the autonomous role of OPEC, and for the relationship between producers inside and outside the organization. Concerning all these issues, incompleteness of information has led actors to behave in ways other than they probably would have with complete information.[3]

Third, the study has included investigations into the political processes leading to actors' individual or joint decisions or behavior. These point to the importance of not only the characteristics of the decisions or behavior of actors but also how these decisions or actions came about. As pointed out by Robert Keohane (1989:30), "world politics is path dependent. . . . Where we are depends not merely on the state of contemporaneous demographic, institutional, economic and military factors but also on how we got there; and how we got there may itself have been strongly affected by random or conjunctural events." This points to an important difference in approach between this study and studies of the oil market based on economic theory. In this study, idiosyncratic factors have been included in the analysis, while they are usually explicitly excluded in economic models. This is prominent in several aspects of the discussion in this book, such as the information problem, the importance of the Gulf wars for the political relationship between the key oil producers, and the way in which the Iranian revolution changed the position of Iran. Especially in the case studies of Saudi Arabia and Norway, idiosyncratic factors behind the cooperative behavior of the oil producers were identified.

Levels of analysis have been the basis for several theoretical debates in the study of international politics. Most textbooks in the field include one or more chapters that discuss the different levels of analysis. When conducting empirical studies, the analysis becomes simplified if it is conducted at one level, or if at least one level is given priority over the others. This study has taken another approach, as it has tried to combine theories and analytical approaches at different levels of analysis. The study thus forsakes the beauty of simple, elegant models in order to grasp the dynamics of the interplay between factors at different analytical levels. This is seldom the case in economic studies.

The empirical analysis in this book clearly shows how explanations at different levels of analysis increase the understanding of the dynamics of the international oil market in general and the oil-producer cooperation more specifically. The interplay between the market structure and OPEC's price increases in the seventies can hardly be understood without the combination of the theory of industrial organization and bargaining theory. Taking it a step further, one could argue that an analysis of all of the actors' policy formations would have developed the explanation even more. This was pursued for only two actors, Saudi Arabia and Norway. An illustration of the range of the dynamics of the explanations proposed in this study is how changes in the structure of the oil market influenced the political debate in the Norwegian parliament, which in turn contributed to a change in the behavior of this country. This again contributed to changes in the bargaining between the oil producers inside OPEC, and thus affected the market structure. For obvious reasons, not every aspect of all such dynamics has been explicitly analyzed, but the illustration suggests that a multilevel approach has the potential to discover more fine-grained aspects of how and why oil producers have behaved cooperatively than "single level-single theory" approaches.

Having argued for the benefits of the approach of this study, it is important to note that theoretical approaches are not true or false, but more or less appropriate. I strongly believe that many different theoretical approaches are valuable in the study of the international oil market. Arguing for the merits of the one chosen in this study is not a disqualification of other approaches with other explanatory aims.

Underdal (1984:73) suggests four criteria for evaluation of the fruitfulness of a model:

1. *Generality:* the set of phenomena to which a model claims applicability.
2. *Conclusiveness:* the extent to which the model produces precise, specific, and non-trivial propositions.
3. *Validity:* the extent to which the model succeeds in capturing the essence of the real-world phenomena it is intended to represent.
4. *Parsimony:* the costs of operating the model.

There are inherent contradictions between these criteria. If one increases the generality of the model, it becomes more difficult to produce specific and precise propositions. Underdal (1984:73) also describes the trade-off between validity and parsimony: "Although validity is a crucial criterion, some trade-off most often has to be made between validity and parsimony." Dismissing all models that do not have a high score on all criteria would be demanding too much. However, validity is crucial. It is meaningless to discuss the score on the other criteria if the validity approaches zero. Thus, a certain level of validity is necessary before it can be included in trade-offs with other criteria. Furthermore, Underdal suggests that generality is important only as long as it does not disrupt the score on the other criteria: "Other things being equal, we would prefer a more general model to a less general one" (Underdal 1984:73). I thus find it reasonable to give priority to conclusiveness and validity at the expense of generality and parsimony.

How does the theoretical approach applied in this study score on these criteria? It was the stated intention of the approach developed in Chapter 1 to increase the validity in comparison with the more parsimonious models of the oil-producer behavior prominent in the economic literature in this field. At the same time, the study aimed at capturing a substantial, but moderate, number of empirical events as it explains the oil-related parts of a dozen countries' policies over a thirty-year period. In addition, the approach sought to apply several concepts from different theoretical strains to the topic of oil-producer cooperation. As Underdal (1984:73) points out, "In empirical studies, conclusiveness implies that the core concepts of the model can be translated into operational terms." Every chapter of the study, excluding the introduction and conclusion, includes such operationalization of different aspects of the theoretical approach outlined in Chapter 1. Taken together, this means that parsimony has been sacrificed to increase not only the validity but also the generality and conclusiveness of the theoretical approach.

At this point it is fair to suggest a counterargument regarding the conclusiveness and generality of the multilevel, multi-theory approach of this study. Although the chapters, or in some instances the sections of a chapter, represent different operationalizations of the theoretical approach presented in Chapter 1, the multitude of aspects discussed may have reduced the coherence of the study as a whole. This is something other than parsimony, as it can be questioned to what extent the study is *one* study and not several independent explanations of oil-producer cooperation. The conclusiveness of the different parts of the theoretical approach may be high, while the conclusiveness of the approach or model as a whole may be diminished as the arguments in the different parts at times contradict one another, or the way they are related to one another becomes unclear. If so, the generality and conclusiveness of the theoretical approach as a whole are results of how the model is constructed rather than what the model is constructed of. This could have been a problem had the research question not narrowed the focus of this study both empirically and regarding the relevant explanatory factors included. In line with the way James Rosenau (1990:25) argues in favor of the multilevel approach, I argue that the present study "is not lacking a distinctive point of view." Rosenau (1990:24) also points out how the different aspects of a multilevel approach should relate: "The crux of this approach is to confine theorizing to those parameters that normally are sufficiently constant as to be operative across time and place but that precipitate . . . repercussions during those periods when they do undergo transformation." This study has indeed focused on factors that have such characteristics (see section 10.1) and thus constitute the core of a fruitful multilevel approach.

10.4 Theoretical Implications

Having claimed that this study contributes to our understanding of the international oil market, the next question is: To what extent does it also contribute to our understanding of international relations in general? The primary ambition of this study has been empirical: to try to explain the extent of cooperation among oil-producing countries. It can, however, tell us something about certain aspects of different theoretical approaches or topics in the theoretical debates in the literature on international relations. Having started out from the tradition named International Political Economy (IPE), it seems reasonable to make some comments on some of the topics of the debates in this tradition. First, it seems appropriate to recapture what IPE is. In a special issue published in 1998 of the journal *International Organization*, the history and present status of this theoretical field was scrutinized (Katzenstein et al. 1998). At the outset the editors make a distinction between the "substantive issues of international political economy" and the "subfield of work . . . that evolved from the study of international political economy" (Katzenstein et al. 1998:645). Around 1970 the economic interdependence of states was empirically identified, and the development of transnational relations theory soon followed. A decade later the focus of IPE turned to the how such transnational relations were governed, and the concept of international regimes emerged. By this the institutional and interactional aspects were developed. Keohane (1989:30) called for the inclusion of domestic factors: "The next major step forward in understanding international cooperation will have to incorporate domestic politics fully into the analysis." The cumulative effects of these building blocks of IPE are improvements in the theoretical foundation of the role of international institutions, and the inclusion of nonstate and subnational actors, in the study of transnational relations. It follows that most, although not all, students of IPE tend to be in opposition toward the state-centric perspective of realism. Likewise, the research program is at least skeptical to the structural determinism of neorealism. Even a general discussion of these theoretical issues would require another book. In this section, the aim is to relate the present study to a few key issues in these theoretical debates.

Politics and Economics

Politics and economics are two spheres of social interaction. In the first sphere, political actors, often states, allocate available resources, while in the other, economic actors exchange goods and services. Ideally, the objectives of political actors are essential in determining outcomes in the political sphere, and in the economic sphere the relative prices determine outcomes. Weaknesses of political systems and market failures makes actual outcomes differ from the ideal situation. The important point for this study, however, is that the two spheres are not isolated. Gilpin (1987:9) identifies an "interaction of the state and markets as the embodiment of politics and economics in the modern world . . . Neither state nor market is primary; the causal relationships are interactive and indeed cyclical."

The relationship between politics and economics can be approached in at least three different ways. One can regard them as separate domains of human interaction that are distinct and, at least for analytical purposes, can be kept apart. A study of politics can be conducted without the inclusion of economics, and vice versa. Another way of approaching the relationship between the two concepts is to regard them as intertwined—inseparable in life *and* for analytical purposes. A study of politics is a study of economics, and vice versa. The third way is to regard the two concepts as distinct but highly "inter-influenced" phenomena—separable but, at least for analytical purposes, fruitfully combinable. This study places itself in the third category. In the introduction to Chapter 3, the difference between wealth and power was discussed, highlighting the difference between states' interests in profit and security. To grasp the relationship between these aspects, one has to be able to distinguish between them. Only then can they be analytically combined. This is an important lesson, since it is far too easy to discard economics by considering politics as primary, or vice versa. By arguing that politics and economics are intertwined, as might be empirically correct, the concepts lose their analytical value as distinctions between them are abolished. In order to study the interaction of politics and economics, we have to be able initially to separate the concepts analytically. This study is an illustration of such a "separation-in-order-to-combine" approach. This is easier to see when using the other, but similar distinctions, instead of politics and economics. Examples are: state and market; power and wealth; or hierarchies and exchange. These concepts suggest that the way resources or goods are allocated and distributed are different in the political and economic spheres, by authoritative decisions in the political sphere, or by exchange between more loosely coupled actors in the market sphere. Different factors and characteristics of actors lead to success in the different spheres.[4]

In this study, a distinction was made between the fundamental rationale behind the behavior of firms, the maximization of profit, and the more complex rationale behind the behavior of states. This difference constitutes a fundamental divide between *political* economy and economics. "For the economists, efficiency in the creation of wealth, the maximization of benefits and the minimization of costs—both calculated in purely economic terms—still constitute the prime criterion of good policy, whether applied at the national or global level" (Strange 1995:156). As Strange clearly points out, the narrow assumption of the economists makes their analysis incapable of fully understanding the motives, interests, and behavior of political actors, even though these actors operate in the marketplace. It is thus necessary, not only to identify the different spheres, politics, and economics, but also to understand the different behavioral logic dominant in the two spheres. In Chapter 5, it was assumed that the political authorities in these states were "single minded," as their only aim was increased income from oil exports. Even when framed by this assumption, the analysis revealed a *political* bargaining process between the oil producers. In Chapters 3, 6, and 9, the interests of the oil-producing countries were more complex, and thus created more complex political processes, both on the international level (Chapters 3 and 6) and on the national level (Chapter 9). In these chapters the complexity of states' interests, and the political processes leading to a single state's action, were demonstrated more fully. These important aspects in the understanding of the cooperative behavior of oil-producing countries could not fruitfully have been included in economic models of the oil market. The economists' criteria of good policy, pointed out by Strange (cf. preceding citation), also miss the importance of grasping the complexity of the formation of states' cooperative or conflictual behavior toward other states. Some OPEC members have actually been at war with one another while at the same time conducting economic cooperation in the setting of the OPEC organization. This has important bearing on the understanding of how we should study the relationship between politics and economics.

The Agent-Structure Debate

The dominant debate in international relation theory during the 1980s has been between neorealism and neoliberalism. There are many variations of this theme, but one of the aspects of this debate with relevance for this study is the structural realists' emphasis of "the effects of the structure of the international system on the behavior of nation-states" (Baldwin 1993:3). The structural realist approach was developed by Kenneth Waltz (1979), who defines the structure according to the ordering principle, the functional differentiation of units, and the distribution of capabilities across units (Waltz 1979:88). The international system is characterized by an anarchic ordering principle and no functional differentiation of units, which makes the distribution of capabilities the essential factor in determining state behavior. One of the many challenges to this structural approach is the liberal approach, which has recently been revitalized by Andrew Moravcsik. He emphasizes the primacy of societal actors, and claims that states are representing these societal actors and behave purposively in world politics, while the "configuration of interdependent state preferences determines state behavior" (Moravcsik 1997:520).

This study has found structural changes in the international oil market highly important in the explanation of the oil-producer cooperation (see section 10.2). However, the findings do not suggest a deterministic role of structural changes, neither market structure nor political structure. Substantial importance has been ascribed to actors' behavior, interests, and to some extent identities (see section 4.3). In particular, the role of Saudi Arabia, a powerful actor in the oil market, has been considered important for the outcome of the oil-producer cooperation. In the case study of Norway (see Chapter 9), the role of societal actors in defining the Norwegian government's policy toward other oil producers were emphasized. Although a thorough discussion of domestic factors have been conducted for only one oil producer, the findings clearly show that states' behavior in international negotiations or bargaining relations are likely to be influenced by domestic politics. The dynamic relationship between the international relations a state is engaged in and domestic deliberations concerning related issues is an important aspect of the understanding of both state behavior and international cooperation.

This study, thus, cut across the different theoretical positions in the neorealist–neoliberal debate. With an aim of understanding real-world phenomenon, a strategy of combining theoretical approaches in order to increase the explanatory power and the empirical validity seems fruitful. This nondogmatic approach to the relationship between structure and agent is in line with the argument of Joseph S. Nye (1988:238):

> The sharp disagreement between Realism and Liberal theory is overstated. In fact, the two approaches can be complementary. Sophisticated versions of Liberal theory address the manner in which interactions among states and the development of international norms interact with domestic politics of the states in an international system so as to transform the way in which states define their interests. Transnational and interstate interactions and norms lead to new definitions of interests, as well as to new coalition possibilities for different interests within states.

It should be emphasized that "complementary" is quite different from the argument by Wendt (1987:360) that agents and structures are "mutually constitutive . . . each is in some sense an effect of the other; they are 'co-determined.'" This understanding brings back the problem discussed regarding the concepts "politics" and "economics." Although it might very well be so that structure and actors are inseparable in reality, the analytical fruitfulness of the concepts presupposes that we can distinguish between them. "We would no longer be able to study the constraining effects of structure by theoretically holding the units and their preferences constant while varying the structure in which they interact. If units and structure are inseparable so that each is at least partly the effect of the other, then variation in the structure will also change the units" (Powell 1994:321).

The Role of International Institutions

Another hot topic in the theoretical debate in the international relations literature is the role of international institutions. Neither realists nor liberals see international institutions as important in explaining states' behavior in the international political system. "Realist theory . . . argues that international institutions are unable to mitigate anarchy's constraining effects on inter-state cooperation. Realism, then, presents a pessimistic analysis of the prospects for international cooperation and of the capabilities of international institutions" (Grieco 1988:485). The liberalism, or intergovernmentalism, advocated by Moravcsik (1993b:481) sees government acting in the "international arena . . . on the basis of goals that are defined domestically." Robert Keohane has vigorously advocated a key role of international institutions. His principal thesis is that "variations in the institutionalization of world politics exerts significant impacts on the behavior of governments . . . [because] institutional arrangements . . . affect the flow of information, opportunities to negotiate, the ability of governments to monitor others' compliance . . . and prevailing expectations about the solidity of international agreements (Keohane 1989:2).

The institutional functions of OPEC discussed in Chapter 4 showed that even organizations with little formal autonomy, like OPEC, can play a vital role at crucial moments in the cooperation between states. The fact that the institution of oil-producer cooperation was intact even when member countries were at war with one another strengthens the conclusion that "institutions matter." This further implies that international cooperation between states is influenced by issue-specific factors. General theories of cooperation between states have to be supplemented with studies focusing on cooperation in different issue areas. Security cooperation, economic cooperation, and environmental cooperation all have some features in common and some mechanisms that do not work similarly in the different issue areas.[5] The study thus suggests that explanations should be based on a combination of general propositions regarding cooperation between states and specific aspects of the issue area in question.

However, the main focus of this study has not been on institutional change but on the bargaining processes among oil-producing states. Susan Strange has argued that the bargaining approach, to some extent, contradicts the institutional or regime approach (see section 4.1):

> An alternative focus [from the regime focus] on the bargains—domestic and international, political and economic, corporate and inter-state—underlying the regimes, rather than the regimes themselves would give better results. . . . There is also in regime analysis a certain bias towards static analysis of organizations. . . . Since it is obvious that the balance of bargaining power is apt to shift over time and that the objectives of those doing the bargaining are also apt to change, an analytical method based on bargains is more likely than regime analysis to take dynamic factors into account. (Strange 1995:160)

Both the changes in the "balance of bargaining power" (Chapter 2) and the changing objectives of the actors (Chapters 5 to 9) are all in all more powerful explanations of the oil-producer cooperation than factors highlighted by theories of international regimes. Not withstanding this, the study again suggests potential gains from an open approach seeking explanations by combining different theories. The role of OPEC in forming the individual members' perceptions of the market through constructing a common identity among the members is an aspect that is hard to detect when applying theories focusing only on actors' rational or intentional choices in international bargains. The study suggests a common ground where theories focusing on actors' identity and theories focusing on actors' interests can be combined and where synergistic effects can increase the understanding of actors' behavior. The potential for states' preference formation in interaction with other states, inside or outside international institutions, is lost by the liberal and realist approach. At this point there is potential for further exploration of the "combination" of different theoretical approaches as advocated by Nye (1988:238). Institutional factors can be important for states' formulation of interests, perception of opportunity-sets, and the utility connected to possible policy options. States' pursuits of self-interests are conducted "within a formal and informal institutional framework that constrain the egoistic behavior of state representatives" (Claes 1999b:15–16).

This study has brought together the logic of market exchange, the imperative of national security, institutional constraints, bargaining dynamics, and the role of domestic political processes in an analysis of a case of international cooperation. The empirical consequence of this complexity is the lack of clear-cut predictions. The theoretical consequence is that the study does not support any individual theoretical hypothesis or a particular theoretical perspective. Although the study to some extent started out with "realist-like" assumptions, these were soon broken down when the role of international institutions, the complexity of states' interests, and the role of a hegemonic power were included in the analysis. Thus, the study does not lend itself to any one theory or perspective. The further advancement of the broad and somewhat eclectic theoretical framework of this study is not found in endless debates over terminological differences and the reformulation of models and approaches. Rather, it is found in a continuous search for fruitfully combinable aspects of different theories or perspectives guided by the old proverb "Who gains wisdom?–He who is willing to receive instruction from all sources" (Polano 1978:302).

Notes

1. In Chapter 7, a successful cooperation was taken to be a situation where the net income of oil producers was raised above what would have been the revenue in a competitive market.

2. This question cannot be answered with certainty unless the same author conducts studies of identical empirical material with different approaches. Differences in explanatory power between this study and studies of oil-producer cooperation by other authors may be due to different measurements, analytical skills, and so on among the authors, rather than characteristics of the approaches chosen. Thus, this evaluation has to be suggestive rather than definitive on this question.

3. Morrow (1994:63) defines complete information as a game where "all the players' payoff is common knowledge" and incomplete information as a game where "some player's payoff is its private information." Common knowledge is defined as a situation where "all players know it, all players know the other players know it, and so on" (ibid.:61). Private information is a situation where a "piece of information known to a player ... is not common knowledge" (ibid.).

4. A situation parallel to the difference between the "numerical democracy and corporate pluralism" in national political systems, where Rokkan concluded, "votes count, resources decide" (Rokkan 1966).

5. This is a study of the politics of oil cooperation. Along these lines are aspects that are not possible to generalize to other economic sectors or to other issue areas. For instance, the demand elasticity of oil is not common among traded goods. The geographical concentration of low costs of production and the virtually global demand are other features that are special to the oil industry.

References

Abir, Mordechai. 1993. *Saudi Arabia: Government, Society and the Gulf Crisis.* London: Routledge.

Adelman, Morris A., and Manij Shahi. 1989. "Oil Development-Operating Cost Estimates, 1955–85." *Energy Economics* (January):2–10.

Adelman, Morris A. 1972. *The World Petroleum Market.* Baltimore: Johns Hopkins University Press.

Adelman, Morris A. 1977. "Producers, Consumers, and Multinationals: Problems in Analyzing a Non-competitive Market." Working paper, MIT-EL 77-038WP (World Oil Project).

Adelman, Morris A. 1982. "OPEC as a cartel," in *OPEC Behavior and World Oil Prices,* edited by James M. Griffin and David Teece. London: George Allen & Unwin.

Adelman, Morris A. 1986. "The Competitive Floor to World Oil Prices." *The Energy Journal* 7(October):9–32.

Adelman, Morris A. 1987. "Economic Theory of Mineral Depletion with Special Reference to Oil and Gas." Paper presented at the IAEE Ninth International Conference, Calgary, July.

Adelman, Morris A. 1993a. *The Economics of Petroleum Supply.* Cambridge, MA: MIT Press.

Adelman, Morris A. 1993b. "Modeling World Oil Supply." *Energy Journal* 14(1):1–33.

Adelman, Morris A. 1995. *The Genie out of the Bottle—World Oil since 1970.* Cambridge, MA: MIT Press.

Al-Alkim, Hassan Hamdan. 1994. *The GCC States in an Unstable World.* London: Saqi Books.

Al-Chalabi, Fadhil J. 1989. *OPEC at the Crossroads.* Oxford: Pergamon Press.

Allison, Graham T. 1971. *The Essence of Decision: Explaining the Cuban Missile Crisis.* Boston: Little, Brown & Co.

Al-Naqeeb, Khaldoun. 1990. *Society and State in the Gulf and Arab Peninsula: A Different Perspective.* London: Routledge.

Alnasrawi, Abbas. 1985. *OPEC in a Changing World Economy.* Baltimore: Johns Hopkins University Press.

Amen, Timothy G. 1996. "The IPE of Energy and Oil," in *Introduction to International Political Economy,* edited by David N. Balaam and Michael Veseth. Englewood Cliffs, NJ: Prentice-Hall.

Amuzegar, Jahangir. 1999. *Managing the Oil Wealth—OPEC's Windfalls and Pitfalls.* London: I. B. Tauris Publishers.

Anderson, Irvine H. 1981. *Aramco, the United States, and Saudi Arabia: A Study of the Dynamics of Foreign Oil Policy, 1933–1950*. Princeton: Princeton University Press.

Arrow, Kenneth. 1983. "Behavior under Uncertainty and Its Implications for Policy," in *Foundations of Utility and Risk Theory with Applications*, edited by Bernt P. Stigum and Fred Wenstøp. Dordrecht: Reidel.

Axelrod, Robert, and Robert Keohane. 1986. "Achieving Cooperation under Anarchy: Strategies and Institutions," in *Cooperation under Anarchy*, edited by Kenneth A. Oye. Princeton, NJ: Princeton University Press.

Axelrod, Robert. 1984. *The Evolution of Cooperation*. New York: Basic Books.

Baldwin, David A. 1979. "Power Analysis and World Power." *World Politics* 31:161–194.

Baldwin, David A. 1993. "Neoliberalism, Neorealism, and World Politics," in *Neorealism and Neoliberalism: The Contemporary Debate*, edited by David A. Baldwin. New York: Columbia University Press.

Bates, Robert H., et al. 1998. *Analytical Narratives*. Princeton: Princeton University Press.

Battley, Nick. 1989. *An Introduction to Commodity Futures and Options*. London: McGraw-Hill.

Baumol, William. 1959. *Business, Behavior, Value and Growth*. New York: Macmillan.

Bergesen, Helge Ole, Olle Bjørk, and Dag Harald Claes. 1989. *The World Oil Market in the 1990s: Is a New Order Possible?* Report 005, Fridtjof Nansen Institute.

Bergesen, Helge Ole. 1982. "Not Valid for Oil: The Petroleum Dilemma in Norwegian Foreign Policy." *Cooperation and Conflict* 17(2):105–116.

Bergesen, Helge Ole. 1988. "The Impact of Oil on the Foreign Policies of the Superpowers—And Ramifications on the Oil Market." Working paper, 003, Fridtjof Nansen Institute.

Bergsten, Fred, et al. 1975. "International Economics and International Politics: A Framework for Analysis." *International Organization* 29(1): 3–36.

Bjørk, Olle. 1988. "The Interdependence between the Oil Market and the Iran-Iraq War." Working paper, Fridtjof Nansen Institute.

Blair, John M. 1976. *The Control of Oil*. New York: Vintage Books.

Bromley, Simon. 1991. *American Hegemony and World Oil: The Industry, the State System and the World Economy*. Oxford: Polity Press.

Bull, Hedley. 1977. *The Anarchical Society—A Study of Order in World Politics*. London: Macmillan.

Bull-Berg, Hans Jacob. 1987. *American International Oil Policy: Causal Factors and Impact*. London: Frances Pinter.

Buzan, Barry, et al. 1993. *The Logic of Anarchy—Neorealism to Structural Realism*. New York: Columbia University Press.

Buzan, Barry. 1991. *People, States and Fear—An Agenda for International Security Studies in the Post–Cold War Era*. New York: Harvester-Wheatsheaf.

Callahan, L. P., et al. 1982. *Describing Foreign Policy Behavior*. Beverly Hills, CA: Sage.

Caporaso, James A. 1992. "International Relations Theory and Multilateralism: The Search for Foundation." *International Organization* 46(3):599–632.

Carlsnæs, Walter. 1992. "The Agency-Structure Problem in Foreign Policy Analysis." *International Studies Quarterly* 36:245–270.

Caves, Richard. 1980. "Industrial Organization, Corporate Strategy and Structure." *Journal of Economic Literature* 28(March):64–92.

Church, Frank. 1974. *Multinational Corporations and United States Foreign Policy. Hearings before the Subcommittee on Multinational Corporations of the Committee of Foreign Relations.* U.S. Senate 93. Congress 2nd session, 11 volumes.

Claes, Dag Harald. 1986a. "'After Hegemony'—The Hegemon Is Still There." *Fridtjof Nansen Institute Newsletter* 6(1):40–46.

Claes, Dag Harald. 1986b. "OPEC and the North Sea: Producers in a Diminishing Oil Market." *Fridtjof Nansen Institute Newsletter* 6(3):12–18.

Claes, Dag Harald. 1990. *Friend and Foe—A Study of the Relationship between OPEC and Norway in the International Oil Market.* Report 005, Fridtjof Nansen Institute.

Claes, Dag Harald. 1994. "Lojalitet, kompetanse og representativitet i internasjonale byråkratier." ["Loyalty, Competence and Representativeness in International Bureaucracies."] Working paper, Department of Political Science, University of Oslo, October.

Claes, Dag Harald. 1995. "Norsk Olje- og Gasspolitikk" ["Norwegian Oil and Gas Policy"], in *Norges Utenrikspolitikk [Norwegian Foreign Policy]*, edited by Torbjørn L. Knutsen, Gunnar M. Sørbø, and Svein Gjerdåker. Oslo: Cappelen Forlag.

Claes, Dag Harald. 1999a. "Talking Oil—A Study of Speech Acts Performed by Saudi Arabian and Norwegian Oil Ministers." Working paper, ARENA, no. 13, 1999.

Claes, Dag Harald. 1999b. "Can We, in the Study of European Integration, Do Without the Model of the State as a Rational, Unitary Actor?" Paper presented to the 7th National Conference in Political Science, Røros (Norway), January 1999.

Coase, Ronald H. 1960. "The Problem of Social Cost." *Journal of Law and Economics* 3(1):1–44.

Cohen, Kalman J., and Richard M. Cyert. 1975. *Theory of the Firm.* Englewood Cliffs, NJ: Prentice-Hall.

Cordesman, Anthony H., and Abraham R. Wagner. 1990. *The Lessons of Modern War—Volume II: The Iran-Iraq War.* Boulder: Westview Press.

Cox, Robert, and Harold K. Jacobson. 1973. *The Anatomy of Influence.* New Haven: Yale University Press.

Crémer Jacques, and Djavad Salehi Isfahani. 1991. *Models of the Oil Market.* Chur: Harwood Academic Publishers.

Crystal, Jill. 1990. *Oil and Politics in the Gulf: Rulers and Merchants in Kuwait and Qatar.* Cambridge: Cambridge University Press.

Crystal, Jill. 1994. "Authoritarianism and Its Adversaries in the Arab World." *World Politics* 46:262–289.

Dahlman, C. J. 1979. "The Problem of Externality." *Journal of Law and Economics* 22(1):141–162.

Darmstadter, Joel, with Perry D. Teitelbaum and Jaroslav G. Polach. 1971. *Energy in the World Economy—A Statistical Review of Trends in Output, Trade, and Consumption Since 1925*. Baltimore: Johns Hopkins Press.

Davidson, Donald. 1980. *Essays on Actions and Events*. Oxford: Clarendon Press.

Davidson, Donald. 1984. *Inquiries into Truth and Interpretation*. Oxford: Clarendon Press.

Davies, James C. 1962. "Toward a Theory of Revolution." *American Sociological Review* 6 (1):5–19.

Dawes, Robyn M., and Richard H. Thaler. 1988. "Anomalies—Cooperation." *Journal of Economic Perspectives* 2(3):187–197.

Dummett, Michael. 1973. *Frege: Philosophy of Language*. London: Duckworth.

Dyrdal, Dag Anders. 1990. *Konsumenter, produsenter eller strategiske argumenter— USA's interesser og atferd overfor norsk utenriks oljepolitikk [Consumers, Producers or Strategic Arguments—The U.S. Interest and Behavior towards Norwegian Foreign Oil Policy]*. Report 143. Oslo: Norwegian Institute of International Affairs.

East, Maurice A., and Leif-Helge Salomonsen. 1981. "Adapting Foreign Policy-Making to Interdependence: A Proposal and Some Evidence from Norway." *Cooperation and Conflict* 16(3):165–183.

EIA. 1998. *Russian Oil and Gas Exports Fact Sheet*. Energy Information Administration, U.S. Department of Energy, June 1998. (http://www.eia.doe.gov/emeu/cabs/nonOPEC.html)

EIA. 1999a. *East Asia: The Energy Situation*. Energy Information Administration, U.S. Department of Energy. (http://www.eia.doe.gov/emeu/cabs/eastasia.html)

EIA. 1999b. *Non-OPEC Fact Sheet*. Energy Information Administration, U.S. Department of Energy. (http://www.eia.doe.gov/emeu/cabs/nonOPEC.html)

Elster, Jon. 1983. *Sour Grapes—Studies in the Subversion of Rationality*. Cambridge: Cambridge University Press.

Elster, Jon. 1985. *Making Sense of Marx*. Cambridge: Cambridge University Press.

Elster, Jon. 1989a. *Solomonic Judgements—Studies in the Limitations of Rationality*. Cambridge: Cambridge University Press.

Elster, Jon. 1989b. *The Cement of Society*. Cambridge: Cambridge University Press.

Elster, Jon. 1989c. *Nuts and Bolts for the Social Sciences*. Cambridge: Cambridge University Press.

Engesland, Bente Egjar. 1989. *Norges forhold til OPEC: fra konflikt til samarbeid ? analyse av en beslutningsprosess [Norway's Relationship to OPEC: From Conflict to Cooperation? A Decision-making Process Analysis]*. Report 001, Fridtjof Nansen Institute.

Estrada, Javier. 1988. "National Oil Companies of Oil Exporting Countries: Downstream Integration Strategies in International Markets." Working paper, Fridtjof Nansen Institute.

Evans, John. 1990. *OPEC and the World Energy Market: A Comprehensive Reference Guide*. Essex: Longman.

Farr, James. 1987. "Resituating Explanation," in *Idioms of Inquiry: Critique and Renewal in Political Science*, edited by Terence Ball. New York: State University of New York Press.

Fesharaki, Fereidun, and Hossein Razavi. 1986. *Spot Oil, Netbacks and Petroleum Futures.* Report 1063, Economist Intelligence Unit.

Fesharaki, Fereidun. 1981. "World Oil Availability: The Role of OPEC Policies." *Annual Review of Energy* 6:267–308.

Finon, Dominique. 1991. "The prospects for a New International Petroleum Order." *Energy Studies Review* 3(3):260–276.

Frank, Helmut J. 1966. *Crude Oil Prices in the Middle East.* New York: Praeger.

Frankel, Paul H. 1946. *Essentials of Petroleum.* London: Chapman & Hall.

Freedman, Lawrence, and Efraim Karsh. 1993. *The Gulf Conflict.* London: Faber & Faber.

Friedman, James W. 1971. "A Non-cooperative Equilibrium for Supergames." *Review of Economic Studies.* 38(1):1–12.

Friedman, James W. 1986. *Game Theory with Application to Economics.* New York: Oxford University Press.

FTC. 1952. *The International Petroleum Cartel.* Staff report to the Federal Trade Commission, Washington, D.C.

Furubotn, Eirik, and Rudolf Richter. 1991. "The New Institutional Economics: An Assessment," in *The New Institutional Economics—A Collection of Articles from the Journal of Institutional and Theoretical Economics,* edited by Eirik Furubotn and Rudolf Richter. Tübingen: J. C. B. Mohr.

Føllesdal, Dagfinn. 1971. "Quantification into Causal Contexts," in *Reference and Modality,* edited by L. Linsky. Oxford: Oxford University Press.

Gately, Dermot. 1984. "A Ten-Year Retrospective: OPEC and the World Oil Market." *Journal of Economic Literature* 22:1100–1114.

Gately, Dermot. 1995. "Strategies for OPEC's Pricing and Output Decisions." *Energy Journal* 16(3):1–39.

George, Alexander L., Philip J. Farley, and Alexander Dallin. 1988. *U.S.-Soviet Security Cooperation: Achievements, Failures, Lessons.* New York: Oxford University Press.

Ghanem, Shokri. 1998. "The Role and Impact of OPEC's Market Share." *OPEC Bulletin* 29(6): 4–8.

Gilpin, Robert. 1981. *War and Change in World Politics.* Cambridge: Cambridge University Press.

Gilpin, Robert. 1987. *The Political Economy of International Relations.* Princeton: Princeton University Press.

Gilpin, Robert. 1991. "The Transformation of the International Political Economy." Jean Monnet Chair Papers, The European Policy Unit at the European University Institute.

Gochenour, D. Thomas. 1992. "The Capacity Shortfall—The Constraints on OPEC's Investment in Spare Capacity Expansion." *Energy Policy* 20(10):973–982.

Golub, David B. 1985. *When Oil and Politics Mix—Saudi Oil Policy 1973–1985.* Harvard Middle East Papers, no. 4, Harvard University.

Gourevitch, Peter. 1986. *Politics in Hard Times: Comparative Responses to International Economic Crises.* Ithaca: Cornell University Press.

Greer, Douglas F. 1984. *Industrial Organization and Public Policy.* New York: Macmillan.

Grieco, Joseph M. 1988. "Anarchy and the Limits of Cooperation: A Realist Critique of the Newest Liberal Institutionalism." *International Organization* 42(3):485–507.

Haas, Peter. 1992. "Knowledge, Power and International Policy Coordination." *International Organization*, special edition, 46(1).

Halliday, Fred. 1991. "The Gulf War and Its Aftermath: First Reflections." *International Affairs* 67(2):223–234.

Hamm, Keith. 1994. "The Refining Industry in the North Atlantic." *The Energy Journal* 15(Special Issue):179–193.

Hanisch, Tore Jørgen, and Gunnar Nerheim. 1992. *Norsk Oljehistorie—fra vantro til overmot? [Norwegian Oil History—From Disbelief to Presumption]*. Volume 1. Oslo: Norwegian Petroleum Society.

Harsanyi, John C. 1986. "Advances in Understanding Rational Behavior," in *Rational Choice*, edited by Jon Elster. Oxford: Basil Blackwell.

Hartshorn, Jack E. 1962. *Oil Companies and Government*. London: Faber & Faber.

Hartshorn, Jack E. 1993. *Oil Trade—Politics and Prospects*. Cambridge, MA: Cambridge University Press.

Hasenclever, Andreas, Peter Mayer, and Volker Rittberger. 1997. *Theories of International Regimes*. Cambridge: Cambridge University Press.

Heikal, Mohammed. 1993. *Illusions of Triumph—An Arab View of the Gulf War*. London: HarperCollins Publishers.

Hermann, C. F., et al. 1973. *CREON: A Foreign Events Data Set*. Beverly Hills, CA: Sage International Studies Series 02-024.

Hermann, Charles F. 1969. "International Crisis as a Situational Variable," in *International Politics and Foreign Policy*, edited by James N. Rosenau. New York: The Free Press.

Hiro, Dilip. 1989. *The Longest War—The Iran-Iraq Military Conflict*. London: Grafton Books.

Hirsch, Fred, and Michael Doyle. 1977. "Politicization in the World Economy," in *Alternatives to Monetary Disorder*, edited by Fred Hirsch, Michael Doyle, and Edward L. Morse. New York: McGraw-Hill.

Hodgson, Geoffrey M. 1991. *After Marx and Sraffa—Essays in Political Economy*. Basingstoke: Macmillan.

Hollis, Martin, and Steve Smith. 1991. *Explaining and Understanding International Relations*. Oxford: Clarendon Press.

Hotelling, Harold. 1931. "The Economics of Exhaustible Resources." *Journal of Political Economy* 39(2):137–175.

Hovi, Jon, and Bjørn Erik Rasch. 1996. *Samfunnsvitenskapelige analyseprinsipper [Analytical Principles of the Social Sciences]*. Bergen, Sandviken: Fagbokforlaget.

Hovi, Jon. 1992. *Spillmodeller og internasjonalt samarbeid: oppgaver, mekanismer og institusjoner [Game Theoretical Models and International Cooperation: Functions, Mechanisms and Institutions]*. Doctoral thesis, Department of Political Science, University of Oslo.

Hovi, Jon. 1996. "Making International Threats Credible. An Overview." Unpublished paper, Department of Political Science, University of Oslo.

Hume, David. 1739 1960. *A Treatise of Human Nature*, edited by L. A. Selby-Bigge. New York: Oxford University Press.

Huntington, Samuel P. 1968. *Political Order in Changing Society.* New Haven: Yale University Press.

Hutchinson, Terence. [1984] 1991. "Institutionalist Economics Old and New," in *The New Institutional Economics—A Collection of Articles from the Journal of Institutional and Theoretical Economics,* edited by Eirik Furubotn and Rudolf Richter. Tübingen: J. C. B. Mohr.

Hveem, Helge. 1977. *The Political Economy of Third World Producer Associations.* Oslo: Universitetsforlaget.

Hveem, Helge. 1994. *Internasjonalisering og politikk—Norsk utenriksøkonomi i et tilpasningsperspektiv [Internationalization and Politics—Norwegian Foreign Economy in an Adaptational Perspective].* Oslo: Tano.

Hveem, Helge. 1996. "Wirtschaftstheorie und Internationale Politik." *Internationale Politik* 8.

Iklâe, Fred C. 1964. *How Nations Negotiate.* New York: Harper & Row.

Ismail, Ibrahim A. H. 1995. "Raising Oil Output in Major Producing Regions—The Financial Implications." *OPEC Bulletin* 26(10):14–19.

Jacob, Phillip E., and Henry Teune. 1964. "The Integrative Process: Guidelines for Analysis of the Bases of Political Community," in *The Integration of Political Communities,* edited by Phillip E. Teune and James V. Toscano. Philadelphia: Lippincott.

Jacobson, Harold K. 1984. *Networks of Interdependence: International Organizations and the Global Political System.* New York: McGraw-Hill.

Jaggers, Keith, and Ted Robert Gurr. 1995. "Tracking Democracy's Third Wave with the Polity III Data." *Journal of Peace Research* 32(4):469–482.

Jenkins, Gilbert. 1986. *Oil Economists' Handbook.* London: Elsevier.

Jervis, Robert. 1970. *The Logic of Images in International Relations.* Princeton: Princeton University Press.

Kaplan, Roger. 1996. *Freedom in the World: The Annual Survey of Political Rights and Civil Liberties 1995–1996.* New York: Freedom House.

Karawan, Ibrahim A. 1994. "Arab Dilemmas in the 1990s: Breaking Taboos and Searching for Signposts." *Middle East Journal* 48(3):433–454.

Karl, Terry Lynn. 1997. *The Paradox of Plenty—Oil Booms and Petro-States.* Berkeley: University of California Press.

Karlsson, Svante. 1993. *USA, Oljan och Världsordningen [U.S., Oil and World Order].* Stockholm: Nerenius and Santérus.

Karns, Margaret P., and Karen A. Mingst. 1986. "International Organizations and Foreign Policy: Influence and Instrumentality," pp. 454–474, in *New Directions in the Study of Foreign Policy,* edited by Charles F. Hermann, Charles W. Kegley, Jr., and James N. Rosenau. Boston: Allen & Unwin.

Karns, Margaret P., and Karen A. Mingst, eds. 1990. *The United States and Multilateral Institutions: Patterns of Changing Instrumentality and Influence.* Boston: Unwin Hyman.

Katzenstein, Peter J. 1985. *Small States in World Markets: Industrial Policy in Europe.* Ithaca: Cornell University Press.

Katzenstein, Peter J., Robert O. Keohane, and Stephen D. Krasner. 1998. "International Organization at Fifty: Exploration and Contestation in the Study of World Politics." *International Organization* 52(4).

Kechichian, Joseph A. 1990. "The Gulf Cooperation Council and the Gulf War," in *The Persian Gulf War—Lessons for Strategy, Law, and Diplomacy*, edited by Christopher C. Joyner. New York: Greenwood Press.

Keohane, Robert, and Joseph Nye. 1972. *Transnational Relations and World Politics.* Cambridge, MA: Harvard University Press.

Keohane, Robert, and Joseph Nye. 1973. "World Politics and the International Economic System," in *The Future of the International Economic Order: An Agenda for Research*, edited by Fred Bergsten et al. Lexington.

Keohane, Robert, and Joseph Nye. 1977. *Power and Interdependence—World Politics in Transition.* Boston: Little, Brown & Co.

Keohane, Robert. 1975. "International Organization and the Crisis of Interdependence." *International Organization* 29(2):357–367.

Keohane, Robert. 1979. "US Foreign Economic Policy toward Other Advanced Capitalist States," in *Eagle Entangled: U.S. Foreign Policy in a Complex World*, edited by Kenneth Oye et al. New York: Longman.

Keohane, Robert. 1984. *After Hegemony—Cooperation and Discord in the World Political Economy.* Princeton: Princeton University Press.

Keohane, Robert. 1989. *International Institutions and State Power: Essays in International Relations Theory.* Boulder: Westview Press.

Keohane, Robert. 1990. "Multilateralism: An Agenda for Research." *International Journal* 45:731–764. Kissinger, Henry. 1982a. *Years of Upheaval.* Boston: Little, Brown & Co.

Kissinger, Henry. 1982b. "Foreword," in *The Critical Link: Energy and National Security in the 1980s*, edited by Charles K. Ebinger. Cambridge: Ballinger.

Krasner, Stephen D. 1978. *Defending the National Interest—Raw Materials Investments and U.S. Foreign Policy.* Princeton: Princeton University Press.

Krasner, Stephen D. 1982. "Structural Causes and Regime Consequences: Regimes as Intervening Variable." *International Organization* 36(3): 185–205.

Krasner, Stephan D. 1988. "Sovereignty, an Institutional Perspective." *Comparative Political Studies* 21(1):66–94.

Krause, Keith. 1996. "Insecurity and State Formation in the Global Military Order: The Middle Eastern Case." *European Journal of International Relations* 2(3):319–354.

Levy, Marc A., Oran R. Young, and Michael Zürn. 1995. "The Study of International Regimes." *European Journal of International Relations* 1(3): 267–331.

Levy, Walter S. 1982. "Oil and the Decline of the West." *Foreign Affairs* 36(2):999–1015.

Lieber, Robert J. 1992. "Oil and Power after the Gulf War." *International Security* 17(1):155–176.

Lindøe, John Ove. 1987. "Intervjuer med fem statsråder" ["Interviews with Five Ministers"], in *Olje og Energi i ti år 1978–88 [Oil and Energy during Ten Years, 1978–88]*, edited by Egil Helle. Oslo: Ministry of Oil and Energy.

Luciani, Giacomo. 1990. "Allocation vs. Production States: A Theoretical Framework," in *The Arab State*, edited by Giacomo Luciani. London: Routledge.

Luciani, Giacomo. 1995. "The Dynamics of Reintegration in the International Petroleum Industry,", in *Oil in the New World Order*, edited by Kate Gillespie and Clement Moore Henry. Gainesville FL: University Press of Florida.

Lynch, Michael C. 1995. "The Analysis and Forecasting of Petroleum Supply—Sources of Error and Bias." Presentation for "Energy Outlook after 2000: Issues of Fuel Choice and Priorities." International Research Center for Energy and Environment Development, Boulder, Colorado.

Mabro, Robert. 1987. "Netback Pricing and the Oil Price Collapse of 1986." Working paper WPM 10, Oxford Institute for Energy Studies.

Mabro, Robert. 1992. "OPEC and the Price of Oil." *Energy Journal* 13(2):1–19.

Mabro, Robert. 1998. "Rethinking OPEC." *Oxford Energy Forum* 33(May).

Maktabi, Rania. 1993. "Liberated Kuwait—Change and the Regime's Quest Towards Internal Stability," in *Golfkrisen i Perspektiv [The Gulf War in Perspective]*, edited by Nils Butenschøn. Research report 01, Department of Political Science, University of Oslo.

Malnes, Raino. 1983. "OPEC and the Problem of Collective Action." *Journal of Peace Research* 20(4):343–355.

March, James G., and Johan P. Olsen. 1989. *Rediscovering Institutions: The Organizational Basis of Politics*. New York: The Free Press.

March, James G., and Johan P. Olsen. 1994. "Institutional Perspectives on Governance," in *Systemrationalität und Partialinteresse: Festchrift für Renate Mayntz/Hans Ulrich Derlien*. Baden-Baden: Nomos Verlagsgesellschaft.

March, James G., and Johan P. Olsen. 1996. "Institutional Perspectives on Political Institutions." *Governance: An International Journal of Policy and Administration* 9(3):247–264.

Mead, Walter J. 1986. "The OPEC Cartel Thesis Reexamined: Price Constraints from Oil Substitutes." *Journal of Energy and Development* 11(2):213–239.

Mikdashi, Zuhayr. 1986. *Transnational Oil—Issues, Policies and Perspectives.* London: Frances Pinter.

Mill, John Stuart. 1909. *Principles of Political Economy*, edited by W. J. Ashley. London: Penguin Books.

Milner, Helen. 1993. "International Regimes and World Politics: Comments on the Articles by Smouts, de Senarclens and Jönsson." *International Social Science Journal* 138:491–497.

Milner, Helen. 1997. *Interests, Institutions, and Information.* Princeton: Princeton University Press.

MNC Hearings. 1974. *Multinational Corporations and the United States' Foreign Policy.* Hearings before the Subcommittee on Multinational Corporations of the Committee on Foreign Relations, United States Senate, Ninety-third Congress. Washington, D.C.: U.S. Government Printing Office.

Moran, Theodore H. 1981. "Modeling OPEC Behavior: Economic and Political Alternatives." *International Organization* 35(2):241–272.

Moravcsik, Andrew. 1993a. "Introduction," in *Double-Edged Diplomacy—International Bargaining and Domestic Politics*, edited by Peter B. Evans, Harold K. Jacobson, and Robert D. Putnam. Berkeley: University of California Press.

Moravcsik, Andrew. 1993b. "Preferences and Power in the European Community: A Liberal Intergovernmentalist Approach." *Journal of Common Market Studies* 31:473—524.

Moravcsik, Andrew. 1997. "Taking Preferences Seriously: A Liberal Theory of International Politics." *International Organization* 51(4):513–553.

Moravcsik, Andrew. 1998. *The Choice for Europe: Social Purpose and State Power from Messina to Maastricht.* London: University College London Press.

Mork, Knut Anton. 1994. "Business Cycles and the Oil Market." *Energy Journal* 15(Special Issue on The Changing World Petroleum Market):15–39.

Morrow, James D. 1994. *Game Theory for Political Scientists.* Princeton: Princeton University Press.

Mossavar-Rahmani, Bijan. 1986. "OPEC Trading Tactics and the Collapse of Crude Oil Prices." Working paper e-86-12, Energy and Environmental Policy Center, John F. Kennedy School of Government, Harvard University.

Mossavar-Rahmani, Bijan, et al. 1988. *Lower Oil Prices: Mapping the Impact.* Cambridge, MA: Energy and Environmental Policy Center, Harvard University.

Ness, Gayl D., and Steven R. Brechin. 1988. "Bridging the Gap: International Organizations as Organizations." *International Organization* 42(2):245–274.

Neumann, Iver B. 1996. "Self and Other in International Relations." *European Journal of International Relations* 2(2):139–175.

Niblock, Tim, ed. 1982. *State, Society and Economy in Saudi Arabia.* London: Croom Helm.

Nicholson, Michael 1992. *Rationality and the Analysis of International Conflict.* Cambridge: Cambridge University Press.

Noreng, Øystein. 1978. *Oil Politics in the 1980s—Patterns of International Cooperation.* New York: McGraw-Hill.

Noreng, Øystein. 1997. *Oil and Islam—Social and Economic Issues.* Chichester: John Wiley & Sons.

Norman, George, and Manfredi La Manna. 1992. *The New Industrial Economics—Recent Developments in Industrial Organization, Oligopoly and Game Theory.* Aldershot: Edward Elgar.

North, Douglass C. 1990. *Institutions, Institutional Change and Economic Performance.* Cambridge: Cambridge University Press.

Nye, Joseph S. 1971. *Peace in Parts.* Boston: Little, Brown & Co.

Nye, Joseph S. 1988. "Neorealism and Neoliberalism." *World Politics* 15(2):235–251.

Nye, Joseph S. 1990. *Bound to Lead—The Changing Nature of American Power.* New York: Basic Books.

Odell, Peter. 1986. *Oil and World Power.* Middlesex: Penguin Books.

Odell, Peter. 1991. "Global and Regional Energy Supplies: Recent Fictions and Fallacies Revisited." Paper. Eurices.

Odell, Peter. 1994. "World Oil Resources, Reserves and Production." *Energy Journal* 15(Special Issue on The Changing World Petroleum Market):89–114.

Odell, Peter R. 1996. "Book Review of M. A. Adelman's *The Genie out of the Bottle: World Oil Since 1970* (1995, Cambridge, MA: MIT Press)." *The Journal of Energy Literature* 2(1):38.

Oliver, Pamela, et al. 1985. "A Theory of the Critical Mass. I. Interdependence, Group Heterogeneity, and the Production of Collective Action." *American Journal of Sociology* 3:522–556.

Olsen, Johan P. 1989. *Petroleum og Politikk—det representative demokratiets møte med oljealderen [Petroleum and Politics—The Representative Democracy Meeting the Oil Age].* Oslo: Tano.

Olson, Mancur. 1965. *The Logic of Collective Action*. Cambridge, MA: Harvard University Press.

OPEC. 1990. *Official Resolutions and Press Releases—1960–1990*. Vienna: The Secretariat of the Organization of the Petroleum Exporting Countries.

Otterå, Magne. 1982. *Data om Fraksjonsmerknader i komiteinnstillinger til Stortinget [Data on Parliamentary Committee Remarks in the Norwegian Parliament]*. NSD Report no. 66.

Paine, Robert, ed. 1981. *Politically Speaking: Cross-Cultural Studies of Rhetoric*. Philadelphia: Institute for the Study of Human Issues.

Palmer, Michael A. 1992. *Guardians of the Gulf—A History of America's Expanding Role in the Persian Gulf, 1833–1992*. New York: The Free Press.

Pearce, David W., ed. 1983. *The Dictionary of Modern Economics*. London: Macmillan.

Penrose, Edith. 1968. *The Large International Firm in Developing Countries*. London: Allen & Unwin.

Penrose, Edith. 1987. "The Structure of the International Oil Industry: Multinationals, Governments and OPEC," in *The International Oil Industry: An Interdisciplinary Perspective*, edited by Judith Rees and Peter Odell. London: Macmillan.

Pindyck, Robert. 1978. "OPEC's Threat to the West." *Foreign Policy* 30(Spring):36–52.

Pindyck, Robert. 1982. "OPEC Oil Pricing and the Implications for Consumers and Producers," in *OPEC Behavior and World Oil Prices*, edited by James Griffin and David J. Teece. London: Allen & Unwin.

Polano, H. 1978. *The Talmud: Selections from the Contents of That Ancient Book, Its Commentaries, Teachings, Poetry and Legends; Also Brief Sketches of the Men Who Made and Commented upon It*. Translated from the original by H. Polano. London: Frederick Warne & Co.

Powell, Robert. 1994. "Anarchy in International Relations Theory: The Neorealist–Neoliberal Debate." *International Organization* 48(2):313–344.

Putnam, Robert D. 1988. "Diplomacy and Domestic Politics: The Logic of Two-Level Games." *International Organization* 42(3):427–461.

Quattrone, George, and Amos Tversky. 1988. "Contrasting Rational and Psychological Analyses of Political Choice." *American Political Science Review* 82(3):719–736.

Ramberg, Bjørn T. 1989. *Donald Davidson's Philosophy of Language—An Introduction*. Oxford: Basil Blackwell.

Ramm, Hans Henrik. 1989. "Rasjonell egeninteresse—en politikk som forstås" ["Rational Self-interest—A Policy Understood"], in *Norwegian Oil and Foreign Policy*, edited by Ole Gunnar Austvik. Oslo: Vett & Viten.

Richardson, J. L. 1990. "Informal Theories of Rationality." Paper presented at the International Studies Association, 31st annual convention, Washington, D.C..

Riggs, Fred W. 1993. "Fragility of the Third World's Regimes." *International Social Science Journal* 45(2):199–243.

Robinson, Jeffrey. 1988. *Yamani—The Inside Story*. London: Simon & Schuster.

Rochester, J. Martin. 1986. "The Rise and Fall of International Organization as a Field of Study." *International Organization* 40(4):777–814.

Roeber, Joe. 1993. *The Evolution of Oil Markets: Trading Instruments and Their Role in Oil Price Formation.* London: Royal Institute of International Affairs.

Roeber, Joe. 1994. "Oil Industry Structure and Evolving Markets." *Energy Journal* 15(Special Issue):253–276.

Rokkan, Stein. 1966. "Norway: Numerical Democracy and Corporate Pluralism," in *Political Oppositions in Western Democracies,* edited by Robert A. Dahl. New Haven: Yale University Press.

Roncaglia, Alessandro. 1985. *The International Oil Market.* Basingstoke: Macmillan.

Rosenau , James N., and Ernst-Otto Czempiel, eds. 1992. *Governance without Government: Order and Change in World Politics.* Cambridge: Cambridge University Press.

Rosenau, James N. 1990. *Turbulence in World Politics.* New York: Harvester-Wheatsheaf.

Rostow, Walt W. 1967. *The Stages of Economic Growth: A Non-Communist Manifesto.* Cambridge: Cambridge University Press.

Rugh, William A. 1996. "The Foreign Policy of the United Arab Emirates." *Middle East Journal* 50(1):57–70.

Sampson, Anthony. 1975. *The Seven Sisters: The Great Oil Companies and the World They Made.* London: Hodder and Stoughton.

Samuelson, Paul A. 1954. "The Pure Theory of Public Expenditure." *Review of Economics and Statistics* 36:387–389.

Schelling, Thomas. 1978. *Micromotives and Macrobehavior.* New York: W. W. Norton & Company.

Schelling, Thomas. 1980. *The Strategy of Conflict.* Cambridge, MA: Harvard University Press.

Scherer, F. M., and D. Ross. 1990. *Industrial Market Structure and Economic Performance.* Boston: Houghton Mifflin.

Schneider, Steven A. 1983. *The Oil Price Revolution.* Baltimore: Johns Hopkins University Press.

Schumpeter, Joseph A. [1918] 1954. "The Crisis of the Tax State" [original title: "Die Krise des Steuerstaats—Zeitfragen aus dem Gebiete der Soziologie," Graz and Leipzig]. Translation published in *International Economic Papers,* no. 4.

Scruton, Roger. 1982. *A Dictionary of Political Thought.* London: Pan Books.

Searle, John R. 1983. *Intentionality.* Cambridge: Cambridge University Press.

Seymour, Ian. 1996. "Oil Price Outlook through 2000." *Oxford Energy Forum* 24(February).

Shepherd, William G. 1990. *The Economics of Industrial Organization.* Englewood Cliffs, NJ: Prentice-Hall.

Simon, Herbert. 1976. *Administrative Behavior.* New York: The Free Press.

Simon, Herbert. 1985. "Human Nature in Politics: The Dialogue of Psychology with Political Science." *American Political Science Review* 79:293–304.

Skeet, Ian. 1988. OPEC: *Twenty-five Years of Prices and Politics.* Cambridge: Cambridge University Press.

Skånland, Hermod. 1988. "Norge og oljen—gamle eller nye utfordringer" ["Norway and Oil—Old or New Challenges"]. Lecture at Sosialøkonomenes forening's petroleumsseminar.

Sluglett, Peter, and Marion Farouk-Sluglett. 1982. "The Precarious Monarchy: Britain, Abd-al-Aziz ibn Saud and the Establishment of the Kingdom of Hijaz, Najd and Its Dependencies, 1925–1932," in *State, Society and Economy in Saudi Arabia*, edited by Tim Niblock. London: Croom Helm.

Smith, A., et al. 1986. "Re-shuffling the Decks of Domestic Reserves: Are Zealous Acquirers Picking Clean Bones?" Paper presented at the 8th Annual American IAEE Conference, November.

Smoke, George. 1975. "National Security Affairs," in *International Politics, Handbook of Political Science*, edited by Fred I. Greenstein and Nelson W. Polsby. Vol. 8. Reading, PA: Addison-Wesley.

Snidal, Duncan. 1985. "Limits of Hegemonic Stability Theory." *International Organization* 39(4):579–615.

Snyder, Glenn H. 1972. "Crisis Bargaining," in *International Crisis: Insight from Behavioral Research*, edited by Charles F. Hermann. New York: The Free Press.

Stein, Arthur A. 1990. *Why Nations Cooperate—Circumstance and Choice in International Relations*. Ithaca: Cornell University Press.

Stevens, Paul. 1982. "Saudi Arabia's Oil Policy in the 1970s—Its Origins, Implementation and Implications," in *State, Society and Economy in Saudi Arabia*, edited by Tim Niblock. London: Croom Helm.

Stewart, David W., and Michael A. Kamins. 1993. *Secondary Research—Information Sources and Methods*. Newbury Park, CA: Sage.

Stocking, George W., and Myron W. Watkins. 1948. *Cartels or Competition? The Economics of International Controls by Business and Government*. New York: Twentieth Century Fund.

Stokke, Olav Schram. 1997. "Regimes as Governance Systems," in *Global Governance—Drawing Insights from the Environmental Experience*, edited by Oran R. Young. Cambridge, MA: The MIT Press.

Strange, Susan. 1988. *States and Markets*. London: Pinter.

Strange, Susan. 1995. "Political Economy and International Relations," in *International Relations Theory Today*, edited by Ken Booth and Steve Smith. Cambridge: Polity Press.

Sydnes, Anne Kristin. 1984. "Norwegian Oil Policy—Economic Interests versus Foreign Policy Considerations." *Fridtjof Nansen Institute Newsletter* 4(4):23–31.

Sydnes, Anne Kristin. 1985. *Norges stillingtagende til nord-syd konflikten i oljemarkedet: Petroleumøkonomiske interesser og utenrikspolitiske orienteringer [Norway's Attitude to the North–South Conflict in the Oil Market: Petroleum Economic Interests and Foreign Policy Orientations]*. Report 004, Fridtjof Nansen Institute.

Sykuta, Michael Earl. 1994. *Real Effects of Futures Markets on Firm and Industry Behavior: A Study of Institutions and Contracting in the Crude Oil Industry*. Ph.D. dissertation, Washington University, Department of Economics, St. Louis, MO.

Sæter, Martin. 1987. "Det dramatiske petroleumsåret 1986." Working paper 381. Oslo: Norwegian Institute of International Affairs.

Sørensen, Georg. 1996. "Individual Security and National Security: The State Remains the Principal Problem." *Security Dialogue* 27(4):371–387.

Taylor, Michael. 1987. *The Possibility of Cooperation*. Cambridge: Cambridge University Press.

Terzian, Pierre. 1985. OPEC: The Inside Story. London: Zed Books.

Tourk, K.A. 1977. "The OPEC Cartel: A Revival of the 'Dominant-Firm' Theory." Journal of Energy and Development 2(Spring):321–328.

Tranøy, Bent Sofus. 1993. Styring, selvregulering og selvsosialisering: staten, bankene og kredittpolitikken 1950–1988 [Governance, Self-regulation and Self-socialization: The State, the Banks and the Policy of Credit Control, 1950–1988]. Thesis for the Cand. Polit. degree in political science, University of Oslo.

Turner, D.F. 1962. "The Definition of Agreement under the Sherman Act: Conscious Parallelism and Refusals to Deal." Harvard Law Review (February).

Tversky, Amos, and Daniel Kahneman. 1986. "Rational Choice and the Framing of Decisions." Journal of Business 59(4):251–278.

Tversky, Amos, Paul Slovic, and Daniel Kahneman. 1990. "The Causes of Preference Reversal." American Economic Review 80(1):204–217.

Udgaard, Nils Morten. 1989. "Norway between IEA and OPEC: Oil Prices and Foreign Policy," in Norwegian Oil and Foreign Policy, edited by Ole Gunnar Austvik. Oslo: Vett & Viten.

Underdal, Arild. 1983. "Causes of Negotiation 'Failure.'" European Journal of Political Research 11:183–195.

Underdal, Arild. 1984. "Can We, in the Study of International Politics, Do without the Model of the State as a Rational, Unitary Actor? A Discussion of the Limitations and Possible Fruitfulness of the Model, and Its Alternatives." Internasjonal Politikk 42(temahefte I):63–81.

Underdal, Arild. 1987. "International Cooperation: Transforming 'Needs' into 'Deeds.'" Journal of Peace Research 24(2):167–183.

Underdal, Arild. 1992. "The Concept of Regime 'Effectiveness.'" Working paper 2, CICERO.

Underdal, Arild. 1994a. "Leadership Theory—Rediscovering the Arts of Management," in International Multilateral Negotiation—Approaches to the Management of Complexity, edited by I. William Zartman. San Francisco: Jossey-Bass.

Underdal, Arild. 1994b. "Measuring and Explaining Regime Effectiveness," in Complex Cooperation—Institutions and Processes in International Resource Management, edited by Peter M. Haas et al. Oslo: Scandinavian University Press.

U.S. Department of State. 1993. Foreign Relations of the United States—1958–1960, Vol. XII: Near East Region; Iraq, Iran; Arabian Peninsula. Washington, D.C.: U.S. Government Printing Office.

Veblen, Thorstein Bunde. 1909. "The Limitations of Marginal Utility." Journal of Political Economy 17:235–45.

Vetlesen, Johan. 1989. North Sea Oil and OPEC, Cooperation and Conflict: The Case of the UK. Report 004, Fridtjof Nansen Institute.

Viner, Jacob. 1948. "Power versus Plenty as Objectives of Foreign Policy in the Seventeenth and Eighteen Centuries." World Politics 1(1):1–29.

Waltz, Kenneth. 1979. Theory of International Politics. Reading, MA: Addison-Wesley.

Waltz, Kenneth. 1986. "Reflections on Theory of International Politics: A Response to My Critics," in Neorealism and Its Critics, edited by Robert O. Keohane. New York: Columbia University Press.

Wendt, Alexander. 1987. "The Agent-Structure Problem in International Relations Theory." *International Organization* 41(3):335–370.

Wendt, Alexander. 1994. "Collective Identity Formation and the International State." *American Political Science Review* 88(2):384–396.

Willett, Thomas D. 1979a. "Structure of OPEC and the Outlook for International Oil Prices." *The World Economy* 2(1):51–65.

Willett, Thomas D. 1979b. "Conflict and Cooperation in OPEC: Some Additional Economic Considerations." *International Organization* 33(4):581–587.

Williamson, Oliver. 1975. *Markets and Hierarchies: Analysis and Antitrust Implications.* New York: The Free Press.

Williamson, Oliver. 1979. "Transaction Cost Economics: The Governance of Contractual Relations." *Journal of Law and Economics* 22:233–261.

Williamson, Oliver. 1988. "The Economics and Sociology of Organization—Promoting a Dialogue," in *Industries, Firms, and Jobs: Sociological and Economic Approaches,* edited by George Farkas and Paula England. New York: Plenum Press.

Wilson, Ernest J. 1982. "The Politicization of World Oil Markets: 1970–1982." Paper presented at the IPSA conference, Rio de Janeiro, August.

Wilson, Peter W., and Douglas F. Graham. 1994. *Saudi Arabia—The Coming Storm.* New York: M. E. Sharpe.

Wæver, Ole. 1989. "Security the Speech Act: Analysing the Politics of a Word." Working paper. Copenhagen: Center for Peace and Conflict Research.

Yamani, Ahmed Zaki. 1986. "Oil Markets: Past, Present, and Future." Paper presented as A. J. Meyer memorial lecture, Harvard University, September.

Yergin, Daniel. 1991. *The Prize—The Epic Quest for Oil, Money and Power.* London: Simon & Schuster.

Young, Arthur N. 1983. *Saudi Arabia—The Making of a Financial Giant.* New York: New York University Press.

Young, Oran R. 1982. *Resource Regimes: Natural Resources and Social Institutions.* Berkeley: University of California Press.

Young, Oran R. 1991. "Political Leadership and Regime Formation: On the Development of Institutions in International Society." *International Organization* 45(3):281–308.

Young, Oran R. 1994. *International Governance: Protecting the Environment in a Stateless Society.* Ithaca: Cornell University Press.

Additional References

Statistical and Other Data Sources
BP (Amoco) Statistical Review of World Energy (London, UK)
Foreign Relations of the United States (FRUS), Department of State (Washington, DC., USA)
International Energy Agency (Paris, France)
Militarized Interstate Disputes (MIDS) database, ICPSR 9044 (correlates of War Project, University of Michigan, USA)

Norwegian Ministry of Oil and Energy (Oslo, Norway)
Norwegian Social Science Database, NSD (Bergen, Norway)
Official reports of the proceedings of the [Norwegian] Parliament (Oslo, Norway)
OPEC *Annual Statistical Bulletin* (Vienna, Austria)
Polity III database, ICPSR 6695 (University of Colorado, USA)
Saudi Arabian National Center for Financial and Economic Information (Riyadh, Saudi Arabia)
Ministry of Foreign Affairs (Oslo, Norway)

Energy Journals
Energy Insider (Washington, USA)
Geopolitics of Energy (Calgary, Canada)
Middle East Economic Survey (Nicosia, Cyprus)
Oil and Gas Journal (Tulsa, USA)
OPEC *Bulletin* (Vienna, Austria)
Petroleum Economist (London, UK)
Petroleum Intelligence Weekly (New York, USA)
Platt's Oilgram News (New York, USA)
Platt's Week (New York, USA)

Newspapers
Aftenposten (Oslo, Norway)
Al-Musawwar (Cairo, Egypt)
Arbeiderbladet (Oslo, Norway)
Asharq al-Awsat (Jeddah, Saudi Arabia)
Dagens Næringsliv (Oslo, Norway)
The Economist (London, UK)
Financial Times (London, UK)
The Independent (London, UK)
International Herald Tribune (Hague, Netherlands)
New York Times (New York, USA)
Newsweek (New York, USA)
The Observer (London, UK)
Stavanger Aftenblad (Stavanger, Norway)

Index

Abd al-Aziz, King, 208, 212
Abu Dhabi, 24(table), 68, 92(n10)
Abu Musa, 129(n25)
Africa, 114
Agent-structure debate, 12
Aghazadeh, Gholamreza, 350(n45)
Alaska, 75
Alberta, Canada, 295(n3)
Alfonzo, Juan Pablo, 211
Algeria, 24(table), 57, 61, 92(n12), 110, 218, 219
  and market shares, 41(figure)
  and oil prices, 173
  and oil production, 172, 194
American Petroleum Institute (API), 43
Amoco, 85
Amuzegar, Jamshid, 92(n10)
Analytical narrative, 1–2
Angola, 75, 291, 310
API. See American Petroleum Institute
Arab Cooperation Council, 107
Arabian American Oil Company. See Aramco
Arabic peninsula, 53
Arab-Israeli conflict
  and OPEC, 33(n17)
Arab-Israeli war
  1967, 61, 218
  1973, 7
Arab League, 61, 108, 128(n9)
Arab radicalism
  and Gulf Cooperation Council, 123
Arab summit meeting (1990), 107
Aramco, 68, 92(n15), 92(n16), 209–210, 221–222
Arnstad, Marit, 315, 316, 336

Asia, 114, 193, 197
  and oil consumption, 194
As-is-agreement, 53
al-Attiah, Abdullah bin Hamad, 314
Auction plan, 219, 238(n4)
Autocracy, 354
  in OPEC countries, 114–115, 117
Azerbaijan, 75
Aziz, Tariq, 108

Bahrain, 92(n12)
Barriers to entry, 43, 57
  and market power, 45
Berge, Gunnar, 310, 344
BNOC. See British National Oil Corporation
Boycott, UN
  of Iraq, 234
BP. See British Petroleum
Brent oil, 80, 81, 196(figure), 330(figure), 336
British National Oil Corporation (BNOC), 186, 289, 303, 304, 344
British Petroleum (BP), 53, 84–85, 87, 91(n1)
Brundtland, Gro Harlem, 310
Bucher-Johannesen, Olav, 352(n93)
Bush, George, 109, 216–217, 343, 347

Cambodia, 75
Camp David accords, 224
Canada, 295(n3)
  and market shares, 39, 41(figure), 42(figure), 43
  and oil production, 287
Capacity utilization, 33(n16)

Cartelization
  of international oil, 241, 242(table)
  and market conditions, 240–243,
    240(table)
Cartel(s), 240–243
  behavior of, 243–247
  and collective action, 360–361
  definition of, 240
  and size, role of, 264–265, 279(n15)
  success of, 243–247, 246, 278(n1)
  See also OPEC
Cartel theory, 171, 358
Carter, Jimmy, 222
Carter administration
  and Iranian crisis, 216
CFP. _See_ Compagnie Francaise des
    Pétroles
Al-Chalabi, Fadhil, 183
Chemical weapons, 102
Chevron, 92(n15), 209
Chicken game, 266, 266(figure)
China, 291
  and Iran-Iraq War, 103
  and market shares, 39, 41(figure),
    42(figure), 43
  and oil consumption, 287,
    288(figure)
  and oil production, 287, 288(figure)
Church commission, 47
Coal reserves, 57
Collective action, 90, 239, 264,
  358–359, 360–361, 366
Collective good, 239, 246, 264, 278(n1)
  and oil prices, high, 246, 278(n1),
    294
Collective identity
  and OPEC, 147–148, 160–161,
    168(n13)
Colombia, 291
Commons, John, 167(n2)
Compagnie Francaise des Pétroles
    (CFP), 57, 91(n1)
Competition, 132, 363
  and cooperative behavior, 378(n1)
  vs. cooperative behavior, 239,
    269–273
Consumer countries, 46, 353, 354

  taxation policy of, 50
  See also Oil consumption; _under_
    particular countries
Contract sales, 78
Cooperative behavior
  and competition, 378(n1)
  vs. competition, 239
  conditions for, in Norway, 321–323,
    322(table)
  costs of, 5, 363
  vs. defect, and oil quotas, 262,
    279(n13)
  definition of, 3–5, 14
  depth of, 5, 362
  effectiveness of, 5, 362–363
  between firms, 2, 366
  institutionalization of, 355, 364
  and market context, 361–364
  and market power, 50–51
  and market structure, 44
  and non-OPEC countries, 292–295
  and norms, 293, 295(n6)
  between OPEC and Norway,
    297–299
  OPEC vs. non-OPEC, 289–292
  and profit, 269–273
  between states, 2, 3–4, 4–5
  substantive scope of, 5, 361–362
  understanding, 1–2
Correlates of War data, 101
Cuba, 75, 128(12)
Custodian of the Two Mosques, 108

Defect
  vs. cooperative behavior, and oil
    quotas, 262, 279(n13)
Defectors, 152, 169(n16)
Delors, Jacques, 343
Demand elasticity, 44, 363–364
  and market power, 45
Demand level
  and cartels, success of, 246, 278(n1)
Democracy Indexes, 29, 115(table)
Democracy movements, 120
Democratic regimes
  of OPEC countries, 114–115,
    115(table), 116(figure), 126–127

Dikko, Alhaji Yahaya, 106
Discount factor
and oil quotas, 262, 279(n13)
Downstream integration, 90
Downstream market, 82–84, 83(table),
87, 92(n26)

Economic institutional approach,
136–137
Economic institutionalists, 167(n2)
Economic models, 1, 2, 20–27, 366
and politics, 7, 32(n6)
Economics
and political science, 8, 366–370
and politics, 96, 372–374
Economic sanctions
against Iraq, 108, 109, 128(n13), 192,
356, 357
Economic security, 99
Ecuador
and oil prices, 173
and OPEC membership, 192–193,
199(n19), 199(n20)
Egypt, 92(n12), 291, 310
Ekofisk, 327, 339
Energy consumption
1950 and 1995, 59(figure)
See also Oil consumption
Energy demand
growth in, 56–58, 58(figure)
ENI. *See* Ente Nazionale Idrocarburi
Ente Nazionale Idrocarburi (ENI), 57,
332
Environmental activism, 31(n1)
Equilibrium points, 4, 31(n3), 206, 260,
262
EU. *See* European Union
Europe
and oil consumption, 194
European Union (EU)
oil consumption in, 71, 72(figure)
and oil prices, tax share of,
74(figure)
Evensen, Jens, 338–339
External shocks, 49
Exxon, 53, 75, 84–85, 85, 91(n1),
92(n15), 92(n18), 209

Fahd, King, 109, 227
as Crown Prince, 219, 220–221
as Prime Minister, 216
Faisal, King, 212, 214, 215, 218, 219,
220
al-Faisal, Saud, 103, 237
Farmanyan, Farman, 61
Financial reserves
of OPEC countries, 85, 86(figure)
Fleischer, Carl August, 338
Forward market, 80, 92(n24)
France, 57
and Iran-Iraq War, 102
Free-riding, 297, 361
Frøysnes, Torbjørn, 309
Frydenlund, Knut, Foreign Minister,
341, 342
Futures market, 80–81

Gabon, 198(n5)
and oil prices, 173
and OPEC membership, 192–193,
199(n18)
Game theory, 20–21, 32–33(n13)
and Norway, 299
GATT. *See* General Agreement on
Trade and Tariff
GCC. *See* Gulf Cooperation Council
General Agreement on Trade and
Tariff (GATT), 168(n8)
Germany
and international oil companies, 52
Getty Oil, 57
Government income
and oil production, politics of, 97
Great Britain, 198(n4)
and Norway, 302–303
and Saudi Arabia, 207–208, 212–213
See also UK
Greater Tunb, 129(n25)
Grisanti, Arturo Hernandez, 309, 310,
312
Gulf, oil capacity, 91(n1)
Gulf Cooperation Council (GCC),
121–126, 293, 354, 364
and Iran-Iraq War, 103, 106, 126
and Saudi-Qatari problem, 129(n26)

Gulf countries, 354
  and external threats, 122
  and Iraq-Kuwait War, 112, 130(n28)
  political cooperation between,
    121–126
  See also particular countries
Gulf plus pricing system, 53
Gulf wars, 360. *See also particular*
    wars
Gullfaks, 309
Gulnes, Nils, 338

Hammadi, Sadoon, 92(n10)
Hance, Kent, 295(n3)
Al-Haram al Sharif Mosque, 178
Hedging, 81
Hegemonic stability thesis, 48
Hegemony, 204–207
  benevolent and coercive, 206–207
  and collective action, 360–361
  definition of, 48
  and leadership, 237(n1)
  and market shares, 234–237
  and Saudi Arabia, role of, 201–202,
    206–218, 358–359, 360–361
Herrington, John, 343, 345
Holst, Johan Jørgen, 352(n93)
Horizontal market structure, 39–43.
    See also Market structure
Hotelling rule, 21–24, 33(n14), 88
Hotelling Valuation Principle, 21
House of Saud, 223
Human rights, 31(n1)
Hussein, King, 107

IEA. *See* International Energy Agency
IGO. *See* Intergovernmental
    organization
Indonesia, 24(table), 106, 110
  and market shares, 41(figure),
    42(figure)
  and oil prices, 173 ı
  and oil quotas, 194
Industrial economics, 20–21
Industrial organization

of international oil market, 25–27,
    27(figure)
Information
  complete, 368, 378(n3)
  incomplete, 134–136, 167(n6)
  private, 378(n3)
Institutionalization
  of cooperative behavior, 355, 364
Institutional theories, 131–142,
    144–164, 364, 366
Institutions
  and market structure, 13–14
  and OPEC, 131–142
  and rational choice, 131–134
Interest-based theories, of
    international regimes, 141
Intergovernmental organization
    (IGO), 152
Inter-group relations
  cooperative aspects of, 46, 47–48,
    48(figure), 49(figure)
Internal threats, 114–121, 354
  and Gulf Cooperation Council, 123
International cooperation
  and hegemony, role of, 202–203
  theories of, 141
International Energy Agency (IEA),
    46, 175–176, 302
  and Norway, 341
  Oil Sharing Agreement, 110
International institutions
  and international relations, 4–5
  role of, 375–377
  study of, 137–140
International oil
  cartelization of, 241, 242(table)
International oil companies (IOC),
    91(n4), 348(n2), 353, 354
  history of, 51–60
International oil market
  industrial organization of, 25–27,
    27(figure)
  institutions of, 13–14
  and Norway, 299–301
  and state interaction, 14–16, 32(n4)
  structure of, 10–13, 32(n8)

International organizations
  role of, 165–166
International Petroleum Exchange
  (IPEX), 92(n19)
International Political Economy (IPE),
  1, 6–8, 371–372
International regimes
  theories of, 140–142, 168(n8)
International relations, 371
  and international institutions, 4–5
Intra-group relations, 46, 48
IOC. *See* International oil companies
IPC. *See* Iraq Petroleum Company
IPE. *See* International Political
  Economy
IPEX. *See* International Petroleum
  Exchange
Iran, 24(table), 57, 61, 92(n10), 198(n5),
  218, 221, 237, 369
  and Gulf Cooperation Council,
    123–125
  and market shares, 41(figure),
    42(figure), 236(figure)
  and oil prices, 173, 177, 178
  and oil production, 65(figure), 104,
    105(figure), 106, 125(figure), 174,
    175(figure), 194, 234, 278(n7)
  and oil quotas, 183, 185, 186, 187,
    189, 194, 198(n5), 199(n8)
  and security threats, 95–96
  and Seven Sisters, 56(table)
  and United Arab Emirates, 122,
    129(n25)
Iran, shah of, 69, 214, 222, 225, 234
Iranian crisis, 216
Iranian revolution, 174, 238(n15)
  and Saudi Arabia, 222–225
  United States during, 198(n2)
Iranian revolution (1979), 7
Iran-Iraq War, 7, 70, 101–107, 111, 113,
  126, 174, 179, 238(n15), 354, 364
  and Gulf Cooperation Council, 121,
    122
  and Saudi Arabia, 222–225
Iraq, 24(table), 53, 61, 68, 91(n4),
  92(n10), 92(n12), 128(11), 218, 221,
  237

  boycott of, 234
  economic sanctions against, 108,
    109, 128(n13), 192, 356, 357
  and Gulf Cooperation Council,
    123–125
  and market shares, 41(figure),
    236(figure)
  and oil prices, 173, 278(n8)
  and oil production, 104, 105(figure),
    106, 113, 113(table), 125(figure),
    172, 175(figure), 234
  and oil quotas, 183, 189
  and Seven Sisters, 56(table)
Iraq-Kuwait War, 7, 100, 107–113, 126,
  128(n14), 129(n20), 217, 227, 232,
  234, 235, 238(n17), 354, 356, 357
  and Gulf Cooperation Council,
    122–123
  and Gulf countries, 130(n28)
  and Norway, 314, 347
  OPEC during, 189–192
Iraq Petroleum Company (IPC), 53, 68
Irwin, John N., 214
Islamic fundamentalism, 222–224
  and Gulf Cooperation Council, 123
Israel, 172, 218
  and OAPEC, 64
Italy, 57, 332

Japan
  and Iraq-Kuwait War, 191
  oil consumption in, 71, 72(figure)
Johnsen, Arve, 130(n29), 310

Kahled, King, 220
Kharg Island, 102, 103
Khomeini, Ayatollah Ruhollah, 69
Kissinger, Henry, 341–342, 347
Knowledge-based theories, of
  international regimes, 141
KOC. *See* Kuwait Oil Company
Kraayenhof, Klynveld, 154
Kristiansen, K[aovercircle]re, 304,
  306–307, 308–309, 311, 319,
  348(n14)

Kuwait, 24(table), 53, 61, 68, 92(n10),
    92(n12), 128(n9), 128(n11),
    129(n20), 216
  and downstream market, 82,
    83(table), 92(n26)
  and Iran-Iraq War, 102, 103–104
  and market shares, 41(figure),
    42(figure)
  and oil prices, 173, 178
  and oil production, 65(figure), 113,
    125(figure), 179, 181, 251,
    252(figure)
  and oil quotas, 186, 192
  and Seven Sisters, 56(table)
  See also Iraq-Kuwait War
Kuwait-Iraq War of 1961, 101
Kuwait Oil Company (KOC), 68

Laos, 75
Larak, 103
Leadership
  and hegemony, 237(n1)
League of Nations, 52
Lebanon, 91(n4)
Lesser Tunb, 129(n25)
Libya, 24(table), 57, 61, 92(n12), 108,
    110, 213–214, 218
  and downstream market, 82
  and market shares, 41(figure),
    42(figure)
  and oil prices, 173, 178
  and oil production, 172, 251,
    252(figure)
  and oil quotas, 185, 186
Libyan affair, 63
Libyan Producers Agreement, 214
Lie, Trygve, 338
Løddesøl, Leif Terje, 338
Lukman, Rilwanu, 312, 324

Maadi Pact, 61
Mabrouk, Ezzedine, 61
Magnussen, Einar, 352(n93)
Malaysia, 291, 310
Market behavior, 353
  and security interests, 126

Market concentration, 39, 40(figure),
    45
Market conditions
  and cartelization, 240–243,
    240(table)
Market context
  and cooperative behavior, 363–364
Market Monitoring Committee, 153,
    157–158, 164, 169(n20)
Market power, 35, 44–49, 60–63, 353
  and cooperative behavior, 50–51
  definition of, 45
  and OPEC, 68–71
  and trading mechanisms, 77–81
  vertical, 85–88
Market-related pricing, 80
Market shares, 39
  and hegemony, 234–237
  and non-OPEC countries, 281
  and Saudi Arabia, 234–237,
    236(figure)
  See also under particular countries
Market structure, 10–13, 32(n8), 35,
    36–43, 353, 358–359
  and cooperative behavior, 44, 88
  definition of, 36
  horizontal, 39–43
  and military operations, 56
  and oil prices, 71–77
  and state behavior, 16–18
  vertical, 36–39, 45
Martinez, Carlos, 349(n37)
Mattei, Enrico, 91(n1)
McCloy, John J., 214
Mecca uprising (1979), 121
Mesopotamia, 52, 91(n4)
Mexican Gulf, 53
Mexico, 87, 195, 233, 291, 292, 310
  and downstream market, 92(n26)
  and market shares, 39, 41(figure),
    42(figure), 43
  and oil production, 194, 287
  and oil quotas, 193
Middle East, 23, 57, 114
  and international oil companies, 52,
    91(n4)
  oil reserves in, 237(n4)

and Seven Sisters, 55–56, 56(table)
Militarized Interstate Disputes data,
  101
Military conflicts, 364
  and oil production, 124, 126,
    278(n7)
  and OPEC, 124, 126, 354, 359–360
Military operations
  and oil market structure, 56
Military security, 95, 99
Ministerial Executive Council, 154
Ministerial Monitoring Committee,
  169(n20)
Mitchell, Wesley, 167(n2)
Mobil, 85, 91(n1), 92(n15), 209
Monopolization, 31–32(n4)
Monopoly profit, 45
Monopoly theory, 24
Mozambique, 75
Mubarak, Hosni, 107, 128(n9)
Multilevel approach, 1, 8–20

al-Naimi, Ali, 195, 233
Nasser, 123
National Iranian Oil Company
  (NIOC), 57, 68, 174
National security, 99
Nazer, Hisham, 109, 314
Neoliberalism
  and neorealism, 374–375
Neorealism
  and neoliberalism, 374–375
Nessim, S., 61
Netback pricing, 80, 92(n23)
Netherlands
  and OAPEC, 64
New institutionalists, 131, 167(n2)
New York Mercantile Exchange
  (NYMEX), 80, 92(n19)
Nguema, Nan, 302
Nigeria, 24(table), 110, 303
  and market shares, 41(figure),
    42(figure)
  and oil prices, 173, 186
  and oil production, 179, 180, 251,
    252(figure), 289

and oil quotas, 182, 194, 198(n4)
NIOC. *See* National Iranian Oil
  Company
Nixon, Richard M., 215, 347
Nixon doctrine, 215
Non-OECD countries
  oil consumption in, 73(figure)
Non-OPEC countries
  and cooperative behavior, 292–295
  and market shares, 281, 283,
    284(figure), 287, 289
  and oil prices, 74–76
  and oil production, 282–283,
    282(table), 290–291, 291(table)
  oil reserves in, 282–283
  vs. OPEC cooperation, 289–292
  and overproduction, 267, 267(table)
  See also particular countries
Norbec, 198(n5)
Nordli, Odvar, 342
North Africa
  oil exploration in, 61
North America
  and oil consumption, 194
North Sea, 23, 75, 198(n4), 303, 327,
  329, 344–345
  and oil production, 289
Norvik, Harald, 352(n93)
Norway, 87, 195, 198(n4), 290, 292, 361,
  367, 374
  and cooperative behavior,
    conditions for, 321–323, 322(table)
  and downstream market, 82
  foreign policy in, 341–346
  and GDP, petroleum sector share of,
    327, 331–332, 333(figure)
  and International Energy Agency,
    341
  and international oil companies,
    348(n2)
  and market shares, 39, 42(figure)
  and oil exports, 327, 331–332,
    333(figure)
  and oil prices, 187, 329, 330(figure)
  and oil production, 289, 324–326,
    325(figure), 327, 328(figure)

and OPEC, 8, 130(n29), 299–326,
    320(table)322(table), 348(n2),
    349(n28), 357–358
party politics in, 332–338,
    335(table), 336(table), 337(figure)
and Saudi Arabia, 319, 356–357, 369
and taxation, 74, 74(figure)
and United Kingdom, 343, 344–345,
    347
and United States, 341, 343, 345, 347
and Western Europe, 341
Norwegian Broadcasting Company,
    307
Norwegian Central Bank, 310
Norwegian Continental Shelf, 241
NYMEX. *See* New York Mercantile
    Exchange

OAPEC (Organization of Arab
    Petroleum Exporting Countries),
    92(n12)
and oil embargoes, 64–68, 279(n20)
Oasis Group, 57
Occidental, 57, 61, 213–214
OECD (Organization for Economic
    Cooperation and Development),
    25
OECD (Organization for Economic
    Cooperation and Development)
    countries, 71
and oil consumption, 73(figure)
and oil prices, tax share of,
    74(figure)
Øien, Arne, 310–311, 312, 348(n14)
Oil
and security, 99–101
Oil companies
dependence on, 61–62, 62(table)
and downstream market, 82–84
and upstream market, 84–85
Oil consumption, 71–74
and taxation strategies, 74,
    74(figure)
See also Energy consumption; *under
    particular countries*
Oil distribution, 38–39
Oil embargo(es)

1973, 172, 213, 218–220
and OAPEC, 64–68
Oil exploration, 37
in North Africa, 61
Oil exports
Norwegian, 327, 331–332,
    333(figure)
Russian, 283, 285(figure), 287
Oil income
and political regimes, 118–119
Oil overproduction
and non-OPEC countries, 267,
    267(table)
and OPEC, 255, 259, 259(table), 262,
    263(figure), 264, 265(figure), 267,
    267(table), 269
and Saudi Arabia, 255, 259,
    259(table), 267–268, 268(table)
Oil-price data, publishing of, 80
Oil prices
behavior of, 20
and cartels, success of, 243, 244
high, and collective good, 246,
    278(n1), 294
increases in, structural effects of,
    71–77
and non-OPEC producers, 74–76
and oil production, correlation
    between, 247–251, 248(table),
    250(table)
and oil quality, 251, 278(n9)
and product differentiation, 43
setting of, and OPEC, 247–253
See also under particular countries
Oil price war
and Saudi Arabia, 220–222
Oil producers, 353, 354
non-OPEC, characteristics of,
    290–291, 290(table)
number of, 44
and technological skills, 43
Oil producing countries
and major companies, dependence
    on, 61–62, 62(table)
Oil production, 37
and cartels, success of, 243, 244–245
history of, 51–60

and military conflicts, 124, 126, 278(n7)
and oil prices, correlation between, 247–251, 248(table), 250(table)
and oil quotas, correlation between changes in, 255, 259(table)
politics of, and security threats, 95–96
in Saudi Arabia, history of, 207–218
See also under particular countries
Oil quality
and oil prices, 251, 278(n9)
Oil quotas
and cooperative behavior vs. defect, 262, 279(n13)
and discount factor, 262, 279(n13)
and oil production, correlation between changes in, 255, 259(table)
and OPEC quota system, 7
See also under particular countries
Oil refining, 38
Oil reserves
control of, 51–60
exhaustible vs. inexhaustible, 20–25
and Iraq-Kuwait War, 111
in Middle East, 237(n4)
and non-OPEC countries, 282–283
proven, 22(table), 33(n15), 57
in United States, 84
Oil transportation, 37–38
Oligopoly
tight, 39
trilateral, 46–49
Oman, 291, 292, 310
Omar, Ahmed El-Sayed, 61
OPEC Board of Governors, 143–144
OPEC Conference, 143–144, 148–149
ministerial committees of, 144, 146(table)
Sixty-third, 153
Sixty-fourth, 153
Sixty-fifth, 106–107
Sixty-seventh, 107, 186
Seventy-second, 153–154
Seventy-fourth, 154–155
Seventy-eighth, 155

OPEC membership, 142–143, 168(n9), 168(n10)
criteria for, 143, 168(n11)
and Ecuador, 192–193, 199(n19), 199(n20)
and Gabon, 192–193, 199(n18)
OPEC (Organization of Petroleum Exporting Countries), 2, 6–8, 32(n4), 33(n17)
as arena for negotiations, 145, 148–149
and cartel strategies, 247, 247(table)
and collective identity, 147–148, 160–161, 168(n13)
and cooperation, institutional aspects of, 131–142
and cooperation and profit, 269–273
and decisionmaking rule, 147, 150–152, 155–160
and defectors, 152, 169(n16)
financial reserves of, 85, 86(figure)
formation of, and Saudi Arabia, 210–212
GDP, 226–227, 228(figure), 231, 238(n17)
as information agency, 145–146, 149–150
institutional functions of, 131–142, 144–164, 364, 366
and Iran-Iraq War, 104–107, 109–113
and Iraq-Kuwait War, 189–192
and market power, 60–63, 68–71
and market shares, 188–198, 236(figure), 283, 284(figure), 287, 289
and military conflicts, 124, 126, 354, 359–360
and monitoring, 147, 152–155, 155, 156(figure), 165
vs. non-OPEC cooperation, 289–292
and Norway, 130(n29), 299–326, 302–308, 320(table)322(table), 348(n2), 349(n28), 357–358
and oil income, 270, 272(figure)
and oil prices, 66(figure), 68–71, 171, 172–182, 180(figure), 198(n1), 251, 270, 271(figure), 274(figure)

and oil production, 65(figure), 155,
156(figure), 165, 171, 180(figure),
184(figure), 188–189, 190(figure),
194–198, 198(n1), 253, 254(figure),
255, 258(figure), 259(table, 264,
265(figure), 269, 270, 271(figure)
and oil quotas, 7, 151–152, 155,
156(figure), 165, 182–188,
184(figure), 192–194, 253–269,
256(figure), 258(figure), 259(table)
organizational structure of, 142–144,
355
organs of, 143
and overproduction, 255, 259,
259(table), 262, 263(figure), 264,
265(figure), 267, 267(table), 269
and price and production policies,
356
and price setting, 247–253
principal aim of, 143
and revenue, 270, 271(figure)
and Saudi Arabia, 276–278, 279(n20)
secretaries-general of, 144,
145(table)
and state power, 151, 151(table)
success of, 273–278
and trading mechanisms, 77–81
and transaction costs, 133
See also Non-OPEC countries;
particular countries
OPEC Secretariat, 143–144, 149–150,
168(n12)
Operation Desert Shield, 109
Operation Desert Storm, 109, 217
al-Oraibi, Qassim Taki, 312
Organization for Economic
Cooperation and Development.
See OECD
Organization of Arab Petroleum
Exporting Countries. *See* OAPEC
Organization of Petroleum Exporting
Countries. *See* OPEC
Osmundsen, Terje, 303–304
Otaiba, Maneh Said al, 157, 159
Output allocation
and cartels, success of, 243, 245–246

Palestine, 91(n4)
Palestinian Liberation Organization
(PLO), 108
Paper barrels, 92(n19)
Parsimonious models, 8–9
Patience, role of
and oil production, 262, 279(n16)
PDVSA. See Petróleos de Venezuela
SA
PEMEX. *See* Petróleos Mexicanos
Pérez Alfonzo, Juan Pablo, 60–61
Persian Gulf, 62, 183
and Iran-Iraq War, 102–103
Petróleos de Venezuela SA (PDVSA),
303
international program, 93(n26)
Petróleos Mexicanos (PEMEX), 87,
93(n26)
Petroleum Act, 307, 308
Petroven, see Petróleos de Venezuela
SA
Phillips Petroleum, 57, 327, 338
PLO. *See* Palestinian Liberation
Organization
Political cooperation
between Gulf countries, 121–126
Political regimes
classification of, 117(table)
and oil income, 118–119
and OPEC, 114–117, 126–127
Political science, 8
and Economics, 366–370
Political security, 99
Political threats, 114
Politicization, 96–99, 354
categories of, 97, 98(figure)
definition of, 96–97
and economic models, 7, 32(n6)
and economics, 96, 372–374
in Norway, 332–338, 335(table),
336(table), 337(figure)
Polity III project, 29
Powell, Colin, 109
Power-based theories, of international
regimes, 141
Primary research, 27–31

Prisoner's dilemma game, 260–261,
  279(n11)
Product differentiation, 43
Production capacity, 33(n16)
Production chain, 36–39, 88(figure),
  89(figure)
Production quotas. *See* Oil quotas
Profit
  and cooperation, 269–273

al-Qadhafi, Muammar, 61
Qatar, 24(table), 68, 92(n10), 92(n12)
  and oil prices, 173
  and oil production, 65(figure), 179
  See also Saudi Arabia-Qatar problem
Quotas. *See* Oil quotas

Ramirez Sanchez, Illitch, 349(n37)
Rational choice, 15, 134–136, 167(n4)
  and institutions, 131–134
Reagan, Ronald, 347
Reagan administration, 216
Red Line Agreement, 53, 55(figure)
Refinery capacity, 38(table)
Religious fundamentalists
  and oil production, politics of, 97
Replacement costs
  of oil reserves, 23–24, 24(table)
Research
  primary vs. secondary, 27–31
Reserves. *See* Oil reserves
Richardson, Bill, 233
Riyadh, 127(n5)
Rockefeller empire, 36
  and Standard Oil, 51
Roosevelt, Franklin D., 213
Rouhani, Fuad, 150
Royal Dutch//Shell, 53, 75, 84–85,
  91(n1), 92(n18)
Royal Saudi Air Force
  and Iran-Iraq War, 103
Rumaila oil field, 108, 128(n10)
Russia, 195, 292
  and oil exports, 283, 285(figure), 287

Al-Sabah, Ali Khalifa, 198(n4)
al-Sabah regime, 119

Sadat, 224–225
Saddam Hussein, 107, 110–112, 123,
  128(n9), 189, 232, 234
Salman, Mohamed, 61
Sampson, Anthony, 91(n1)
San Remo agreement, 52, 53, 91(n4)
Saudi Arabia, 24(table), 61, 62, 92(n10),
  92(n12), 92(n15), 92(n16), 292,
  367, 374
  and Aramco, 68
  and downstream market, 82,
    92(n26)
  formation of kingdom of, 207–209
  GDP, 226–227, 228(figure), 231,
    238(n17)
  government budgets, 227,
    229(figure)
  and Great Britain, 212–213
  hegemonic role of, 201–202,
    206–218, 358–359, 360–361
  history of, 207–218
  and Iranian revolution, 222–225
  and Iran-Iraq War, 102, 103–104,
    107, 127–128(n5), 127(n4),
    222–225
  and Iraq-Kuwait War, 7, 108–113,
    191–192
  and market shares, 41(figure),
    42(figure), 234–237, 236(figure)
  and Norbec, 198(n5)
  and Norway, 302–308, 319, 356–357,
    369
  and OAPEC, 64
  and oil embargo, 1973, 218–220
  and oil prices, 68–70, 80, 172, 173,
    177, 178–179, 186, 220–222, 227,
    230(figure)
  and oil production, 65(figure), 95,
    104, 113(table), 125(figure), 174,
    175(figure), 179, 180, 189,
    190(figure), 194–195, 227,
    230(figure), 231–234, 255, 259,
    259(table), 267, 289
  and oil quotas, 185, 187, 193–194,
    255, 259, 259(table), 267
  and OPEC, 210–212, 276–278,
    279(n20)

and overproduction, 255, 259,
259(table), 267–268, 268(table)
power capabilities of, 100
and Seven Sisters, 56(table)
as swing producer, 187–188,
225–231, 356
and United Kingdom, 213
and United States, 212–218,
218–220, 224–225, 368
Saudi-Qatari problem, 101
and Gulf Cooperation Council,
129(n26)
Scarcity, perception of, 88
and oil reserves, 23
Schlesinger, James, 175
Schultz, George, 343–344
Secondary research, 27–31
Security
categories of, 99, 127(n1)
definition of, 99
and internal threats, 114–121
and oil, 99–101
Security interests, 354, 364, 367
of Gulf countries, 124
and oil-market behavior, 126
Security threats
and oil production, politics of,
95–96
Self-denying clause, 53
Semi-paper market, 80
Seven Sisters, 36, 54–56, 91(n1), 354
and Middle East, 55–56, 56(table).
See also particular companies
Seymour, Ian, 195
Shah of Iran, 69, 214, 222, 225, 234
al-Shanfari, Said Bin Ahmed, 314
Shell, see Royal Dutch/Shell
Sirri, 103
Situational model, 9–10
Skånland, Hermod, 310, 349(n32)
SoCal. *See* Standard Oil of California
Sociological institutional approach,
136–137
South America, 114
Soviet Union, 39, 53
and Iran-Iraq War, 103

and market shares, 41(figure),
42(figure), 283, 284(figure), 287
and oil production, 289
Spot markets, 77–80
Standard Oil, 51–52, 56, 91(n6)
Standard Oil of California (SoCal),
91(n1), 92(n15), 212
Statoil, 87, 304, 310, 332, 344
Stoltenberg, Jens, 314
Strait of Hormuz, 102, 198(n5)
Structural realist approach, 374–375
Suez Canal, 61
Suez crisis (1956), 61
Swing producer
Saudi Arabia as, 187–188, 225–231,
356
Syria, 91(n4), 92(n12), 183, 224–225
and Iran-Iraq War, 106
Syrian-Iraqi unity plans, 224

Tariki, Abdallah, 61, 211
Taxation, 50
and Norway, 74, 74(figure)
and oil consumption, 74, 74(figure),
354
and political regimes, 117–118
Technological skills
and oil producers, 43
Tehran-Tripoli agreement, 7, 62, 63, 64,
172, 211, 213–214
Tertiary market, 78
Texaco, 91(n1), 92(n15), 209
Texas, 295(n3)
Texas Railroad Commission, 295(n3)
"Tit for tat" strategy, 260
Tondguyan, Javad, 104
Trading mechanisms, 50, 77–81,
79(table)
Transaction costs, 132–133
Tripoli agreement. *See* Tehran-Tripoli
agreement
Truman, Harry S., 213
Turkey, 53
Turkish Petroleum Company, 52–53,
53
division of, 54(table)

UAE. *See* United Arab Emirates
Udgaard, Morten, 309–310, 319
United Arab Emirates (UAE), 61,
  92(n12), 129(n25), 221, 222
  and Iran, 122, 129(n25)
  and Iran-Iraq War, 104
  and Iraq-Kuwait War, 108, 111
  and market shares, 41(figure),
    42(figure)
  and oil prices, 173, 178
  and oil quotas, 185
United Kingdom, 39, 87, 304
  and international oil companies, 52,
    91(n4)
  and market shares, 39, 42(figure)
  and Norway, 343, 344–345, 347
  and oil production, 287
  and Saudi Arabia, 213
United Nations, 356, 357
United Nations Security Council
  and Iran-Iraq War, 103
  and Iraq-Kuwait War, 109
United States, 39, 53, 295(n3)
  and downstream market, 82–84
  and international oil companies,
    52–53
  and Iranian revolution, 198(n2)
  and Iran-Iraq War, 103
  and Iraq-Kuwait War, 108–113
  and market shares, 41(figure),
    42(figure)
  and Norway, 341, 343, 345, 347
  and OAPEC, 64
  and oil consumption, 71, 72(figure),
    283, 286(figure), 287
  and oil imports, 283, 286(figure),
    287
  oil policy in, 2–3
  and oil production, 283, 286(figure),
    287
  oil reserves in, 84
  and Saudi Arabia, 212–218, 218–220,
    224–225, 368
Upstream market, 84–85, 87

Veblen, Thorstein, 167(n2)

Venezuela, 61, 63, 169(n21), 210, 218,
  233, 292, 303, 332, 349(n37)
  and downstream market, 82,
    92(n26)
  and market shares, 41(figure),
    42(figure)
  and oil prices, 173
  and oil production, 179, 194
  and oil quotas, 185, 193
Vertical market power, 85–88. *See also*
  Market power
Vertical market structure
  and market power, 45
  See also Market structure
Vietnam, 75

Warfare. *See* Military conflicts
Weak states, 120, 129(n22)
Wealth
  and power, 95
Western Europe
  and downstream market, 82
  and Norway, 341
Western Texas Intermediate (WTI), 80,
  81
Willoch, Kåre, 304, 343–344
World commission on Environment
  and Development, 342–343
WTI. *See* Western Texas Intermediate

Yamani, Ahmed Zaki, 64, 69, 92(n10),
  289, 349(n21)
  kidnapping of, 349(n37)
  and Norway, 302–303, 304, 305, 308,
    310–311, 312, 348(n14), 349(n41),
    350(n49)
  and OPEC price and production
    policy, 173, 177, 178, 186, 197,
    198(n4), 211–212, 219, 220–221,
    226, 237(n5)
Yemen, 128(12)
Yom Kippur War, 216
Yousfi, Youcef, 195